Praise for Ian Johnson's

THE SOULS OF CHINA

"Compelling. . . . A seminal piece of work taking the reader well beyond the prejudices and clichés that so often mark writing about religion in East Asia."

—*The Times Literary Supplement* (London)

"With a subtlety born of years spent in China, Johnson explains how traditional rituals help people overcome urban anomie and answer the 'pragmatic but profound issue of how to behave.' . . . He sees believers' recurrent invocation of 'heaven' as an aspiration for justice and respect, couched as an appeal to a power higher than the government." —*The New Yorker*

"Produces deep insight into China's multifaceted religious revival. . . . Distill[s] the results of broad scholarly research with gentle humor and quiet emotion." —*Foreign Affairs*

"Absorbing and often surprising." —*Financial Times*

"A deeply knowledgeable, eminently readable and important book that reveals a side of China that foreigners rarely explore."

—*The Christian Science Monitor*

"[Johnson] is at his best, showcasing his mastery of immersive reporting as he travels with Buddhist pilgrims and lives with Chinese Christians." —*Foreign Policy*

"Takes us on an extraordinarily rich and intimate journey. . . . Johnson shows us what is really in Chinese souls and hearts. This vividly written, deeply researched book will be the primary work about religious faith in China for years to come."

—Leslie T. Chang, author of *Factory Girls*

"A fascinating panorama." —*The Economist*

"A rich, informative, and timely book. . . . A tremendous accomplishment." —Ha Jin,
National Book Award–winning author of *Waiting*

"This entrancing and engaging book challenges the modern assumption that religion is a thing of the past; on the contrary, the dramatic resurgence of spirituality in China, after a century of violent persecution, suggests that it is an irrepressible force that may in some sense be essential to humanity."
—Karen Armstrong, author of *Fields of Blood*

"In Ian Johnson . . . the faithful have found an ideal chronicler. With the patience of the ethnographer, and the precision of a journalist, Johnson has produced an enduring account of China's inner life at a time of disorienting social and economic change."
—*Asian Review of Books*

"Remarkable. . . . Recounts extraordinary tales of courage and heartbreak." —*The Irish Times*

"Captivating. . . . *The Souls of China* is written like top-flight journalism—it is driven by the stories of real people, and the analysis flows out of their lives. At the same time, a reader who knows the literature (and who reads the endnotes) will see just how thoroughly grounded Johnson is in the broader range of scholarship."
—*Current History*

Ian Johnson

THE SOULS OF CHINA

Ian Johnson is a regular contributor to *The New York Review of Books* and *The New York Times*; his work has also appeared in *The New Yorker* and *National Geographic*. During more than twenty years of working in China he has won the Pulitzer Prize for International Reporting and the Shorenstein Lifetime Achievement Award for covering Asia. An advising editor for the *Journal of Asian Studies*, he also teaches university courses on religion and society at the Beijing Center for Chinese Studies. He is the author of two other books that also focus on the intersection of politics and religion: *Wild Grass: Three Stories of Change in Modern China* and *A Mosque in Munich: Nazis, the CIA, and the Rise of the Muslim Brotherhood in the West*. He lives in Beijing.

www.ian-johnson.com

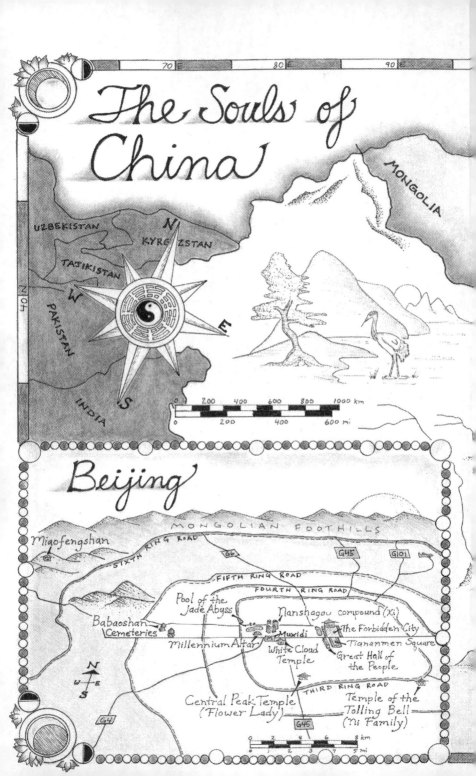

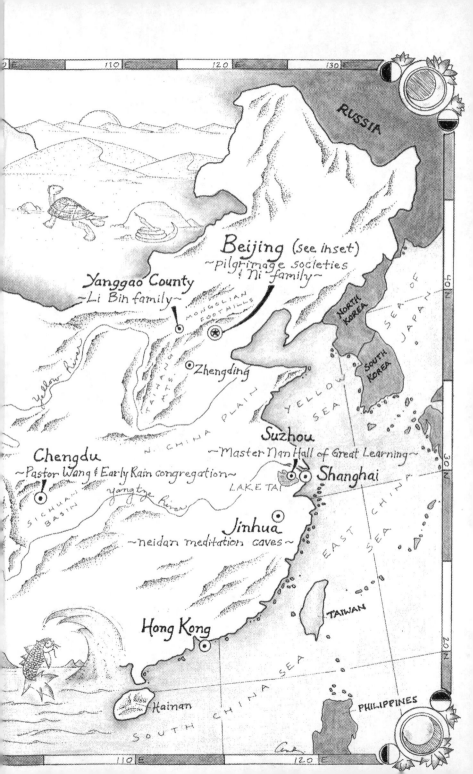

THE SOULS OF CHINA

THE SOULS OF CHINA

The Return

of Religion

After Mao

Ian Johnson

VINTAGE BOOKS
A Division of
Penguin Random House LLC
New York

FIRST VINTAGE BOOKS EDITION, MARCH 2018

Copyright © 2017 by Ian Johnson

All rights reserved. Published in the United States by Vintage Books, a division of Penguin Random House LLC, New York, and distributed in Canada by Random House of Canada, a division of Penguin Random House Canada Limited, Toronto. Originally published in hardcover in the United States by Pantheon Books, a division of Penguin Random House LLC, New York, in 2017.

Vintage Books and colophon are registered trademarks of Penguin Random House LLC.

Owing to limitations of space, permissions to reprint previously published material can be found following the index.

The Library of Congress has cataloged the Pantheon edition as follows:
Name: Johnson, Ian, [date].
Title: The souls of China : the return of religion after Mao /
Ian Johnson.
Description: First Edition. | New York: Pantheon Books, 2017. |
Includes bibliographical references and index.
Identifiers: LCCN 2016036412
Subjects: LCSH: China—Religion—20th century.
China—Religion—21st century.
Classification: LCC BL1803 .J645 2017
DDC 200.951/09051—dc23
LC record available at lccn.loc.gov/2016036412

Vintage Books Trade Paperback ISBN: 978-0-8041-7339-1
eBook ISBN: 978-1-101-87006-8

Author photograph © Sim Chi Yin
Map by Angela Hessler
Book design by Betty Lew

www.vintagebooks.com

Heaven sees as my people see.
Heaven hears as my people hear.

—BOOK OF DOCUMENTS

But now they desire a better country,
that is, a heavenly one. Therefore God
is not ashamed to be called their God,
for he has prepared for them a city.

—HEBREWS 11:16

Contents

Cast of Characters

THE BEIJING PILGRIMS

Ni Zhenshan, or Old Mr. Ni: the family patriarch and head of a pilgrimage association that runs a shrine on Miaofengshan, Beijing's holiest site.

Ni Jincheng: the older son who becomes a reclusive Buddhist.

Ni Jintang: the younger son who helps run the pilgrimage association.

Qi Huimin: the tough manager of the association and devout believer.

Wang Defeng: the Communist Party official who led the reconstruction of Miaofengshan and remains its influential manager.

Chen Deqing, or Old Mrs. Chen: founder of a shrine on Miaofengshan and patron saint of a summertime pilgrimage to the Temple of the Central Peak.

THE SHANXI DAOISTS

Li Bin: the ninth-generation Daoist *yinyang* man, or funeral master, fortune-teller, and geomancer. He moves into the city against his father's wishes.

Li Manshan, or Old Mr. Li: the father of Li Bin, he stays in the family's ancestral village.

Li Qing: the Li family's late patriarch, who revived traditions after the Cultural Revolution.

THE CHENGDU CHRISTIANS

Wang Yi: the former human rights lawyer and pastor of Early Rain Reformed Church.

Jiang Rong: Wang Yi's wife and early convert to Christianity.

Zhang Guoqing: Early Rain's liaison to marginal groups in society.

Zha Changping: the cerebral pastor of the Spring of Life Reformed Church.

Peng Qiang: former entrepreneur and Communist Youth League member who runs the Grace and Blessings Reformed Church.

Ran Yunfei: "Bandit Ran," a mercurial essayist and Chengdu's best-known public thinker, who is drawn to Christianity.

THE MASTERS

Nan Huai-chin: Buddhist meditation guru and interpreter of Chinese classics, he lives in a hermitage on Lake Tai.

Wang Liping: charismatic practitioner of a Daoist meditation technique called *neidan,* or internal alchemy, who teaches courses in the caves of southern China.

Qin Ling: Wang's chief disciple in Beijing.

Xiao Weijia: Qin's husband and scion of an important Communist Party family.

THE MOON YEAR

The Moon Year begins with no moon. The sky is black but for the stars; the moon lies unlit on the other side of the earth, invisible to our eyes. The Chinese call this the Lunar New Year, but it is best known as the Spring Festival, the celebration of a new season. The name seems wrong: the holiday falls in the winter month of January or February. It is cold and dark; the days still short. In northern China, snows can blanket the land. In the south, chilly rains penetrate every room, every layer of clothing. We feel gripped by the hopelessness of winter and wonder how this calendar ever functioned: How did it order time in one of the world's oldest continuous civilizations?

In the nineteenth and twentieth centuries, Chinese patriots had similar questions. They worried that their country was so backward that it would be torn apart by foreign powers. One of these reformers' chief targets was China's traditional culture, especially its systems of belief, which they thought were superstitious relics that dulled people to the potential of science and progress.

The old-style calendar was an easy target. Few practices are as important to a society as how it measures time. In traditional China, calendars were made by artisans who used wood-block printing on tissue-thin paper to create colorful pieces of art decorated by gods and saints. They listed key holidays and reminders when certain ceremonies had to be carried out. On Chinese New Year's Eve, the old calendar was scraped off the wall and the new one pasted up.

The traditional calendar was based on the moon's orbit around the earth. It started on the second new moon after the Winter Solstice, which meant the traditional year began in late January or early

February. Each month was one orbit of the moon around the earth. To China's modernizers, all of this seemed ridiculously out of date. By 1929, the forces for change were so strong that the government formally discarded the lunar calendar and replaced it with the Western Gregorian calendar—the solar calendar, based on the earth's orbit around the sun. Since then, the year in China begins on January 1 and has 365¼ days, just like elsewhere.

And yet, with time, you notice that the lunar calendar still underpins how many Chinese dress, eat, worship, and pray. Even Chinese New Year's other name, the Spring Festival, begins to make sense. In the West, spring starts on the Vernal Equinox—the date in mid-March when day and night are about equally long. But in China, events are anticipated earlier; here, the buildup is the key. Late January or early February might seem too early to welcome spring, but in fact the days are warming. In January, Beijingers will tell you that if you want to skate on one of the city's lakes, you had better go now: after the start of the Moon Year, the ice will melt.

You shrug your shoulders but later think back to holidays that are now mostly forgotten in the West, such as Candlemas or Imbolc. They too fell around this time and used to herald the beginning of spring. And then, a week or two later, even you, a city person who has lost touch with the seasons, you notice that the weather actually has turned. The coldest days are past. Winter's edge has blunted. The ice is melting. And it doesn't seem so odd to look again at the Chinese calendar and notice its upcoming markers: Awakening of the Insects, Clear and Bright, Grain Rain, Summer Harvest.

Today, on the first day of the New Year, the moon is already swinging around in its orbit, soon to reveal the faintest sliver of its sunlit face. Over the coming fifteen days of the Lunar New Year celebrations, the moon will wax into a crescent, then a half globe, each day gaining in power. Finally, on the fifteenth day, it will appear in full force, lighting the darkness, dwarfing the other heavenly bodies. This day is called *Yuanxiao*—the First Night, the first full moon of the first month, the sky relit, the fires rekindled. Pyres are set ablaze, devils driven off, and the year unfolds as always: a series of heavenly events ordered by the sun and the moon and the meaning we give them.

Beijing: The Tolling Bell

I n the southeast corner of Beijing is a neighborhood called Fen-zhongsi, or the Temple of the Tolling Bell. According to local legend, the name came from the story of an old widower who was kind and pure of heart but childless. In traditional China, that meant he had no one to support him in old age. His fellow villagers took pity and offered him a small job as the community's night watchman. His task was to walk around the village every two hours, marking time by beating clappers. He accepted the job but refused pay, saying the villagers should save their money to cast a bell that would replace him when he died.

Over the years, the locals saved their money, while he carried out his duties to unusual effect. During the last watch, just before dawn, he would sound his clappers especially loudly in front of the doors of lazy people, hoping to wake them and get them off to work. In front of the doors of the diligent, he was as quiet as could be, allowing them a few more minutes of sleep in the knowledge that they would get up on their own. As time went by, some villagers said his clappers anticipated the changing seasons or warned of coming storms. When they heard the steady beat, they knew what they had to do—not just when to work or sleep, but how to live their lives, following good and avoiding evil. Eventually, the old man died, the money was counted, and the bell cast. When it was rung, it had the same miraculous effect, a bell tolling for each person.

The bell, the temple that was later built around it, and the village—all were torn down long ago, leaving only a story and the name of a highway overpass, a subway stop, and a neighborhood of tenement homes about to be demolished. Over the past decades, this wave of destruction has rolled over the rest of the capital as well, eliminating a vast medieval city of twenty-five square miles. Beijing had once been made up of *hutongs*—narrow alleys that passed between walled homes, interspersed with hundreds of temples. Superimposed over these communities was an imaginary landscape of holy mountains and deities who linked the city into a sacred bond of myth and faith. For centuries, this urban landscape epitomized the political-religious state that had run China for millennia.

Beijing's cosmology changed in the twentieth century, especially after the Communist takeover in 1949. Many of the temples and *hutongs* were destroyed to make way for the new ideals of an atheistic, industrial society. Starting in the 1980s came economic reforms and uncontrolled real estate development, which has wiped out almost all the rest of the old city and pushed most of Beijing's original residents out of the city center. In the few fragments of the historic city that survived, migrants moved in. Some were poor workers from the countryside, others rich gentrifiers from afar. With them came new foods—spicy dishes from the interior or nouvelle cuisine from abroad—and new customs, such as the mass exodus out of Beijing during holidays to rural hometowns or tropical beach resorts. Lost was a way of life, just as the local cultures of other great cities have been swamped by our restless times.

I had watched this transformation since first coming to Beijing in the early 1980s. Like many people, I was disheartened and felt the city and its once-great culture were lost. But in recent years I began to realize I had been wrong. Beijing's culture was not dead; it was being reborn in odd corners of the city like the Temple of the Tolling Bell. It was not the same as in the past, but it was still vibrant and real— ways of life and belief that echoed the sounds of the past.

The Temple of the Tolling Bell was the home of the Ni (pronounced "NEE") family, ordinary Beijingers who had once lived in the old city near one of its most famous landmarks, the Temple of Heaven. Next door to their old home had been a much smaller temple to Our Lady of the Azure Clouds, or *Bixia Yuanjun*, an important Daoist goddess. The Ni family children used to play in the temple's three courtyards, and the family was friends with an old priest who lived there. In 1992, their house and the Daoist temple were slated for demolition to make way for the headquarters of the General

Administration of Sport of China, a government agency charged with creating national glory. Faced with such a strong opponent, the Ni family did the wise thing: it yielded. As compensation, the family was given money and land to build new homes in the Temple of the Tolling Bell neighborhood. It was from this new encampment outside the old city that they helped orchestrate the revival of Beijing's spiritual life.

On the second day of the Lunar New Year, I paid a visit to the Ni family's eighty-one-year-old patriarch, Ni Zhenshan. Two nights earlier, Beijingers had heralded the Year of the Dragon with loud and endless fireworks against the dark, moonless sky. Yesterday, the first day of the New Year, had been quiet. Traditionally, it is a day for staying home with one's family, cooking big meals, and recuperating from the previous night's excitement. The second day is given over to social calls, and so here I was, plodding past spent firework casings and charred paper, doing what any gentleman is supposed to do on this day: pay respects to one's betters and elders.

Compared with me, the Nis were both. Old Mr. Ni and his fifty-six-year-old son, Ni Jincheng, weren't just older; they understood infinitely more. They knew all the holidays on the traditional calendar, the right way to kowtow before a statue, how to recite sutras, which cigarettes to smoke, and which grain alcohol to drink. They knew which fruits to eat in April and why you never make a gift of a knife or a plum. They had stylish clothes made by a dead tailor, second homes acquired for a song, calligraphy from a colonel, teapots from a royal kiln, and a flock of European racing pigeons. When I asked why or how or when, they would look at me as if I had missed the point: there was no reason; this was how you lived.

Like any good gentleman, Jincheng was waiting for me at the street corner as I got out of the taxi. He was broad shouldered, with a beefy face and a thick head of hair that was combed back in a rakish wave. In his normal life, he had a desk job at the Ministry of Construction but had spent most of his career out in the field, managing projects or inspecting them for safety defects. His speech was distinctive, in part because of its volume: this was a man whose work called for him to communicate over the roar of a jackhammer.

But he also peppered it with a patois of ur-Beijing dialect laden with religious expressions. He talked about karmic retribution (*baoying*), and when someone died, he spoke of the dark gate (*xuanmen*) closing. His clothes reflected his double life. Draped over his shoulders was a green army greatcoat that could have been worn by a worker, but underneath was a tailored collarless jacket made of brown silk and patterned with a stylized version of the character *shou*, or longevity. His cheeks were redder than usual, and he motioned for me to follow him.

"You'll catch a cold out here," I said.

He grunted. "Wang Defeng was here visiting the old man. Everyone was drinking."

Wang Defeng was a government official who ran the most important religious site in Beijing, Miaofengshan, or the Mountain of the Wondrous Peak, located about forty miles west of the city center. I had met the Ni family there a year earlier during the annual pilgrimage to worship Our Lady of the Azure Clouds, the same goddess whose temple had also been next to the Ni family's old home. During the pilgrimage, the Ni family ran a small shrine next to the main temple. It was dedicated to another popular goddess and had a stand offering free tea to pilgrims. This is known as a pilgrimage association and is meant to help the faithful by providing them with physical and moral sustenance as they climb the mountain. About eighty of these groups exist in Beijing. Some provide food and drink, while others honor the gods with acrobatics, stilt walking, humorous skits, and martial arts. During the two-week pilgrimage, many of these volunteers live on the mountain, bunking out six to a room or, like the Ni family, sleeping on cots in the back of their shrines.

The temple is owned by the government, but neither it nor Manager Wang controls the pilgrimage associations. They are independent, with an authority that comes from tradition and faith rather than power and money. Over the course of many generations, the pilgrimage associations have been handed down through clans and families, and they have developed arcane sets of rules and regulations. They choose who can ascend Miaofengshan and how to behave on the mountain. They even decide how you should greet another association member on the street. And they are crucial to the pilgrimage's financial success. If the groups participate, then the Miaofengshan fair is a genuine spiritual event and a destination for tens of thousands of pious pilgrims. If the groups stay away, then it's nothing but a carnival.

Manager Wang had not come to ask the Ni family to attend this year's pilgrimage; no man of culture would come at the start of the Lunar New Year on such a crude mission. Instead, he was paying a courtesy visit. A cynic might view this as the same thing, but this would be too narrow. Personal contact is how life is organized in China, whether running a pilgrimage, business, or political party. All of these have rules, regulations, or bylaws, but what really holds them together is a web of relationships that rarely fits on a flowchart. It includes who is related to whom and who has done whom a favor, when, and under what circumstances. It is about who has the personal charisma and prestige and who has donated the most money, but also it is about who is sincere in carrying out obligations—something even the poorest person can do. Mr. Wang had visited because he was an able administrator wanting to make the next fair a success, but he didn't think in such unsophisticated terms; he was here because visiting Old Mr. Ni was the right thing to do. The patriarch was a great man in Beijing's religious scene. Not visiting him on the second day of the New Year would have been unthinkable.

Jincheng led me down a side street, turning in to an alley too narrow for a car. He pushed open the second door on our right, and three small dogs charged out, barking and wagging their tails. He walked through the first room, where his wife and several other women were playing mahjong on a dark rosewood table. They looked up and called out greetings, offering tea and sunflower seeds, which I waved off. Jincheng slid open a glass door, and we entered the back room, where his father sat waiting for me on a heavy, carved wooden chair—a throne for one of the noblemen of Beijing's religious life.

Old Mr. Ni had a shaved head and thick dark eyebrows that seemed permanently arched upward in a sign of surprise and humility. He loved to talk about catching crickets, collecting gourds, and raising dogs. When I had visited him a few months earlier, we had chatted for a couple of hours about everything from calligraphy to the construction industry, where he had worked since his youth. He had told me that he had cancer but he was certain that he would recover. Now, though, I could see that the illness had overwhelmed his body.

His hands clutched the armrests, as if struggling to keep his body upright. His head was bowed and immobile; when I approached, he did not move. It took him a moment to open his eyes and gesture for me to take a seat next to him. Then he summoned his energy and issued a command.

"If you want to write a book, be accurate. You don't want to be spouting nonsense like people on television, filming this or that, and making all sorts of misleading statements about us. Don't lead people astray. Do you understand?"

I thought back to my visits to Miaofengshan. State-run television often filmed the colorful festival and aired reports on how everything was well and good with traditional Chinese culture. It rarely showed people worshipping, and avoided mentioning that this was primarily a religious event. It usually seemed like a report on a new theme park. I nodded.

"I am not so strong anymore and am not sure I can explain everything. If I lead you astray, then you will write errors and others will be misled. We'll get further and further from the truth.

"But I want you to mark this: All temples are not the same. Some are fake. When you're writing, you have to know the distinction. You have to know which permit pilgrims and which do not. Miaofengshan does allow them. It's why our tea association goes there."

Jincheng leaned over and whispered in my ear, reminding me how his family's tea association had been founded. It had been 1993, and Old Mr. Ni had been ill with kidney cancer. Surgery was imminent. He vowed that if he lived, he would make a trip to Miaofengshan to thank Our Lady of the Azure Clouds. She had looked after the family in their old home, and he was sure she would help him now. Back home, Jincheng had lit incense and prayed.

The surgery had gone well, and Old Mr. Ni had recovered. The next spring, he went to Miaofengshan to fulfill his vow. Although the family had lived next to the temple of Our Lady of the Azure Clouds, they had never made the pilgrimage to her mountain. Old Mr. Ni had been just eight years old when the Japanese invaded and twenty when the Communists took power. In such tumultuous times, the flow of pilgrims had slowed to a trickle, with people worried about safety and generally too poor to afford the long trip through the mountain roads. After Mao took power, his zealots destroyed the temple. But by the mid-1990s it had been rebuilt, and the pilgrimage had resumed.

On his way down the mountain, Old Mr. Ni told Jincheng that he had an idea. He wanted to set up his own pilgrimage association to offer pilgrims tea. In a literal sense, pilgrimage associations are superfluous; nowadays, a pilgrimage usually just takes a day, and no one needs free tea or food. But the associations survive because the idea behind them is more important than their function. They symbolize piety—a gathering of people who have enough faith to sacrifice the thousands of dollars and weeks of time that it takes to run a pilgrimage association.

Jincheng had paused for a minute to think. This venture would cost a huge amount of money. They would need a shrine with a beautiful statue and an altar. In front of it they would need to set out expensive porcelain teapots and cups to symbolize their offering. Of course they would also need a lot of tea, and not cheap tea but something that would honor the goddess. And then they would need volunteers to staff their stall so pilgrims could get tea anytime of the day. It would cost tens of thousands of yuan, which especially back then was a lot of money for working-class people. But Jincheng was in private enterprise then and had begun to make money in the construction industry. He also knew he could count on family and friends to help out. He looked at his father and nodded. During the 1995 pilgrimage, with their own savings and donations from friends and colleagues, they began offering tea and steamed buns at Miaofengshan.

Now I looked over at Old Mr. Ni and nodded: I knew the story, and I knew that it was because of Miaofengshan that he had established the tea association.

"You were healed twenty years ago, perhaps it can happen again?" I ventured.

He shook his head: this wasn't the time for empty talk. He was dying, and he wanted to get across something important. His voice, which even last summer had been so strong and clear, was now hoarse. He struggled to gather the air in his lungs.

"You have to decide if you're writing about practices to make money or if you're writing about belief." He stared down at the floor. Then he took a deep breath and brought up something no one liked to talk about: the Cultural Revolution, a decade of chaos and attacks on religion. Temples like those on Miaofengshan had been razed, while priests, monks, and nuns had been humiliated and dispersed. When the chaos ended with Mao's death in 1976, religious life slowly resumed.

"After the ten years of calamity, the government didn't approve rebuilding Miaofengshan, but it didn't oppose it. There was no document saying it was approved. You see what I mean? It was done by ordinary people.

"'Folk,' this word," he said, pausing, to let the word *minjian* hang in the air for a few extra seconds, "it means it doesn't matter who you are. You can be a farmer, it doesn't matter."

"But now," I said, "that first generation that reopened the temples is getting old. Will its children carry on this work in the future?"

"Humans . . ." He trailed off, trying to find the right way to put it. "There's no end to doing good deeds; there's no final point. You're a Westerner. It doesn't matter if you're Catholic, or Protestant, or any religion. If you've been doing something for thirty years, you don't quit. You don't fold. Impossible. Mark this: with faith, if you've gone half the road, you'll go the distance. The next step, your sons and daughters will take up the things you left behind. It's the same with Christianity."

"Or any religion," Jincheng added.

"You get what I mean? It's the same principle. There's nothing mysterious about it. Of course we all have our own cultures. Chinese literature, or other parts of culture, well, it's pretty big. If you're going to eat and drink culture, that's not easy. That's a complicated topic.

"But faith is different. The basic point is simple. It's only the specifics that are different." The old man wheezed and pushed hard on his hands to keep himself upright. Jincheng's wife, Chen Jinshang, walked in and put her arms around his shoulders to steady him.

"Dad, take a rest," Jincheng said quietly. The old man shook his head.

"Talking to me is just wasting your time if you want to know about high culture." He laughed and perked up. "I don't like to talk nonsense. If I know something, I'll tell you. If not, I won't. Ask."

"I want to ask why you still run the tea association," I said. "You wanted to thank Our Lady of the Azure Clouds, to pay her back for saving your life." He nodded and I continued. "But why do you still go, year after year? Haven't you paid her back already?"

"There is a need. People are unsettled. They come to the mountain, so we should be there for them. We are carrying this on to the next generation. I feel it is our duty."

He paused to formulate the words.

"There is another reason. The temple on Miaofengshan, its history, is like a great story. Many famous people went there. Do you know Cheng Yanqiu? He's one of the four big names in the history of Peking opera. He was fantastic. He gave an incense burner. It's well-known. It's part of the story.

"Those are famous people, but you, what have you left behind?" he said, addressing himself. "Who's going to recognize what you've done? What have you left of value?"

Then he answered his own question.

"Unless it's participating in the pilgrimage association? Our tea association has a name that's unique. It's the Whole Heart Philanthropic Salvation Tea Association. It's based on charity.

"What are you going to leave behind?" he said again, and then replied in a different, deeper voice.

"Well, you've got your tea association.

"Ah! Right! In the Beijing district of Fengtai, in the Temple of the Tolling Bell neighborhood, is the Whole Heart Philanthropic Salvation Tea Association. Oh, right . . . so you can leave that.

"I, Ni Zhenshan, I can leave that. Otherwise who will remember you?"

Jincheng looked down at the ground. His father was already talking about the time after his passing. He was upset; who would run the pilgrimage association if his father died?

"Dad, what are you talking about? What nonsense!" Jincheng's wife blurted out. Chen Jinshang was a lively woman of fifty-six, with short permed hair and a great pealing laugh. But her father-in-law's talk troubled her.

The old man was patient; this was his daughter-in-law, a member of his family for over thirty years, a good, loyal woman who had cared for him day and night over the past months. How to make her understand? Then he thought of the family's stele—a stone tablet about four feet high that stood outside the temple, an honor given to his tea association for its service to pilgrims. Chiseled on the front was the association's name. On the back were the names of the founding family members, including hers. He looked at her softly.

"Think of it like this. Long in the future, even if times change, our stele will remain at the temple. They'll see your name and say, 'Hey, who is that Chen Jinshang?' Then they'll know, 'Oh, that's one of the founders of the tea association.' If you don't have something like this, you won't make it into history as a personage."

"But, Dad, after a while steles fall down," Ms. Chen said. "They break."

"Yes, you can think of it like that. But heaven knows what you have done. And if your grandson goes to Miaofengshan and carries on the tea association, if he sees that the stele is broken, he'll fix it or put up a new one—copy the names from the old one and reerect it. His children will know that their great-grandmother was called Chen Jinshang and she was a pilgrim to Miaofengshan and erected a stele here, and so they'll take care of it. This is what's known as 'passing down for ten thousand years' or 'through the ages of a thousand autumns.'"

"Dad wanted to write a book about the family," Ms. Chen said to me.

"I'm afraid I don't have much to offer," Old Mr. Ni said. "I don't have that much higher education. I'm afraid that I'll tell you a lot of nonsense and your book will be full of errors."

"A book like yours," his son said, nodding sagely, "could be boundless."

"What aspect of the pilgrimage associations do you want to understand?" the old man said to me.

"You need direction," his son added.

"What *are* you writing?" Ms. Chen said with a big laugh, and we all joined in.

"I want to describe this rebirth of faith," I said to them. "It seemed to start recovering after the Cultural Revolution but really took off in recent years."

"That's my case," Old Mr. Ni said. "I encountered an illness and wanted to express my faith. For the first time in our lives, we had money, so I decided to donate tea. It was 'a thought harbored in my breast but never spoken.' I just went to the mountain and saw some-thing was missing and the next year helped out a bit. I just wanted to see what could be done. We offered green tea."

"In my dad's day, green tea was expensive, and so we offered it," Jincheng said. "That's why. But our principles are different from some of the other groups' that you might see. We follow the Bud-dhist idea of *dana*"—the practice of giving, or charity.

"A lot of this new stuff is just for making money," Jincheng added. "It's rubbish."

Then his father surprised me by disagreeing.

"No," he said, shaking his head firmly, his eyebrows knit together tightly as if pondering the idea and then rejecting it. "Not all new things are bad. Sometimes new things rise up and they stay. After a while they become old. Then they become tradition."

2

Ritual: The Lost Middle

Pilgrims like the Ni family underpin one of the great religious revivals of our time. Across China, hundreds of temples, mosques, and churches open each year, attracting millions of new worshippers. The precise figures are often debated, but even a casual visitor to China cannot miss the signs: new churches dotting the countryside, temples being rebuilt or massively expanded, and new government policies that encourage traditional values. Progress is not linear—churches are demolished, temples run for tourism, and debates about morality manipulated for political gain—but the overall direction is clear. Faith and values are returning to the center of a national discussion over how to organize Chinese life.

This is not the China we used to know. For decades, we have been accustomed to thinking of China as a country where religion, faith, and values are marginal. Our images of Chinese people are overwhelmingly economic or political: of diligent workers in vast factories, nouveau riche flaunting their wealth, farmers toiling in polluted fields, or dissidents being locked up. When we do hear of Chinese people and faith, it is either about victims—Chinese Christians forced to worship underground—or exotic stories of wacky people walking backward in parks, hugging trees, or joining scary cults.

All of this exists and is true but misses a bigger point: that hundreds of millions of Chinese are consumed with doubt about their society and turning to religion and faith for answers that they do not find in the radically secular world constructed around them. They wonder what more there is to life than materialism and what makes a good life. As one person I interviewed for this book told me, "We thought we were unhappy because we were poor. But now a lot of us aren't poor anymore, and yet we're still unhappy. We realize there's something missing and that's a spiritual life."

Most surprisingly, this quest is centered on China's heartland: a huge swath of land running roughly from Beijing in the north to Hong Kong in the south, Shanghai in the east to Chengdu in the west. This used to be called "China proper" and for twenty-five centuries has been the center of Chinese culture and civilization, the birthplace of its poets and prophets, the scene of its most famous wars and coups, the setting for its novels and plays, the home of its holiest mountains and most sacred temples. This is where Chinese civilization was born and flourished, and this is where the country's economic and political life is still focused. We have long known that China's ethnic minorities—especially the Tibetans and Uighurs—have valued religion, sometimes as a form of resistance against an oppressive state. But now we find a similar or even greater spiritual thirst among the ethnic Chinese, who make up 91 percent of the country's population. Instead of being a salve for China's marginal people, it is a quest for meaning among those who have benefited most from China's economic takeoff. This is why this book focuses on ethnic Chinese, also called Han Chinese. They dominate China's economic, political, and spiritual life; their journey, for better or worse, is China's journey.

Not all Chinese see this quest in spiritual terms. Government critics often view it as purely political: the country needs better rules and laws to solve society's ills. Reformers inside the system see it more technocratically: if they had better administrative structures and provided better services, apathy and anger would abate.

But most Chinese look at the problem more broadly. China needs better laws and institutions, yes, but it also needs a moral compass. This longing for moral certitude is especially strong in China due to its history and tradition. For millennia, Chinese society was held together by the idea that laws alone cannot keep people together. Instead, philosophers like Confucius argued that society also needed shared values. Most Chinese still hold this view. For many, the answer is to engage in some form of spiritual practice: a religion, a way of life, a form of moral cultivation—things that will make their lives more meaningful and help change society.

All told, it is hardly an exaggeration to say China is undergoing a spiritual revival similar to the Great Awakening in the United States in the nineteenth century. Now, just like a century and a half ago, a country on the move is unsettled by great social and economic change. People have been thrust into new, alienating cities where they have no friends and no circle of support. Religion and faith offer ways of looking at age-old questions that all people, everywhere, struggle to answer: Why are we here? What really makes us happy? How do we achieve contentment as individuals, as a community, as a nation? What is our soul?

Understanding this spiritual tumult requires making a detour back in time to its cause, one of the greatest antireligious movements in world history, one that affected all major faiths in China: Buddhism, Christianity, Daoism, folk religion, and Islam. Because China has been run by a Communist Party for such a long time, it might seem like a typical case of atheistic Communists attacking religion, and to a degree it was. But the campaign against religion did not originate with the Communists' takeover in 1949. Instead, it began a century earlier, when China's traditional civilization began to collapse.

This breakdown was triggered by a crisis of confidence. For most of its history, China dominated its neighbors. Some were militarily stronger, especially the nomadic peoples to its north, such as the Xiongnu, the Mongols, and the Manchus. But even when these groups got the upper hand and conquered China, Chinese rarely doubted the superiority of their civilization. Chinese were often self-critical but believed that their ways of life would prevail.

China's encounter with the West shook that self-assurance. Starting with the First Opium War of 1839, China suffered a string of military defeats. Many in power were at first unfazed, figuring that they only needed better technology, especially arsenals, ships, and cannons. But when China kept losing battles and territory, a sense of crisis developed. Chinese looked around the world and saw how the West had carved up the Americas and Africa and subjugated India. Was China next?

By the end of the nineteenth century, a growing number of Chinese began to believe that their country needed more than superficial changes. They realized that China lacked modern science, engineering, education, public health, and advanced agricultural methods. All of these things were products of a radically different way of ordering society, one based primarily on science. As the crisis deepened, increasingly radical ideas took hold. China didn't just need new policies, or even a new dynasty. It needed to abolish the emperor. It had to overthrow the entire political system of running China. And that meant destroying the religious system that was its most important pillar.

Why religion? Couldn't China have simply revamped its schools and modernized its economy without gutting its traditional faiths? Today, China is a rising power and traditional religions are widespread. The two do not seem incompatible. But the role of religion in traditional Chinese society was very different from today, something we are only beginning to appreciate. Until the past few decades, scholars thought Chinese religions were somewhat analogous to the Abrahamic faiths. Instead of Christianity, Judaism, or Islam, China had Buddhism, Daoism, and Confucianism. That was wrong. Instead, as the historian C. K. Yang put it, religion was "diffused" in Chinese society. It wasn't one pillar next to secular society and could not be defined as one particular thing you did once or twice a week, at a certain place, under the guidance of a certain holy book—the way many world religions are organized. Instead, Chinese religion had little theology, almost no clergy, and few fixed places of worship. But this didn't mean Chinese religion was weak. Instead, it was spread over every aspect of life like a fine membrane that held society together.

Work, for example, was sacred. Almost every profession venerated a god: carpenters worshipped Lu Ban, a historical figure who invented many woodworking and building techniques; martial artists worshipped the general Lord Guan or the monkey king Sun Wukong; medical professionals honored Hua Tuo, a doctor from the third century who pioneered brain surgery; sailors worshipped the goddess Mazu. The list is inexhaustible: dyers, vintners, tailors, makers of musical instruments, musicians and actors, cooks, barbers, and even professional storytellers; in a survey of twenty-eight craft guilds in Beijing in the 1920s, only four did not worship a patron god. In Chinese cities, almost every street corner had a temple or shrine. In her survey of religious life in Beijing, the historian Susan

Naquin estimates that the city had roughly one thousand temples in 1911. The rest of China was similar: every village had a temple or two; many had half a dozen.

Many people might wonder, what religion are we talking about? Are these Buddhist or Daoist practices? In most cases, the answer would be neither. Thanks to the predominance of the Abrahamic faiths in the West, we think in exclusive terms: this person is Catholic, that person is Jewish, another is Muslim. These faiths have clearly defined stories about their beliefs, as well as set places of worship, a holy book, and, quite often, a clergy. Most important is that belief in these faiths is absolute and exclusive; it's one or the other. One doesn't celebrate Passover, fast during Lent, and go on the hajj. New Agers notwithstanding, dabbling is heretical.

Traditional Chinese religion is different. This is why pollsters have a hard time figuring out if Chinese people are religious. Asking "what faith do you believe in?" seems like a simple question for people who define religion according to monotheistic norms. They expect a clear-cut answer, like "I am a Buddhist" or "I am a Daoist." But for most of Chinese history, this sort of question would have been strange. Religion was part of belonging to your community. A village had its temples, its gods, and they were honored on certain holy days. Choice was not really a factor. China did have three separate teachings, or *jiao*—Confucianism (*rujiao*), Buddhism (*fojiao*), and Daoism (*daojiao*)—but they did not function as separate institutions with their own followers. Primarily, they provided services: a community might invite a priest or monk to perform rituals at temples, for example, and each of the three offered its own special techniques—Buddhist Chan meditation or devotional Pure Land spiritual exercises, Daoist meditative exercises, or Confucian moral self-cultivation. But they were not considered separate. For most of Chinese history, people believed in an amalgam of these faiths that is best described as "Chinese Religion."

In fact, the concept of thinking of oneself as part of a discrete and clearly definable religious system was so foreign to Chinese that when modernizers wanted to reorganize society using Western norms one hundred years ago, they had to import the vocabulary from the West. Turning to Japan, which had started a similar discussion a generation earlier, they imported words like *zongjiao* (religion) and *mixin* (superstition). Before that, there was little idea of religion being separate from society or government. It was all one and the same. It was how you lived. It was what you did.

This is reflected in theology's small role. In religions like Christianity, theologians argue passionately over issues like the Trinity or original sin, using tools provided by Greek logic and metaphysics. The same goes for Judaism or Islam, where scholars argue over doctrines or ways of behaving, engaging in epic debates. China has a long history, so it is possible to find exceptions—such as a famous debate in the court of a sixth-century emperor between proponents of Buddhism and Daoism (the Daoists lost, and the Buddhists wrote a book called *Xiaodaolun,* or "Laughing at the Daoists"). By and large, however, these kinds of discussions were rare. Most people saw them as pointless.

What did interest Chinese were rituals—in other words, the pragmatic but profound issue of how to behave. As the historian David Johnson puts it in his book *Spectacle and Sacrifice,*

> *Chinese culture was a performance culture . . . Chinese philosophers were concerned more with how people should act, and what counted as good actions, than with using logic to prove propositions. Ritual was the highest form of action or performances; every significant life event, social, political, or religious, was embedded in and expressed through ritual.*

These rituals helped organize Chinese society. In traditional China, the imperial bureaucracy was tiny by today's standard, and most officials sent out by Beijing only made it to the county seat, which meant one person oversaw hundreds of villages and tens of thousands of people. More important was the role of prominent local people, often called the gentry or literati because most of them had an education in the Chinese classics. Temples and religious practice united these people and formed a structure for them to rule. A key committee in every village was one that ran the local temples. These often doubled as bodies that united a community for other purposes as well, such as building irrigation systems or raising militias to fight off bandits. Temples also provided a physical space for government rule. Local elders might meet, read proclamations, or carry out punishments there. A local temple could be like the cathedral and city hall of a medieval European town rolled into one. In the words of the historian Prasenjit Duara, religion was society's "nexus of power."

But religion was more than a method for running China; it was the political system's lifeblood. The emperor was the "Son of Heaven," who presided over elaborate rituals that underscored his semidivine nature. These included praying at temples to ensure good harvests, making sure that ancestors were honored, and worshipping the holy mountains that held up the four corners of the universe. Officials duplicated many of these rites at the local level, especially by praying at temples to the local City God. From the fourteenth century onward, the government mandated that every district of the empire have its own City God temple. Officials had to worship there on certain days, and it was often a center of local life and politics. The City God was an official of the spiritual world, which was organized on hierarchies similar to the traditional political world. The realm of spirits was an extension of this world, co-opting each other for legitimacy.

With all this in mind, it becomes easier to understand why reformers and revolutionaries took on religion. They wanted to create a new political system, and to do that, they had to grab power from where it lay—in the political-religious system that ran China.

This is not as unusual as it might sound. In other countries, religion also played a key role in governing societies. For much of European history, politics and religion were inseparable. The rise of the nation-state in the seventeenth century changed this, diminishing and compartmentalizing religion. The bureaucratic state took over schools and hospitals and destroyed legal privileges enjoyed by the church. The rise of Protestantism played an important role too, with the binary terms of authentic "religion" and taboo "superstitions" used to discredit Catholic practices. This fed into Christianity's long-standing appeal to logic: true religion could be defended by reason; everything else was superstition and should be destroyed.

As the world globalized in the nineteenth and twentieth centuries, these ideas spread. When the Ottoman Empire collapsed after

World War I, the new Turkish state abolished the caliphate—the ruler of all Muslims—and even converted some mosques into museums. In the Middle East after World War II, political movements like the Ba'ath Party in Iraq and Syria tried to scale back Islam as well, seeing it as a cause for their region's colonization by the British and French. In India, too, modern Hinduism was created by streamlining a variety of diverse faiths into something more like an Abrahamic religion. All these movements were united by one desire: a strong state to imitate and fend off Western countries.

In China, this movement gained ground as the Qing dynasty crumbled in the late nineteenth century. China had an estimated one million temples around the turn of the century. A movement for political reform in 1898 called for many temples to be converted to schools. Although this reform plan was defeated, many local governments took steps on their own, and today many of the best-known elementary and high schools across China are located on the grounds of former temples. Most notable was the destruction of the old City God temples. As the prime representatives of the old system of political-religious power, they were first taken over by the modernizing Chinese state and then destroyed; in fact, only a handful of City God temples exist today. The wrath of reformers was almost boundless; even before the Communist takeover in 1949, half of these one million temples had been destroyed, shuttered, or converted to other uses.

What of the monotheistic faiths? Islam entered China more than a millennium ago via traders along its coast and up through the Grand Canal to Beijing, as well as along the Silk Road from Central Asia. But Islam was mainly confined to China's geographic periphery, including regions like Xinjiang, Gansu, and Ningxia that were only occasionally under Chinese control. Even today, with these regions firmly ruled by Beijing, Islam counts at most twenty-three million believers, or 1.6 percent of the population. Conversions almost only happen when people marry into Muslim families—a result of government policies to define Islam as a faith that is practiced by only ten non-Chinese ethnic groups, especially the Hui and Uighurs. Islam sometimes provides an identity for people who do not want to be ruled by China—a situation we find today among the Uighurs in China's far western province of Xinjiang—but its marginalized position means it rarely enters the contemporary national debate on faith, values, or national identity.

The impact of Christianity was radically different. It entered China later but spread among Han Chinese, causing much angst around the turn of the century. One popular saying then was "One more Christian; one less Chinese" (*duo yige jidutu; shao yige zhongguoren*)—the idea was that the religion was incompatible with being Chinese. But its influence was huge, helping to define modern China's religious world. One basic reason for Christianity's influence was its presence in the West. Chinese reformers realized that Western countries were Christian and concluded that it was not incompatible with a modern state. Some, like the Nationalist Party leader Chiang Kai-shek, even converted. But more influential was the decision by almost all modernizers of China to adopt the Protestant distinction between religion and superstition. "Real" religion was like Christianity and allowed to survive; the rest was superstition.

The result was traumatic. For Buddhism and Daoism, only a handful of large or famous temples managed to win approval as "religion," or *zongjiao*. These were mostly monasteries or temples on holy mountains or near big cities. They had a clergy, regular ceremonies, and volumes of scriptures that could be defined as something similar to the Bible. It was also fairly easy to describe them as coming from a great and long tradition. Of the two, Buddhism fared better. It has a long philosophical tradition with several schools that early on were introduced to the West via Japan. It also had a history of proselytizing and easily gave birth to energetic reformers in the twentieth century who quickly adapted to the new paradigms. They linked temples into nationwide associations that lobbied for their rights.

But most Chinese religion did not fare so well. Confucianism had been too closely tied to the old system to survive, despite efforts in the early part of the century to organize it into a religion, or even to declare it China's "national" religion, much as Japanese reformers had done with indigenous religious practices that became known as Shinto. As for Daoism, it survived, but only barely. Because it was less hierarchical than Buddhism, most of its temples were not organized and ended up being closed or destroyed, leaving just a few of the great monasteries in the countryside or remote mountains.

Most tragically, folk religion was all but wiped out. These were the innumerable small temples or shrines that were locally managed and not linked to the major faiths—in other words, the vast majority of temples in China. They were declared "superstitious." Hundreds of thousands of temples were obliterated, an immense wave of auto-cultural genocide.

At first, this religious cleansing happened haphazardly, often through individual actions. A telling example involves Sun Yat-sen, who would eventually help overthrow the Qing dynasty and establish the Republic of China in 1912. One of his first acts of rebellion was to go to the local temple in his hometown and smash its statues. When Sun's Nationalist Party took power, the pace picked up. His successor Chiang Kai-shek launched the "New Life" movement to cleanse China of old ways of doing things. Along with trying to eradicate opium, gambling, prostitution, and illiteracy, the Nationalists launched a "campaign to destroy superstition" as part of a broader effort to *jianguo*, or create a nation. In a precursor of Mao's Red Guards, Nationalist Party youth organizations sent groups out to destroy traditional temples, and the government issued regulations with the ominous name "Standards to Determine Temples to Be Destroyed and Maintained." The Nationalists effectively controlled China for only ten years, so the impact of their measures was limited, but the course was set: Chinese religion was a social ill that needed to be radically reformed or destroyed in order to save China.

In 1949, the Communists defeated the Nationalists in China's civil war, bringing to power the most radical group that wanted to change China. Initially, the Communists organized religion as they did other non-Communist groups in society: by co-opting them under the "United Front." These were non-Communist groups that the party thought could be useful or could at least provide the facade of a pluralistic society. The party set up associations for the five religions that had coalesced out of the wreckage of the old system: Buddhism, Daoism, Islam, Catholicism, and Protestantism. These five groups were allowed to run their faiths' surviving temples, churches, or mosques. But everything was firmly guided by the party. Key personnel decisions (important abbots, priests, bishops, cardinals, or imams) all had to be approved by the Communist Party. Most property was confiscated, such as Christian-run schools and hospitals or the landholdings that had supported the great Buddhist and Daoist monasteries in the countryside. Foreign ties were especially suspect, and all missionaries expelled. But religion wasn't banned, and many of the surviving temples or churches stayed open.

This system only lasted a few years. By the late 1950s, Mao embarked on a series of wildly radical policies that suppressed most religious activity. By the time the Cultural Revolution was launched in 1966, the attack was among the most furious in world history. Virtually every place of worship was shuttered and clergy driven out. In the Catholic stronghold of Taiyuan in Shanxi Province, the central cathedral was turned into a "living exhibition" of how backward religion was. Priests and nuns were held in cages and local residents ordered to troop by and watch them. Across the country, Buddhist, Daoist, and Catholic clergy who had taken vows of chastity were forced to marry.

Almost no place of worship survived unscathed. Family shrines were dismantled and thrown out. Temples that had endured the attacks in the late Qing and Republican periods were gutted, torn down, or occupied by factories and government offices. A few were of such historic importance that moderates in the government were able to protect them, but most were damaged or destroyed. Almost all were emptied of their statues, which were pitched into bonfires or smuggled down to Hong Kong to be sold off through antiques dealers. This is one reason why so many temples in China lack the great works of art that characterize many ancient places of worship around the world.

During this period, religion went underground. Churchgoers met in secret, while Buddhists and Daoists tried to save their scriptures and ritual manuals by burying them or committing them to memory. Open practice of physical cultivation—Tai Chi, meditation, or even martial arts—were not allowed, although people did so at home, or even in prison.

In public, all that was allowed was the cult of Mao. In the Republican period, Sun Yat-sen and Chiang Kai-shek were venerated but the Cultural Revolution took this to a new level. People wore Mao badges, waved his book of sayings like a Bible, and traveled to his hometown as if on a pilgrimage. Some people prayed to Mao, asking for his instructions in the morning and reporting back to him in the evening. It is hard to gauge how much to make of this because many of these reports are propaganda. Coercion was endemic; not showing the right revolutionary zeal could result in prison or death. But especially among the youth who had grown up since the Communist takeover, some fervor was real—an ecstatic outpouring of emotion, an ersatz religion for a country that had destroyed its own.

There was one problem with Mao as a living god: he died. When that happened in 1976, the country went into shock. Some people were thrilled—finally, the dictator was gone—but many were crushed. Genuine tears flowed, and the country ground to a halt. With traditional religion decimated and Mao dead, where could one channel one's faith?

The party responded by trying to turn the clock back to the early 1950s. On March 31, 1982, as part of a more general accounting of the destruction wrought by the Cultural Revolution, the Communist Party issued a ten-page paper called "The Basic Viewpoint and Policy on the Religious Question During Our Country's Socialist Period." It is better known as Document 19 and is an astoundingly candid analysis of China's religious crisis and the legal basis for China's religious revival. It states that for nineteen of Mao's twenty-seven years in power, "leftist errors" took hold—a startling admission of how the party had fumbled religious policy during its first three decades in power. It admitted that the radicals who ran the country "forbade normal religious activities," "fabricated a host of wrongs and injustices that they pinned upon these religious personages," and "used violent measures against religion that forced religious movements underground."

After admitting its errors, the party went on to describe religion in sympathetic language, arguing forcefully that religion would disappear but only very gradually: "Those who expect to rely on administrative decrees or other coercive measures to wipe out religious thinking and practices with one blow are even further from the basic viewpoint that Marxism takes toward the religious question. They are entirely wrong and will do no small harm."

Instead, the document said the party's long-term policy was "respect for and protection of the freedom of religious belief." That meant it was permissible, either in places of worship or at home, for "Buddha worship, scripture chanting, incense burning, prayer, Bible study, preaching, Mass, baptism, initiation as a monk or a nun, fasting, celebrations of religious festivals." Even Christian house church meetings were tacitly approved: "In principle this should not be allowed, yet this prohibition should not be too rigidly enforced."

As for how religion should be controlled, Document 19 ordered a return to the old system set up in the early 1950s: the five religions would be run by associations that would report to the government. Places of worship could reopen, and a new generation of clergy be trained. This was the foundation of China's religious revival.

This does not mean that China's religious life is normal. Government control of major temples, churches, and mosques is resented by many, who turn to underground places of worship free from government control. In the public sphere, religion is also tightly circumscribed. It is all but banned from the media; religious leaders, for example, almost never comment on the great issues of the day, or even interact with each other. Interreligious dialogue is all but unknown.

The turmoil of the past century and a half has also made people uncomfortable about expressing their religiosity. In fact, most people shun the word "religion," which is seen as a sensitive term, something extremely formal, hierarchical, and political. This results in colossal misunderstandings when outsiders try to use these terms to gauge religious or spiritual life in China.

One government survey in 2012, for example, showed that only 10 percent of respondents said they had a "religious belief," with 89.6 percent saying they had none. International polling firms seem to reflect similar low levels of belief. In 2014, for example, the Pew Research Center issued a major study on global views about religion. It came to the startling conclusion that in China only 14 percent of respondents believed that morality was linked to belief in religion. This led some Western commentators to write of "the atheists of Beijing." In 2015, a WIN/Gallup International poll went further, reporting that 61 percent of Chinese identified themselves as atheists—versus the worldwide average of just 11 percent atheists.

These studies are absurdly flawed. Almost all try to get people to define their behavior based on the loaded Western vocabulary, especially *zongjiao*—do you believe in a *zongjiao*? Put this way, almost all Chinese will say no.

Instead, it is much more useful to ask people how they act or whether they believe in specific ideas. In a 2007 study of over three thousand people, 77 percent said they believe in moral causality, or *baoying*, a key pillar of traditional Chinese belief. It also reported that 44 percent agreed with the statement "life and death depends on the will of heaven," while 25 percent said they had experienced the intervention of a "Buddha" (*fo*) in their lives in the past twelve months.

Other surveys capture this religious surge. A 2005 survey by East China Normal University in Shanghai found that 31 percent of the country's population, or about 300 million people, are religious: two-thirds were worshippers of Buddhism, Daoism, or folk practices, in addition to 40 million Christians, with the rest divided among other faiths. The key reason for the high response rate was that the survey used the word *xinyang*, or faith, instead of *zongjiao*, or religion. Another study, the China Spiritual Life Study, led by Fenggang Yang at Purdue University, gave similar numbers: 185 million consider themselves Buddhist, while another 17.3 million have formal ties to a temple (making them the equivalent of lay Buddhists). As for Daoism, 12 million say they are Daoist, and another 173 million say they engage in some Daoist practices.

The most obvious sign of China's religious revival is the growing number of places of worship. A government survey from 2014 found half a million Buddhist monks and nuns in thirty-three thousand Buddhist temples and another forty-eight thousand Daoist priests and nuns affiliated with nine thousand Daoist temples—twice the number of temples reported in the 1990s. That might seem like impossibly fast growth, but it matches what I have observed in dozens of cities across China. Even in Beijing, the most politicized and atypically atheistic city in China, the number of Daoist temples has increased from two in 1995 to over twenty today. That is still a fraction of the hundreds that existed in the past but indicates the speed of change.

As for Christianity, the picture is bifurcated. Until 1949, Catholicism was the strongest Christian group, numbering three million, or three-quarters of Christians in China. But since then, Catholicism has fared poorly. The chief culprit is Catholicism's greatest strength and weakness: its hierarchy. Before 1949, that top-down structure allowed the church to channel money from abroad into China to build hospitals and schools and send missionaries to far-flung corners of the land. But when the Communists took power, this hierarchy was decapitated, and the money supply cut off. The new government broke ties with the Vatican and expelled foreign missionaries. In their place, the government installed government functionaries, giving the state control over the Catholic religious apparatus.

These problems were compounded by the Catholic Church's failure to localize its clergy. Before 1949, virtually all Catholic leaders—cardinals, bishops, heads of hospitals and schools—were foreigners. When they were forced out, Catholics were left leaderless, and the religion devolved into a clan-based faith, with conversions taking place only when people married into a Catholic family—much like Islam, but with fewer believers. This is why Catholicism remains the weakest and least influential of China's five official religions. Even if one accepts upper-end estimates of twelve million, that is still less than 1 percent of the population and barely above China's population growth (which has more than tripled since 1949). The religion has a colorful history in China, and the decades-long courtship between the Vatican and Beijing attracts much foreign media coverage. But the reality is that Catholicism plays a minor role in China's religious life.

Protestantism, by contrast, took off after 1949 and is often described as the fastest-growing religion in China. From 1 million adherents in 1949, the official figures show that 20 million Protestants are members of government-run churches. Almost all independent estimates, however, show the true number to be several times that, especially because of the popularity of churches that are not part of the government structure—"underground" or "house" churches. In 2008, the Beijing sociologist Yu Jianrong estimated that Protestants number around 60 million. In 2011, the Pew Forum on Religion & Public Life estimated 58 million Protestants. Because the government does not permit independent studies of religious belief, figures on unofficial activity are at best educated guesses, but round-number estimates of 100 million have to be seen as at the very upper end, and so I think it reasonable to exclude them. Even so, it is worth noting that since 1949 the number of Protestants has increased at an annual rate of 7 percent. Straight-line projections are risky—some extraordinary factors, such as the turmoil of the early years of Communist rule might have driven high numbers of people into Protestant Christianity—but even at just a 4 percent growth rate, the number of Protestants should top 100 million by 2030. The exact numbers are in any case not so important. The key is that Protestantism has become a dynamic part of China's religious landscape, especially in its biggest cities and among its best-educated people.

Altogether, we can say that China has roughly 200 million Buddhists and Daoists, with another 50 to 60 million Protestants, 20 to 25 million Muslims, and about 10 million Catholics—in other words, about 300 million people, which matches broader estimates, such as the Shanghai study. This excludes the 175 million who follow some sort of Daoist or folk religion practices and the many Chinese who follow smaller spiritual practices, such as Baha'i, Gandhiism, Yoga, and esoteric practices imported from the West. All told, this is a remarkable recovery, especially considering the destruction of religious infrastructure and knowledge, the continued political suppression, and the broader difficulties of defining one's spirituality.

This does not mean that the party has suddenly allowed religious freedom. Document 19 and subsequent rules and regulations make it clear that religion is supposed to be apolitical and regulated by the state. Underground activities might be tolerated but are still illegal. So, too, are ties with foreign organizations—a taboo that often leads to persecution.

The biggest example of official intolerance took place in 1999, when the government banned the Falun Gong spiritual movement. This group was an outgrowth of a return to traditional spiritual and physical cultivation, but the group was seen as a challenge to the government. When it refused to disband, a crackdown followed. Human rights groups estimate that about one hundred practitioners died in police custody, while thousands were incarcerated without trial, many spending years in labor camps.

However terrible, the suppression of Falun Gong might have created space for other religious organizations. Since the crackdown, the government has loosened its policy toward established religions, perhaps feeling that it is better to allow religiosity to be channeled into groups that it can control, rather than see it erupt in independent movements like Falun Gong. Government favor is especially pronounced toward Daoism, folk practices, and most forms of Buddhism.

Groups with foreign ties have fared less well. Hence the ongoing troubles for Tibetan Buddhists who emphasize ties to the exiled Dalai Lama, Muslims inspired by global Islamic movements, or Christians who look abroad for guidance and leadership. But if focused, led, and financed inside China, religious life has been granted huge leeway.

This has led to an uneasy balance. Traditional values and practices are encouraged as a source of stability and morality. But faith is also feared as an uncontrollable force—an alternative ideology to the government's vision of how society should be run. In the past, state and religion were united, forming a spiritual center of gravity for China. That old system is now gone, but nothing new has taken its place. With no clear course, the country percolates with sects and saviors but has no system to hold it all together—or as the historians Vincent Goossaert and David Palmer describe it, "a Middle Kingdom that has lost its Middle."

3

Shanxi: First Night

The Taihang Mountains begin west of Beijing, where Miaofeng-shan abuts the Mongolian plateau like a pillar holding up the northern edge of the Chinese world. From there, the range runs south through the historic heartland of the Chinese people like a primordial scar. Centuries ago, people looked to the peaks and believed them to be the birthplace of Nüwa, the matriarchal creator of humans. Military strategists cast a colder eye, finding value in narrow passes that could be easily defended. Nowadays, industrial-ists see the richness of the mountains in the vast deposits of metal and coal that have made the region one of the world's greatest con-centration of steelworks. To the east lies the North China Plain, a great grain-growing area that extends to the coast. To the west is the province of Shanxi, which literally means "west of the mountains." It is home to Mount Heng, one of the five holy mountains of ancient China and one of the greatest concentrations of historic relics in the country.

In the northeast corner of Shanxi, wedged in between the Taihang and the Mongolian plateau, is a plain little county of 280,000 people called Yanggao. A bit of the Great Wall runs through its northeast-ern corner, but it is hard to reach and not developed for tourism. Its most famous temple is in ruins and used as a storage shed for stacks of smashed Buddha heads and steles. No famous officials, generals, poets, or painters made Yanggao their home. And in a region where coal is about as common as oil used to be in Texas, it is the only county in Shanxi without a mine. It relies on agriculture, but water is so scarce that farmers still look to the clouds, hoping that the spring clouds will bring rain. To be safe, they grow cash crops that do well in arid climates: apricots, nuts, and chrysanthemums.

Seen on a map, though, Yanggao tells a more remarkable story. The county is a blur of 267 villages, their names running one into the other—an incredible density of rural life. For thousands of years, Chinese civilization has been anchored in areas like this. Its population was spread out evenly, with no major metropolitan centers. Travel was by foot, so life centered on the village and local traditions. That fostered a communal life of agricultural work regulated by the lunar calendar, punctuated by annual festivals at the hundreds of local temples—many of them huge and imposing, dotting the countryside like castles or cathedrals in Europe. This was village China, for centuries venerated as the ideal form of society.

Today, this rural idyll exists only on paper. A new ideology called urbanization has left many of those villages empty. Some farmers have left for China's big cities, but many ended up in the county seat, Yanggao Town, which by 2015 had sucked in half the county's population. An awkward city of weedy roundabouts and potholed boulevards, it bustled with two-stroke tractors and wrong-way drivers. People sauntered across the roads, oblivious to the horns and shouts, owning the street as if it were their families' fields. On each side of the road were two-story buildings of upstairs apartments and shop fronts offering services no one needed on the farm: hairdressing, security doors, and lottery tickets.

The front of one store was decorated with a bright red sign and white letters that read, "Funerals from Head to Toe," and in smaller characters the owner's qualifications: "Upper Liangyuan Village Ninth-Generation *Yinyang* Man Li Bin." In a city rushing forward, the sign's descriptions were personal and idiosyncratic—history by the number of generations, geography by the name of a village. The store was like a fruit tree in a village orchard: its top cut off and grafted onto something new—an effort to transplant the past into the future.

Two weeks ago, the Chinese New Year had begun on the dark night of a new moon. Now it was nearly full, and Li Bin was about to celebrate the holiday's end with the "Lantern Festival," a tame-sounding name for what is also called *Yuanxiao,* First Night, or Primal Night, a name that harks back to the festival's origins as a time of purging and exorcism. This is when the year really begins, when the visits and ceremonies end and daily life resumes: a new moon, a new start.

The festival began the next day, and Li Bin intended to spend it mingling with friends in town. It was the dead of winter, just five degrees above zero, but as he stepped outside his store, he didn't bother wearing an overcoat or hat. That was the outfit of people back in the countryside where he used to live, the cautious, careful people who hoarded their calories until warmer days arrived. He wasn't so timid. He was tall and strong, with quick eyes and a sharp sense of humor. He spoke like a city person, confidently and directly, not with the pregnant silences and meaningful looks of village people. He was accustomed to living amid strangers; he knew that he could no longer assume that everybody knew who he was and what he was thinking. He still understood that smaller world but was a city man now, dressed in black loafers, black corduroys, and a black leather jacket unzipped to show off a thick dark gray sweater. He cut a good figure, a thirty-five-year-old stepping out into a new world.

Li Bin's profession, though, seemed a throwback. A *yinyang* man is a cross between a geomancer, a fortune-teller, and a funeral director—a form of family-based Daoism that was how the religion was originally practiced before new schools of the religion arose about a thousand years ago that emphasized celibacy and monastic living. In those days—and still today across wide swaths of rural China—Daoist masters were not affiliated with a temple, and they certainly were not part of a government association. They lived in local communities as priests, passing their knowledge down from father to son. In many parts of China, these priests are simply called *daoshi,* or Daoist priests, but the local term is much more evocative: *yinyang* priests are masters of the *yin* world—the dark world of death—but also the *yang* world of brightness and life.

For nine generations, an unbroken chain of Li family men had provided religious services. The world of their authority was small; they rarely traveled more than a dozen miles to perform a funeral or tell a fortune. But many became famous in this small corner of rural China. Mao's Red Guards had tried to burn all the religious manuals in the region, but Li Bin's grandfather had miraculously recovered them, helping to rebuild local religious life. Li Bin's father was a respected fortune-teller, carefully listening to people's problems before offering measured advice. As for Li Bin, he had his own gift: vision. He could see that Chinese were leaving the villages for the towns. He also knew that these new city people were hungry for belief.

So despite his father's opposition, he had recently moved to Yang-gao Town. Then he started acting like the other small-business people there. He handed out name cards wherever he went and invited anyone of note for a meal and a bottle of grain liquor.

The efforts had paid off. Now he was traveling across provincial boundaries for his clients and had recently buried the director of a government office. That had been a financial bonanza: most country people could afford just two wreaths of paper flowers, but the official's family had ordered seven. Li Bin and his wife, Jing Hua, had stayed up all night making the wreaths, their hands rubbed raw from bending bamboo into wooden frames and gluing on the paper flowers. But they were clearing more money in a week than his father did in a month back in the village, and the business kept coming; the couple could barely get six hours of sleep a night. Many days, they asked relatives over to help.

The work was challenging in other ways, too. Rural people knew their roles and what was expected of them. Li Bin and his father gave them a standard two-day funeral, complete with music, complex rituals, and periods of intense emotion when family members could express their loss. It was a tried-and-true way of dealing with death and one that had brought respect to his family. But this new era was different. City people wanted things faster, simpler, and on their own terms. Not only that, but everyone assumed that everyone else was on the make. That bothered Li Bin; the suspicion and the endless haggling of city life wore him out.

But before he could meet his city friends, he had to bury a dead man. China might be urbanizing, but half the population still lived on the land. The deceased had been a well-regarded farmer, and his children and grandchildren had returned from across China to see him off. Wanting it done right, they had hired the Li family. Tomorrow was the big holiday, with a parade, floats, and massive bonfires. Li Bin was looking forward to that. But like in much of Chinese religious life, the dead held precedence over the living.

He walked over to his car, a tiny Chinese-made sedan that always seemed close to collapse. Its starter whirred and whined in protest against the cold, but eventually Li Bin coaxed it awake. He stepped on the clutch, put the car in gear, and crawled down the rutted street to the first intersection, turned left, and headed back into the countryside.

I first met Li Bin at Carnegie Hall. It was 2009, and the New York institution was holding a series of concerts about Chinese cultural life. There was an evening dedicated to marionettes, another to puppets, and one devoted to sacred music. On that evening, Li Bin and his troupe performed with another group, their different styles knitted together by the story of a Chinese-American named Wu Man, who was a master of the *pipa*, a Chinese-style lute. A film about Wu Man at the start of the concert explained how she had gone back to China to see if folk music still existed. Later, during the concert, she joined the groups to perform. I had heard Daoist music before and knew it as something that primarily accompanied rituals, many of them very long and complex. But these pieces were short, neat, and digestible.

Afterward, I went backstage to introduce myself. Li Bin handed me a business card, inviting me to visit him back in China. I doubted I would go. They seemed like nice people, but I had hoped to find something authentic and assumed that any world music that found its way to Carnegie Hall had to be fake. The brochures were slick, the advertising effective, the audience polite; how could this be connected to the rough world along the Taihang range?

A year and a half later, I was traveling in Shanxi and realized I was near Li Bin's home. I called him, and he said the group was about to perform; come on over. I arrived at his store in Yanggao Town, and the two of us set out for the countryside in his beat-up car. I had no idea what was going on; I thought it was a concert in a village or maybe a rehearsal. We arrived in the village, stopped in front of a farmhouse, and walked in. Everyone was wearing white—white robes over their ordinary clothes, white hats, and white paper pasted to their shoes. We were at a traditional Chinese funeral.

"What the heck are you doing here?" I asked him.

"We're performing," he said to me. "This is what we do for a living."

Li Bin's father and other members of the troupe marched out of a side room, dressed in black gowns and black peaked caps decorated with the outline of a red sun on the front (symbolizing *yang*) and the moon on the back (symbolizing *yin*). They walked past me into a small tent that had been set up by the front door. In the middle was a temporary altar laden with fruits and snacks—offerings for the afterlife. Behind it was a big oak coffin, and on it was the picture of a dead man. The musicians sat down on folding chairs, three on each side of the altar, and began playing. Two were on cymbals and gongs, and three played the *sheng*, a handheld instrument made of a dozen pipes protruding from a wooden base. Another played a *guanzi*, a kind of valveless clarinet. One of the men playing the cymbals also sang prayers, while the hypnotic music built up in intensity and volume. It was strange, unsettling, sad, and so different from anything I had heard in Carnegie Hall.

I spent the day listening to them perform for short stretches in front of the coffin, punctuated by breaks, when I could ask them questions. I began to realize that I had completely misunderstood the concert in New York. The story implying that Wu Man had discovered them was a harmless fiction designed to give American audiences something to hold on to. She is indeed a great *pipa* player, who has recorded with famous groups like the Kronos Quartet. And she is genuinely interested in traditional Chinese music. But she was part of a decades-long effort by outsiders to transform Daoist ritual practices into a musical product that could be marketed to modern audiences. The problem is that Li Bin and his family were not primarily musicians; they were Daoist ritual specialists who used music to carry out funerals or celebrations of a god's birthday. They were priests.

The Li family became pigeonholed as musicians in the 1980s. That is when a Chinese scholar named Chen Kexiu found them while conducting field research in Shanxi in the 1980s. He and other scholars discovered that fourteen similar Daoist *yinyang* groups exist in the greater Datong area—a hidden religious life that would not be obvious if one just drove through the area. In China, these rural folk practices are often called "living fossils" and romanticized as something that has not changed in centuries—like a brontosaurus bone dug out of a pit that had suddenly come to life.

Chen decided to see if he could make the dinosaur dance. He streamlined their music and gave them a fanciful name: Hengshan Daoist Music Group, named after the nearby holy mountain. The group had never been to Mount Heng, but no matter; it was better than not having a name. Then Professor Chen helped organize a concert in Beijing in 1990. A music group was born.

Then another stroke of luck: one of the people in the audience was a young Englishman, Stephen Jones. He was a Baroque violinist and a budding ethnomusicologist, fluent in Chinese. He visited the Li family back in Shanxi and interviewed Li Bin's grandfather Li Qing and included some of their story in two broad surveys of folk religion and Daoism in northern China. Jones also became their overseas manager. I got to know Steve over the years as a formidable scholar who understands the entirety of the Li family's work—their rituals and their fortune-telling, as well as their music. But to make the music palatable to a concert audience, Steve continued Chen's work of reshaping it. He arranged it all into a forty-five-minute program. He later took them to Amsterdam, introduced them to Wu Man, traveled with them to the United States, and soon to Italy.

In the early years of the twenty-first century, this transformation began to feed back into China. The government adopted a term coined by the United Nations Educational, Scientific, and Cultural Organization called "intangible cultural heritage," or *feiyi* as it is known by its Chinese acronym. This is meant to protect not monuments like the Great Wall and the Forbidden City but to help more elusive traditions like music, cuisine, ritual, drama, and martial arts. By the second decade of the twenty-first century, it had become a national craze, with *feiyi* designations offered by each level of government: neighborhood, city, province, and nation. In 2010, the Li family were designated as one of twelve hundred national-level *feiyi* organizations and received a onetime payment of 150,000 yuan (or about $25,000 at current rates) to teach their craft to future generations.

In exchange, the Li family had to show that ye ancient olde musick was alive and well—no matter what was actually going on. That meant performing a few concerts a year during big holidays. And for that they used the musicologists' repertoire of a few shortened pieces from funeral or other rituals. So this creation of Chinese and foreign scholars became the government's benchmark for the survival of rural Daoist folk music. It was as if a church organist from West Virginia were asked to play a concert in New York devised by scholars to assure American city people that Appalachian culture was alive and well.

But all of these outside interventions were unknown to the Li family's clients. No one hired the Li family to perform a funeral or tell their fortune because they had performed at Carnegie Hall or were designated as a national-level heritage group. They hired them for the same reason that people had hired Lis for nine generations: because they knew how to bring a dead person over to the other side.

We set up for the old man's funeral in what is grandly known as the Scriptures Hall. This was actually just a room given to the troupe by the family, a place where the musicians could rest and write the calligraphy that adorned the coffin and altar. Today, that meant a room in the home of one of the deceased's sons, a poor corn farmer. The son farmed just 10 *mu*, or about 1.6 acres, of land, and his home consisted of a small compound surrounded by broken, rammed-earth walls and a rickety gate that opened to a pigsty that took up half the yard. The humans filled their half with empty beer bottles, a couple of motorbikes, and their home, a brick bungalow with a corrugated-metal roof. The building was divided into three rooms: a small vestibule in the middle behind the front door that was used for storage, and one room on either side, each about twelve by twelve feet. The Scriptures Hall was the left-hand room.

As in most northern Chinese farmhouses, about a third of the room was occupied by a *kang*, a three-foot-high platform used as a multipurpose living, eating, and sleeping area, and heated underneath by a coal stove. The other members of Li Bin's troupe were already there, sitting on the warm *kang* or readying to perform. As usual, they were six: Li Bin, his father, their star musician, Wu Mei, and three other men who joined in depending on who was free.

Our host was absent, but we were made comfortable by his wife

and daughter. They busied themselves boiling water for tea and offering us plates of peanuts, hard candies, and roasted sunflower seeds.
The wife was in her forties, a bright, talkative woman who peppered
the musicians with questions: How often did they perform? (Almost
every day for Li Bin and his father, a few times a month for the
others.) How much could they make? (Almost 1,000 yuan each for
the two- to three-day event.) How did they learn their instruments?
(From family members or on their own.)

But the real star was the daughter, a twenty-three-year-old with
long bangs that fell over her eyebrows and the rest of her hair pulled
back in a ponytail. She had her mother's small, sharp features, but
they were softened by her youth. She was the first in her clan to have
made it to college, although it had been a hard road. She had failed
two grades, one in middle school and one in high school, and she
had failed the college entrance exam twice. But she had persevered
and was now in Datong University's Chemistry Department. The
men buzzed with approval; they understood what a rare feat it was
for a poor farmer's daughter to get into college.

"Respect!" Wu Mei called out after hearing her story, and everyone nodded vigorously. Li Bin remained silent, keeping his thoughts
to himself. His son was eleven. Where would he be in a decade?
Sitting in a farmhouse burying someone's parent? On his way to a
college education? Or was it possible to imagine a life in between,
cultivating a tradition that was respected and also fairly paid?

He looked up and asked the young woman, "Do you think you
will be able to find a job in the coal bureau?"

She was framed by the cracked adobe wall, papered over with ads
for pesticides and genetically modified seeds. "It is my goal," she said
softly. Li Bin looked at her face, taking in her features—the gaze of a
professional fortune-teller. Then he nodded thoughtfully. "I predict
you will."

The winter sun slanted through the warped glass onto the back of
Li Bin's father. The women had gone to help prepare for the funeral,
and the musicians had left to scope out the village. Li Manshan, or
Old Mr. Li as I called him out of respect, was only sixty-one but

looked much older: small and wrinkled, a man of few words but deep intensity. His love was his profession, a fidelity to the past that won him more work than he could handle.

He crouched on his hands and knees, leaning forward, a Chinese writing brush in his right hand hovering over a blank piece of paper three feet long and two feet wide. *Yinyang* men say they have three tasks: fortune-telling, reciting scriptures, and making music. But to me their most amazing skill was calligraphy. It seemed a small miracle that these men, with so little formal education, could be so adept at the rich and dense language of classical Chinese. They write hundreds of characters a day by hand with a writing brush and paper, penning odes to the dead, exhortations to the spirit world, and talismanic symbols.

The task at hand was an announcement of the good man's death. It had to be told from the perspective of the eldest son. Old Mr. Li started down the middle of the paper writing from top to bottom:

> *Informing of the death*
> *of my late father*
> *LIU*
> *respectfully, his given name a taboo,*
> *CHENG*
> *on this day*
> *has reached longevity*
> *with*
> *seven decades*
> *and*
> *eight years*
> *of age.*

The characters were written in different sizes. The family name, Liu, and his given name, Cheng, were bigger. Other characters, like *gong hui*, were smaller. This phrase meant that his given name was to be said respectfully—in fact that uttering it was a taboo. It was almost like an aside to the readers, a reminder of their duties.

Old Mr. Li worked quietly and concentrated completely. An overflowing ashtray lay next to him, but his cigarettes were stashed; the words were now the key. He added the dates of the man's life: his birth, known as "happy event," and his death, or the "great limit." Off to the side, he wrote out useful information for visitors:

> *In-laws are not banned.*
> *Mourning dress for children is not discouraged.*

Li Bin walked in and quietly told his father that the family had incorrectly told them the time of the patriarch's birth. It had been the early morning, the second watch, not in the late afternoon.

"This changes everything," Old Mr. Li said, the only words he would speak this hour. He hastily consulted a ragged notebook of tables and formulas. Then he carefully wrote in the time that the coffin could be lowered—tomorrow morning, fifteen minutes earlier than he had previously calculated. It was a good thing his son had asked, or else the announcement would have to be rewritten. Li Bin left and Old Mr. Li went back to the announcement, writing in the names of the sons and expressing their sorrow.

Quiet time in the Scriptures Hall was an important part of the funeral. Rural funerals usually last two days. The troupe arrives around eight in the morning of the first day and sets up. One of the first tasks is the announcement, which Old Mr. Li was now completing. At around nine o'clock, they don their Daoist robes, either black or red and green, depending on the ceremony, and put on their mortarboard hats with a sun on the front and a crescent moon on the back. They form a line headed by Old Mr. Li and march single file through the village from the Scriptures Hall to the family home, where the deceased lies. There they play pieces that last about fifteen minutes to half an hour and are often accompanied by the singing of scriptures. The pieces have names like "Opening the Scriptures," "Delivering the Scriptures," and "Circulating the Offerings," culminating with the body's burial the next day. In between, Old Mr. Li or Li Bin writes out magical symbols on red strips of paper that will be used to seal the coffin. Sometimes, people came by to have their fortunes told. Oftentimes, the men simply rest, tune their instruments, smoke a cigarette, or nap.

Wu Mei came in and sat down silently on the *kang*. A handsome man in his early forties, he was quick-witted and loved to crack jokes. But he was dead serious about his music and the profession. When he saw Old Mr. Li writing the funeral announcement, he quietly pulled out a broken reed and began repairing it with a pocketknife.

Wu Mei had been with the family for thirty years. As a teenager living in one of the poorest and driest villages in the county, he had been so fascinated with the profession that one day he walked ten miles to the Li family home and begged Li Bin's grandfather Li Qing to accept him as his disciple. The old man had agreed, and Wu Mei moved in and began to learn to play music, although not all the skills of a *yinyang* man, such as fortune-telling. Still, he was now the group's best musician, able to play any instrument. His solos were inspiring, and he could bring a crowd to its feet. He had also learned a conventional profession, welding, but in recent years the Li family's business had grown so quickly that he could quit welding and devote himself to Daoist ceremonies full-time. After fiddling with his instrument for a while, he lay on his back and napped; the drowsiness of spring was arriving.

The sun rippled through the old glass over the milky paper and the black ink. Old Mr. Li tucked his legs underneath his torso and leaned forward to start a new line. He carefully dipped the writing brush in a saucer of black ink, filling the page with strong, clear characters. After consulting his book, he added a list of people whom he identified by the zodiac year in which they were born. They were advised to keep a safe distance because their presence might clash with the dead man's spirit.

> *Inauspicious people belong to these four signs*
> *Tiger, Monkey, Snake, and Swine.*

Old Mr. Li straightened up and looked at his work. The silence was a pleasing part of their routine; they had done this so many hundreds of times that no one needed to say anything. Soon they would go out for the first performance of the day, "Reading the Scriptures," and then come back for a break, then another, and another, and then lunch. They were like artisans working on a sculpture, but their craft left no traces.

Old Mr. Li readied a cigarette in his mouth, but before lighting it, he added with a flourish two large characters at the bottom:

Solemn
Announcement.

Liu Hexuan zigged dizzily through the dining tent until he saw what he wanted: me, the foreigner. He was the fifty-four-year-old second son of the deceased, wiry and tough, with thin lips and watery red eyes. Dressed in a white cotton jacket and trousers over his winter clothes, and wearing a white hat decorated with hemp, he was in mourning for his father. The upheaval, however, had also unleashed other emotions. He saw me and for a moment his spirits soared: here was a foreigner, really, a foreigner, a f-o-r-e-i-g-n-e-r for God's sake— here in China, in Shanxi, in Yanggao, in his father's compound, today, here, now, eating with him. This was going to be great fun.

We sat at a small table overflowing with liquor and beer bottles as he poured out an endless series of questions: Where is Canada? Is it a big country or a small one? What about the United States? How many harvests do you get a year? Corn or millet? Sorghum?

Mr. Liu did not really expect answers, only that I drink with him. After refusing many times, I finally accepted a bottle of beer. He wrenched off the cap with his teeth, laughing at my wide eyes. For himself, he opened a bottle of grain alcohol, and we began toasting each other. In China, one isn't supposed to drink alone, so I was doing him a favor, but not really: I was drinking 4 percent beer and he 43 percent grain alcohol, so I was able to match him cup for cup, my head fairly clear, while he plowed forward, the questions coming in a constant stream: How much do people earn in foreign countries? Are foreign people poor? Poorer than here?

He kept insisting that I eat and drink up, again and again, his urgency bordering on panic. I asked him to slow down, but he wasn't listening.

"Why are we here? Foreigner, tell me."

I said that I had no answers, figuring that he would move to another subject. But Mr. Liu was insistent.

"Why are we here?" he said again. "Why?"

I shrugged but said nothing, had no answers. He looked at me in silence, his mourning costume framing his face, hardened by the weather but softened by the drink. Our eyes finally met, but he didn't see me; he was already in another realm. At that moment, he achieved his goal: he put his head on the table and passed out cold.

Today was the solar term *lichun,* or Spring Commences. This was a key day in the calendar, and people stopped by after lunch to ask for advice. Li Bin was adept at fortune-telling, but they gravitated to his father; age was synonymous with wisdom.

First came a stout neighbor with short hair, curled and dyed orange. She climbed up on the *kang* and sat across from Old Mr. Li. She was worried and hoped for solace. He wrote down her birth date and time and had her throw three coins. He then consulted a chart and silently counted some numbers off on his fingers.

"I don't know," he said. "It's not that great."

"But the numbers aren't that bad, are they?"

"This is going to be a strange year, a tough year. It won't be easy. There might be a drought."

"Okay." The stout woman leaned forward toward Old Mr. Li. "Can you be more concrete? Is it just the weather?"

"No, it's not the weather. It's more than that. The numbers don't add up. I'm puzzled."

I had been to fortune-tellers before, and most of them offered some banal uplifting advice and then it was over. But this was more like a negotiation. The fortune itself wasn't in doubt; it was clear from the expression on Old Mr. Li's face that it was bad. And what would somebody expect in a place like this? A bright answer would have been dismissed as nonsense. The sensitive part was how this message would be conveyed.

"I don't know," Old Mr. Li said, looking directly at the stout woman.

"It's all right," she said. "I'm okay if it's difficult. I knew it would be. Thank you."

She seemed almost relieved to say it. And in a way, Old Mr. Li's hesitancy had granted her power; she was the one who spoke the fortune. She knew it; it belonged to her. She looked pleased and placed a pack of cigarettes and 5 yuan, or a little less than a dollar, on the *kang.* Her session was over, but she didn't leave. In the countryside, even if your fortune was bad, there was at least some benefit in having it told early, because then you could stay there and listen to your neighbors' woes. She slid over to the side and waited.

Our inquisitive hostess was up next. Mrs. Wei was a petite woman with faint eyebrows and tinted-red hair. She had thin lips and small eyes, but her features were fine and light. Like her intelligent daughter, she looked as if she belonged somewhere else. She asked politely if she could pose a question. Old Mr. Li nodded and smiled *of course*.

"I can't stand my husband. We fight all the time. Should we divorce?"

Old Mr. Li put down the coins. He looked down at the *kang* in silence for a moment, and then he asked, carefully, "Do you want to get divorced?"

"If he doesn't change, I will. He's terrible." She laughed, and the stout woman smiled sadly. She knew; everyone in the village did.

"Only you can decide this. If you feel you must, then you should."

Silence. Old Mr. Li stared at his hands in his lap. He had wrapped the three coins in a piece of paper, and now he pressed the packet together firmly. This was not a question the coins could answer.

"It's up to you. The numbers can't tell it. Only you know."

Then he turned to the stout woman. She had been staring at him intently. On the surface, the fortune-telling had moved on, but she still hadn't; she was turning it over in her mind. She looked tired. Old Mr. Li seemed to know what she was thinking.

"You can get through it," he said. "You can. You can release the poison."

"I can? How?"

"There's no how. It's not like that. You can get through this."

"I will," the woman said relieved. I imagined the regular droughts, the emptying land, the exhaustion. "Thank you," she said. "Thank you."

These women probably had such ideas on their own, but the presence of Old Mr. Li—an outsider, a person of faith and tradition—allowed them to speak it out. In a village, everybody might know each other, but closeness is not the same as intimacy. Opening up is a risk; it means telling your secrets to someone you will see every day for the rest of your life. Old Mr. Li wasn't just wise; he would be gone tomorrow.

The two women began chatting about the rest of the day's events. Their relief was palpable, but so was Old Mr. Li's exhaustion. It was a tiring life, always on call, staying in people's homes, burying their dead, eating their banquets. The questions never stopped—an avalanche of new challenges and problems that were overwhelming these old villages.

Ever since he was a young boy, Li Bin knew what his fortune would bring: working as a *yinyang* man in the countryside, just like his father. His family's history guaranteed it. When he was a boy, he learned the *sheng* from his grandfather Li Qing, and when he failed to test into high school, he began working with his grandfather and father full-time, learning the trade and traveling around the county. In 1999, his grandfather died and Li Bin continued to work with his father, even after his own son was born in 2000. Six years later, though, the boy was ready for school, and Li Bin realized it was a chance to make a move. Village schools are almost always inferior to town schools, so he could say it was for the boy's sake, even if it was also for his own. That year, they moved into Yanggao Town.

In town, Li Bin was thrust into a world that was far from his father's village but much more in line with China's future. He was immediately one of the most reputable *yinyang* men in the county seat—the family's reputation had followed him into the town—and now he could schmooze with government officials regularly. He knew all the officials in the cultural affairs office as well as in Public Security—powerful figures in towns like Yanggao. His uncle, who worked in the county government's legal affairs office, made the introductions, and he also got to know people at concerts. That brought business and a feeling of being part of things.

"Definitely, I get more work in the town because of this," he told me during a break. "We've expanded our geographic area to about five counties. It started when I began handing out name cards at concerts and while traveling. We'd start getting calls from various places, even in other provinces like Hebei and Inner Mongolia. But even just here in Yanggao, we have more business. Townsfolk have more money. That's new business we wouldn't have gotten before."

His son's education had not been quite so successful. The school he had attended folded, so Li Bin had to send him to a boarding school in another county. He could have moved back to the village at this point but had no intention of doing so, even though he knew his father needed help.

"We used to do everything together—all the funerals, fortune-telling, and so on. But now I'm in the town, he's left with quite a bit of work on his own in the village. He's getting older and would like to rest more."

He was bothered by it but saw no choice. City clients were also difficult: they asked more questions and did not blindly follow precedents. But the money was much better, and, anyway, what would happen when all the old people in the villages died off? He did not want to be the last *yinyang* man in the countryside.

By the early evening the sky was black and the moon nearly full, lighting the village with unnatural intensity. Inside the compound, the Li family was performing in front of the casket, but no one under thirty was watching. Instead, these young people, who worked in big cities as cooks, waitresses, construction workers, and truck drivers, were crowded outside the front door, watching a husband-and-wife team sing on the flatbed. The woman was tough looking and the man sang in a falsetto. Their repertoire included popular songs and opera excerpts backed by recorded music—a kind of professional karaoke.

The couple left, and several of the dead man's grandchildren jumped onto the stage. One granddaughter, whose white funeral clothes set off her bright red-dyed hair, crooned a song. People from the village began to gather. This was interesting: children in mourning singing onstage. In another era, their parents would have dragged them off the stage and thrashed them, but now people just watched. In fact, the deceased's eldest son had hired the truck, knowing that his children, nieces, and nephews would want this. The crowd watched silently.

"She's a prostitute," one young woman in the audience said, casting a hard, calculating look.

"Are you sure?" a friend next to her asked.

"Everyone knows; how else can she send so much money home?"

The young woman looked up at the stage silently, taking in the scene.

Later, disco music was put on, and all the young people jumped on the stage, stamping up and down to a popular song, "You Didn't Know I Was That Kind of Girl." They bounced so hard that the stage rocked back and forth on the truck's suspension. This was their performance, as if to say, look at us; this is the future.

The second son had awoken from his lunchtime binge and was now sitting at a small table, eating a late dinner. He had missed a key ceremony that had just ended—burning a paper house and paper effigies of material goods from this world to provide for those in the netherworld. It had been beautiful: the moon shining on the frozen fields, the family kneeling on either side of the three-foot paper house as it vanished in flames. All of it had been built by Li Bin's wife the day before, and now it was gone, a profound experience that left the group silent as it walked back home on the hardened-mud path. Perhaps because he had not participated, Mr. Liu sat alone. He chewed quickly, a glass of clear grain alcohol next to him. He had no one to drink with, until he saw me across the room and waved me over.

Mr. Liu laughed but was not in a jesting mood. The alcohol had done nothing but delay the questions.

"Tell me, foreigner, why are we here?"

"It's too deep of a question. I don't know."

"Isn't it so we can eat and drink and have fun? What more is there to life than that?"

"Do you really believe that?"

"Believe, ha, I don't know. What more is there? Foreigner, tell me."

He slammed down a drink. I poured myself a Coke to accompany him, but he didn't care. He ripped the plastic pouring spout off the top of his bottle so the liquor would chug into his plastic cup faster. He slugged it back, time and again, laughing and cursing.

He sank lower into his chair and kept asking me why, and I knew he meant it all: the big questions and the small, the death of his father and the injustice of having had to stay behind to tend the family farm while his siblings had moved to cities to earn money. He gripped the table to steady himself, and then he slumped forward once again. Li Bin and I dragged him to bed, and then we drove home in the unnaturally bright moonlight.

Tomorrow, Li Bin would finally have his big night out. *Yuanxiao*, the First Night, would be celebrated with floats through town and a giant, thirty-foot bonfire at the center of a major intersection. He would walk through the town, talking to police officers, government officials, businesspeople, handing out cards, and taking in the sort of pageantry that never occurred in a village. But now he was tired and drove silently, until I finally asked him a question that had been bothering me.

"So which son was he—the drunk?"

"You haven't figured it out yet?" Li Bin kept his eyes on the road, his face lit up by the dashboard's glow. "He owned the place where we stayed."

"You mean, his wife was the woman who asked about the divorce? And his daughter was the one who got into college?"

It had been a long day, a series of intense scenes that had little connection until now, when I finally saw them clearly: a woman asking about her marriage; three coins wrapped tightly in paper; a young girl talking about her studies while everyone nodded in admiration; a man opening a beer bottle with his teeth and asking, over and over, "Why are we here?"

Li Bin nodded.

"How did the girl manage that?" I asked him. "With such a father, I mean."

Li Bin sighed. He didn't say anything for a while. Then he spoke: "Sometimes if you want something, you just make it happen. You create your own fate."

4

Chengdu: Long Live Auntie Wei

When Wang Yi addressed his congregation, he looked like an explorer surveying new horizons. He would grasp his pulpit with both hands, leaning forward on the balls of his feet, his eyes squinting through thick glasses as if focusing on a speck in the distance. He had rosy cheeks and a winning smile, and when he spoke, it was in a strong and forceful voice, his words as clear as his arguments. Earlier in life, he had been a popular blogger on cinema and had written two books analyzing Hollywood and European movies. Trained in law, he had also been one of China's most prominent civil rights lawyers before the government detained or drove most of those people out of their profession. By the time that happened early in the second decade of the twenty-first century, Wang Yi had already found a new calling. He had converted to Christianity in 2005 and founded Early Rain Reformed Church, quickly establishing himself as one of China's best-known preachers. His church was independent of government control, but that made it all the more dynamic. Videos of his sermons circulated on social media. His plans, ideas, and ambitions seemed boundless. Protestant Christianity was China's fastest-growing religion, and Wang Yi was one of its stars.

But at times he had been accused of arrogance and talking over people's heads, of giving theoretical sermons about theological issues that no one could understand. Like most Chinese pastors, he was mostly self-taught in the Bible and tended to bring his lawyer's argumentative nature to church matters. In 2011, he had kicked one of his closest associates out of his church, saying his advocacy of an equal role for women risked allowing "Satan" into the church.

Tonight, though, was a chance to shine. Behind him on a screen was a picture of a dead woman whom people had come to mourn. She deserved more than an abstract talk. Her name was Wei Suying, a popular member of the church, known to everyone as Auntie Wei. She had died of cancer at age sixty-two, leaving two daughters and two infant grandchildren. Her family had come to the funeral, as well as many church members eager to show their solidarity. The service had started out with a touching slide show of her life. Then her daughters testified about how she had persuaded them to convert to Christianity. Both said how it had changed their lives, helping them see through the materialism of contemporary society. They had become better people, less obsessed with money, and more concerned about helping others. A few people began sobbing; her death had been sudden, and the grief was raw.

Now it was Wang Yi's turn. A few hours earlier, he had been thinking about how the Communists exalt famous people by saying *wansui,* or long live, like "Long Live Chairman Mao." *Wansui* (wansway) was a term everyone in China knew. It was almost a prefix before the Communist Party's name, a formulaic chant meant to guarantee that its rule would never end. Auntie Wei's death made him realize how much he hated that term. It was an offense to God and to ordinary people like Auntie Wei, whose lives truly deserved exaltation. Talking about this was a bit abstract, but he thought it might work. He stood up to speak, as usual without notes. He started softly, forcing everyone to listen carefully.

"Auntie Wei was someone I think it would be fair to call a simple woman. She was a mother and had a hard life. She raised two daughters mostly on her own. Her husband had died young." One of the daughters began sobbing. People in the church began nodding but caught themselves as Wang Yi continued.

"She was not someone who heard the word *wansui* too often. If she heard it, she would have thought it applied to China, or the Communist Party, or Chairman Mao. *Wansui:* that's almost always reserved for them. This is wrong. *Wansui,* this word, if it belongs to anyone, it belongs to Auntie Wei." A couple of people looked up startled.

"I tell you that she can hear *wansui* now because she is *wansui;* she is immortal because of Jesus. It's not the government that can confer this word. It's God, and it's us by how we live our daily lives. It's the choices we make despite the immoral society we live in. This is what real *wansui* is. It's nothing that the Communist Party can provide. It's something we can make ourselves."

Suddenly people were smiling; this was why they came to Early Rain Reformed Church. It was different from the anodyne churches sponsored by the state. It was warm and direct, but most of all it was relevant. It was for people who didn't want the status quo, who were searching for alternatives to the life around them. Wang Yi was dressed in a suit, with short cropped hair and an earnest expression—a nice, modern young man, a perfect son-in-law. And yet here he was standing in front of them, telling them directly how to challenge the official way of looking at their country.

When I had visited Old Mr. Ni in Beijing a few weeks earlier, he had also described religion as a kind of immortality, but one that was achieved through private faith and recognition from the community. In Shanxi, the *yinyang* man Li Bin was also part of this world of rituals, even as he faced demands from city people for something fresher and newer. Here in churches across China, this push for a modern spirituality was probably furthest along. It was a direct relationship with God, unmediated, that didn't shy away from political implications.

"Auntie Wei was one of our sisters," Wang Yi said, winding up his eulogy. "We loved her. But it's she who possesses eternal life, not the government. She created it for herself by living a good life, by being our sister in the church, and resisting the immorality around her."

Now I could see why Wang Yi had made the choice to become a pastor. When he was a public intellectual, most of his words were censored. But here, speaking to one hundred people in a room, he was helping a grieving family and also teaching the congregation how to live a different life. He was contributing to a sense that it was ordinary people who possessed real power in a country where all authority seemed to belong to the state.

After the service, a son-in-law of Auntie Wei's walked up to Wang Yi and did something Chinese almost never do: he hugged him. And Wang Yi, blinking back his own tears, looked bewildered but then happy. This was truly his flock, and he was their pastor.

Wang Yi's church is located in Chengdu, capital of the vast, mountain-ringed province of Sichuan. The terrain makes it hard to reach and for centuries has isolated Sichuan from the rest of China. Nowadays, highways and rail lines cut through the mountains, and airlines serve its cities, but the region is still the most remote big concentration of Chinese in the country; to its north and west is the Tibetan plateau, while the south is dominated by the historically tribal lands of Yun-nan. Sichuan produced some of China's best-known poets, painters, officials, and soldiers, but a feeling remains of being apart from the big cities to the east. It is as if the mountains and distances and history diminish the laws and orders and rules promulgated in the faraway capital.

You can sense this in Chengdu's street life. Beijing is defined by walls—the Great Wall to its north, the sentries around the leadership compound in the Forbidden City, and the *hutongs*, lined with walls, behind which daily life plays out. Chengdu lives outdoors, especially in its teahouses. Some are noisy, public spaces in big parks or temples. Others are simply a slew of tables and chairs strewn under a canopy of trees. Most are quiet storefronts found on almost every block, where regulars come and go at various times of the day, chatting with friends and discussing the latest news and gossip.

Chengdu percolates with an argumentative air that is different from the cautious, curtained world of Beijing. It has the biggest group of thinkers and dissidents outside the capital, and during periods of unrest, such as the 1989 protests, it had the second-most-tumultuous rallies. Nowadays it is China's capital of alternative lifestyles, with a thriving gay scene, hippie communes, and independent history museums. Its cuisine is peppery, its countryside lush, and its people libertarian.

For a while, Chengdu became my second home. As I followed the Moon Year and its unfolding cycle, I lived there for weeks at a time, finding a lively counterpoint to the rural life of Li Bin's Yanggao County and a valuable corrective to the incestuous world of Beijing and its hyper-politicized life. In the capital, government policies were so amplified that they took on an importance they did not deserve as predictors of China's future. In Chengdu, Chinese society was unfolding at its own pace, and predictions of a new totalitarianism seemed less likely.

Two weeks after the Lunar New Year festival ended with the burning pyres in Li Bin's hometown, the second month of the New Year
was upon us. This year, it coincided with the beginning of Lent, the
solemn forty-day period of fasting and prayer leading up to Jesus's
crucifixion and resurrection during Easter.

Lent starts on a Wednesday—Ash Wednesday—when people
used to paint crosses on their foreheads with ashes. The day before is
known as Shrove Tuesday. As kids growing up in a Protestant household, my sister and I marked the holiday by eating pancakes. The idea
was to use up butter and other luxuries before Lent, when people
were supposed to prepare for Easter by giving up things they liked—
dessert, alcohol, or tobacco—or by praying each day. In Catholic
countries, the holiday is even more important, known in some places
as Mardi Gras, or Carnival—an almost *Yuanxiao*-type street festival
of purging at the start of a new season.

But in Chinese Christian communities, this religious calendar
was unfamiliar. Lent? No one in Wang Yi's church knew the Chinese
word for it, *dazhaijie*. Finally, I found one church member who was
taking a course in theology. He said, yes, he knew it, but it seemed as
if I were speaking in Aramaic.

On Ash Wednesday, I visited the church to meet some friends.
Early Rain looked different from most churches I have known, a
function of its strange legal status. China does have churches with
steeples and stained glass, but most were built by missionaries in the
nineteenth and early twentieth centuries. Since the Communist takeover in 1949, these established churches—Catholic and Protestant—
have been run by the government.

Early Rain was not part of that world of official religion. It was
an unregistered church, which are sometimes called "house churches"
or "underground churches." In the past, those terms made sense
because these congregations usually met in people's homes or somewhere in secret. But increasingly, churches like Early Rain are big and
public. In fact, these unregistered churches make up about half of
China's fifty to sixty million Protestants, forming one of those gray
areas that defines much of religious life in China. Like the temples
on Miaofengshan that were rebuilt in the 1980s, Early Rain wasn't
permitted but also wasn't banned. The government knew it existed
but wasn't prepared to close it down. It operated openly but couldn't

buy a plot of land to build a proper church. That forced Early Rain and hundreds of other unregistered churches across China to find space in buildings like the River Trust Mansion.

The mansion was actually a seedy office tower in an older part of Chengdu near the Jinjiang River. It was dank and covered with tiles, and only one elevator usually worked. In 2009, the church bought several rooms on the nineteenth floor as a place to hold services, but police officers barred members from entering. The congregation met at a park along the Jinjiang River for several weeks. Eventually, the authorities let the church take possession of its office floor. The reasons are still unclear: perhaps officials feared the repercussions of alienating hundreds of mostly white-collar professionals, or perhaps they would only take such a drastic step if instructed from Beijing and never got a directive. In any case, since then the church has been housed in the River Trust Mansion—invisible to the public but the center of spiritual life for hundreds of people in Chengdu.

The church occupied half of the nineteenth floor. The biggest room was where the congregation met on Sunday, but this only sat about 150 so the service was video streamed into an adjoining room where another 70 people sat. A second service in the afternoon took care of another 100 or so. There was no stained glass, no wooden pews, and only a simple lectern serving as the pulpit. But the church pulsed with energy all week long. People came to buy books, or meet friends, study the Bible, pray, or organize to help victims of human rights abuses. As the year unfolded, they would set up a seminary, launch a campaign to challenge the government's birth-control policy, form an alliance with other like-minded parishes, and establish a second place of worship in another part of Chengdu.

The only indication of these ambitions was Early Rain's green-and-white logo on the wall by the entrance: a cross sheltering two people, a symbol of how the church saw its role in Chinese society. Next to this logo was a corridor adorned with a time line of Protestant Christian history, one that was sharply at odds with the government's version of the past. It began conventionally enough in 1384, with the publication of John Wycliffe's English-language Bible, and then moved to Martin Luther, John Calvin, and other great figures from church history.

When the chart reached the twentieth century, the white faces gave way to a more diverse array of people, and the story began to become more subversive. Some of the figures portrayed included Wang Mingdao, the revered preacher who spent decades in the Communists' gulag for refusing to join the official church. Closer to the end was Stephen Tong, an ethnic Chinese revivalist preacher from Indonesia whose lectures are popular in the Chinese-speaking world. None of these people were recognized by China's government-run church but instead formed an alternative history emphasizing the independence of Chinese Christianity. The government-run media sometimes presents Christianity as a foreign faith; here, the religion was portrayed as indigenous as in any other country.

On this Ash Wednesday morning, I walked past the faces on the wall, turned left, and saw that Wang Yi was in his office. He looked up and waved me in. As always, he was disarmingly frank. I asked him about his plans to set up a seminary. The idea made me nervous, and I wondered how he felt. Had the government approved that?

"Well, no, they won't approve it, but the question is if they'll shut it down. We don't think so. They asked us if it's internal, and we said yes, so they seemed okay with that."

"So the idea is that it's only to train Early Rain church members," I said. "But will they go out to preach?"

"Definitely; the idea is people from here will become missionaries. They'll learn here."

"But isn't this a sensitive year? You know . . ." I trailed off, wondering if his office was bugged.

"You mean the big leadership issue?" Wang asked with a twinkle in his eye. "Every year is something special. Last year was some anniversary, and a few years ago were the Olympics. Next year will be something else. Right now the Communist Party is not so stable. We can't know what is going on inside. They may feel they need quiet at all costs, and we'll have trouble. Or they could also say that they need quiet so will ignore us; after all, we're not challenging them. Or they may be too preoccupied with their struggles to notice us. It's hard to say. We just trust in God and let Him decide."

As we were talking, a policeman walked in. I thought at first it was just one of the many workers or deliverymen in China who sometimes wear blue uniforms. Then I noticed the insignia. Wang Yi stood up, greeting the officer warmly by name, and quickly led him out. Ten minutes later, Wang Yi returned.

"The local police officer. He comes every week to get the list of those who attended church. We give them this information; we have nothing to hide, and the congregants are okay with that too. In fact, it's a precondition for joining our church. You have to give your name, address, and contact information and be willing for us to share it with the authorities. We don't want to be stuck in the old underground-church mentality. It's not healthy."

He pointed to a whiteboard on the wall, which was covered with notes and numbers. "There's the figure for the Sunday morning service: 222. And the afternoon: 92. So the total was 314. We can only seat around 220, so that's why we have the second service."

I asked about Lent.

"It's hardly celebrated here at all. We had this break in our history—you know, the missionaries being expelled in 1949 and then the antireligious campaigns—so a lot has been lost. A lot of people don't really know too much about Lent. We had a service trying to reintroduce the idea and explain it, but there's very little celebration. Nothing on Shrove Tuesday or Ash Wednesday."

I later realized it was more than Lent; the church calendar itself was hardly known. But at the same time, Chinese Christians often rejected the traditional lunar calendar. At most, they might celebrate Chinese New Year, but the other festivals and holidays were treated as pagan.

We talked about my upbringing and how in my family we marked Lent by eating simply. My mother used to make a big show of giving up dessert for Lent. We knew she was partly motivated by wanting to lose weight, and we joked about whether she could last the forty days until Easter. But the effect was real: we did think about Lent and were aware of it. It was hard to convey the naturalness of this; it was cultural and not learned formally. Some Chinese Christians envied this, while others rejected it in a fundamentalist way. To them, all that mattered was reading the Bible. The good book didn't tell people to eat pancakes or put ashes on their foreheads, so these were as irrelevant as the fires of *Yuanxiao*. But an increasing number of churches were like Wang Yi's. They wanted all the traditions and imported them as a package, assembling them like a model airplane.

"You'll find that Christmas is the biggest difference," Wang Yi said. "In the West, you celebrate at home with your family. Not us. For us it's too good an opportunity to proselytize. We try to bring people to the church—to get members to invite friends and have a big celebration. Many churches in Chengdu have over one thousand people at the services, even though they might just have a couple of hundred regular worshippers. Christmas will be quite different from what you're used to."

In a little room near the front door was the church's library and bookstore. Its walls were lined with glass cabinets holding magazines published by unregistered churches, or reference works, such as various translations of the Bible or primers in classical Greek. In the center of the room was a table with a display of about fifty books on Christianity, many of them translated works of charismatic American pastors. Wang Yi's sermons were on sale too. These talks were what had initially drawn me to Early Rain. Although they were long—forty-five minutes was the norm—they were among the best I had heard in any language, and I dreamed of having them translated and posted online. Wang Yi was fast on his feet, referring to verses from the Bible that we had read earlier in the service, while also inserting current events and humor. He created a coherent and orderly world in contrast to the one racing blindly by on Chengdu's streets outside.

I wondered how long he could continue preaching before he would get in trouble. It wasn't really his sermons that made me wonder. Instead, it was that his church was a parallel realm outside the party's control. It had its own nursery school, day care, seminary, and elementary school—all located on this floor that it owned. It handled its own finances, rejecting all foreign money. It held its own elections and annual meetings—just like the government's, but more transparent and inspiring. The Beijing social commentator Li Fan once wrote a monograph on Christianity in China declaring that China's unregistered churches were the only real example of civil society—in other words, organizations independent of government control that tried to change or improve society.

This was clearest in Early Rain's social work. Independent activism is anathema to the government, which worries that even innocent-sounding groups might morph into something political. This is not as far-fetched as it seems. In 2008, Sichuan was hit by a terrible earthquake that left thousands dead. Spontaneously, people across China volunteered to help or send money. But they quickly noticed that the first buildings to collapse had been schools. Critics such as the Chengdu activist Tan Zuoren began to ask pointed questions about corrupt building practices, a theme amplified by the Beijing activist-artist Ai Weiwei. What had started as charity had transformed into something political. Within weeks of the earthquake, most independent helpers had been sent home, and Tan was later locked up.

Early Rain, however, persisted. Wang Yi's congregation set up charities to help street people and even families of political prisoners. The church claimed it wasn't siding with the prisoners, just acting from purely humanitarian grounds. That was probably true, but it was skating close to the edge.

As I sat flipping through Wang Yi's sermons and books, a friend stopped by. He was Zhang Guoqing, a local businessman in his late forties, still not married but hoping to find a Christian wife. He was always busy with work, which involved setting up concerts, conferences, and big public events. That and his heavy involvement in Early Rain had left him single. He often spoke to me longingly about finding a *duixiang*—a partner, someone to share the joys and trials of life. For now, the church filled his time, and he was its unofficial liaison with every thinker in town, as well as the *guobao* security agents who kept watch.

"You need to understand Chengdu a bit better if you want to write about it," he said to me. "You want to meet Ran Yunfei?"

The famous author and blogger who had been detained in 2011 for retweeting something about the Jasmine Revolution in North Africa? Authorities had held him for six months without trial before finally releasing him. Since then, he had been under close watch. I nodded vigorously. Of course I was interested.

"His wife is a member of Early Rain. We're old friends, and of course Ran and Pastor Wang are old buddies. We know him well. We'll go early to avoid the *guobao*," Zhang said. "I'll pick you up at 7:00."

I laughed. "The *guobao* doesn't start work until after 7:00?" I had thought that state security worked round the clock.

"This is Sichuan! And it's just old Ran. But you're right, 6:30. No, 6:00. He won't be expecting us."

"The *guobao* or Ran? Are you sure he wants to see us?"

Zhang laughed and slapped me on the back. "For me, he'll do anything. We're brothers."

"Christians?"

"Ran isn't exactly a Christian, but he's like one. See you tomorrow."

Ran Yunfei lived in an old Communist-style apartment complex from the 1950s, a series of low-slung buildings made of brick but crumbling like an old temple. It was canopied by gingko trees that seemed to have been planted centuries earlier. They enveloped us, holding in the early morning mist like a rain cloud. We slithered over smooth paving stones, wet and mossy, as morning broke gray and chilly.

This was what was known as a *danwei* apartment complex. Until the 1990s, most Chinese in cities worked for a "work unit," or *danwei*—a company, a government agency, a university—some sort of organization that provided cradle-to-grave benefits. Gradually, the *danwei* system broke down as China adopted market economics. The biggest step was when the government started selling these apartments to their residents in the 1990s, an often underestimated step that gave people a huge sense of freedom. Ran's *danwei* was *Sichuan Literature*, a government-run magazine where he still held a token job writing occasional articles about classical Chinese texts. His *danwei* housing was typical: poor construction, five stories up with no elevator, and extremely dingy. The stairway was dark and littered with junk that people no longer wanted in their homes. Public spaces tended to be like this in China—littering, spitting, and abusing public property were the rule; after all, there was always a migrant laborer to sweep it up.

As Zhang predicted, the *guobao* wasn't around, and Ran wasn't expecting us either. He opened the door of his fifth-floor apartment in his pajamas, stared at us for a second, and burst into a staccato laugh, as if to say, well, if the *guobao* didn't see you, what can I do? He was a compact man—five feet six—with a shaved head and a dark complexion. A member of the Tujia minority from the mountains near the Yangtze River, he called himself a "bandit"—"you know, short, dark, angry" was how he put it—and he used it as his social media handle: *Tufei Ran*, Bandit Ran. He spoke fast and stuttered, often adding a few *dui, dui, dui*—right, right, right—at the end of his sentences, as if one word couldn't adequately convey his agreement or cover up his doubts. He shook my hand and pulled me into the room, then quickly excused himself to brush his teeth, change his clothes, and put the kettle on.

He lived with his wife and daughter, who were rising to get ready for work and school. They stayed in the back until Ran appeared with our tea and led us up a small internal staircase to the roof of the building, where he had built a glass-walled room that served as an office. It was lined with a wonderful array of books, stacked every which way like games of pick-up sticks. Between the bookshelves were a work desk, sofa, easy chairs, and several large wooden chests that seemed salvaged from a sunken Spanish galleon. As dawn broke, we looked out over the polluted city, its buildings rising from the smog like trees in a misty forest. Objectively, it was ugly, but so abstract that it could have passed for a classical Chinese painting of a mystical landscape.

"You're looking good," Zhang said perkily, as if his friend had just come back from vacation.

"I read lots of the classics in jail. They don't allow the Bible, because it's considered subversive, but they allow the classics, which have a lot of subversive material! Of course they can't read the classics. They don't know. But it was very instructive."

He handed me a small blue book with the picture of a temple on it. It was called *The Lungs of Old Sichuan: The Story of the Temple of Great Charity*, a methodically researched history of one of Chengdu's most famous Buddhist temples. I marveled at the production quality. It was a beautiful paperback, with a rough, textured cover.

"It shows how the monks were attacked after liberation and declared Rightists"—a term used in the Mao era for those who were considered not left-wing enough. "A monk as a Rightist! What nonsense, but that's how it was. It's all in there, but I don't go out of my way to rub the government's nose in it. It's just stated factually. That's how I like to write books: factually and clearly."

"And you got it published?" I asked him.

"It was in the publisher's warehouse, but after I was released from prison, they wouldn't distribute it. I told this to the *guobao*, and they said, 'You haven't been convicted, so you can publish.' I said, 'Good, so can you tell the publishing house this?' They said, 'No, we can't tell the publisher or else we'll frighten them to death! But you can tell them our views.' So I did and they released the book, but it's not available anywhere. We had a press run of five thousand, and I've sold about two thousand, mostly directly through the temple."

"Why did you pick a Buddhist temple to write about?" I asked. "Are you a believer?"

"No, no, no. Not a Buddhist. But I do have a lot to do with Christianity. My wife is a Christian. I've been influenced by Christian thought through Wang Yi. I'm not a believer, but I'm not an atheist, because I know the value of spirituality. I don't deny the value."

He and Wang Yi were old friends. When Ran had been detained in 2011, Wang had written an emotional, open letter called "Now I Must See My Friend Ran Yunfei Become a Prisoner." The title was darkly humorous. In the past, Wang and Ran had discussed religion so vigorously that Wang Yi had jokingly said that he couldn't stand the idea of Ran becoming a Christian; if Ran did, Wang would see too much of him and they would argue all the more. But now he had to bear a much worse thought: his dear friend behind bars. "I am heartbroken for my country," Wang Yi wrote. "I call out for righteousness."

Ran's wife came up the stairs with a bowl of black peanuts for us to munch on. "You amuse yourselves while I go out." She was polite but weary: her husband was at it again, talking to people he probably should avoid.

We were silent for a minute, and then Ran picked up his train of thought, the ideas coming out rapid fire as he laughed, joked, and satirized the government's view of religion.

"The Communists really destroyed religion. They don't understand it at all. Look at Tibet. I told the *guobao* that they have gone too far. You don't allow the Tibetans to hang pictures of the Dalai Lama. You don't have faith, so you don't understand. So the Tibetans get very angry and depressed. And then you go into temples and instead hang pictures of Mao. You've gone overboard! This isn't right. Think about it. No wonder they set themselves on fire."

I asked him what else religious groups provide; is it mainly solace?

"No. It's much more. If this government wants China to develop well, it needs faith. It also needs nongovernmental organizations. I've often said that Chinese don't get NGOs. They think it's 'good people doing good works.' But this is wrong. NGOs are necessary because society can't just be the government doing stuff and we either support or oppose it. It has to be us doing stuff on our own, not just reacting to the government. You see what I mean?

"Churches are like this. The unregistered churches are public spaces. They're maybe the only real public space in China right now. Also, I have to say I've learned to think more clearly thanks to them."

"Churches make you think clearly?" I asked.

"I'm cursed by people online all the time. But I've learned to accept this."

"To turn the other cheek?"

"Yes, or just trying to be civil. I'm like this: I've got rules for arguing. One, I don't care if you curse me. Two, I won't praise you or kiss your ass. Third, I'm magnanimous. I don't fight with the secret police, for example. Of course, we have differences of opinion"—he broke out into guffaws, wiping his mouth to try to recover—"but we discuss things. I don't treat people as enemies. We're polite to each other. Nowadays in China few people don't curse. Public intellectuals are constantly shouting and cursing. That's why public discussion is so trashy in China."

"So why are you writing about education? What does it have to do with this bad public discourse and this lack of spiritual values?"

"You have a society where the educational materials are all about loving the party, so of course it leads to a spiritual crisis."

"I don't get it."

"Everything they teach you to admire is fake. Right now they're pushing Lei Feng again," he said, referring to the Communist hero who for decades has been held up as a model of selflessness.

"But everyone knows that Lei Feng is fake. His story is mostly made up. It's bullshit. He was supposed to be an ordinary soldier, but somehow a Xinhua photographer was there to take perfect pic-

tures of him? And his beautifully written diary? It's an insult to people's intelligence. All of their model heroes are fake: Wang Jie, Liu
Wenxue, Lai Ning, fake, fake, fake. So when they teach morality,
their teaching tools are fake. Completely fake.

"After a while the students learn that Lei Feng is a fake. This is
destructive; it destroys everything you've been taught. You feel that
nothing is real. How can they teach virtues? It's impossible. You find
out that the things you're supposed to admire the most are fake. So it
seems nothing is real. Faith is a foundation, but the government has
no foundation: they will say anything or do anything. The only way
the party can succeed is by cheating you. That becomes their biggest success—by how much they can cheat you. That's whom you're
ruled by."

"How do you combat that?"

"The main thing is you have to learn how to argue. Too few public intellectuals can argue logically in China. They don't learn how
to do this, and they end up cursing each other all the time. If there's
one thing I've learned from Christianity, it's that one shouldn't curse
everyone all the time. I'm a hothead, but I'm trying to calm down. I
think it's taught me that. To be rational."

That was an interesting twist. Secularists say religion is irrational,
and if they have any sympathy for it, it's as a mystic, illogical part
of human life that at best we have to accept. And yet as Old Mr. Ni
had also said a few weeks earlier, faith can be a simple proposition:
doing good deeds and living a straight life. Wasn't this the universal
basis of real happiness?

By contrast, the society that China's radical secularists had set
up seemed much more convoluted—not only the fake moral heroes,
but even things like Ran's own job: a job that wasn't a job. A person
arrested for a blog post, freed, but somehow still under house arrest.
I asked Ran why he didn't quit his job.

"They don't let you! They say, 'Oh no, you can't quit,' and they
keep paying your salary, no matter what letters you write or what
you say. The secret police here in Sichuan want you to be part of the
system. They won't let you leave."

"Because it's easier to control you?"

"It's not so direct. If something happens, then the *guobao* don't need to deal with you. It's much more refined. Let's say you have a good boss, you like him. So they go to him. His daughter is going to college. So he asks you, really embarrassed, 'Do you really have to publish this or that thing? Do you always have to be so critical?' And so you feel, 'Don't I want his daughter to go to college?' "

"So you get $250 a month for doing nothing?"

"It's a crazy society. Okay, let me give you an example. Wang Yi hasn't been in jail but I have. But Wang can't publish but I can. They have some sort of blacklist, but I'm not on it and he is. Why? I was in jail and he wasn't. You figure it out."

"Because he's a preacher? He has a congregation?"

"Right! You can't underestimate the role of house churches in Chinese society. They're the only real NGOs in China right now. People like Wang Yi have their own followers. These are real followers. It's not like on social media, which they can switch off when they want. I joked to Wang Yi that the government is more afraid of him than of people like me. They are real civil society."

We talked for another hour and left without encountering the feared *guobao*. My mind wandered back to Wang Yi's church and the sense that it might not last. In his open letter about Ran's detention, Wang had predicted his own imprisonment. Even though that had not happened, the letter contained a startling passage in which he talks to his wife, Jiang Rong, about his likely arrest:

My wife said, "I thought that you would be arrested before Ran Yunfei." Beginning on Wednesday, I fasted for three days and discussed with my wife various eventualities. In my prayers, I reached the certainty that I had been called.

No matter where I go, whether voluntary or involuntary, it will be for the sake of spreading the Gospel. My wife, no matter what, is a minister's wife. Human forces can easily alter the time, place and manner of our service but cannot change our basic mission of serving God.

So Jiang Rong asked me if I am arrested, what could she do? I answered, "Go to prison as if you were going to Africa. I am still a missionary, you are still a minister's wife. The Gospel was our life yesterday and it will be our life tomorrow. This is because the One who called us is the God of yesterday and the God of tomorrow."

P
A
R
T

II

AWAKENING OF THE INSECTS

One reason that China's modernizers rejected the lunar calendar was that it slowly goes off course. Twelve lunar cycles is just 354 days. That's about ten days short each year. The calendar is corrected every three years by adding a leap month, but this still means that events on the lunar calendar shift relative to the solar calendar from year to year. Sometimes Chinese New Year is in January, sometimes in February.

This might seem insignificant; after all, other religious calendars have shifting dates for their holidays, too. But China's calendar did more than track religion; it set the pattern for work as well. In agricultural societies like traditional China, farmers needed reliable guideposts to the seasons: when the earth would warm, the rains fall, or the frosts arrive. To figure this out, people had to gauge where the earth was relative to the sun, not the moon.

They did that by tracking the way the sun appears to move through the stars. From the earth's position as we revolve around the sun, the stars behind the sun appear to be moving. This idea is familiar to Westerners through the signs of the zodiac, which tell which constellation is passing behind the sun. Of course, it is we who are moving around the sun—not the sun through the stars—but the basic idea is right: it tells the earth's location on its annual 360-degree circuit around the sun. The movement is exact and predictable: about 1 degree around the sun each day of the year.

Ancient Chinese used this principle to group days into fifteen- to sixteen-day mini-seasons called *jieqi*, or solar terms. Each year has twenty-four—six for each season—and each of the twenty-four has its own special weather patterns, poems, aphorisms, and even rules about which foods to eat—which ones, for example, would cool the body in the summer, warm it in the winter, or replenish fluids in dry months. Their names evoke another, rural era: Grain Rain, Summer Harvest, Frost Descends, Lesser Snows, Greater Cold.

In recent years, these solar terms have made a comeback as cultural symbols. In the 1990s, artists began to use them allegorically for political and cultural events. Around 2010, consumer culture discovered them. Magazines devoted special issues to the solar terms, reintroducing readers to the traditional calendar and suggesting the appropriate food, tea, and clothing. In Beijing, a grocery store chain hired folk culture experts to devise a line of special foods for each of the twenty-four solar terms: minced-garlic pies to fight off the increased bacteria in the warming air of the Vernal Equinox; cooling green-bean cakes for Lesser Heat; and a hearty pig's elbow to build up one's constitution for the cold days of Autumn Commences. Books and apps explained the poems, myths, and fables associated with them. Elementary schools invited guest lecturers to explain the concept. Friends started signing e-mails with a greeting for key solar terms: A Peaceful Winter Solstice to You!

One of the most evocative solar terms is *jingzhe*, or the Awakening of the Insects. It occurs in early March when spring thundershowers were believed to waken dormant insects. The last of the six winter solar terms, it falls when the earth is 345 degrees around its orbit and planting is just around the corner. After the excitement of the New Year celebrations has faded, the world rouses itself. Tao Yuanming, a reclusive Daoist poet of the fourth century, put it like this:

> *Spring approaches, bringing timely rains*
> *Early thunder, erupting from the east*
> *Hibernating animals, hidden but shocked awake.*
> *Plants and trees, across the land, slowly open up.*

5

Ritual: Awakening the Past

The golden age of China's past was the Zhou dynasty, a legendary era that began three thousand years ago and lasted eight centuries. Philosophers like Confucius praised its early kings as paragons of wisdom who ruled by virtue and inspired their subjects without resorting to force. In one of the dynasty's many actions that were emulated through the ages, the first Zhou king is said to have built a structure known as the Hall of Light, which was meant to be a symbolic building to unify the new kingdom. A hymn from that time recounts how the people were so inspired that they built it quickly and spontaneously:

> All the people worked at it,
> In less than a day they finished it.
> When he built it, there was no goading;
> Yet the people came in their throngs.

In 1959, the Communist Party created its own hall. To celebrate the tenth anniversary of its rule, the party ordered for Beijing Ten Great Projects of pharaonic scale: a new railway station, a massive new sports stadium, huge exhibition centers, a national museum, and a hall of political power, the Great Hall of the People. The party mobilized seventy thousand workers, employing almost everyone in the construction industry, including Old Mr. Ni and his father. They worked twelve-hour shifts to complete the gargantuan structures in just a few months. Everywhere, gangs of workers toiled as in ancient days: by hand, hauling bricks and stones day and night. Then, as millennia earlier, the party emphasized speed and spontaneity: the buildings were a sign that the masses supported the party's right to rule. Or, as one of the architects put it, people "welcomed this glorious assignment . . . throwing themselves into a mighty collective campaign of architectural creation."

Of the ten projects, the most enduring is the Great Hall of the People. Many of the other buildings have been sidelined one way or another—surpassed by bigger stations, fancier museums, and showier stadiums. But the Great Hall is still the public focus of Chinese politics, a monumental granite block of massive columns that extends twelve hundred feet along the west side of Tiananmen Square. It is where the country's leaders appear in public to display their power. It is a backdrop for state banquets, receptions of foreign dignitaries, and symbolic political meetings. It is their throne room, their sacred space. It is a manifestation here, in the public world, of decisions made in murkier realms.

These parallels to China's old political-religious state are not accidental. The building's severe lines mirror China's Stalinist policies of the 1950s, when it largely followed the Soviet model. But the details are traditional. The pillars that stretch across the front sit on lotus petals, a Buddhist symbol of purity and uprightness. They number twelve, which purposefully equals the twelve columns of the Hall of Supreme Harmony, the central building in the Forbidden City. The usable floor space, which exceeds forty-two acres, was expanded from more modest dimensions so it would exceed the area of the entire Forbidden City.

In a nod to traditional Chinese geomancy, or *fengshui*, the building is not positioned directly in the middle of the square's west side. That would have put its entrance directly across from a memorial in Tiananmen Square to people who died for the Communist revolution—an inauspicious symbol of death. Instead, the entire structure was moved to the north. As the chief architect put it, "The living should not face the dead."

Inside, too, the Great Hall reflects a traditional view of how the political center views and unites its territories. Four thousand years ago, China's first dynasty, the Xia, cast bronze vessels decorated with symbols of its provinces and their tribute goods. In the Great Hall of the People, this confederation is symbolized by rooms for each

of China's thirty-four provinces, regions, or provincial-level munici-
palities, each room featuring local products and symbols. The Hong
Kong room is dominated by an imposing painting of the night scene
of Victoria Harbor to display its role as China's most cosmopolitan
city. Antique bronzes fill the Hunan and Shaanxi Halls to showcase
these provinces' ancient heritage. The Xinjiang Hall boasts "the largest Oriental carpet in Beijing," while the Tibet Hall is decorated with
Thangka-like murals.

Uniting these far-flung territories are emblems of the Communist Party. The most prominent is a giant red star on the ceiling of
the grand auditorium. On Mao's instructions, the auditorium was
designed to seat ten thousand people; the number ten thousand, or
wan in Chinese, is synonymous with infinity, just like in the saying for
eternal life, *wan sui*, literally meaning "ten thousand years." According to a statement by the architectural team, the curved ceiling

> alludes to the infinite space of the universe. In its center, an
> illuminated red star made of plexiglass stands for the lead-
> ership of the Party. The star emits radiating rays of golden
> light, and is encircled by gilded sunflower patterns and again
> by waves outlined with recessed light. The message of the dec-
> orative scheme is clear: all the people unite themselves around
> the Party, following the Party to advance the revolution from
> one victory to another.

Each year around the solar term Awakening of the Insects, under
this galaxy of heavenly lights, the party launches its most important
public display of power: a ten-day ritual called the Two Meetings.
One of them is a session of a consultative conference where Communist Party leaders confer with entrepreneurs, movie stars, religious
figures, and academics. It is meant to show that people "from all
walks of life" are part of the sacred mission of ruling China.

The other gathering is the annual session of the National People's Congress, a ritualized version of a parliament. The congress
has deputies, but they are unelected. It passes bills, but the decisions
are drafted elsewhere. It promulgates laws, but their enforcement is
arbitrary. Like the bright halls or bronze vessels of ancient times, it
is a statement of intent—of plans that will only slowly become clear.

This year, the Great Hall was an especially apt setting because China, its leaders announced, would revive its spiritual life.

Like all one-party states, China is obsessed with "culture." This does not mean subsidizing opera houses or philharmonic orchestras, although it does that, but instead something more akin to the modern management term of "corporate culture"—the ideas and philosophies that make an organization tick or that inspire people to action. It's not just authoritarian countries that face this challenge. In the premodern era, many societies were held together by hereditary rulers who had some sort of divine power or right to rule. When that collapsed, new nation-states often adopted an identity around ethnicity and a shared history: Germany was the land of Germans, France of the French, and so on. Today, most countries recognize that they are multiethnic and strive for broader identities. Germany has adopted the character of a country determined to confront its past. France emphasizes the ideals of the French Revolution. The United States, Canada, Australia, and other countries with a strong tradition of immigration tend to stress equality and basic human rights.

Forging a national consensus is always difficult, especially for countries run by authoritarian systems. A lack of free expression and assembly means that national discussions and debates are stunted, so leaders often impose some sort of national myth, with varying degrees of success. China's official identity is a multiethnic state where all peoples, beliefs, and traditions are equally respected. The problem with this story is that Han Chinese run the country and it is their values, their dreams, and their traditions that define the national vision—not China's fifty-five other ethnic groups. Coming up with a more credible national dream is complicated by China's modern history. Its last dynasty, the Qing, was created by invaders from the northern steppes, Manchus. During their rule from 1644 to 1911, they massively expanded China's boundaries to include far-flung peoples who in the past had only been under Chinese rule for short periods or in a very loose fashion. It was also a truly multiethnic empire, with many documents and public monuments written in several languages, such as Chinese, Manchurian, Mongolian and

Tibetan. What held the Qing together was hereditary rule and the old Chinese political system imbued with religious power.

When the Qing collapsed in 1911, the Republic of China and then the Communists—both dominated by ethnic Chinese—inherited the Manchu Empire's borders but struggled to come up with ideals and values to replace it.

Part of Mao's solution was to put himself forward as a godlike figure: the Great Helmsman, or the sun rising in the east. But because his rule was marked by a string of catastrophes, his successors were saddled with a lack of credibility. Their solution was to focus on economics, making the national credo economic development. Later, patriotism was added to the mix. Students had to undergo mandatory military training, and the government pushed a story that China had been humiliated until it was saved by the Communist Party.

Even so, a sense of malaise began to take hold in the 1980s and '90s. By the early twenty-first century, it had become widespread—a lack of social trust that infuriated so many Chinese and was reflected in opinion polls and studies. Some in the government thought that religion—if carefully controlled—could be an answer. One of these officials was Ye Xiaowen, a controversial figure who headed the State Administration for Religious Affairs, the government body that sets policies, appoints senior religious leaders, and determines which temples, churches, or mosques can be built. Ye was a close political ally of the former Chinese leader Jiang Zemin and made head of religious affairs work in 1995, at the relatively young age of forty-five. He held the position for fourteen years—easily making him the most influential figure in the party's religious work in the reform era.

In the West, Ye is widely seen as a hard-liner, but Ye was a complex figure who had some understanding of religion. In the party's early years, it had either tried to ban religion or grudgingly respected it as something important to minority groups like the Hui and Tibetans, and so best left alone. Ye was more sophisticated. He had grown up in one of China's poorest provinces, Guizhou, and in the 1970s studied sociology. For many years, this discipline had been banned as unnecessary because Communist ideology was supposed to be able to explain all phenomena in society. So trained sociologists like Ye were in short supply and quickly rose through the ranks. By 1980, at age thirty, he was already director of the provincial society of sociology. Five years later, he headed the province's branch of the Communist Youth League and in 1990, right after the Beijing massacre, he was brought to Beijing to work in the Communist Party's United Front Work Department. This organization is supposed to win over and control non-Communist groups in society—like religions. As the party was trying to repair its links to society after the massacre, its role was crucial.

Ye was firm but outgoing. In 2003, he went on a tour of the United States to explain China's religious policy and "fielded questions like a used-car salesman"—standing before a group of skeptical reporters in Los Angeles and colorfully explaining that there was no contradiction for an atheistic Communist Party official like himself to run religious policy. As he later put it, "If I believed in a religion, other religions would be unhappy. As I show respect for all religions and don't believe in any religion, I can serve them."

But Ye's tenure was less impartial than this. While cracking down hard on religions with foreign ties, he was supportive of belief systems—especially Buddhism, Daoism, and Confucianism—that were considered indigenous. In 2005, he lent his imprimatur to the newly founded Center for the Study of Confucian Religion by attending its opening. Soon, scholars critical of Confucianism as a religion were moved out of key research institutes and replaced by those who supported its revival. Soon after, universities, high schools, and elementary schools across the country set up institutes or classes teaching the value systems of Confucianism, Daoism, and other traditional schools.

In keeping with the Communist Party's new emphasis on economics, Ye argued that religion could promote development by creating social trust and smoothing over tensions in society. "Religious force is one of the most important social forces from which China draws its strength," Ye told an international conference on Buddhism in 2006.

In 2004, the party began to step up promoting its own values, coining "harmonious society," a traditional term that recalled Daoist ideas of living in harmony with the world. In 2006, it adopted another archaic-sounding phrase called the "Eight Honors and Eight Shames," a list of dos and don'ts for party officials.

These words might sound empty, but they actually marked the beginning of an important transformation. Under Mao, Communism was based on the idea that society had to be in a state of permanent revolution. Deng replaced revolution with "reform," a softer term but one that still involved painful changes. So it was actually a radical idea that in the twenty-first century the party should define its role not as an agent of social transformation but as a mediator that smoothed over conflicts with traditional ideas.

The slogans' apparent superficiality was deceptive for another reason. This is because content always comes slowly to Chinese projects. China is the land of soft openings: projects are first announced to big fanfare, structures erected as a declaration of intent, and only then filled with content. In this sense, developing a new ideology to unify China is similar to building a shopping mall: the deal is publicized, the building goes up, a few stores open, but only years later are all the shops and restaurants open for business, and only after a number of anchor tenants have gone bankrupt. This makeshift model differs from how Westerners like to see projects—envisioned and planned thoroughly, then completed according to that design. But it has its own logic. If viable, the project goes ahead; if not, backing out is easier.

The content for these new missions began to arrive five years later, in the autumn of 2011, at the last big annual Communist Party meeting under the old administration of President Hu Jintao and Premier Wen Jiabao. The communiqué issued by that meeting frankly described a society where "in a number of areas, morals are defeated, sincerity is lacking, the view of life and value system of a number of members of society is distorted."

The solution was to educate people in "Core Socialist Values." These were mainly anodyne terms ("patriotism," "honesty," "thrift"), but they began to be supplemented with ideas from the old political-religious system of Han Chinese thought, such as filial piety, or *xiao*, and a political utopian term, *datong*, often translated as "great harmony." In fact, the report called China's traditional heritage "a common spiritual garden for the Chinese nation." Now as a new political

era began, these were the terms to be brought alive in a ceremony at
the Great Hall.

In traditional Chinese religion, a *fashi,* or ritual master, recites a set
of phrases that are designed to turn an ordinary space into a sacred
area where the gods descend to receive prayers and rejuvenate the
community. The rite can last days, with breaks and feasts, until the
rites end and secular life resumes. In Chinese politics, the spring ceremony is the National People's Congress, and its *fashi* is the premier.
He kicks the session off with a speech and ends the meeting with
a mock press conference. The premier's role indicates the symbolic
nature of the session. Real power in the Communist Party is held
not by the premier but by the party's general secretary. The premier
is usually chosen for his ability to operate the vast bureaucracy that
runs the country. But he is only the public face of power, not the
ultimate arbiter of the shadowy committees and cliques that make
the decisions. He is useful but replaceable.

Even though these religious-like political rituals are annual events,
each year is unique. The year 2012 marked the transfer of power from
Party Secretary Hu Jintao and Premier Wen Jiabao to the new government under Xi Jinping and Li Keqiang. In the autumn, Hu would
conduct his own farewell ceremony. Now, during the National People's Congress, it was Premier Wen who would first say good-bye.

Like every other annual session of parliament, the 2012 National
People's Congress had been so tightly scripted that one could follow it from last year's agenda. It had begun punctually, on March
5, the first day of the Awakening of the Insects, with Premier Wen's
work report. This is an hour-long talk that usually repeats the decisions made at the previous autumn's Communist Party plenum—in
this case, the pledge to adopt new values and to promote traditional
Chinese culture. As always, he followed the document so closely that
there was no need to listen to him; the speech had already been made
public an hour beforehand, and by the time he gave it, journalists had
already written their articles and were only following to make sure he
didn't forget to read a line.

In the days that followed, the session unfolded as always. One perennial feature was the discussion of bills, as if the congress were a true deliberative body that might just take up a new idea and debate it. This year, delegates asked for a ban on television advertising, while others suggested that the government encourage young women to marry older men. The reason: only older men can afford apartments in Chinese cities. Another serious proposal came from a delegate who suggested that rural children not be allowed to attend university. If they did, the sponsor said, they would not return to their ancestral homes, and traditions would be lost. Needless to say, all of these bills were killed before entering committee; they were just part of the show.

Each year, the party documented its ceremony in almost identical fashion. The front pages of five major party newspapers—*People's Daily, Enlightenment Daily, Workers' Daily, Liberation Daily,* and *Economic Daily*—were indistinguishable. This year the flagship *People's Daily* offered a front page with the headline "National Consultative Congress Eleventh Session Fifth Plenum Ends." The year before the headline was "National Consultative Congress Eleventh Session Fourth Plenum Ends." The year before that it was the third plenum that had ended. This year, last year, and the year before all had the same photographs: Top center was a panorama shot of the carefully festooned rostrum with the same faces, the same suits, the same dyed hair. A photograph center right showed the head of the congress standing in front of a microphone, a sheet of paper in his hands. Both appeared to be exactly the same pictures as the year before.

The ten-day ceremony wound up with the final press conference, which this year was Premier Wen's exit from the national stage, just as it had been for Premier Zhu Rongji ten years earlier and would likely be for the incoming premier, Li Keqiang, ten years later. Wen was a thin, almost ascetic man whose neck shriveled into the collar of his shirt and whose lips always seemed pursed like a priest contemplating a particularly embarrassing confession. In his earlier years, Wen had supported reformers in the party and looked the part: the punctilious, careful, good-hands man, or as the local press liked to call him "Uncle Wen." This abstinent image, however, was misleading. As foreign journalists later proved, Wen's family was loaded with money. His old mother had been used to list shell companies, while siblings had taken cushy jobs abroad. At the very least, he was incompetent, or a bad example of the Confucian admonishment to first regulate one's home before regulating the affairs of society.

Wen's press conference went on for three hours; he did not seem to want to leave the stage. At the time, most attention in the politically incestuous capital was focused on a political scandal that involved a provincial leader named Bo Xilai whose wife had allegedly murdered a British businessman, Neil Heywood. Wen seemed to be alluding to this when he issued an "urgent" appeal for political reform—not democracy, of course, but some sort of fairer, more transparent system, one ruled by laws and not tyrannical local bosses.

Wen's personal wishes and political warnings were interesting but irrelevant. The real significance of this year's ceremony under the Great Hall's stars was its call for cultural renewal. This was the program that the party would adopt over the course of the year—its new foundation for power. At the end of his press conference, Wen trudged offstage, a defeated man. This was not the era of political reform; it was the beginning of an appeal to China's mystical, powerful history. And it was driven by a widespread desire across China for a more stable, moral society based on traditions culled from the past.

6

Beijing: You Can't Explain It

Ni Jincheng was in purgatory, lying flat in bed, in excruciating pain, waiting for a miracle. As often happened when he was stressed, he had thrown out his back. The cause was not hard to find: his father's terrifying illness. The cancer had spread, and his body was bloated with water. The old man lay on a cot in a side room next to the hall where he had greeted me at Chinese New Year, now barely able to move. Family members changed him and tried to spoon-feed him, but he was declining rapidly. Across the hall from his sickroom was another small chamber used as a family shrine. It contained a large table covered in silk. On top were scores of statues of smaller deities centered on a two-foot-high bronze statue of the Buddhist goddess of mercy, Guanyin. In front of the altar was a red padded kneeler and next to it a big brass bowl and a wooden mallet. Every morning at five, Jincheng went there to perform his morning prayers. He would light three sticks of incense, strike the bowl with the mallet, and kowtow, repeating a prayer for his father's health. The bowl would vibrate like a deep-registered bell, tolling across the hall for the old man to hear.

Old Mr. Ni's illness had made Jincheng head of the clan, but he was not sure he wanted to lead the Ni family's Whole Heart Philanthropic Salvation Tea Association. He was the older son and had helped his father found the pilgrimage group fifteen years earlier. He had donated generously and joined the group each spring when it set up a shrine during the fifteen-day pilgrimage to Beijing's holiest mountain, Miaofengshan, the Mountain of the Wondrous Peak. There they provided tea to pilgrims, a symbolic act of generosity and piety.

But truth be told, his father had done most of the work. His faith had inspired people to donate their time and money. His recovery from cancer had seemed a miracle. He possessed a quiet charisma and the authority that comes simply from having lived a long time. He had seen the old temples before they had been torn down. He knew the old Daoists who had lived in the temple next to the family home. He understood things that a younger person could not. Compared with him, who was Jincheng but a wealthy and pious son, a mere fifty-six years old, born after the Communist revolution, a youngster when the Cultural Revolution had been unleashed? How could he manage to bring the family together without his father? And now, as if fate were testing him, he had slipped a disk while moving a box, just weeks before the pilgrimage.

After days of intense pain, he had admitted himself to the Titan Orthopedic Hospital. It was a small clinic, not very famous, but it was located near their old home. Its name carried the story of the Ni family's expulsion from the old city to the Temple of the Tolling Bell neighborhood. Pronounced "tee-tan," it was made up of two abbreviations: "Ti" for the sports commission whose construction in 1992 had meant the destruction of their old home, and "tan" for the Temple of Heaven, a landmark near the old home. The name could have been an unpleasant reminder of their loss, but Jincheng didn't think so. For him, it created a link to the past, a sense of continuity at a trying moment.

Like any gentleman, he insisted on meeting me at the door to his room. But he was bent over, and his black hair had gone gray at the roots, a sign that he had not been able to get to a barber in a while. I followed him as he shuffled to his bed. He perched gingerly on the edge, looking down at his hands, embarrassed at his predicament. Then he gathered himself and issued a command: "Use my other mobile number next time. The one you called is issued by the government. They're listening in."

"The government is listening to *your* cellphone?" I knew that Jincheng had strong views on social issues, but he was not a political person. "No way! Why?"

"Corruption. You know what I mean? A lot of people are corrupt in the government. A bunch of my colleagues have been sent off for reeducation. Who can resist it? There's so much money at stake. The companies can't avoid offering bribes. Many take it."

Jincheng began telling me about his worries. As a civil servant with the Ministry of Construction, he worked on a team that inspected large-scale projects. When the team found problems, they fined the construction companies, sometimes millions of dollars. But the inspectors made only about $1,000 a month. Like elsewhere in the system, that had led to widespread corruption. Now the government had launched a crackdown in a way only an authoritarian state can. All members of the team assumed their cellphones were tapped and their bank accounts monitored.

"But you're not involved, are you?"

"Ha, me? Look at how we live. You've seen our house. Does it look like I take bribes?"

I thought of the family's reduced circumstances. In imperial times, the Ni family had been Manchu soldiers who settled in the area of the Temple of the Tolling Bell, founding the Ni Family Village, which no longer exists but can still be found on city maps. In the late nineteenth century, they became prosperous by staging weddings and funerals and then moved into the city, buying the home near the Temple of Heaven. They became the equivalent of lay religious leaders. They set up temporary altars at funerals and weddings, invited Daoist priests or Buddhist monks to carry out ceremonies, and made sure the complex sequence of events over several days ran smoothly. All of this had made Jincheng's grandfather a godfather in the community: if a respected widow died poor, he made sure she had a proper send-off, financing everything out of his own pocket.

That changed in the Communist era. Once prosperous small-business people, they became state employees. Jincheng's grandfather and father had helped build Tiananmen Square and the Great Hall of the People. Later, Jincheng and his brother followed them into the trade. All lived in the old family home near the Temple of Heaven. Like much of Beijing, the house survived the first decades of Communist rule because the government was too poor to carry out its plans of radically changing China's urban landscape.

Then came economic reforms in the 1980s and 1990s. The state got wealthy and had the money to carry out its program of "transforming" (gaizao) cities across China. In Beijing and hundreds of other cities, that meant clear-cutting old neighborhoods and building apartment towers, shopping malls, elevated highways, and prestige projects like the sports commission. The Ni family was expelled from the sacred capital, ending up in almost the same neighborhood where their ancestors had lived a century before. For his father, Jincheng built the bungalow I had visited a few months earlier at Chinese New Year. For himself, he constructed a narrow four-story building. They rented out the bottom two floors and lived on the third floor.

The fourth floor was a tacked-on penthouse, cheaply made, but in Jincheng's hands a hermitage atop the city. A back room had a shrine bigger than the one in his father's home, dominated by a three-foot bronze Guanyin that would be carried to Miaofengshan in a few weeks. Out front was a living room with an enormous ceramic bowl filled with fat goldfish, and next to it a room stocked with cages of racing pigeons, which cooed and strutted throughout the day. A balcony looked over the city's sprawling southern suburbs. The materials were cheap and temporary, but when we sat there, drinking tea and smoking dollar-a-pack Great Qianmen cigarettes, it felt otherworldly, as if we were transported back to a time when the Temple of the Tolling Bell still stood and its message still resonated with the townsfolk.

"I know, you live simply," I said, thinking also of the meals I had had at his home: noodles, cold cuts, and a $2 bottle of grain alcohol. "But it is still a dangerous time."

I mentioned the upcoming government meetings and government campaigns against corruption, but he laughed as if I were warning him about the weather: predictable but unalterable forces that you could cope with but not change.

"Faith makes you realize that these things are not important. But others . . . you can see from how they live that something isn't right. I don't want to say more than that."

He had chosen his words carefully, but his workplace sickened him. He felt that almost no one was clean and that you were a fool if you didn't take bribes. So he had started simply not going to work, using his seniority to his advantage. The ministry had a rule that when it issued a fine over 8 million yuan, or about $1.25 million, an inspector with more than thirty years' experience had to sign off. Because of China's construction boom, the ministry was constantly inspecting and fining. Senior managers like Jincheng were at a premium. His superiors needed his signature so badly that they tolerated his coming to work only once a month. The rest of the time he said he was sick, traveling, or on vacation. No one seemed to care as long as he signed the stack of papers on his desk once in a while.

"I'm happy about it so I can look after my father. Also I don't have to deal with those officials who just want to make money. They don't have a *dixian*."

That word, *dixian* in Chinese, was tough to translate. It literally meant "bottom line," but in the sense of a minimum moral standard, below which one would not stoop. Without a bottom line, the means always justify the ends. For Jincheng and many—maybe even most—Chinese, this is how their country felt: a place where anything went.

Jincheng experienced this whenever he left home and had to encounter the outside world. Growing up in 1950s and early 1960s Beijing had felt simpler. Even though this was after the Communist takeover, many of the old *guiju*, or rules, still survived. They ranged from small rules of personal politeness (don't spit at the table) to respecting privacy (don't enter a room without knocking or a person's home without first calling out a polite greeting). But bigger principles existed too: You treated religious figures with respect. You didn't flaunt your wealth. You worked hard because you didn't want to shame your family, friends, or master.

"People today don't know anything," he said as we sat in his small hospital room, "except how to push you out of the way."

It reminded me of another pilgrimage leader, Zhao Baoqi, whose group performed martial arts at Miaofengshan. When I asked him once what the key was to understanding the pilgrimage societies, he also repeated that word: *guiju*. This was what society lacked: rules, standards, ties. Chinese society was like a sailboat unmoored, its centerboard broken, its sails full, flying wildly across the water—exhilarating to watch from the shore but terrifying to ride.

"Who are our enemies? Who are our friends? This is a question of the first importance for the revolution." This is the first line of the first essay of the first volume of Mao Zedong's collected works—the genesis of the violent world that Chinese like Jincheng are trying to escape. Mao's words set up a binary world of friends and enemies.

Anyone opposing the revolution was an enemy, and enemies were killed. This was not metaphorical. Violence was endemic in the Mao era. Millions of so-called landlords—often the literati who had held traditional society together for centuries, but many of them little more than smallholding farmers with tiny plots of land—were buried alive, decapitated, or beaten to death by villagers, often whipped up by Communist Party agitators.

Just a decade later, the Cultural Revolution continued this brutalization. Like millions of homes across the country, Beijing's old courtyards were ransacked by Red Guards. The Ni family lost all their statues, and the Daoist temple next door was vandalized. When the army was sent in to Beijing and other Chinese cities to restore order, it made things worse, savagely beating and killing even more people than the Red Guards. Then the soldiers brought in hundreds of thousands of their relatives who occupied the old courtyard homes and the *danwei* housing compounds, or the once-majestic old temples. Suddenly people were surrounded by strangers, in a society where basic rules of human conduct had largely been destroyed. Trust became limited to one's immediate family and circle of friends.

When the Cultural Revolution ended, many wondered if they could ever trust anyone again. Some hoped that a kinder, gentler society might replace the violence of the Mao era. Throughout the 1980s, people wrote and argued for an ethical awakening. Writers like Ba Jin, for example, called for a Cultural Revolution museum to commemorate and warn against the horrors of the past.

Instead, public discussion was throttled; the 1989 massacre of demonstrators further stifled any open debate about how to organize society. As economic reforms accelerated in the early 1990s, the country was ordered to direct its energies into getting rich. But underlying this new era of prosperity was a sense of anger and violence. One senses this in online forums, where even by the low standards of Internet civility, disputes quickly take a brutal turn, often ending with online mobs posting humiliating personal details about their opponents—the modern-day version of the Mao era's denunciations. As the Peking University ethicist He Huaihong wrote, "We can feel the overlay of savagery in our ordinary lives."

We should not forget that the reforms were a godsend to many people. The new policies allowed hundreds of millions to lift themselves out of poverty. Horizons opened for many more. Farmers migrated to the coast for paying work in factories, young people received an education and embarked on new lives, and millions entered the middle class and traveled abroad for the first time in their lives. For many, the reform era has been an optimistic time.

But the disquiet remains and has become more pronounced now that the thrill of prosperity has faded. In traditional society, schools and medical care were based on local relationships with a teacher and a doctor. In the *danwei* system, these sorts of services were provided by the work unit. In the post-Communist system, everything is for sale—not just obvious things like a hospital bed, a place in a school, and a government job, but also health-inspection certificates, book reviews in the newspaper, and scientific articles. Standards—of hygiene, of professional pride, of academic rigor—degenerated.

Trust had to be triangulated. I can trust that this bottle of liquor is not a fake because my cousin's brother-in-law works at the distillery. This rice doesn't have pesticides because it is from a village where an old classmate still has relatives. This doctor won't toss me out of his office after thirty seconds, because she's my eighth cousin's daughter. Even if people did not really believe that these tenuous ties amounted to anything, they clung to them, hoping they weren't being cheated, even though they knew they were: the only really safe food was served in the Zhongnanhai leadership compound; the only really good doctors saw patients at outrageously expensive private clinics; decent public schools required under-the-table "donations" of $10,000 or more each year.

People's powerlessness was especially humiliating. Many countries have similar problems but also mechanisms for ordinary people to express their frustration or even change the system. But China has no lobby groups, unions, or free media. Nongovernmental organizations are allowed to exist only if they restrict their activities to providing services, such as disaster relief. Organizing to change society is forbidden. So too are protests and independent political parties. People are left on their own. They can hope that the Communist Party might take action on a given issue, or they can rely on their personal network. This sense of helplessness is captured in numerous opinion polls. One 2014 study cited "loss of trust" as the top problem facing China, with 88 percent agreeing with the statement that China was beset by "a social disease of moral decay and lack of trust."

In place of principles, China has "hidden rules," or *qian guize*, in the phrase of Wu Si, a prominent historian and former editor of the influential magazine *China Through the Ages*. Success is based on connections, favoritism, and unethical deal making. It is analogous to a Hollywood actor's getting roles through sexual favors—except this sort of crass quid pro quo is widespread in Chinese society.

Jincheng's beloved apartment was a typical example of these hidden rules. The government was threatening to tear down the neighborhood of the Temple of the Tolling Bell—not just one or two buildings, but dozens of city blocks to make way for scores of new housing towers. Residents could get apartments in the new project, but it meant negotiating a murky bureaucracy. Government officials would almost certainly get the best units, but if Jincheng played his cards right, the family might end up with two or three bright, comfortable apartments, maybe even one that he could turn into a prayer hall. If not, they would be reduced to one miserable apartment. The family's fortunes hung on getting this right. "I have to find someone to figure this out," Jincheng said to me one day at his apartment.

"Find someone"; that was another special Chinese phrase. To find someone, or *zhaoren*, meant you couldn't rely on asking the government if your home was going to be torn down. You had to have an insider who could slip you some advice—all for a reciprocal favor, of course: Yes, your home is going to be torn down, and the government absolutely will not offer more than so-and-so much a square meter. So if it offers less, you can expect more, but if you hold out for more, you will be penalized and receive a smaller unit. And make sure your daughter is married off by next summer because then she can qualify for her own apartment. Later than July 1 and she won't qualify. Yes, the July 1 date is certain. No, it hasn't been made public. I'm telling you this as a friend. Friend, or *pengyou*, another Chinese word that acquired a warped meaning: I'm telling you this, and now you owe me something. In the past, connections mattered, but ties and obligations were more predictable and tempered by moral values and rules. Today's society was in a way simpler: what mattered was power and money. The rest was rhetoric.

All this drove Jincheng to distraction and made him appreciate the pilgrimage association. Here were thirty people who trusted one another. Most were relatives of some sort, but outsiders joined and became friends. They were like a big clan, something that most Chinese lost when they left their ancestral village and were then subjected to family-planning controls. They quarreled, feuded, and argued loudly. But they were bound by faith in Our Lady of the Azure Clouds, and they looked out for one another. Without saying it—because who needed to say or even think this sort of thing?—they loved one another as people do in a rambling, mildly dysfunctional family.

I had brought with me a newly published Chinese edition of *Zen Baggage*, a book by the American writer Bill Porter. For years, Porter had worked as an indigent translator of Chinese poetry and Buddhist scriptures, getting by on meager royalties and occasional donations from pious Buddhists who appreciated his work. Living in rural Washington State, Porter was so poor that some of his books acknowledge help from the U.S. Department of Agriculture—for its food stamp program. But in 2010 one of his travel books on hermits in China was translated into Chinese. He became a star. Eager to learn how a foreigner sees their religion, Chinese bought hundreds of thousands of copies of his book. He held book signings where people waited for hours for a signature. State television made a documentary on him, and he had fans who put money into a bank account that he could spend when he came to China.

Jincheng was delighted. He held the book up and pressed the spine against his forehead. "Thank you; this is an offering," he said, and then placed it next to a piece of yellow silk that was covering something on his night table.

I said it was quite simple and he'd probably not learn much from it.

"No, I don't agree. He's looking at things from the heart, and that's the most basic. It has nothing to do with being Chinese. If he does things like I do them, then I don't learn anything."

He pulled away the bolt of yellow silk next to the book. Under it was a small portable altar made of rosewood. Inside was a small wooden stand holding a bronze mirror. Next to it were two laminated pieces of paper the size of playing cards. On the front of one was a many-armed Buddha and on the back was a mantra, "Cundī Dhāranī," a short chant of ten words meant to be said aloud. Jincheng explained that this was really powerful but only if you said it often.

"How often?"

"Twenty thousand to start. Eight hundred thousand to achieve enlightenment."

"Who has time for that?"

"You're supposed to say it 108 times a day. That's 54 in the morning and 54 in the evening. It just takes ten minutes to say it 54 times."

"How long do you spend on prayers?"

"An hour in the morning and an hour in the evening. You can do the 20,000 in half a year. It's not a lot if you're devout. If you can't manage that, you don't have much."

We talked about this year's pilgrimage. It started on the first day of the fourth lunar month, which this year fell on April 21. He cautioned against going too late. It was important to get there the night before it started—so on the thirtieth day of the third lunar month. That way you were there at midnight when the first day of the fourth month began. That was the high point. What mattered was the buildup. By the time it started officially, the best was over.

I looked at him and thought, the two weeks up on the mountain, is this your calling? Your family shrine, the racing pigeons, the balcony, the hours of prayer, isn't this where you belong?

"Maybe you shouldn't go," I ventured politely. "You're sick."

"Well," Jincheng said slowly, as if considering this for the first time. "No, I have to go, but don't forget, get there early! No one gets there late. If you get there at midnight, you've missed it."

He reached into his satchel and pulled out a tattered booklet. It was his official papers as a lay Buddhist. It listed his master, at a temple in Beijing where he had taken a short course in Buddhist ideas and history. Becoming a lay Buddhist or Daoist was increasingly popular. Some prominent Chinese, like the singer Faye Wong, were lay Buddhists. Wong, a onetime sex symbol and torch-song singer, had carved out a new identity with music featuring esoteric and explicitly Buddhist lyrics.

Others signed up for Tibetan Buddhism, which they viewed as a purer form of the religion because it came from what they thought of as an unspoiled part of China—the Tibetan plateau. The interest, though, did not translate into sympathy for Tibetans, many of whom wanted more autonomy or even independence. At heart, it was a kind of selfishness, and if it had a political meaning, it was as expropriation—much in the way Native Americans were first conquered, their land despoiled, then their beliefs hijacked by pop culture. For Chinese, Tibetan Buddhism was like a more efficacious form of medicine and for some even a status symbol: I've got my own master from Lhasa, or my Rinpoche from Sera. Jincheng watched some of these masters in online videos but spent his money on the tea association and focused his piety inwardly.

Jincheng pointed out that the bronze mirror had one patch that was shinier than the rest.

"I haven't touched it. It's shinier because of the praying. It's one of those things—you can't say for sure or not for sure. You say it's not scientific, but then you see this happening. You can't explain it."

He pointed to a glass jar in front of the small altar. It was filled with water and had a metal lid screwed on.

"I drink this water once a day, and my blood pressure is perfect and my heart rate is perfect. How do you explain it? You can't explain it."

He said he had brought the jar over from the altar in his home. You weren't meant to drink all the water at one time. Instead, you drank half of it and refilled it. That way the old holy water made the added water efficacious.

"The jar doesn't matter. It's because it's in front of the altar. The prayers make it special; otherwise it's just water in a jar. Why does it work? You can't explain it.

"Let me give you another example: the old man. He's really sick, yes, but after Wang Defeng went up and prayed for him last year, he got another year. He should have died last year, but he's still alive now. How do you explain that? You can't explain it.

"You can find a lot of things that you can't explain unless you understand this," he said, pointing to his heart. "This explains it."

7

Ritual: The Caged Master

Chinese culture originated in the country's north, near the Yellow River and mythic mountain ranges like the Taihang. But climate and geography long ago pulled the center of Chinese civilization south, to Jiangnan, or south of the river, the area around the Yangtze. Here, the milder weather and plentiful rain created the prosperity that produced more officials, scholars, painters, and writers than any other place in China. Even today, it is the country's economic motor, with the two provinces of Jiangsu and Zhejiang along with the mega-city of Shanghai forming an economic zone that is at the level of a middle-income country. Although not as boisterous as Sichuan or as politically connected as Beijing, its wealth and sophistication are unrivaled.

The heart of Jiangnan is Lake Tai, a strangely half-round body of water that is home to some of China's most coveted products: ink brushes from Huzhou, clay teapots from Yixing, silk from Suzhou, tea from the hills of Zhejiang, and limestone "scholar" rocks from Dongting Mountain. Although its shape is sometimes attributed to a meteor impact, it functions more like a railroad turntable, sending goods and ideas racing across the region and up through the Grand Canal to the country's politically rich but economically arid north.

Lake Tai was also the home to China's most famous contemporary sage, ninety-four-year-old Nan Huai-chin. His life spanned most of modern Chinese history, taking him from being heir to a prosperous family on coastal China to the peaks of a holy mountain, a career in the military, political trouble that required him to flee to Taiwan, the United States, Hong Kong, and now, toward the end of his life, back to mainland China.

It was a sojourn worthy of Confucius, who had bounced around the known world of his time, seeking a ruler who would accept his advice. Master Nan, though, had achieved recognition in his lifetime. On the mainland, he had become famous as a Zen Buddhist master and author of books explaining China's traditions in folksy, accessible language—something like Will and Ariel Durant's *Story of Civilization,* a multivolume work of mostly Western ideas that was in the bookcase of every middle-class American family in the mid-twentieth century. Master Nan's books are more idiosyncratic and personal—he did not nod to scholarship or try to cover China's tradition in a systematic way—but he has sold over sixty million copies, and government-run bookstores feature his works prominently. Through a foundation, he also helped revive classical education in public schools and started his own traditional-style school.

Most interesting to me was that here, on the shores of Lake Tai, he had a close-knit coterie of followers, admirers, and rich donors who competed for his time every evening, hoping to get answers to the confusing reality around them. Up in Beijing, political leaders were just beginning to embrace traditional Chinese values and beliefs, but here, under Master Nan's tutelage, these ideas had been nurtured for over a decade. I was curious to find out how.

So on the day of the start of the Awakening of the Insects solar term, I arrived on the shores of Lake Tai to meet Master Nan. His Lake Tai Great Hall of Learning was comfortable, made of several traditional-style buildings and flower gardens on the shores of the lake. But it also felt like a minimum-security prison: Guards and dogs were stationed around the complex, and the grounds were often eerily empty. Visitors were carefully selected by a former central government employee. Master Nan published many books but never gave media interviews. He forbade his speeches to be recorded and distributed. He didn't allow his students to teach his ideas. And he cultivated the role of an enigmatic recluse, keeping questioners at arm's length with stories and riddles.

At the end of my first day there, I met him: short, slender, with combed-back hair that emphasized his birdlike features, wearing a dark blue Chinese gown, with a hand-carved walking stick in one hand and a Panda-brand cigarette in the other. He was a nonagenarian but witty and funny, as solicitous as any good host should be. How did I like his hermitage?

I said I liked it but felt perplexed. The empty campus, the guards and the disciples, the strange combination of fame and obscurity: What did it all mean?

He planted his cane between his legs like a sword, looked past me toward the lake, and laughed.

"Your story should be written like this. You came across this giant lake, one of the largest in China, and on the edge of it was an old guy who talked all kinds of nonsense. That should be how you tell your story."

Master Nan was born in 1918, when ancient China had all but vanished. The last emperor had abdicated in 1911, and a new, modernizing government under the Nationalist Party, or Kuomintang, was about to unify the country. But like most people of his generation, he attended a traditional school, which meant learning the classics by heart. His teachers were old men who had come of age in the mid- to late nineteenth century and imbued him with the traditional way of looking at Chinese culture: as an unbroken string going back twenty-five hundred years to Confucius. It wasn't a critical appraisal of traditional China but a massive download of information, assumptions, and accepted ways of viewing the world that had shaped Chinese for centuries.

And yet Master Nan wasn't oblivious to the outside world. Angered by Japan's steady encroachment onto Chinese territory during the 1930s, he joined the military. At twenty-one, he was commanding his own unit of several thousand men. He was short but trim and powerful, with dark eyebrows and an ability to lead.

Then came one of the odd, unexplained twists that have defined his life. Even though China faced invasion by Japan, Master Nan abandoned his military training to pursue a spiritual path. He eventually retreated to Mount Emei in southwest China's Sichuan Province, living as a Buddhist hermit for three years. When he descended from the mountain in 1943, he found the unfamiliar smell of humans repulsive. He took up smoking to shield himself from their odor and for the rest of his life still puffed on cigarettes, blowing the smoke out in front like a protective shield.

When the Communists won China's civil war and took power in 1949, Master Nan was one of the more than two million Republic of China loyalists and soldiers who fled to the island of Taiwan. It remained under control of the tradition-oriented Nationalist Party government and became a refuge from the radical social experiments that Mao carried out on the mainland. A charismatic and forceful public speaker, he gathered around him some of Taiwan's most celebrated intellectuals and powerful political figures. These connections proved dangerous. In the early 1980s, Taiwan was still under martial law, and some of his students angered the regime. Master Nan was warned that he was in danger. In 1985, he fled to Washington, D.C., where he lived in relative anonymity. He stayed for just three years, eventually moving to Hong Kong.

In 2000, he finally returned to China to great fanfare. His books had already been printed in samizdat form and were popular among the country's growing middle class. Most of them discuss one great book, such as Confucius's *Analects* or Laozi's *Daodejing*. Academics often gripe that Nan gets his facts wrong—misidentifying poems or misstating references. And scholarship—forget it; his books have virtually no footnotes or references to textual analysis or archaeological finds. But he resonated with Chinese. They had been through more than one hundred years of brutal policies to catch up with the West. They had discarded their traditions wholesale and tried out new ideologies like suits of clothes: warlordism, fascism, and Communism. Now they had found a hybrid authoritarian-capitalist system that had brought prosperity to many people, but were left with an urgent question: With so much lost, what makes them Chinese? Master Nan wasn't another scholar expounding a turgid point or a glib television star able to talk about the traditions but with no real credibility. Instead, his age, his education, and his reputation make him an authentic master who could explain the country's complex past and offer a vision of the future.

So when he returned, it was hailed as a momentous event: here was one of the Chinese-speaking world's great masters of *guoxue*, or traditional learning, choosing to return to China, proving that the

People's Republic was the legitimate heir to the country's glorious past. Then the reality of living in China set in. He moved to Shanghai and tried to buy property but was repeatedly rebuffed by the government, which controls the real estate market. Two years later, in 2001, one of his students encouraged him to look at a shorefront property on Lake Tai. After a four-hour drive from Shanghai, Master Nan and his entourage found that the property was swampland. They turned back.

Just a few minutes into their trip home, their motorcycle police escort veered off course, leading them to a local hotel. Officials had laid out a red carpet and a giant red banner announcing his purchase of the swampland. As with so many things in China, a decision had been made by someone somewhere. Master Nan was welcome to return, but he was to live here, hours away from China's urban centers. He was back home, but in another form of exile. Undeterred, he began to rebuild his life at age eighty-three. His weapon was his voice, and his battleground was his dinner table.

Days at the Lake Tai Hall of Great Learning began sharp at six o'clock in the evening. That was when Master Nan held court at the dinner table. Today, a Tianjin real estate developer had come to seek Master Nan's advice on where he should invest his money. Flush with cash, he wanted to earn more; he explained that there was an opportunity to put money into a cure for Alzheimer's. But he was unsure of the ethics of such a deal—did the ninety-three-year-old master have an opinion on Alzheimer's?

"You shouldn't invest in that," Master Nan replied firmly. He questioned the cure's efficacy, especially because China is rife with medical scams. Then he looked around the table, where a dozen people had gathered. "To become old and not die is like being a thief," Master Nan said. He paused to make sure the aphorism had sunk in. "People get old," he explained. "There's nothing to be done about it."

The real estate developer nodded, but like any good Chinese entrepreneur he was able to shift gears in an instant. "I've also got a chance to invest in electric car batteries . . . ," he said, his voice trailing off expectantly.

"That sounds better," Master Nan said. "That's future oriented."

The man nodded gratefully and held up a glass to toast Master Nan's wisdom. It was filled with dark rice wine, and he downed it in one shot to show his sincerity. Master Nan also held up a glass. A decade ago, it would have been filled with whiskey, and he would have downed it, too. But age had caught up with him, and now it held only a dark tea. He took a sip and nodded back.

The dinners were festive gatherings, with visitors seated around several large round tables. We ate home-cooked food, drank red wine, and listened to Master Nan, his voice amplified through a microphone, while a Buddhist nun wrote out his key points on a whiteboard. After a while, Master Nan would rest, and followers would demonstrate traditional skills: reading from the classics, performing a tea ceremony, or playing a traditional instrument like the Chinese zither.

Up to fifty people usually attended: airline executives, bank managers, young scholars, architects, and the well-connected children of senior leaders. Many were part of a new hereditary elite that has coalesced over the past few decades—the *hong er dai,* or red second generation. These are children and grandchildren of the Communist Party leaders who founded the People's Republic in 1949. Few of them believe in Communism, and many have become proponents of traditional culture. To them, Master Nan was like a time traveler from the era before the Communist revolution that their parents had launched. He had appeared, almost miraculously, to tell them what life had been like before their parents had suppressed Chinese faith and values.

When I attended the retreat, the audience included a daughter of a senior politician, the son of China's top financial regulator, and three other wealthy businesspeople. For entrepreneurs like the Tianjin real estate magnate, Master Nan's advice was revolutionary. It had to do not with rates of return or who would have to be bribed to pull off a deal but with the potential benefit to society. During the discussions, he often called into question China's tunnel-vision focus on economic development. He blamed this on the destruction of China's traditional past, which he said had left the country without a counterweight to materialistic goals of wealth and power. China, he said, had copied everything from the West, leaving it with nothing of its own.

"Chinese are like spiritual beggars," he told the group before getting up to go, "asking for handouts from everyone else."

Part of Master Nan's appeal is that he is critical without being a dissident. He never speaks disparagingly of the government in public and is forceful in arguing that Taiwan and troubled regions like Xinjiang and Tibet are inalienable parts of China. And on a deeper level, his books and lectures support the government's idea of fostering pride by trumpeting the idea of an immutable, glorious Chinese past. For many Chinese scholars, this is a dangerously simplistic way of looking at Chinese history.

One skeptic is Zhu Weizheng, a famous scholar of classical texts at Shanghai's prestigious Fudan University. I met Zhu during an earlier stay at the Hall of Great Learning, driving over to spend the day with him and then returning for dinner with Master Nan. I met Professor Zhu in the Shanghai Tumor Hospital, where he had been a cancer patient for several months. He would die the following year, but on this day he was still alert and gracious, giving me one precious afternoon while his wife came and went, tending to his needs.

"I oppose some of the uses of *guoxue*," he told me. "I don't think it should be used to promote Chinese nationalism."

Zhu was born in 1936 in Wuxi, a city on Lake Tai. He attended Fudan University and had a meteoric rise up the academic ladder until the Cultural Revolution. Like most educated people, he was sent to labor and lost the next decade of his career. Rehabilitated in the late 1970s, he began publishing again on the Chinese classics in the 1980s.

By the 1990s, China was gripped with *"guoxue* fever." Classic texts were reprinted and studied on mainland China for the first time in two generations. The following decade saw the arrival of popularizers, notably the government-approved television lecturer Yu Dan, whose breezy discussions of Confucius's works glossed over historical controversies and gave a rosy view of the past. Major universities also set up lucrative *guoxue* centers that offered pricey weekend courses (and a big framed certificate) to businesspeople and enthusiasts eager to prove their erudition. The government also used the idea to promote China abroad, setting up Confucius Institutes around the world.

But Zhu had blocked his university from setting up a *guoxue* center. China has such a long tradition that scholars should, he argued, be delving deeply into the past instead of pushing a simplified version of Confucianism to make money or curry favor with the government. When Chinese talk of returning to Confucian principles, he asks, do they mean Confucianism's love of hierarchy or its promotion of social justice? Harmony or the right to rebel?

Zhu told me that the very idea of *guoxue* was foreign. Like the term for religion, it originated in Japan, which had already developed a vocabulary for these challenges. The idea was to save traditional culture and faith by separating it from the old political-religious system that ruled the country. Great powers needed to boast of their great culture, so *guoxue* gave Chinese something that they could use even after deposing the emperor and the traditional education system in the following decades.

"In the early *guoxue* movement in the early twentieth century, people did original research that we still rely on," Zhu said. "They were incredibly well educated. But in the following decades we destroyed these old books so much that people here, even of my age, don't really understand them. It's like a foreign culture to most Chinese."

He pointed to Confucius's *Analects* as a key example. People like Master Nan, he said, teach it simplistically, as a received text that Confucius had really written. Scholars, he said, widely accept that the work was heavily edited and is likely a compendium of sayings and anecdotes written down by various followers. I asked him what he thought of popularizers like Yu Dan.

"She talks about passages she doesn't understand," he said. "She can't even put the punctuation in correctly. These are people who serve the government."

And Master Nan?

"He is different. He isn't as overtly political. That old gentleman is interesting, but he's not a scholar."

The problem with *guoxue,* he said, is that it has become a political project. The state sponsored a lavish film adaptation of the life of Confucius, and China's cabinet voted in 2012 to establish a national *guoxue* center in Beijing to coordinate and spread the tradition. Zhu said, however, that much of this is superficial: despite embracing the past, the government doesn't allow the sort of academic freedom necessary to explore it with an open mind.

"It's almost impossible to have a neutral debate about issues in China. All the publishing houses are controlled by the government. The universities are controlled by the government. The foundations are controlled by the government. The government increasingly wants to use *guoxue* for its own purposes."

Whatever the merits of his books, Master Nan was still a magnetic force in the small-group sessions at Lake Tai. This was when his charisma was strongest and, despite his advancing years, it was possible to see why he had been such a popular figure in the Chinese world for so long.

The talks were always at night: Master Nan worked and meditated through the night, slept in the morning, and got up in the afternoon to handle correspondence. Dinner was when he made his first appearance, striding into the room with the lithe step of a former martial artist. His eyes had started to fail, so he was forced to read large-print versions of the classics that his students had specially printed for him. But he still dominated a room. He invariably made straight for the control panel on the dining room wall and adjusted the lights and air-conditioning like a director making sure the stage was set just so.

Most nights, Master Nan started out by quizzing us on what we had accomplished during the day. One man was an architect who spent his time at Master Nan's Hall of Great Learning fasting and hallucinating.

"Master, I have broken the barrier between waking and sleeping!"

"Yes, you appear to have done so," Master Nan said dryly.

Another meditated most of the day in a large Zen meditation hall that Master Nan had built just for this purpose.

"Don't spend so much time meditating," Master Nan admonished him. "It's a tool, not a goal."

Several other people had busy jobs and tried to perform e-mail triage, breaking away from work to help Master Nan's staff figure out how to implement his charitable projects. One evening, Master Nan asked a question that has baffled Chinese thinkers for the past century.

"In the past one hundred years, China used Western thinking, not Chinese thinking," Master Nan said. "Communism is Western, not Chinese. Capitalism is also Western. Socialism is also Western. What is Chinese?"

His guests shifted uncomfortably in their chairs. Master Nan waited, watching carefully.

"This is why we have to read the classics," ventured a young man who had just spent a year as a hermit and was now opening a Buddhist temple. "We don't know what is ours."

"Exactly," Master Nan said. "Read the classics." Then he quickly lightened the mood. "You can at least start with something concrete: your clothing!"

He segued into one of his favorite stories. Once, many years ago, he had been stopped in the San Francisco airport by U.S. customs agents who queried him on his need for an entire suitcase full of Chinese medicine. What won them over was that he was wearing his trademark blue gown, a sign that he respects his own culture and that they should respect him.

"It was the power of the gown," he said with a laugh.

Everyone held up small glasses of liquor and toasted him. Then we took a break to listen to the mellifluous voice of one of Master Nan's disciples, a Shanghai television host who read classics to the group. The man had a warm, inflected reading style, but like most modern Chinese he had a shaky grasp of the classical idiom. In the middle of the text, he made a string of errors that visibly irritated Master Nan, who had been following with his eyes closed. He opened them and looked around the room, annoyed at what he saw.

Then he heard something that made him relax and lean back in his chair. It came from the other side of the main building, the location of a boarding school. The children were performing their nightly chanting of the classics—part of his traditional curriculum. I thought of something Master Nan had told me once: children can memorize the silliest pop song or advertising jingle; why not instead have them commit the *Daodejing* or another classic to heart? True, they don't understand it, but in time they will, and when they sit down to write one day in the future, their brains will have been hardwired by the beauty of Laozi's language instead of the clichés of a Hong Kong songwriter.

The children were chanting excerpts of Confucius's *Great Learning*. Some were just first graders, so small they could barely hold the book open to the right page. Teachers walked around patiently, making sure they weren't daydreaming and keeping them in sync. The young voices rose like a prayer, one that has been recited in China for thousands of years in hopes of a better future:

> *Their thoughts sincere, their hearts were rectified.*
> *Their hearts rectified, their persons were cultivated.*
> *Their persons cultivated, their families were regulated.*
> *Their families regulated, their states were rightly governed.*
> *Their states rightly governed, the kingdom was tranquil.*

Toward the end of my stay, Master Nan invited me to his apartments to discuss what I had learned. Located in a spacious villa on one end of the campus, his residence included a two-story personal library, as well as several studies decorated with original calligraphy by famous Chinese. I began asking him the usual questions about whether Chinese culture can really be revived.

"The Cultural Revolution dug out its roots," he said. "How can anything recover without roots? There is an old root, but he's dying soon."

"But your students," I said, but he cut me off.

"They are just sprouts. We don't know whether they can grow."

After another fifteen minutes of this, he grew tired and closed his eyes. But he suddenly revived with a glint in his eye.

"In foreign countries, everything has to have a point. Your articles and books all have to have a point. I find it annoying."

"Well, I'm curious about . . . ," I said, but he cut me off.

"In ancient China we have other ways of writing. The author talks about the flowers and the grass. And then you can cite a poem and everyone will know what you mean. It is more subtle than your way.

"You should consider this poem," he said, reciting a verse by the poet Bai Juyi, who was born in 772:

Jiangnan is beautiful
Long ago I knew the scenery:
At sunrise, the river's flowers red like fire
In spring, the river so green it is almost blue.
Who wouldn't miss Jiangnan?

I looked at him quizzically and he sighed. Another cultural illiterate who needed even a simple poem spelled out.

"It is about the past," he said. "About missing something that you can't recover."

8

Practice: Learning to Breathe

The room was dark, and the four of us sat quietly on small round mats of thick woven straw. Through the corner of a heavy curtain the faint artificial lights of the city cast an orange glow. We were half an hour into our meditation, in the phase of sitting quietly. The session had begun with Qin Ling talking to us in her soothing, soft voice, preparing us to turn inward.

> Sit cross-legged.
> Your shoulders, arms, elbows, two wrists, two hands—
>   everything is relaxed.
> Your spine upright.
> Your lips lightly closed.
> Your teeth not clenched.
> Your tongue on the top of your palate.
> Your chin slightly down.
> Your head upright.
> Open your eyes.

We opened them.

> Your eyes are calm.
> Look far.
> Look beyond the wall.
> Look as far as you can.
> Your thoughts are there.
> Do you see a light? Is it bright?

If you couldn't visualize a light, Qin Ling allowed us to scrunch our eyes so the blood and nerves made a burst of light appear, but that was usually not necessary. In a dark room, if you stare straight ahead, light always comes.

Slowly pull the light back to you.
Pull it back to a point between your two eyebrows.
Very softly, close your eyes.

Now you were inside your own body, floating in a space where you could get lost. So she made sure we were fixed in the here and now:

Think: How big is this room?
What's in it?
How many people are in it?
Where are they?

We were in a small apartment facing south toward the White Cloud Temple, the center of Chinese Daoism. Twelve stories below a few car horns honked faintly. The west of Beijing. The center of government. The place with few foreigners. The ministries, the housing compounds, the military. Spring seeped in: the warming air, the insects stirring, the spring winds from the north. But all of that was outside, behind a wall, beyond our bodies.

We were breathing normally, in and out, our chests expanding when air flowed in and contracting when it left. But we needed to push the air, the qi, down into our lower abdomens. So Qin Ling had us start reverse breathing—a common meditation technique of expanding our abdomens when exhaling and contracting when inhaling.

Inhale, pull the qi from all directions into all your body's
     expanding pores.
Exhale, push the qi from all your body's pores out in all directions.
Inhale, pull in your body.
Exhale, push out your body.
Inhale, make yourself small, smaller.

Exhale, make yourself big, bigger.
Inhale, pull the room into you.
Exhale, push the walls of this room, expand it.
Inhale, make yourself small.
Exhale, make yourself big.
Inhale, exhale.
Return to natural breathing. Relax your body. Sit quietly.

That had taken about a quarter of an hour. Now was the roughly thirty minutes of quiet sitting, of emptying our minds. That was easier said than done. Qin Ling told us to let our thoughts run through our heads like a film reel hurtling forward. Don't think of new things, but let what's there play itself out. At some point, the reel comes to the end and the tape click, click, clicks into nothing. The screen goes blank.

I thought back to an opening section of our textbook:

The Dao has neither name nor force. It is the one essence, the one primordial spirit. Essence and life cannot be seen. It is contained in the Light of Heaven. The Light of Heaven cannot be seen. It is contained in the two eyes.

This is where it started: in the eyes. They brought in the light and turned it inward to reveal our inner thoughts. If we purified our thoughts, we could achieve what so many religions seek: immortality. We sat and waited for our minds to empty, our thoughts and ideas still whirring forward toward plans unrealized and back to a past we couldn't change.

I had met Qin Ling a year earlier through a young man I had gotten to know at one of Master Nan's dinners. The young man's family members were descendants of the first generation of Communists who had founded the People's Republic, and he was a child of one of the "Great Courtyards," the *dayuan* of western Beijing where the children of Communist Party leaders had played together. Over a dinner at Master Nan's retreat, he mentioned to me that one of the family's masters knew how to project energy out of his body—*fa qi* (fah-chee) in Chinese. His power was so strong that he could cause people to bounce up and down on the floor, and his knowledge so deep that students across China followed him.

"This master can *fa qi*?" I asked. That sounded like *qigong*, a form of physical and moral cultivation similar to meditation but sometimes involving extraordinary abilities. In the 1980s and 1990s, it had been one of the most dramatic religious movements in modern Chinese history, with millions of people occupying parks each morning, sitting, swaying, levitating, and hugging trees. Some of the nation's most famous universities, such as Tsinghua University, as well as the military studied whether qi—the energy force that Chinese religion and medicine say runs through our bodies—really existed. Messianic *qigong* masters had roamed China, claiming to have answers to the immorality that people felt was enveloping China. But *qigong* had suddenly disappeared from public view after the 1999 crackdown on one of its militant offshoots, Falun Gong. So the young man's story grabbed me, and I asked, "Does anyone dare practice *qigong* anymore?"

"Of course. But now it's called something else."

"Internal alchemy?" I asked, using the Daoist term *neidan* for similar physical practices.

"You're familiar with it? Then when we get back to Beijing, I'll bring you to someone who knows our master. Maybe you can learn from her."

A few weeks later, I met the young man in front of an apartment complex on Beijing's main boulevard. It was about three miles due west of Tiananmen Square, near an intersection called Muxidi. The complex was a dozen stories high and built in the late 1970s to lure back overseas Chinese. That was the end of the Mao era, and some of Mao's enemies were being released from jail. Some had been among the highest-ranking officials in China before their persecution, and the new leadership wanted to make a gesture for their suffering. So they got this complex, and the overseas Chinese were given apartments elsewhere. Its inhabitants included Li Rui, one of Mao's former personal secretaries, nearly one hundred years old and still a vocal voice for liberal political reforms. Most of the other famous people were dead, like Wang Guangmei, the wife of Mao's former number two, Liu Shaoqi, who had died in prison. Red Guards humiliated Wang in public, forcing her to dress up like a prostitute and wear a necklace of Ping-Pong balls. She lived here until her death in 2006.

Back then, the building had been the best the country could offer—modern, spacious apartments just down the street from the Communist Party's headquarters next to the Forbidden City. But it now looked like a low-security prison: crumbling concrete walls, with outdoor walkways between the apartments. The building was long and had six entrances, each one about fifty yards apart. We wanted the second one, but to save money only odd-numbered entrances had working elevators. So we walked down to the third entrance. Inside the elevator, a bored woman in her forties was sitting on a little stool reading a tattered comic book. I smiled: a busybody elevator operator—I hadn't seen one of these in China in years. This was like a time warp. She asked whom we were visiting.

"Mr. Xiao," my friend said. The woman nodded and pushed the button for the top floor. The elevator banged the walls as it struggled up.

The woman eyed me for a moment and then went back to her comics. During sensitive days on the government calendar—congresses, anniversaries, deaths—the building was off-limits to people who did not look Chinese. But today was a normal day, and in any case the Xiao family had always had foreign guests. At one time, before the Mao era had crushed them, they had been one of Communist China's most cosmopolitan couples: Xiao San, a rakish Communist Party poet and propagandist, and his beautiful wife, the German photographer Eva Sandberg. It now belonged to Xiao San's middle son, Xiao Weijia, who had been born in the party's mountain redoubt of Yan'an in 1941.

We got out at the top floor and walked down the corridor that linked the apartments. The hallway was attached to the outside of the building like an afterthought, protected from Beijing's Mongolian winds only by cheap windows that barely shut. Below us were the blinking lights of Muxidi, where some of the worst killing had taken place on the night of June 3–4, 1989. We passed several apartments, then the silent elevator that we should have taken. Finally, we reached the entrance, knocked, and waited for a minute. I was about to knock again when the young man stopped me: "They might be meditating. She'll answer when she can."

Sure enough, a few minutes later we were greeted by Weijia's wife, Qin Ling. She was in her forties, self-assured and stocky in an athletic way, with bobbed hair and dark eyebrows. She spoke with a lilting accent of the south, direct and forthright but playful as if she knew she was teaching something so esoteric that humor was the only way to explain its unconventional ideas.

She led us in through a hallway to the living room. A few people were rubbing their joints; they had obviously just come out of a meditation session. In front of the television was a whiteboard dominated by a diagram of a cross-legged torso overlaid with lines showing where qi flowed.

As her students prepared to go home, Qin Ling told me that her master was Wang Liping. She handed me a small paperback with a turquoise cover showing a faint sun and moon over a hilly landscape. The Chinese title read, *Walking the Great Dao: A Visit with the Reclusive Layman Mr. Wang Liping.* On the back was the price: 5.85 yuan, or about $1.00. The paper was cheap and the pages brittle. I held it gingerly and looked at its publication date: 1991. This had been translated into English as *Opening the Dragon Gate* and told the story of a lay Daoist who had traveled through the mountains with three elderly Daoist priests, evading Red Guards and learning how to meditate.

"Master Wang's teachings are based on a famous Daoist text. Fortunately, it has been translated into foreign languages by Lichade Weilian."

"Who?"

"Li-cha-de Wei-lian." Then she said his name very slowly in English, mouthing the sounds awkwardly. "Ri-cha-rd Wil-helm."

"Then you must be reading *The Golden Flower,*" I said in amazement. This was one of the most famous and difficult works of Chinese meditation.

She smiled faintly and raised her eyebrows in a question: Will you join us? I nodded, then left for home in a trance, wondering what I had gotten into.

This was my introduction to traditional Chinese meditation techniques. It was not ideal—something like a beginner in French being tossed a copy of Proust and given occasional lessons by a disorganized professor. But within a few months, I was hooked. Our textbook was one of China's oldest and most famous guides to meditation, the *Taiyi jinhua zongzhi,* widely known thanks to Wilhelm as *The Secret of the Golden Flower.*

The book is part of a Daoist tradition called *neidan,* or inner alchemy. It stems from an early Daoist goal of freeing people from illness and disease—not life after death, but life without death. The idea of respecting longevity wasn't uniquely Daoist. Judaism, for example, makes much of patriarchs like Enoch and Methuselah, who lived for hundreds of years. What is unique about early Daoism is that followers initially tried to use drugs to increase their life spans. This involved alchemical experiments—not to purify metals as many alchemists tried to do in the West, but to discover the elixir of life. Toxic metals, such as arsenic, lead, and cinnabar, or mercury sulfide, were combined with edible natural products like honey to form a pill of immortality. Ingested, the concoction was supposed to purify the body and stave off death.

Over time—and a few dead Daoists later—these ideas shifted. Some of the alchemical theories and experiments may have helped form the basis of Chinese medicine, whose practitioners experimented with minerals, as well as plants and animal parts, to cure disease. Immortality, meanwhile, became mainly a spiritual quest. Cinnabar—*dan* in Chinese—turned into a synonym for life after death. The pill of immortality became something allegorical that people could develop internally (or *nei* in Chinese) by purifying themselves spiritually with the aid of meditation—hence the term *neidan.* A common form of meditation involved channeling light, or energy, down into the body to the "cinnabar fields," or *dantian,* of the lower abdomen. The light was cycled through the organs like an alchemist's purifying fire, helping to create the flower of immortality that would lead the soul to heaven when the body died. This was more than a purely physical practice. Morality plays a key role, as the *Golden Flower* makes plain:

> *Whoever has done mostly good has spirit-energy that is pure and clear when death comes . . . But if, during life, the primal spirit was used by the conscious spirit for avarice, folly, desire, and lust, and committed all sorts of sins, then in the moment of death the spirit-energy is turbid and confused, and the conscious spirit passes out together with the breath.*

The *Golden Flower*'s fame in the West is due to the 1929 translation by Wilhelm, who was a German sinologist living in China, as well as a commentary by the Swiss psychiatrist Carl Jung. The two had been close friends. When Wilhelm died in 1930, Jung delivered the chief eulogy, calling his contact with Wilhelm "one of the most meaningful events in my life." The book was quickly translated into English and went through numerous print runs. It is now in the public domain and a classic in the New Age scene.

Jung's foreword helped make the book understandable. He made numerous analogies to Christianity, noting that Christian mystics had also used light as a way to purify their minds. Jung also described the *Golden Flower*'s meditation as a kind of proto-psychoanalysis, the discipline that he and Freud had helped launch. The *Golden Flower* showed that other cultures had their own traditions of inward-directed thought.

In an essay preceding his translation of the text, Wilhelm recounts how he came across the book, describing its reappearance as part of China's spiritual crisis in the first decades of the twentieth century. According to tradition, it was originally transmitted orally, with the first extant printed edition found in a monastery in southern China in the seventeenth century. But even then, it was unlikely to have been practiced outside a narrow circle of Daoist priests and their closest disciples. The upheaval of China's religious world in the early twentieth century changed that. Just like Europe during the Reformation, Chinese society was shifting away from the idea that religious knowledge was the monopoly of a clergy. People began to want direct access to sacred texts, and so in 1920 a thousand copies of the *Golden Flower* were printed. In his introductory essay, Wilhelm wrote that he picked up a copy in Beijing's Liulichang, a street famous for its bookstores and antiques shops.

This was also a time when lay religious leaders like those who influenced Master Nan came to prominence. Others rejected any established religions and promoted meditation for well-being—similar to movements around the same time in India, where people like the healer and yogi Tirumalai Krishnamacharya codified and partly secularized Yoga.

The idea of self-cultivation resonated with the political times: through building a self with integrity, many people believed they could also construct a strong modern nation able to withstand the depredations of warlords and foreign armies. These groups have sometimes been called "secret societies," but they were never really secret and a more neutral term is "redemptive societies"—groups that wanted to redeem, or save, society. They had their own philosophical systems (often amalgams of Buddhism, Daoism, and Confucianism, sometimes also including Christianity and Islam) and forms of physical cultivation, such as meditation. Some, like Yiguandao (the Way of Pervasive Unity), were powerful local organizations that controlled large swaths of China. One survey in 1950 showed that eighteen million Chinese belonged to them.

When the Communists took over in 1949, they immediately attacked these newly formed traditions. The new state could tolerate no independent organizations, and so they were declared "counterrevolutionary"—a catchall phrase for any group or individual that government wanted to eliminate. Tens of thousands of members were jailed in one of the first major crackdowns on religion in the new state.

Initially, the Communists were unsure what to call these meditative practices. A committee batted about terms such as "spiritual therapy," "psychological therapy," and "incantation therapy," before settling on "*qigong* therapy." The word *qigong* was a neologism, formed of *qi*, or breath, and *gong*, or practice. The new practice, its proponents wrote in an article, was free from "the superstitious dross of old."

Qigong became part of the traditional medical establishment, taught alongside acupuncture, herbal medicine, and massage. The relationship of master to disciple was replaced by classroom teaching, and practice was moved to clinics. Practitioners conducted experiments, published research, and held conferences. *Qigong*'s acceptance ended in 1964, when it was banned in the run-up to the Cultural Revolution. In that way anything with the slightest association with traditional culture was forbidden, Mao was the only deity allowed.

But when the Cultural Revolution ended with Mao's death in 1976, *qigong* returned in a strange new form: as a public religion. It had been banned, so proponents began teaching it in parks. By the 1980s, self-proclaimed "*qigong* grand masters" began to appear. They had similar tales of *chushan,* or coming out of the mountains—Jesus-like stories of spending time in the wilderness to forge their resolve and later returning to save humanity. This new movement dwarfed the popularizing programs of the prewar era, which had largely been confined to intellectual and upper-class circles. The new *qigong* masters reached hundreds of millions through state-run television, videotapes, and books.

Qigong became a kind of gateway spiritual experience: starting with the fulfillment and joy that accompanies good health, it led many practitioners to profound mystical experiences. People boasted supernatural powers, claims that were supported by much of China's scientific establishment. After a century of China's being seen as a second-rate scientific power, some officials believed that *"qigong* science" would allow the country to leapfrog the West by harnessing extraordinary powers. This echoed similar movements earlier in the twentieth century, such as the Boxers, a group of martial artists who claimed to be able to withstand Western bullets. *Qigong* also appealed to a strain of magical thinking from the Mao era—the desire to bypass the slow, tortuous path to modernity and prosperity that involves educating people, building infrastructure, and other dull steps that take much work and many decades to bear fruit. Instead, Mao embraced romantic shortcuts to national glory, such as the Great Leap Forward, whose backyard steel furnaces and unscientific farming methods launched the catastrophic famine of the late 1950s and early 1960s.

It wasn't coincidental that *qigong* rose shortly after Mao's death. His passing meant the ban on traditional practices was slowly lifted, but the underlying belief in supernatural powers was the same. At a high-level conference in 1979, senior government officials heard reports of how qi could be harnessed not just for medical purposes but to release supernatural abilities. One participant demonstrated how he could hold a book up to his ear and "read" it in a matter of seconds. The conference heard how qi left the body and accomplished these feats. Scientists were treated to performances of qi causing a television set to crackle and pop. At a follow-up meeting five days later, a member of the Chinese Academy of Sciences said all of this reminded him of the discoveries of Galileo. Two years later, researchers from several leading universities presented findings on extraordinary powers (*teyi gongneng*). The scientists left no doubt: *qigong* could unlock extraordinary powers.

Skeptics argued that this was bad science, but *qigong*'s proponents countered by recruiting one of China's most famous scientists, Qian Xuesen, or H. S. Tsien, who had cofounded the Jet Propulsion Laboratory at the California Institute of Technology and returned to China in 1955 to lead China's rocket program. In 1986, Qian persuaded the China Association for Science and Technology to found the China Qigong Science Association. It agreed, with one advocate claiming, "*Qigong* has left religion and folklore to enter the Temple of Science!"

This was part of a broader discussion that echoes today's. The 1990s were a period of debate within the Communist Party about how to move China forward. The 1989 demonstrations shocked many officials, who had thought the government's commitment to economic reform was all that was required to cement the regime's legitimacy. The protests and subsequent crackdown left many party members scrambling for ideas with social appeal, had traditional roots, and which could be co-opted. *Qigong* seemed ideal.

Typically for religion—and many other things in China—*qigong* was successful because it fell into a gray area that allowed it to escape much government control. Unlike the five official faiths (Buddhism, Daoism, Islam, Catholicism, and Protestantism), *qigong* wasn't designated a religion. Instead, it was registered as a martial arts practice. This allowed *qigong* groups to proselytize by handing out flyers, leaflets, books, and video recordings—a practice that was forbidden to religious groups, and still is today.

Soon, parks in Chinese cities were filled each morning with people meditating or moving spasmodically on the ground: crying, jumping, twitching, burping, or sometimes even speaking in tongues. As the anthropologist Nancy Chen wrote in her study of that era, it was a mass psychological release after the pains of the Cultural Revolution when "parks, courtyards, and even streets became spaces where it was all right to cry out or laugh uncontrollably . . . One master aptly concluded a group session of several hundred people by stating, 'Qigong releases the soul of China.'"

Even more challenging to the government was that the grand masters adopted religious cosmologies, explanations, and even homily-like guidelines to proper living. Some developed their own moral codes. One, called Zhonggong, positioned itself as an educational, industrial, and political system with its own trademark—the "supreme whirl," a modified *yin-yang* symbol. The most organized of these groups was Falun Gong. Its founder, Li Hongzhi, wrote two complex books with their own creation stories, heavens, and hell. He advocated clean living, no divorce, no premarital sex, and no lying. Over time, Falun Gong's exercise groups could be seen in almost every park in China, and its reach extended from its homeland in the rust belt of Manchuria to some of the best graduate schools in China's big cities.

By the mid-1990s, Falun Gong's rise had led to increasingly polemical debates. In 1998, several Buddhist magazines attacked it as a "heretical cult," or *xiejiao*, a formerly obscure term that in China had been resuscitated in the late twentieth century to describe foreign groups like the Branch Davidians in the United States or the Aum Shinrikyo doomsday cult in Japan. In 1997, the Ministry of Public Security began an investigation into Falun Gong as an "illegal religion," and the next year labeled it a *xiejiao*.

Slowly, criticisms of the group seeped into the Chinese media. When the group protested these media reports by organizing a sit-down strike in downtown Beijing in 1999—just ten years after the Tiananmen massacre—its fate was sealed. Within days of the protest, the government established a nationwide network of "610 Offices" (for the date on which they were created, June 10) that led the crackdown. Falun Gong members argued that they were patriotic and wanted simply to be able to practice. For nearly two years, they came to Beijing to protest in numbers. Most would try to sit cross-legged on Tiananmen Square, hold up a banner, or begin to practice Falun Gong. Police would swoop in and threw many in illegal holding facilities—infamous "black jails," where they were given a choice: renounce Falun Gong or be beaten. Many refused, and human rights organizations estimate that one hundred people were beaten to death. Tens of thousands of others were detained, and thousands sent to reeducation camps. It remains the biggest uprising since the Tiananmen protests.

Although the government stated that the broader *qigong* movement was not the problem, most of the large *qigong* groups were rolled up along with Falun Gong. What had been one of the most distinctive features of Chinese cities in the 1980s and 1990s—people practicing their odd assortment of exercises and meditations in public parks—vanished. In their place the government used proceeds from a new sports lottery to erect cheap exercise machines brightly painted yellow and blue, and often with a sign calling it "scientific exercise." Falun Gong continued to exist abroad as a kind of dissident movement with its own newspapers and television station, but in China it and the rest of *qigong* seemed dead.

It had now been over a year since my initial trip to visit Qin Ling with the young man. In the intervening months, I had come to this apartment regularly for classes with her and spent hours every week practicing on my own. For me, internal alchemy had two attractions. It was a window into the *qigong* movement of the 1980s and 1990s, but I also knew that for thousands of years this sort of practice has been at the core of Chinese spiritual and religious belief. All traditions have some sort of physical practice—meditation in some Christian orders, for example, or yoga—but in China it is absolutely central. Changing your body could change your soul. Across China, "grand masters" like Wang Liping and Master Nan were attracting millions of followers. The only way I knew how to understand this trend was to join in and observe.

I first became aware of the centrality of physical practice in the 1990s when I met a U.S. businessman based in Beijing, Brock Silvers. He was a committed Daoist who had started a registered charity called the Taoist Restoration Society. The charity helped rebuild Daoist temples that had been destroyed in China's century of turmoil and my role was to help him scout out temples. This was my first encounter with real Chinese believers, and I began to realize that for many people physical cultivation was at the root of their experience. Brock himself meditated and I had tried it, although not regularly. It seemed like something hard to figure out without a teacher. But back then, I didn't know how to find one. So when I was introduced to Qin Ling, I realized this was a special opportunity.

Besides learning this esoteric practice, I enjoyed talking with her about the days in the 1980s and 1990s when Master Wang toured China, filling sports stadiums. One day, she pulled out a DVD to show us what it had been like in the not-too-distant past.

"This is 1990 or 1989," she said as we looked at images taken from the balcony of an auditorium. Scores of adherents were sitting cross-legged on mats, much like ours. A much younger Wang walked between them, moving his arms as if in an incantation, his face smiling beatifically. Slowly, the people meditating began to fall backward, their legs still locked in the full lotus position—cross-legged but with the feet on top of their thighs. Several of Wang's assistants follow him and catch the people or ease them back onto the floor, sometimes placing a pillow under their heads. Occasionally, the camera panned the seats—hundreds were watching intently.

She fast-forwarded, and we saw people facing each other, some crouching, and placing their hands on each other's faces and shoulders, moving their fingers as if massaging in a trance. Wang faced a man standing, his arms at his side, apparently asleep. Like a conductor, Wang swayed back and forth, his hand outstretched, leading the man back and forth in time.

The camera panned past people staring down at Wang as he lectured. Wang was working an overhead projector that showed the Big Dipper and the North Star, which for thousands of years has been the center of heaven, around which we revolve. I suddenly got it: above are the cosmos; we re-create them down here. We are part of them. Man as a microcosm of the universe. The light cycling in our bodies. Pull the room into your body.

As we were watching, her husband, Xiao Weijia, walked in.

"You're watching the classics!" he said with a laugh and sat on the sofa with us. He was tall, with flowing gray hair, seventy, an impressive man with a deep voice. Qin Ling brought him a cup of hot water, and we settled back to watch more. But Xiao's face began to cloud over. He looked at us and then the movie. Suddenly he seemed to feel that this was inappropriate.

"Enough of that," he said sternly. Qin Ling fumbled with the remote, rushing to switch off the film. Xiao turned to us and almost apologetically tried to explain what we had just seen. It had been a glimpse into another China, one just a couple of decades ago but somehow embarrassing. It was a more anarchic, freewheeling time when the country was less settled and the government less in control of spiritual life. Xiao spoke carefully.

"I asked Teacher Wang why he did this. Why go so deep and show so many strange things? Most people in the group surely can't learn this very well, right? So why bother? Most will just learn a little and not get it on a deep level.

"He said this was true but that he wanted to show people that it existed. People said it had been destroyed, but he wanted to show that it was still there and still powerful. Today it still is. It's just changed form again."

P
A
R
T

III

CLEAR AND BRIGHT

After the land awakens but before the summer heat arrives is an interlude when winds blow the skies clear and farmers await the spring rains. This solar term, the fifth of twenty-four, is Qingming (ching-ming), literally "Clear and Bright" or "Pure Brightness," when trees begin to bloom, mice come out of their holes, and farmers prepare to plant their fields. Each season in China gets six solar terms, and of the half a dozen allotted to the spring, Qingming is the most important.

It is best known as the Tomb-Sweeping Festival, the first of the three commemorations for the dead; the others are the Hungry Ghosts Festival on the fifteenth day of the seventh lunar month, and Xiayuan, or the Lower Primordial Festival, on the fifteenth day of the tenth moon. Qingming is the most widely celebrated of the three, perhaps because it coincides with the spring and a sense of rebirth. As the living prepare to plant the crops that will provide the food they need to survive, they dare not forget the dead. The departed are honored by burning paper money, offering food, and kowtowing in front of the tombstone or mound of earth that marks their graves. Qingming is so important that in 2008 it became a national holiday with its date fixed on the modern calendar as April 5.

Like Easter, which also falls around this time, Qingming raises confusing emotions. We might thank those who went before us, but we also sense a darker mood of mourning and of only remote hope. These conflicting feelings are reflected in poems about the holiday, such as this one, simply titled "Qingming," by the ninth-century Tang dynasty poet Du Mu:

Tomb-Sweeping Day, rains shrouding the land,
People trudge the roads, hearts breaking from sorrow.
May I ask where the nearest tavern lies?
Peach Blossom Village, the shepherd boy says, pointing to the far
    horizon.

9

Ritual: Martyrs

t was a blustery day, the blue sky covered by a film of dust whipped up by the Mongolian winds. When the air calmed, it felt like spring. But then a sharp gust would rip through the streets, filling my eyes with cold, runny tears. I searched the road for a black Audi but saw nothing, so I chatted with a few men selling flowers at the side of the road. They asked me what I was doing at the cemetery so early; Qingming was still a week away. I said I was waiting for a friend who couldn't make it on the holiday. They nodded and suggested I buy a wreath. I declined. Xu Jue had the flowers picked out, and they never varied. Every year the ritual was the same: forty flowers, four police officers, two cars, and one old lady.

Xu Jue lived in the western suburbs of Beijing next to the Yong-ding River, one of the last legs of the Grand Canal, the waterway that starts in her hometown of Hangzhou, one thousand miles to the south. Her home in the capital was comfortable: two bedrooms, a kitchen, and a sunny living room—the perks of a good govern-ment job. The geological bureau where she had worked gave it to her in 2000, eleven years after her son was killed in the 1989 Tiananmen massacre and seven years after her husband died of grief. She lived there alone, her home silent except for Saturday nights, when she pulled the dustcover off her upright piano, played church hymns, and drew closer to God.

Xu Jue was a short and vivacious seventy-three-year-old, with dyed-black hair, black trousers, a bright, flower-patterned blouse, and a cardigan. She spoke in a high, almost girlish voice, in short simple sentences as a teacher might to a child. When I went to visit her a few days before Qingming, she happily busied herself, making tea and fussing that she did not have biscuits. But for her, normal life ended in 1989. Her son, Wu Xiangdong, had been twenty when the student protests started. Initially, he had not participated. He had been a good high school student but outspoken. School administrators said they could not recommend that he sit for the college entrance examinations and suggested he look for a job. He found one at the East Wind Electrical Machinery Company and took night classes at the Beijing Institute of Technology. That classified him as a blue-collar worker, while the protests were led by the nation's elite, the university students. But when the government threatened to use force in late May, he and many other ordinary Beijingers went down to argue with the soldiers. At first, they were successful and the soldiers beat a retreat. But on the night of June 3, new units came in, determined to clean the square with force. The young man decided to go again.

"We told him don't go. It's really dangerous. But he wanted to go and stop the tanks."

Xu Jue told the story mechanically and didn't cry. She narrated the tale as a series of mysteries: why her son went, where he died, where his corpse was, where to bury him, how to commemorate him, and how to get to his grave each Qingming.

"When it got to midnight on the third, my husband and I got really nervous. We went out on bicycles. There were no cellphones then, so you didn't know what was going on. We rode down to Xidan. Many people were dead, a lot of them students. Some had been shot; others had been crushed.

"Our hearts were oppressed. We were riding and hoping to find him. That night, June 3, there were a lot of people out looking at the excitement. The moment the guns started firing, they ran into the *hutongs*. The soldiers chased some into the *hutongs*, and when they were cornered, some felt they had no choice and killed the soldiers. They told us that. We rode and rode everywhere, looking for our son.

"We went to Muxidi, and the people there knew him. They said, what a good boy he was, so nice, and trying to stop the army from killing the students. He didn't want the tanks to get in. But the tanks were so big. He was so small. It was too terrible."

The couple rode home. The next day, they set out to solve the next riddle.

"We didn't know where his body was. We went from hospital to hospital. They had lists out. We said, 'Are those the people staying in the hospital?' They said, 'No, those are the dead!'

"Finally, at the Fuxingmen Hospital, we found his name. We had to find a way to get his body out. There were rumors that the soldiers would come and burn them. We pleaded and argued. Finally, someone just let us in. We rented a trishaw and carried him home."

As she spoke, she began unpacking a box, assembling what was left of her son. She laid on the sofa a stained blue work shirt that he wore that night. It had been laundered and then signed by his work colleagues, the ink now blurred into the cotton. She placed a black-and-white photograph of her son where his head would have been. He is young, with Xu Jue's small mouth and intense eyes. His name, Wu Xiangdong, had been taped over the bottom of the photograph.

Then she laid out two thin white strips of cotton. They framed the shirt at angles and met at the top, over the photograph, spreading out like protective halberds. The left one read,

> The spirit of the June Four martyrs will never decay;
> It resides below in the mountains and rivers, above in the sun
> and stars,

and on the right side,

> Blood shed in a just cause may not be rewarded for a thousand
> autumns;
> Its fame lies at the gates of the capital, its merit found in the
> whole world.

On the left, next to the shirt, she placed a Citizen-brand watch that he had worn. Balancing it on the right side, she put a camera in a leather case that he had carried with him. It had no film in it when they got it from the hospital.

"We tried to get him buried, but no one would accept him. They would ask for the cause of death, but what could we say? Finally, someone at the Babaoshan cemetery said yes without any questions."

That was the public cemetery next to the grand revolutionary martyrs' cemetery with the same name. Famous Communists, like Qin Ling's in-laws, were buried at the martyrs' cemetery but the public one was also well-known and not too far outside town. Xu Jue was satisfied with the choice.

"When Xiangdong was young, I had always been working in the field doing research. I had been in the mountains working and got transferred to Beijing for the birth of our son. But just a month after his birth, I had to leave again. So my husband raised him from a month old until he was twenty. Right after Xiangdong died, my husband's hair went white. It was black, and then it turned white. He had been in excellent health, but then he got leukemia and died. But I know what killed him: he died of anger." She said the Chinese phrase over and over: *qiside*. In 1993, she buried her husband, too, in Babaoshan, a section over from her son.

Soon after, Xu Jue went to Germany on a study trip and encountered Christianity through Taiwanese immigrants. They were members of one of the world's largest Pentecostal churches, the True Jesus Church, which had been popular on the mainland before the Communists took power and persecuted it as a cult. Their members worship on Saturdays because Jesus was a Jew and Jews celebrate the Sabbath that day. When she returned to China in the late 1990s, she felt that underground churches were too secretive and cultlike. One said the world was going to end one year on July 7, so she stopped going. The state churches, however, were part of a system that had killed her son. So she started reading the Bible on her own on Saturday nights and singing hymns to herself, banging away on the piano, sometimes playing until late at night. Neighbors complained, but they stopped after plainclothes police were noticed observing her. Nobody wanted to get involved with them.

The police had begun watching her after she got active in a group called Tiananmen Mothers. At the start of every year, the women, at first middle-aged and now elderly, would write letters to the National People's Congress. She and the other mothers hoped that the verdict on the protests would be reversed. Instead of labeling it a counterrevolutionary movement, the government should consider it a protest against corruption.

Each year on the anniversary of the massacre, the mothers try to light candles at the Muxidi intersection, where many of their children died. Of course, the mothers never get close to Muxidi; police always put them under house arrest days or weeks ahead of time.

But the police have a harder time forbidding Qingming ceremonies. The holiday was largely banned or downplayed in the Mao period but survived because it overlapped with the Communists' own veneration of the dead: the cult of the red martyr.

In 1944, a peasant soldier named Zhang Side was killed when a charcoal-producing kiln collapsed. This accident might have gone unnoticed except that Zhang had once served as Mao's personal bodyguard. To honor the twenty-nine-year-old, Mao delivered a famous eulogy:

> *All men must die, but death can vary in its significance. The ancient Chinese writer Sima Qian said, "Though death befalls all men alike, it may be weightier than Mount Tai or lighter than a feather"... To die for the people is weightier than Mount Tai, but to work for the fascists and die for the exploiters and oppressors is lighter than a feather.*

Mao was drawing on a long history of martyrdom in China. One of China's earliest and most famous dissidents was Qu Yuan, a fourth-century B.C.E. poet and minister who committed suicide to protest the corruption that had led to the downfall of the state where he had served. People like him were revered over the centuries as examples of integrity and loyalty. Unlike Qu, however, most Communist martyrs have strangely uninspiring stories. Like Zhang Side, they seemed to have died randomly. The most famous was Lei Feng, the hero who so annoyed Ran Yunfei. Lei Feng also died in an accident, when a telephone pole fell over and smashed him on the head. As Ran noted, his story is doubly uninspiring because the party clearly made up many of his selfless accomplishments—miraculously having documented them with photographers, and turning what was probably the harmless life of a good young man into an epic story of sacrifice and heroism. In the 1950s, Qingming was renamed Martyrs Memorial Day, centered on Lei Feng.

All public memory is influenced by the state, but in China the government's role is overwhelming. In addition to erecting the usual war memorials, Beijing publishes biographies of martyrs. It features them on television. It posts their faces on billboards or bus stop advertisements. In years past, it even conducted public show trials of those allegedly responsible for their deaths.

After the party took over in 1949, it began searching for a location for a martyrs' cemetery in Beijing. It settled on the Nation-Protecting Temple (Huguosi) in the Babaoshan hills west of Beijing. This was a Buddhist temple where old eunuchs went to spend their last days and also where they stored their severed genitalia. In 1956, the temple was seized and demolished. The dozens of eunuchs still living there were each handed a pouch containing their dried genitalia—so they would not be buried without them when they died—and sent off to live elsewhere. Some ended up in other temples, while others lived out their days in poverty.

The party named the new cemetery after the nearby hills: Babaoshan Revolutionary Martyrs Cemetery. Later, it dropped the word "martyrs" because it wanted to include anyone who had made "exceptional contributions to the revolution." This included many senior political leaders, as well as foreigners such as the pro-Communist American journalists Anna Louise Strong and Agnes Smedley. Next to it is the Babaoshan public cemetery where Wu Xiangdong lies.

After Mao died, Qingming reverted to its old name. By 2008, it had become a national holiday, and major political leaders began participating openly. The clearest link between politics and worship of the dead is a ceremony held on Qingming in Shaanxi Province to honor the Yellow Emperor, the mythical ur-ancestor of the Han Chinese. The enormous event takes place at the emperor's tomb, a vast complex of nearly ten square miles that was rebuilt in several phases during the 1990s and the first decade of the twenty-first century for $40 million. The event usually involves an army honor guard, attendance by senior officials, and thousands of onlookers.

But the dead don't always rest peacefully. In 1976, commemorations for Zhou Enlai, the popular premier who was seen as a check on Mao's radical policies, turned into protests against political extremism. And in 1989, mass public commemorations of another moderate leader, Hu Yaobang, expanded into the Tiananmen protests.

The simple thing would be for the government not to allow Xu Jue to sweep her son's tomb. After all, she is under twenty-four-hour surveillance; I only entered her apartment once, because I mistakenly took the wrong entrance into her compound, inadvertently avoiding the secret police. But the government has not banned her from honoring her dead son and husband on Qingming, perhaps because the taboo against not commemorating the dead is too great. So every year, police visit her a month ahead of Qingming. They discuss the upcoming festival and make an offer that she has no choice but to accept: on a quiet morning roughly a week before the holiday, they will escort her to the Babaoshan cemetery and let her tend her husband's and her son's graves. That way the government cannot be accused of preventing her from doing her duty. And so it was this year as I waited outside the cemetery gates.

Xu Jue arrived in a black Audi, followed by a second one. Four plain-clothes policemen got out. Two of the officers stood by their cars while she walked up to the cemetery entrance with the other two. I was standing off to the side by the flower stalls and watched them pass by, then followed them in.

She turned right to her husband's grave. She always goes there first, she says, because they had been married for over thirty years. She also felt that his grave was less problematic; if something went wrong at her son's grave, at least she would have already swept her husband's. *Qiside*, she said to herself as she looked at the tomb: angered to death.

The front of the tombstone was engraved with the three characters that make up his name: Wu Xue Han. On the back was a poem written by a friend with the line "Xuehan's grievance caused his early demise." The explanation came a few lines farther down. They listed the flowers to be laid out in front of the man's grave:

> *Eight calla lilies*
> *Nine yellow chrysanthemums*
> *Six white tulips*
> *Four red roses*

Eight, nine, six, four, or June 4, 1989. The two police officers stood at a respectful distance as she laid down the twenty-seven flowers.

Then she walked back to the main path and over to the section where her son's grave lay, the two officers trailing discreetly. Between every fifth or sixth tombstone, pine trees had grown in, giving the area a quiet, shady feel. She stepped into the grove and found his tombstone: row three, number thirteen. The stone was small and simple, indistinguishable from the other graves. One of the rituals many Chinese perform every year is to touch up the tombstone with red paint, filling in the engraved characters so they stand out.

She pulled a jar of red paint and a brush out of her bag and stooped over to freshen up the three characters of her son's name:

Wu Xiang Dong

Then she went to fill in the smaller lines next to his name, which give his dates of birth and death. But as she bent over, she grimaced. Her back was sore, and she put a hand on her hip, blowing out a sigh of pain and weariness. One of the officers stepped forward and reached out for the jar and the brush. She did not resist. He crouched down and carefully painted in the lines on the upper right:

Born: Year 1968, August 13
Died: Year 1989, June 4

And then in the bottom left:

Father: Wu Xuehan
Mother: Xu Jue

Xu Jue said something, and the police officer nodded. He painted the top and the sides of the tombstone red. Many people do this to brighten their relatives' headstones, and she wanted it done, too. If the symbolism of dark red paint was a little obvious, the officer did not argue. Maybe he wanted to get home, or maybe he was willing to grant her this bit of dignity, or maybe he had a son. He liberally slathered red paint over the top and sides, making it pop out of the row of whitish stones. Some paint splashed on the plinth, but it was a good job. No one spoke. In a week, all the tombstones would look like this, but for now her son's stood out, just as he had in life.

The two men stepped back, leaving Xu Jue alone in front of her son's tombstone. She placed one red and twelve white flowers in front and bowed her head. Then the three walked back to the gate and picked up the other two officers, and the five drove off, their annual ritual complete.

10

Shanxi: The Buried Books

Early April in northern China is strangely quiet. The weather, clear and bright, is perfect for a drive or a hike, but it is still too dry for planting, and so the fields are empty. The next solar term in a couple of weeks, Grain Rain, is the farmer's focal point. Until then people prepare, wait, and honor the dead.

With Xu Jue's ritual completed a week before the holiday, I spent Qingming with the Li family in Shanxi. They live on the other side of the Taihang Mountains, the range that runs south from Beijing to the more fertile watersheds five hundred miles south. I made the drive every couple of months, sometimes staying for a week and following them around their villages as they lived their bifurcated lives: ordinary undertakers and fortune-tellers in Shanxi, Carnegie Hall musicians abroad.

The jammed roads of Beijing thinned out after the famous passes of the Great Wall. The highway heads west toward Zhangjiakou, the city in Hebei Province that will host the 2022 Winter Olympics. The area is sparsely populated and arid—mostly rocks and dry fields waiting for the rains that rarely come. This region was being united into one megacity of 130 million people called Jing-Jin-Ji ("Jing" for Beijing, "Jin" for the port city of Tianjin, and "Ji" the traditional name for Hebei Province, which surrounds the two cities). This conglomeration was being accomplished through amazing infrastructure projects that were drawing the cities closer. Everything was an engineer's dream: smooth, flat, and fast. But it reduced the countryside to a blur, an afterthought to be abandoned or bypassed by hyperlinks of steel and concrete. The land looked bleak, barren, and empty.

That changed five hours and three hundred miles later when I turned off the highway and pulled on to state road 202, a two-lane thoroughfare lined with willows and poplars. As I turned the first bend and entered a long straightaway, spring arrived. The trees were suddenly all around me, rows of them, one behind the other, lining the road toward the horizon. The perspective allowed their faint colors to layer on top of each other like washes of watercolor. The road was haloed with light green—a color-touched photograph from the past.

I wanted to spend Qingming with Li Bin's father. Old Mr. Li had refused to move to the county seat, preferring the homestead in the village. There, he kept the family archives and I heard had set up a new training center for traditional music right next to his farmhouse. So I made straight for Upper Liangyuan Village, located ten miles out of Yanggao Town, where Li Bin lived.

The village's five hundred homes, mostly brick bungalows with tiled roofs, were hidden behind high brick walls arrayed along narrow lanes. This was typical for northern China, where the villages formed a closed-off front against the outside world—a reaction to the featureless geography and a contrast to the more anarchic settlements in China's south.

The main street had been paved recently, but open ditches were filled with water and trash. The town center was a general store that sold the bare necessities: cooking oil, cigarettes, grain alcohol, and Oreo cookies. It was housed in a whitewashed brick building whose only decoration was a stone star that had once been red but was now gray and faded—a relic from the Mao era. It seemed the only trace of that period in the village, an impression I later realized was completely wrong.

The family homestead was at the end of a lane, next to an orchard of almond trees. I pushed open the red door and walked through a yard of fruit trees and vegetables to the bungalow. It was new, made of concrete covered with white tile and capped with a traditional-style roof of yellow tile. The main door led into a hallway. To the left was the bedroom, and to the right was the kitchen and living room, where Old Mr. Li sat on an elevated platform called a *kang*, which doubles as a bed and couch in northern China. He was sitting cross-legged but leaning to one side on an elbow, carefully copying strange symbols from a worn notebook to a new other. With his blue railroad engineer's cap pulled down tightly and a narrow-striped shirt, he looked like an old-fashioned manager of a train station preparing for a busy day.

He lifted his head slowly, gave a big crackly smile, and made his best effort at Mandarin Chinese. Old Mr. Li's wife came out. Yao Xiulian was warm and friendly, but her accent was so thick that we had trouble communicating beyond the barest of phrases. She kept laughing and took leave to prepare food in the kitchen. Old Mr. Li motioned for me to get up on the *kang*. It was his day off, although like anyone from the countryside he never really stopped working. He had set aside today to prepare fortune-telling books. These are small notebooks filled with dates and tables that list the sixty-year cycle of years cross-referenced with other material: cycles of the moon, charts showing the interaction of the Five Elements—an almost infinitely complicated amount of information. He carried these around in his breast pocket all year. Eventually, the cheap paper would wear out and have to be recopied by hand. He carefully put the books in a faded leather satchel and poured me a cup of tea.

"You have visited Li Bin in the county seat," Old Mr. Li stated.

I nodded.

He nodded. He drank his tea thoughtfully, then said nothing.

We both said nothing for a while. Old Mr. Li never said something for no reason. I decided to see what he was thinking.

"Do you go to the town very often?"

"Me?" he replied with feigned surprise.

"The town is bustling," I said. Yanggao Town had 130,000 people, which wasn't a lot by Chinese standards but was nearly half the county's population of 300,000. And it was growing rapidly, with a new district being built to the south. Construction cranes were erecting about thirty new housing towers, each one twenty stories high. Soon, most people in the county would live there. "There's a lot going on there."

"A lot," he said, looking out over his teacup carefully, as if visualizing the town for the first time.

"Have you thought of moving there, too?"

"Me?"

"I bet Li Bin has new customers because he has moved to town."

"You don't get new customers by going to a new place," he said firmly, as if citing a well-known line from *The Analects*. Then, to be accommodating, he added, "But a lot of our old families here have moved to town, and he's there now too."

When Old Mr. Li was a child, Upper Liangyuan Village had about 750 residents. This peaked at nearly 1,000 in the 1980s, a time when economic reforms had given farmers back their land but urbanization had barely begun. Around then, about three-quarters of Chinese still lived in rural communities. Now the official figure was that more than half of Chinese lived in urban areas. Upper Liangyuan Village reflected that shift. It now officially reported 500 families, but many no longer lived in the village. Only old people and their grandchildren were left; the rest had departed for the city.

Li Bin was part of this migration. He had left the village to find a better school in town for his son, Li Binchang. That school had gone bankrupt after two years, but no matter: Li Bin had found a boarding school in another town. The boy was almost invisible in the family's life, coming home just every other weekend, but any sacrifice seemed worth it, if it meant escaping rural life.

"It's a pity that Li Binchang won't learn all of this," I said. Old Mr. Li was the eighth generation, and Li Bin was the ninth. Would there be no tenth? Li Bin had been adamant that his son would not carry it on. When I had seen the boy, playing computer games and dreaming of living in a big city, I was sure Li Bin was right.

"He might. If he passes his tests, he can study at the university. Then he won't be a *yinyang* man. But if he fails . . ."

"But then he'll be around twenty. Isn't that too old to start learning?"

"Even if you're thirty, you can succeed," he said.

This seemed like wishful thinking, but as we kept talking I began to understand that he might be right.

Old Mr. Li's life was defined by a decision made in Beijing in 1958. The country's leader, Mao Zedong, had decided that the normal rules of economic development—of patiently producing, saving, and investing—were outmoded. Instead, faith would let China leapfrog to prosperity. Farmers were ordered to plant crops closer together.

This would result in doubled, in quadrupled, in infinitely higher yields—Sputnik yields, named after the newly launched Soviet satellite. In industry, farmers were told to set up primitive brick kilns to produce more and better-quality steel than the developed countries' modern steelworks.

These delusions led to catastrophe. Planting seedlings closer together caused crop failures, not bumper yields, while the kilns only made the crudest of steel. But because Mao ordered these miracles, proof of their existence had to be found. So officials confiscated what little grain farmers had, even next year's seed grain, in order to boost harvest totals. And because the kilns couldn't make real steel, farmers were ordered to meet production quotas by melting down their hoes, knives, and plows. Rural China was left without grain, without seeds, and without tools.

The resulting famine killed more than thirty million people and tore apart the fabric of rural life. At first, families scrounged for food, desperately eating bark or grass. Some tried to walk to nearby cities, but the government made local travel illegal, punishable by death. People lied, cheated, stole, and killed for food. When that failed, they breached the ultimate taboo: cannibalism. They dug up corpses and carved off the flesh. Families exchanged the carcasses of dead children so they would not have to eat their own offspring. Parents died, and their orphaned offspring killed each other for their flesh. The end of time seemed near. In one village in Sichuan Province, flyers appeared proclaiming, "The heavenly army is coming soon, and Chairman Mao will not last long."

That prediction proved to be wrong. Mao persisted in his policies and the famine grew. It was especially hard on poor grain-growing areas like Yanggao County. Old Mr. Li was eight when the famine hit in 1959 and remembers people dying silently in their homes, too weak to flee.

"People died, so many of them. I was just little, but I knew that no one could have children because they ate too little. Our lives were no good. Maybe one day a person ate three or four *liang* [150 to 200 grams] of grain. No vegetables or meat."

His father had been forced to join a folk music troupe in the nearby city of Datong. That left Old Mr. Li alone on the family farm with his mother and siblings. They almost starved to death, and Old Mr. Li remembers being instructed which grasses you could and could not eat. "Some would plug you up and kill you," he said quietly.

The famine was accompanied by radical policies forbidding traditional culture and religion. In 1958, he said, the first temples in the village were attacked. When the famine ended in 1961, moderate policies were restored but only for three years until a new campaign, the Four Cleanups, again targeted rural religious practices.

I told him I hadn't realized there had been any temples in Upper Liangyuan Village.

"They are all gone. The Hall of the God of Prosperity. Guanyin Temple. The Hall of the Three Purities. The God of Wealth Temple. The Temple of the Five Paths. The Temple of the Three Lords. The Perfected Warrior Temple. Some of the temples were really big like the Hall of the Three Purities. It was on this road, on a little ridge."

Two years later, the Cultural Revolution began, ending performances for ten more years. As accomplished ritual specialists, the Li family had been prosperous before the Communist takeover. Afterward, this worked against them. They were labeled "rich peasants" and during the Cultural Revolution were singled out for attack. I asked him about the Red Guards.

"They said we were Ox Devils and Snake Spirits. They were from the village, from the local school. They weren't outsiders. They burned everything."

"What did they burn?"

"All of our liturgical texts. All our books. The music. The instruments were smashed. The robes were burned."

Old Mr. Li added something else: he said that this is when people stopped respecting each other. Respect for elders, respect for authority, even common decency: the Cultural Revolution was when it ended. When people were beaten, it was forbidden to help them. Neighbors lay crumpled on the side of the street. If you helped, you were guilty too. I thought of the studied indifference in society— the unwillingness to help people outside one's *guanxi* network. Part of it was the deep structure of Chinese culture—the division of people into those inside one's network and those outside—but the first decades of Communist rule had made this worse. It wasn't just unprofitable to help others; it was dangerous.

The Li family was under virtual house arrest, allowed only to plow the fields. Eventually, they were cast out of the family home and forced to live in a shed on the corner of town. Old Mr. Li, who worked the fields, was not allowed to marry until 1973. Four years later, Li Bin was born, and some of the traditions began to resurface.

The traumas of those years radiated out over the decades. Because of the persecution, Old Mr. Li had never learned to play a reed instrument. And the loss of the temples meant that the family's repertoire shrank. Temple fairs used to take place regularly but the lack of temples meant fewer fairs, while other ceremonies, such as traditional forms of thanksgiving that families performed in the winter, have been almost completely abandoned. Yet some of the tradition has survived. Even though Old Mr. Li never learned to play, he learned many of his father's skills. He joined the band and kept time by beating a small drum. He recited the scriptures. He learned fortune-telling and acquired a reputation as a quietly reliable person who would be a good successor to his father. That meant of the five skills that a *yinyang* man needed—blowing (the reed), beating (the drum), writing (funeral notices and talismans), reciting (the scriptures), and seeing (the future and setting dates)—he was able to do four. It wasn't ideal, but it was enough.

This was why he was not willing to say that his grandson would never join the family tradition. Maybe the boy also would not learn an instrument but would find his own way back, just like Old Mr. Li had in his own turbulent era. If he did, it might be as something completely different, perhaps as a more modern kind of funerary expert, or a counselor.

Whatever happened in the future, it would not be the way it was in the past, or even now. In the past, rural funerals were enormous, some lasting five days, compared with the two days common today. Many more rituals were performed. Some were preserved in the liturgical books, but Old Mr. Li said no one was really sure how to perform them. Instead, funerals now took a maximum of two days, with city people's funerals even simpler.

What had not changed so much was fortune-telling. This seemed to reflect deeper needs in society.

"Sometimes when you're asked to tell a fortune, you also offer psychological advice," I said to him. "Do you remember at the First

Night holiday, during the funeral for the old man a woman asked you about a divorce?"

He nodded.

"Fortune-telling depends on which bell is tolling on the clock. You have to know where you are in the calendar and where you are in the day when you tell someone's fortune. Fortune-telling is about influence. Which days influence you the most. Which are appropriate and which are not appropriate. That woman, she was saying, 'I've got something on my chest, and I want to use fortune-telling sticks [in a temple].' You see, if you've got a problem, you can ask the immortals for help. But you have to be sure you want the answer, because when you get it you have to follow it. So she wanted to ask my advice before taking that step. She said her heart was hurting and could she do this? Could she take the next step?"

"And you told her that only she could decide."

"In the end you decide. You can ask for advice, but you decide. That's my advice."

Like all houses in this part of the country, the Li family's was a long bungalow of several square rooms set next to each other in a row. Some opened into each other, so you could walk from the vestibule to the bedroom or the living room without going back outside. But one room at the far end of the homestead opened only to the yard. Over it was a bronze plaque with embossed red letters: HENGSHAN DAOIST MUSIC TRAINING BASE.

Inside was a little classroom of tiny desks covered with glued-on vinyl paper. In front were little red stools, like a farmhouse elementary school. At each seat was a cymbal and carefully stapled notations. The strangest part was the complete absence of dust. In this dry part of the country, everything seemed covered in dust, but this room was as clean as a glassed-in museum exhibition.

Tacked to the far wall was a banner proclaiming the opening of the "Hengshan Daoist Music 2011 Second Term Training Class." Below it were several official plaques. The most important declared the group to be NATIONAL LEVEL INTANGIBLE CULTURAL HERITAGE, a coveted designation.

On the left wall were three placards. The first had six couplets that listed the training session's regulations, a mishmash of the government's obsession with culture and hygiene:

1. *Ardently Love Hengshan Daoist Music; Take Culture as the
   Foundation.*
2. *Study Diligently; Have a Spirit of Enduring Hardship.*
3. *Respect the Teacher; Unite Students.*
4. *Observe Discipline; Work and Rest According to the
   Schedule.*
5. *Have a Civilized Bearing; Pay Attention to Hygiene.*
6. *Love and Protect Public Property; Find Pleasure in Helping
   Others.*

The other two placards listed a series of fanciful plans and events—probably meant to impress visiting government officials: see, even here in Yanggao County we're protecting traditional values. One, dated June 2009, listed previous training sessions, which had supposedly had eighty students. By 2015, a new music troupe was to be formed and become famous throughout the world. That clearly hadn't happened. The other placard seemed even less plausible. It listed the students' study plan. They were to get up at 4:30 each morning and practice for two hours, study until 7:00 p.m., and practice some more.

All of this was bogus, but as so often in China the details weren't important. What mattered was the overall direction, and here the message was that the government had given its seal of approval. Instead of being persecuted as "feudal superstition," the Li family's rituals were approved by the government. Old Mr. Li nodded at the plaque and explained.

"At the time, we had a lot of things that had been passed down many generations. The country was afraid it wouldn't be transmitted to future generations."

I asked Old Mr. Li about the classes, but he was uncertain when they had been held, who taught them, or who had attended. Eighty people? Hmmm. The teachers? Hmmm. The students? Hmmm.

It was no wonder the class had not been held. There are other Daoist music troupes in Yanggao, but they were rivals. The Li family did have part-time musicians who helped out on busy occasions, but they were all capable and practiced. And overall, traditions are simplifying. The classes and plans reflected the city person's desire to create living fossils.

But the room held real treasures, too. At the back in a small metal bookcase with glass doors was a stack of about twenty handwritten books. I missed them at first glance, but Old Mr. Li walked over and took them out. They were small, about three inches by five inches, and just an inch thick each. But I realized that they had made everything possible: these were the handwritten works of Old Mr. Li's father, Li Qing. Unlike dozens of other Daoist music troupes in northern China, the Li family's liturgical works had survived. But how? Hadn't Old Mr. Li just said they had been burned?

I carefully opened each volume and marveled at the penmanship and beauty of each page. Like traditional Chinese books, the bind-

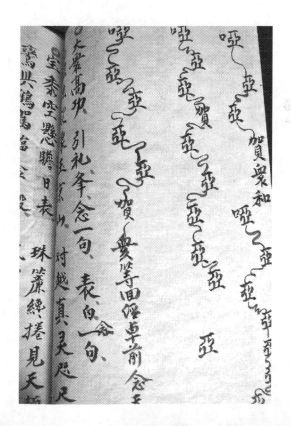

ings were stitched by hand, the pages opened right to left, and the characters were printed top to bottom. And of course the characters themselves were standard Chinese characters, not the simplified ones that the Communists implemented after taking power. Written in classical Chinese, the books were incredibly dense, harder even than reading the Book of Common Prayer with its archaic phrasings. But I could appreciate them aesthetically. The characters were written with a firm, vigorous stroke, and the punctuation—which was usually not used in classical Chinese—was edited in bright red ink, making the pages look like works of abstract art. Some of the books had talismanic symbols that started off like characters but turned into swirling representations of the otherworld. Other books had characters written with large spaces in between and eddying, smokelike lines linking them, as if incense were burning on the pages or mist were carrying them up to heaven. They had titles like *Rang zai jing* (Classic for avoiding disasters), *Zhaoqing quanbu* (Complete book of invitations), *Lingbao daganbu* (The stepping on the Big Dipper), and *Lingbao jinbiao kefan* (The pattern of study of the Numinous Treasure's Advanced Tables)—all classic works used by Daoist priests. If anyone thought that folk religion was superstition devoid of advanced ritual content, this was proof that it wasn't always the case.

Old Mr. Li looked at them, though, as if they were work tools. They were dog-eared and something he consulted, not a work of art belonging in a museum. They reminded me of the Book of Common Prayer that my grandmother had given me, a beautiful pocket-sized volume in a leather binding, but one she had heavily marked up with pencil annotations.

So how had the volumes survived? I had heard that his father had committed all the volumes to memory and rewritten them after the Cultural Revolution had ended.

"No, no. No one's memory is that strong," Old Mr. Li said with a raspy laugh. "Some of them were in other families' homes. He had disciples or people who helped him. Also, relatives like my uncle Li Peisen saved volumes. Some of these are originals, from before the Cultural Revolution. Some were copied out afterward."

And the original books, where had they been burned? Outside in the yard?

"No, in the kitchen. In the oven."

"You had to watch?"

"Yes," he said with a laugh.

We turned to go, but Old Mr. Li stopped me.

"I want to ask you something," he said. I nodded.

In one of the closets was a bottle of grappa and a pack of cigarettes from Italy. What does this mean, he said, pointing at the large, crude script, as mysterious to him as the classical language had been to me. I laughed. *Il fumo uccide.*

"It says, 'Smoking kills.'"

"And what's this?"

"It's a picture of a lung after smoking."

Old Mr. Li puffed on a cigarette and eyed the package. I asked him about the grappa.

"We have plans for that."

We sat in the classroom for a while longer. Old Mr. Li peppered me with questions about Italy. They had just gotten back a few weeks ago, and that strange land was fresh in his mind. He had been impressed by the cathedral in Florence and its enormous dome from the Ming dynasty. He asked me about the wolf that suckled two men, which launched us into a conversation on Chinese mythology. We talked about Western funerals, and I explained the concept of a wake, which he immediately understood. Watching over the dead before burial was a Chinese tradition too.

As we talked, I noticed that he focused on the specifics of our cultures, the microscopic similarities and differences. But I wanted him to generalize. What was it like, I asked, to take all this—the gods, the music, the liturgy—abroad? It was strange, he answered, because in China they are performing rites that a family commissions but that few people really listen to carefully. In the West, they are in auditoriums and everyone is quiet, listening intently, but it doesn't mean anything to them. There is no funeral, no coffin up onstage. Then he was silent for a moment, gathering his thoughts.

"I don't have any feelings about travel, but in our hearts it's our honor to be able to take Daoism out to the world. It's our glory. But you can't say one place is better than another. There, it's not like here, where with one gust of wind there's dust everywhere. Venice was a water city, and we rode boats all day long. We went to an island, and there were birds everywhere. We sat on the shore and ate, and watched the birds. It was beautiful. It was really beautiful, Ian. A very beautiful day. A day I will never forget.

"But I read that this year in the winter, people died because the lagoon froze over. Some people were out drinking and froze to death. They froze to death because no one let them into their homes. Maybe it's the same anytime you leave your home. You don't belong, and then people don't care about you."

Like all proper Chinese homes, Old Mr. Li's faced south for maximum exposure to the sun. Through a big window over his *kang*, we watched the sun setting. The wind had blasted clouds into faint streaks that dusted the sky. On the left side of the horizon, the moon was already rising, so bright that the outline of its unlit section was visible. In two days it would be full.

Mrs. Yao had been making us dinner for hours, and I felt guilty. They were an old and slow couple, both sixty-one but less limber than my eighty-three-year-old father. The two of them lived traditionally: exercise was work, not enjoyment. Daoism was a family trade, not a form of wellness. *Il fumo* was a luxury, not a way to *uccide*.

We sat quietly, Old Mr. Li smoking, thinking, looking out the window, contemplating. He told me he liked to watch television. "She hates how I watch television."

"I disapprove of it!" she yelled from the kitchen.

To prove her right, he turned on the television. We watched a local news program, and his wife cackled in the kitchen.

Mrs. Yao brought in a small feast just in time for the 7:00 p.m. news. We ate in silence, watching the show unfold. A friend of mine in Beijing liked to joke that the national news always has three themes: China is prosperous; the leaders are busy; and foreign countries are chaotic. Tonight's program focused on the first two. The show started off, as it did every Qingming, with Politburo members visiting the countryside to plant trees. The announcer—a stern woman with permed hair and severely plucked eyebrows—said the men had performed their work "conscientiously." All the leaders wore the same uniform: black dress shoes, black dress slacks, and black windbreakers zipped all the way up, as if they were a gathering of nerdy engineers from the 1950s. The jacket had a rounded collar like military men have in China, giving them the prescribed official look. All the men had jet-black hair, almost certainly dyed, and the pallid, sallow complexion of aging men who rarely plant trees. The only contrast was provided by the military men, who wore green dress uniforms adorned with colorful ribbons.

After a while, I noticed that I was the only person watching, like an idiot savant searching for clues about something that no one else cared about. Mrs. Yao was washing up, while Old Mr. Li copied the ancient formulas into a new book.

The sun was up before six, truly a clear and bright day. I walked down to the orchard at the end of the street. It had a few pear trees but mostly almond trees, about fifty of them on a mini-plateau of loess soil that was about five feet above the Li family homestead. This is where Hall of the Three Purities had stood. I clambered up and walked around the trees, which had tiny red buds. Out in the fields, people were already turning the earth, waiting for the next solar term, Grain Rain. Around me was nothing but houses. The temples had been destroyed, their foundations and stories waiting for archaeologists.

Back home, the house was suddenly bustling. Late last night, Old Mr. Li had received an urgent call from a prosperous owner of an iron ore mine, Wang Yicang, who needed Old Mr. Li's geomancy skills at the family graveside the next day. Old Mr. Li said yes, as long as he could be finished in time for his own family's tomb sweeping, which had to be completed in the morning. Mr. Wang had agreed and said he would pick us up at 7:30 a.m.

Mr. Wang showed up in a chrome-plated Nissan sedan. On the drive over to the graves, he explained his problem. Back in the Mao era, rural people were allowed to be buried—then, as now, the party did not insist on cremation as it did for city folk—but it had not allowed tombstones. Mr. Wang wanted to right this wrong. The problem was how the tombstones should be aligned. He also wanted to mark the cemetery properly with a stone pillar at each corner and small pine trees. But the proper boundaries were unclear. These were important considerations: getting the geomancy right meant respecting the dead and making sure they did not interfere with the lives of the living. Old Mr. Li nodded thoughtfully. It was a familiar problem that he had solved many times.

Ten minutes later we arrived at the cemetery, and Old Mr. Li was soon immersed in his work. He squatted on the ground, squinting at a *luopan*, a small square box, about a foot by a foot and an inch thick. In the center was a compass, and radiating out of it were a dozen lines like marks for pie slices. In these segments are characters corresponding to the earthly branches and heavenly stems, which are used to count the years and days in sixty-year cycles. There were innumerable other characters that he looked at, comparing them with the notes in his fortune-telling book, and the birth and death dates of the people under the ground. He was like a land surveyor, but one mapping the spiritual world on the hard, crumbly soil.

It was time-consuming, exacting work, but the weather was comfortable, in the mid-forties, and warming up quickly. Yanggao is in a large basin, with mountains to the east and north—branches of the Taihang Mountains that run from Miaofengshan in the north to China's rainy south. On the north side of our basin was Dragon Phoenix Mountain, its ridges clear and dramatic in the early light. But the lower third of the hills, closest to the settlements, were covered in a gauze of dust and pollution. It made the mountains seem to hover over the fields, cut off from the ground below.

After checking his book many times, Old Mr. Li pulled out a red thread about two feet long and affixed it to the center of the *luopan* where the compass needle rotated. Then he pulled it taut in the direction the needle pointed and looked at which characters it crossed. He moved the thread slightly to the right based on this year's special characteristics—dryness, hardship—that he had read in his booklet. Mr. Wang pulled the thread taut and then tied it to a long rope, allowing him to mark the cemetery's boundaries.

While the men worked, other family members made small altars in front of the two main tombs, which were still just simple mounds of earth about four feet high. As part of the tomb-sweeping ritual, some family members took a spade, carried earth from a nearby field, and dumped it on top of the mound—the idea was to make sure the mounds didn't erode. Others laid cardboard in front of the mounds and placed fruits, cakes, and cookies. Others peeled hard-boiled eggs or bamboo-wrapped glutinous rice balls. Then they burned paper money and scattered some of the food on the grave, taking the majority back home to eat. That way the living and the dead shared a meal.

"This is something I have wanted to do for a long time," Mr. Wang said as we watched Old Mr. Li work. "My heart could not rest easy until this was done. We've got money, but if you don't take care of this, your life can't be stable."

Mr. Wang was fifty-one, and he had three sons and five grandchildren, who raced around chasing each other. He asked me about English classes and immigration possibilities. His sons were poorly educated, but he had high hopes that one of his grandchildren could move to Australia or Canada.

"In those countries, I think if you work hard, you'll be rewarded," he said. "In China, it's complicated. I've got the mine, but in a few years someone else might have control of it. In China, you don't really own a business like this," he said, and I guessed at the bribes and banqueting that underlay his fortune.

After nearly two hours' work, the ground was marked for the posts and tombstones. The Wang family men began digging holes for the posts and the small trees. It would take most of the morning, but they could do that on their own. Mr. Wang said good-bye, and a colleague drove us back to the Li family homestead. He slipped Old Mr. Li 200 yuan for his troubles and drove off.

Li Bin was waiting for us, wearing a black-checked shirt he had bought as a souvenir in Italy. Now it was the Li family's turn to honor its ancestors. We drove out of the village south and along a small range about one hundred feet above town. The road was really just a dirt path with enormous grooves caused by the loess soil's endless erosion. At times it was perilous because the ruts were so deep that the ridge in the middle bumped into the car's chassis. Li Bin steered so the left wheels of his little car were on the middle ridge and the right wheels on the right side of the road. We slipped and slid down the road, sometimes scraping bottom.

After fifteen minutes, we arrived at fields that sloped gently up from the village. Directly below the road was a huge mound: Li Qing's grave. The man who rescued the family's tradition had his own space far from the other family members. This was not a special honor, but just pragmatic: the old graveyard had filled up, and so they buried him here. The family set up the offerings on the southern base of the mound: fruits, biscuits, and stacks of paper money.

Then Old Mr. Li brought out the pièce de résistance: the bottle of Italian grappa. So this was how it would be used.

"Ha-ha, now he'll get some," he said, and poured a cup for his father. Li Bin joined him and helped set up the rest of the offerings. From the road they looked tiny: two dark-clad men against the light-yellow soil, which stretched down into the valley and for miles across the valley to Dragon Phoenix Mountain.

The sky was pale blue, and you could see the wind picking up. It began by hitting us in our faces and causing us to squint. It seemed to be the color white, turning the horizon pale and indistinct, as if the airwaves were so disturbed that they blurred the horizon. The men lit the stacks of paper money, but gusts started to come in waves, blowing the offerings over the scrub-covered hill. Li Bin held the paper down with a stick so it wouldn't fly away, but half a dozen bills—100,000 yuan each, payable to the Bank of the Underworld—cartwheeled across the field. The dry grass began burning. Old Mr. Li picked up a tree branch and beat the flames. I stomped on other flaming tufts of yellowed grass. If the hillside had not been so denuded, it could have gone up in flames.

A silver minivan drove up. It was Li Yunshan, Old Mr. Li's younger brother, who worked as a civil servant in the county government. As a child, he loved to play the *sheng* but gave it up to get into college. But he was still good enough to go with the family on trips abroad and to make it seem as if the tradition were unchanging. With his name on the bill, it seemed as if three members of the Li family were in the troupe. In fact, only Li Bin really played an instrument with any aptitude.

Li Yunshan and his son got out of the van and carried several bags of goodies. They plunked down a golden "money tree," stacks of paper, and two paper wreaths for the grave. Li Bin piled everything— all still in its plastic wrapper—on the fire. The plastic curled and melted away, giving off a worrisome smell. The plastic money tree began to smolder and turn into a hunk of toxic rock that burned for the next fifteen minutes, long after the paper had gone up in smoke. I wondered if the dead choked on smoke too.

While we worked, Li Yunshan's sixteen-year-old son hovered

nearby. "Sure it's interesting," he said of the family tradition. "But I'm too old to learn." He had his sights set on studying physics in the provincial capital. "China has a lot of universities, and most of them are pretty good." I got the message: anywhere but here.

Our work done, we returned to the family home, where Mrs. Yao had been making dishes. The smell was wonderful, and soon we were eating dumplings, tofu, vegetables, and a big stew.

"It will rain soon," Old Mr. Li announced.

I asked how he knew.

"The next solar term is Grain Rain," he said simply.

That sounded improbable, but two weeks later it rained and the planting began.

11

Chengdu: Good Friday

A couple of days after spending Qingming in Shanxi, I was driving through the streets of Chengdu with Zhang Guoqing, a conference planner by trade and leading member of the Early Rain church. In China, many companies organize outings in the springtime for their staff, and Guoqing's job was to arrange their meals, concerts, and team-building exercises. After years of struggling, he was now established in his profession and looked the role of the successful urban professional: jeans, an open-collar dress shirt, and a tan blazer. But he wasn't out to meet a client; today was Good Friday, the day Jesus was crucified, and Guoqing was up early, visiting some of the unluckiest people in Chengdu.

Guoqing was the church's liaison to society's margins. He had participated in the 1989 antigovernment protests in Hangzhou, where he had graduated from Zhejiang University two years earlier. Students had gotten off fairly lightly, a nod to their youth, inexperience, and privileged position in Chinese society. But protesters with jobs were supposed to know better. Guoqing had just demonstrated a few times, but he was held three months. Later he had moved to Chengdu and eventually shifted his energies from politics to religion. But he maintained his contacts with marginal parts of society, helping advise Wang Yi's church on how to stay socially engaged. Today was a day to take stock of several projects, starting with a homeless mission that the church supported with donations of $14,000 a year.

We drove west toward the Third Ring Road, but it wasn't yet finished, and our interchange was several mounds of dirt on either side of the highway. We drove up over a small dirt hill, his Citroën's bottom scraping. Next to us were snaking bridges and ramps, now empty but soon to be clogged with traffic. We bounced along an unpaved road and finally rejoined the highway and headed south.

"The Communist Party only likes to invest in big projects like this," he said of the elaborate flyover. "It's not interested in the people's livelihood."

"Isn't this good for the people?"

"To a degree, yes, but all these projects—the roads, the high-speed rail, and so on—are all given to state firms. There's no way for anyone else to benefit from this. Private companies are cut out. I hear that a lot from my clients."

As if on cue, a large red banner appeared over a bridge: "The Eleventh Department of the China National Rail Corporation Extends Its Regards to the People of Chengdu."

Greetings, Earthlings, from Planet State.

Our destination was Sansheng Village, a small hilly area with teahouses and restaurants in a rustic setting. It was once some of the area's richest farmland, but Chengdu's appetite for land had turned the orchards and vegetable plots into suburban housing develop-ments, equestrian centers, and plots of land for the well-to-do to play at farming. After a bit of searching, we found the shelter, which was housed in a former two-story concrete farmhouse with an eight-foot brick wall and a rusty sheet-metal gate.

Guoqing got out of his car and walked up to the gate. It was chained shut. He pulled at it and yelled through the crack, "Brother Zhang, open up!"

Zhang Bin rushed out to open the gate. It was 9:00 a.m. already, and it probably should have been open; Guoqing looked annoyed. I knew Zhang Bin from the church. He was a trim forty-nine-year-old, ingratiating but somewhat detached and vague, dressed as always in his simple-but-respectable poor-man clothes: scuffed loafers, creased polyester dress slacks, blue flannel shirt, and tattered houndstooth blazer. He was the shelter's manager, just a step up from the men he helped.

The farmhouse was clean but worn. Inside the yard were two gingko trees and two peach trees. The whitewashed walls were deco-rated with dozens of stenciled verses from the Bible, such as "But when you give a feast, invite the poor, the crippled, the lame, the blind, and you will be blessed, because they cannot repay you. For you will be repaid at the resurrection of the just."

Zhang Bin lived here with a dozen men. We wandered through the rooms while Guoqing quizzed him on the numbers and Zhang Bin stumbled through his poorly rehearsed answers.

"Chengdu's homeless people are just men passing through," Zhang Bin said. "We take in about two hundred a year. They mostly just stay a little while, and I encourage them to find work."

"If they're able-bodied, they have to work," Guoqing said in agreement. "The church won't support it otherwise."

"Well, we can't be big anyway, even if we wanted to. The government doesn't want too many people here, so we can't have a big center. They're afraid we'll start something. Anytime we get more than a few," he said nodding to a few residents who had followed us in, "the police come by and make trouble."

The men in the shelter had stories of misfortune and troubles.

Liu Jianyun was a forty-nine-year-old stroke victim whose family kicked him out of his home. "When we found him, he was eating out of a garbage bin," Zhang Bin said. "He could only walk with a cane, but through the power of prayer he now doesn't need it. His hand is also better."

Next to him stood Yu Chenyuan, a sixty-year-old with one eye colored a milky gray. He used to work as a repairman for a company in a provincial town. He had been standing on a ladder fixing a light when a piece of glass broke and went into his eye. His boss refused to compensate him, and the family sued. The boss sent ruffians around to threaten the family, and they killed his wife. Mr. Yu fled in terror and had been homeless for five years.

Two years ago he was taken in by the mission and is now its cook.

"It's had an effect on his mental health," Zhang Bin said. Mr. Yu looked down and smiled. "He's seen so much suffering that he's not able to really hold a job, but he can cook."

The only man with a job prospect was Zhen Changnong. He was thirty-six years old, and very short, well under five feet, with grayish teeth and oily hair, yet smart and well-spoken. When he was a boy, his stepfather beat him constantly, so he ran away from home. He was soon kidnapped by a gang that took him to work as a slave. He escaped and ended up in a village in Hebei Province near Beijing, tending the fields of a corn farmer. He had recently held a job cleaning tables at a restaurant until he and his boss had a falling-out over a trivial matter. From Zhen's own account, it seemed his temper was largely to blame.

Last year, Zhang Bin took Zhen home, and he reconciled with his mother, who was ill. His stepfather was already dead.

"I'm really glad I did it, but I need to find another job. I have to work, and I want to go back and see her."

Zhang Bin looked on proudly as Zhen's story came to its conclusion.

"When I first came here two years ago, I didn't want to be baptized. I left here often and sometimes didn't come back."

"We could see that his heart hadn't settled, so we didn't push it," Zhang Bin said.

"Last April, though, I felt I could do it and was baptized. I am a Christian. I feel really calm now and can handle anything."

"You should get a job," Guoqing said approvingly. "You need to stand on your own two feet, get a place to live, and maybe start a family."

We sat down on old rattan chairs that had been rescued from a dump. Tea was procured, and Zhang Bin got down to business. Early Rain's support was appreciated, but the center needed more—about three times as much. A Norwegian woman provided some money, but foreign money was a bad idea, he said. Guoqing nodded. This was true; outside funding always led to complications. It was the easiest reason for the government to close down a nongovernmental organization.

"You need to reach out to congregations more," Guoqing said. "You come to us once in a while, but you don't really have a good relationship with the church. You only come when you need something."

"We do talk to congregations," Zhang Bin said, then added pointedly, "So many congregations send people here, but they don't really do anything. Everyone wants to come and see this and feel they're part of it and claim credit for it, but they don't do much."

"But why don't you make your books public? People will be more generous if they see what you do. It's not complicated."

"It's hard," Zhang Bin said vaguely. He rambled on about how the bookkeeping was complex. Guoqing and I looked at each other; neither of us understood what he meant.

"It's simple," Guoqing said to Zhang Bin before we left. "People want transparency. If you're getting money from someone, that person has a right to know how it's spent."

Early Rain's social work started with the 2008 Wenchuan earthquake, which killed sixty-nine thousand people. For many activists and Christians, the earthquake was a turning point, as important as the 1989 Tiananmen protests had been to an earlier generation. While government leaders flew in from Beijing to try to direct rescue operations, the main efforts took place across the country as a whole as people spontaneously donated time and money, driving from far-off provinces in cars laden with food and water or renting out trucks to deliver supplies. They were shocked at the government's focus on presenting itself as heroic; many were further alienated by how the government treated them—as an embarrassing reminder of its own failure, rather than an inspiring example of civic compassion. It caused many citizens to look more closely at how society was organized and the values that underlay it.

After the catastrophe, people attending Wang Yi's new church began helping the injured in one of Chengdu's hospitals. They also supported a discount supermarket for poor people in western Sichuan's Ngawa Prefecture, a Tibetan part of the country that had been the epicenter of the earthquake. Its most sensitive project, however, was financial support for families of prisoners of conscience. Chengdu has the highest number of dissidents outside Beijing, and the church tried to help family members coping with having a loved one in jail. This came to a head in 2011, when Arab countries went through the Jasmine Revolution that toppled authoritarian leaders. Voices on social media called for a similar uprising in China. The call was ignored, but the government reacted nervously. It rounded up dozens of dissidents, including Ran Yunfei, the strong-minded writer who was close to the church. His prominence led to his quick release, but others were still stuck in prison. Speaking of the families of the prisoners, Wang Yi once put it to me like this: "In China, the families are like untouchables in India. Often the wife or spouse loses work; the family has little to fall back on. In Chinese society, there's no social force that's independent and organized enough to help these people except the congregations."

A key point that Wang Yi and Guoqing emphasized time and again is that the donations were not from abroad: foreign aid guaranteed that authorities would stop the project. The money was solely from congregation members and it was not anonymous. If the Public Security Bureau wanted to know who donated, the church could provide a list. Guoqing also stressed that it wasn't meant to support the prisoners—just their families, as a humanitarian gesture.

We were now pulling up to the west gate of Chengdu University. Guoqing waved breezily at the guards, and they let us through. After passing several newer sections of campus, we arrived at a quiet corner of half a dozen buildings from the 1970s. They were five-story concrete structures streaked with mold and dirt. A small stand of gingko trees surrounded the buildings protectively, as if hiding something shameful.

Guoqing left the car at the side of the road, and we walked up four flights of stairs in one of the buildings. He knocked at a door and then yelled until a tall, exhausted-looking woman opened it. Wang Qinghua was in her late fifties, with dyed-black hair that was partly pinned up in a bun and partly falling down around her ears. She had an ashen complexion and small, even teeth stained with nicotine.

She and Guoqing knew each other, and he walked right in, closing the door behind us. We sat down at a small wooden table.

"We want to know how your situation is," Guoqing said.

"What part of my situation?" she said.

Mrs. Wang had been living alone for three years, since her husband, Tan Zuoren, had been detained and jailed for five years for opposing construction of a PX chemical plant near a residential area. He was being held at a prison in Ya'an, a town about ninety miles away.

His imprisonment had not been a shock to Mrs. Wang. Tan had participated in the 1989 antigovernment protests in Chengdu and gone underground, fleeing to Shenzhen. "We thought he had died because we had no word from him," she said, smiling at the memory. "Then he called from Shenzhen, and I went down there to marry him."

Tan wasn't arrested, and eventually the couple returned to Chengdu, where he worked as a freelance writer and filmmaker. After the 2008 earthquake, he had been the first to point out the link between corruption and collapsed buildings, and he also set up a database for missing children. His arrest spurred protests in Hong Kong and was later highlighted by the activist-artist Ai Wei-wei. Ai traveled to Chengdu to try to attend Tan's trial and said he was beaten up in his hotel room.

Mrs. Wang related all of this quickly for my benefit, with an air of pride but also exasperation. Then she fast-forwarded to the day when he would be released and what their first words would be.

"I guess he's going to explain first how he was right about being jailed and how he was right about June 4 and how he was right about the earthquake," she said. "He's always explaining how he's right about various things. It's something he does really well."

Guoqing nodded. Easy does it, he seemed to say.

"But he needs to do something else: He needs to get a job. He needs to earn money and support his family!" Her lips were trembling with emotion, and I thought of her daughter, who hadn't been able to attend university because of the family's political problems. Instead, she had taken an online marketing job—poorly paid and with no future. Mrs. Wang had been given early retirement from the phone company at age fifty and now took 600 yuan a month in charity from Early Rain. These were educated people, and they could have had a good life. She tried to speak again but could only gasp.

"That's right!" Guoqing said, cutting in to save her from crying. "He's able-bodied and there's no reason why he can't work. Everyone should work for their food."

Guoqing was talking partly as an administrator of the fund but also out of conviction. Like the Puritans of old, the Chengdu Christians believed in the value of labor. Tan Zuoren was one of China's best-known dissidents, but when he got out of jail, he would still be in his fifties. He should work.

Mrs. Wang took a call. It was her mother. After she got off, she explained, "She's over ninety but worried about me. She knows I'm here, without a husband, and hopes I am okay."

"How does she feel about Tan?" Guoqing said.

"Both my parents were in the underground Communist Party in Chongqing before liberation. My father—it doesn't work too well here," she said, pointing to her head. "But my mother supports Tan Zuoren. She says that some people in China need to speak out. If no one dares to speak out, how will China improve? Everyone can't keep silent and go along all the time. Some people have to speak."

"How is he holding up?" Guoqing asked.

"Depressed," she said.

"Didn't Ran Yunfei write to him?" Guoqing asked.

"He wrote a three-page letter to Tan urging him to keep up his spirits in jail, but they wouldn't deliver it. When Ran tried to read it to him over the phone, they cut the phone line. So Ran gave it to me in person, and I rewrote it, pretending it was from me. Then I sent it to the prison. After a while they gave it to him. The warden told him, 'We didn't want to give it to you, because it's really quite strong stuff, but it's from your wife, so we relented.' But Tan knew it was from Ran. It meant a lot to him."

I thought of the dissident blogger in Chengdu named Huang Qi. He ran an Internet site called 64Tianwang, which carried news from across China about unrest and protests. Of course, the site was blocked in China, but it raised the question of why the state allowed him to publish in the first place. Why not just pull the plug on him entirely and block his Internet access or his VPN? I mentioned this to Mrs. Wang.

"They can't do that," Mrs. Wang said. "They might pull the Internet access during a sensitive period, but it's controlled by another department, the Telecom Ministry. They can tell them to shut down your access for a day and tell you that it's 'broken.' But you'll complain, and by the second day they'll feel embarrassed because everyone's supposed to have Internet access if they pay for it. And so by the third day it'll be up again."

"And don't forget Wang Bin," Guoqing interjected. He was a technician who worked as Huang Qi's right-hand man. He was also a member of the Early Rain Prisoners of Conscience Fund's board of directors. But everyone also believed he worked for state security.

"Huang knows he is state security—we all do—but Huang figures he might as well be transparent. If the state security wants to give you a computer expert, you might as well accept."

It was such a tangled mess. Maybe at their extremes all societies are, but the level of double-talk in China was disorienting. Compared with places like East Germany, where an estimated 3 percent of the population were official secret police informants, China's system was more refined and subtle. It was easy to dismiss or write off as an exceptional part of society, but it underpinned everything else; it was society's rotten core. A government that relies on fear cannot instill morality; it can only enforce behavior. This was why Wang Yi's church stood with people like Mrs. Wang.

"The 600 yuan is a huge amount of money for us," she said, pulling out a fresh pack of cigarettes. She unwrapped the cellophane, crumpled it, and put it on the desk, where it slowly uncoiled.

"But it's not only the money. It's knowing that people care about us and that we're not forgotten. Living here . . . ," she said, her voice trailing off. I looked around the concrete apartment and out the windows at the gingko trees sprouting big flat leaves. "It's not what I expected. I wonder why, what am I doing? Why are we here?"

"The way I see it," Guoqing said quietly, "we're all working for the same thing—for a more open and better China. Some are on the inside. Others are on the outside. I could be there and he here."

For the first three decades of his life, Wang Yi hadn't thought too much about religion. He had studied law at Sichuan University and began teaching at twenty-three. He quickly became known as an idealistic legal-rights advocate, especially through two popular online discussion groups, "Gate to Heaven Teahouse" and "Century Salon." By 2001, he had set up another online forum on constitutional law and a fourth to cover personal interests, like film. Soon he was a nationally known commentator, writing columns in some of China's most influential publications, such as *Orient, Readers, Southern Weekend,* and *Twenty-First Century Economic Herald.* A national magazine called him one of China's fifty most prominent public intellectuals, and his effort at promoting constitutionalism seemed in line with the new policies of the incoming government of Hu Jintao, who had taken over from Jiang Zemin in the early twenty-first century.

In 2002, a friend gave him a copy of a multipart documentary called *The Cross*. It had been made by Yuan Zhiming, who in the late 1980s had helped make a documentary called *River Elegy*. That film had aired on national television in 1988, arguing that China was too inward looking, its culture too insular, and its political path too narrow. The series had a strong effect on students who participated in the 1989 Tiananmen protests. Many credited it as a key to opening their eyes to the need for wide-ranging reforms—not just economic changes, but social transformation. After the crackdown, Yuan had been labeled one of the "black hands" behind the student protests, and he had fled abroad. Like many involved in the protests, he began to wonder if China could have political reform without spiritual change. He converted to Christianity and turned his filmmaking skills to the story of Christianity in China.

"Before that film, I didn't realize that China had a Christian history," Wang Yi told me. "I knew there were one or two churches, but I didn't think it played a role in Chinese history or contemporary China."

We were sitting together with his wife, Jiang Rong, in their home, a small but cozy apartment in a complex near one of Chengdu's biggest temples. Visiting was always tricky: the guards demanded IDs and then made notes. But inside, all of that was far away; their home was decorated with drawings by their young son, and one wall had shelves overflowing with hundreds of DVDs—a reminder of Wang Yi's long-standing interest in film. No wonder that a documentary had awoken his interest in Christianity.

Yuan's series started with the Nestorians, a Christian sect that came to China with Persian traders during the seventh century. Although they faded, others tried to bring the religion to China, culminating in the Jesuits, who arrived in the sixteenth century and established a permanent Christian presence in China. Foreign missionaries came next, after Western gunboats forced China open to the outside world in the nineteenth century. Although this period is uniformly portrayed in Chinese history textbooks, museums, and movies as a period of humiliation, *The Cross* took a different tack. It showed a dynamic time when Christianity spread widely and missionaries helped found many of China's first modern schools and hospitals.

The film's most riveting segments covered the twentieth century, telling the lives of heroic Chinese Christians like Wang Mingdao, a fierce evangelizer who spent nearly three decades in Communist labor camps for refusing to join the government-run church. Others, such as Watchman Nee, died in prison for their faith. Abroad, websites and books tell their stories but in China they are excluded from the historical record. Wang Yi recalls being shocked when he saw those segments: "For me this was a complete blank. I'm a public intellectual and pay a lot of attention to Chinese society, but I didn't know anything about this."

Equally unsettling was how it was Christian faith—not belief in abstract ideas like human rights or democracy—that held out strongest against Mao's totalitarianism. In fact, some liken the persecution to a crucible. When the Maoist era ended in the late 1970s, Christianity, especially Protestantism, took off in popularity. From one million adherents in 1949, when the Communists took over, Protestantism began to count its followers in the tens of millions.

"They were just very simple people from the countryside without education. And yet in the Cultural Revolution they refused to sing Chairman Mao songs or to pray toward his statue. They were sentenced or bullied or beaten. They were much more courageous than the intellectuals. They were the toughest, the strongest. They succeeded. The intellectuals failed."

Another event in 2002 got Wang Yi thinking more about the link between religion and China's future. The township of Buyun east of Chengdu was the scene of an intriguing experiment in local democracy. For several decades, villages in China had been allowed to hold elections for village councils, with varying degrees of fairness depending on the open-mindedness of local officials. Buyun took this to another level. A township of sixteen thousand residents, it comprised a dozen villages. Optimists saw it as a stepping up the ladder toward county and maybe even provincial elections—the sort of slow-but-steady progress that places like Taiwan had seen several decades earlier. That proved too optimistic, and Buyun was the last township to hold such elections. But for Wang Yi, that didn't matter. He found something more significant.

"I noticed the religion. That township had twelve villages, and each one had a religious activity center. Most were Buddhist or Daoist or folk religion, and there was also one Catholic village. Each village had a government office of course—party committee, mayor, and so on—but each village's religious center also had its own financial arrangement and supervisory committee. And not only that, but each religious organization had better financial management than the official side! Each of the twelve villages had a debt of 200,000 to 300,000 yuan, but each of the twelve religious groups had a surplus. And each of the religious groups—they were called clubs [*huisuo*]— they were elected! So the best-run organization in the village wasn't the Communist Party but the local religious association."

This might seem far-fetched, but it reflects what some political scientists have documented in China—that in places where religious groups have status, they can act as a check on government power, holding officials accountable for their actions. Wang Yi began to wonder if political progress required the support of a higher authority, not an ideal or a constitution, but a God who endows all people with the same rights—something that could not be taken away by a political leader.

As he talked, his wife, Jiang Rong, sat next to him on the sofa. The two had known each other since childhood and began courting in college. They married shortly after graduating in 1995. Short and petite, with a pageboy haircut and a determined jaw, Jiang Rong had a sharp mind and followed conversations closely. She was reserved, but when she spoke, she often seemed a step or two ahead of the discussion. Without being asked, she told how Wang Yi's political and religious awakening strained their relationship.

When Wang Yi had started his legal-rights work, she was working at a company that staged concerts. Worried that her husband's activism would cause him to lose his teaching job, she put in overtime to bolster their savings. One day, she went to the office and opened a letter. The letter laid out all of her personal details, her job, her husband's job, and said her husband was evil. If she stayed with him, the letter said, her company would collapse. The anonymous writer suggested she get divorced. She was dumbfounded; it felt like something out of the Cultural Revolution. Soon after, the government audited the company where she worked. Jiang Rong showed the letter to her boss.

"He was really an upright person. He said this wasn't fair. He

said, 'Don't leave this job, you have a job here. I have always admired
Teacher Wang—show me his latest writings! Show me what is causing the problems!'"

Jiang Rong did so and then read Wang Yi's writings herself. She
discovered that she actually hadn't paid too much attention to her
husband's work.

"I began to read carefully. I began to know him. I thought I knew
him but didn't really. I found that our views were different. It was like
we were in different worlds."

Understanding did not lead to agreement. She was especially
upset at his new friends. He was spending more time with "rights
defender," or *weiquan*, lawyers. They were a serious legal movement
that lasted for about a decade in the early 2000s, giving widespread
hope in China and abroad that rule of law might be permitted. They
represented farmers with polluted soil, people illegally arrested, and
others who had run afoul of the system. They didn't challenge Communist Party rule, but they tried to hold the government accountable
to its own laws. About a quarter were Christians—including many
of the movement's most famous members—inspired by the faith's
emphasis on social justice.

"I thought they're doing good work, but I didn't really think it
had to do with me. I really thought, why are they doing stuff the
government doesn't want? They've all got good educations. They're
ruining their lives. What's the point? It's not worth it."

The harassment picked up. She got calls at three in the morning, with the caller using the intimate, diminutive form of her given
name, "Xiao Rong," which would be like saying "my little Betty."
The caller would hang up. Other times, the caller detailed her exact
movements during the day to show he knew everything.

She also got letters saying her husband was having an affair. She
asked Wang Yi, and he said he had been receiving similar letters.

Then the SARS epidemic struck China in 2003. It was a respira-
tory ailment that swept the country, canceling any sorts of public
events. Her company lost business, and employees were given leave.
One day, while she was at home, her husband brought home Yu Jie,
an outspoken Chengdu writer who was living in Beijing. He had just
converted to Christianity and was eager to share his story. He gave
her a book by a Chinese-American woman whose marriage was saved

through Christianity. The woman was visiting Chengdu, and Jiang Rong called her up. They began meeting regularly and were joined by Huang Weicai, a woman a few years older who was also interested in Christianity and who today is a key member of the Early Rain governing committee. By now, it was the spring of 2005, and they met outside in parks, their numbers gradually increasing.

"One day Wang Yi said, 'You're always meeting outside, why don't you start meeting here at home?' It was April, and that's how it started. More and more people started coming on Sunday afternoons."

It was only after she learned about Christianity that she began to understand her husband. She had resented him for his impracticality: as a university professor, for example, he had been offered campus housing but had rejected it. She had thought this foolish. Now she realized it was because he did not want to owe anything to anyone. Slowly, her frustration turned to admiration.

"I realized that this was work that really had to be done. There needs to be people who work for the public benefit."

In August 2005, a visiting Chinese-American pastor from the United States baptized Jiang Rong, Huang Weicai, and several others at an outdoor ceremony in a river. Like the Christians of old, they were dunked completely in water. Wang Yi, though, wasn't quite ready.

"I thought philosophically that Christianity was good, but my heart wasn't opened yet," he said. "They all joked that they had brought an extra set of clothes in case I wanted to be baptized, but . . . ah, I don't know."

Wang Yi asked Yu Jie endless questions, such as where good Chinese from earlier generations went. What about his favorite poet, Su Dongpo? He was one of the great figures in Chinese history—a man of letters and an upright administrator. Had he gone to hell? Yu Jie talked him through his concerns, the two men spending long days together whenever Yu Jie came to Chengdu or Wang Yi traveled to Beijing. Eventually, it happened. On Christmas Day 2005, Yu Jie came home to Chengdu for Christmas. They held a service at Wang Yi's apartment. Nine people converted, including Wang Yi.

By then, over twenty people were meeting regularly in the couple's apartment. They weren't registered with the government. They were a house church, and they wondered what to call themselves. A friend

mentioned one of her favorite verses from the Bible: Deuteronomy
11:14. They read it and named themselves after one of its phrases:

> He will give the rain for your land in its season, the early rain
> and the later rain, that you may gather in your grain and your
> wine and your oil.

A few hours after our visit to Wang Qinghua, the committee that ran
the prisoners of conscience program met to discuss the best way to
help people like her. The Good Friday service had taken place in the
later morning, and now we were just half a dozen, sitting around a
little table that looked out on the Chengdu smog.

Guoqing was there, of course, now dressed more formally for
church in a serge blue suit, red-and-blue striped shirt, and a smart red
tie. He was lively and jocular, putting everyone at ease, eager to share
some of the ideas that had come to him since our visit earlier in the
day with Mrs. Wang and the homeless people. Four others were there
too: an impatient woman with a green trench coat, prim but with
heavy makeup; a quiet man who didn't say much; and a former dissident who now sold real estate—a sad man with oversized glasses,
thinning hair, a blue suit, and an expression that all of this would
end badly for everyone involved; and finally the chairwoman, Huang
Weicai, who had converted along with Jiang Rong. She was in her
early fifties, a bit harried, but humorous and efficient. She was there
to make sure that the families were helped but also that the meeting
didn't devolve into an antigovernment cabal. The church wanted to
send a signal, not get closed down.

After a hymn and a short prayer, we began discussing a book that
the group was reading in translation. It was *Good News About Injustice:
A Witness of Courage in a Hurting World*, a work about Christians who
stood up to human trafficking, forced prostitution, persecution, and
torture. The committee met once a month and read a chapter each
time. They were on chapter 5, which discussed the value of compassion, and everyone took turns reading it paragraph by paragraph.

After half an hour, the sixth member of the committee showed
up: Wang Bin, the man believed to be an informant. Soon after his

appearance in the church a few years earlier, word had spread that he was working for state security. People were concerned, but a consensus soon emerged to let him attend. It was part of Wang Yi's policy of radical openness: let them know exactly what we do and they won't fear us.

Wang sat down at the end of the table and studiously ignored the others. He was fat, in a bright blue polo shirt, drumming his fingers dexterously as if a violinist limbering up. He began fiddling with his thermos of tea and a small Bible. He used the plastic edge of the Bible's cover to push at a tea stain on the edge of the thermos. He scraped and scraped, oblivious to the others, who cast quick glances at him before turning back to the book.

Mrs. Huang asked us what we thought the chapter meant and then offered her view: "How do we deal with injustice? In the past, people didn't talk about individual responsibility as much. Instead, responsibility was collective. If one person committed a crime, then all people were guilty. Injustice was everyone's duty."

She looked at Wang and ordered us to open the Bible to Romans 9:19–26, and then she read it aloud:

> You will say to me then, "Why does He still find fault? For who has resisted His will?" But indeed, O man, who are you to reply against God? Will the thing formed say to Him who formed it, "Why have You made me like this?" Does not the potter have power over the clay, from the same lump to make one vessel for honor and another for dishonor?

I glanced at the informant. The verse seemed aimed at him in a message of forgiveness: the potter made you, too; we shouldn't judge your dishonor. But Wang Bin wasn't reading. Instead, he kept scraping, scraping, scraping, using the Bible like a scalpel on the stainless steel.

> What if God, wanting to show His wrath and to make His power known, endured with much long suffering the vessels of wrath prepared for destruction, and that He might make known the riches of His glory on the vessels of mercy, which He had prepared beforehand for glory, even us whom He called, not of the Jews only, but also of the Gentiles?

I mulled this over: Was mercy possible? Doomed for destruction, could the informant, the police, the state, be a vehicle for glory? And then we read the final lines of the verse, a message of forgiveness.

As He says also in Hosea:
    "I will call them My people, who were not My people, And her beloved, who was not beloved.
    "And it shall come to pass in the place where it was said to them, 'You are not My people,' There they shall be called sons of the living God."

Guoqing spoke up. He said the readings made him think of China. God permits disasters, such as the earthquakes, or political persecution. One way to honor God was to use these troubles to show goodness through charity.

"During this time, we support the [political prisoners'] family members," he said. "In a way, we can say when the whole world is going backward, we are going forward. Through disaster we get to know ourselves; through disaster we get to know God and we improve ourselves."

He said he had recently talked about this with Wang Yi, who had told him that democracy was not the only solution.

"In the beginning, we counted on our leaders, but later we worshiped democracy, but democracy can't solve all problems. In this world, nothing can be relied on."

The group began speaking quickly, in a jumble of voices.

"Right now prisoners of conscience, including those who have left prison, are in a very bad state."

"Some are mentally disordered after getting out of jail."

"One prisoner told me, we don't really need the money. We need love."

Wang Bin kept silent. His fingernails were already bitten to nubs. He began using his pen to poke at the end of his left index finger. Soon it was covered with little dots. He jabbed, while the people spoke around him.

"One of them is a gambler. He's playing mahjong!"

"We need to tell him that gambling isn't good. I know he's not a Christian, but it's not good for anyone."

"But you can't cut him off, because he's a gambler. It's a sickness."

"Look at it this way, we're paying welfare to one of our members. She gets 600 yuan a month from us. But we're giving a non-Christian gambler 1,200 a month. Some people in the congregation might ask why we're doing that."

"These people are in a difficult situation. They're under incredible pressures. It's a question of love, like what we just read."

The last sentence was spoken by Guoqing, who then started to talk about his favorite topic: how Chinese politics were about to enter an era of reform. A party congress was coming later this year. The government was easing off. He was sure of it.

Finally, the informant spoke. Wang Bin's face was pockmarked and jowly, but his voice was cold, clear, precise, logical—the most rational in the room: "This is not reasonable. Yesterday more than one thousand police from Mianyang captured petitioners in Beichuan; the day before yesterday, several hundred police captured petitioners in another place. Why do you say that reforms are coming? This is just hope, not logic."

Guoqing was taken aback but kept his optimistic line.

"There is a saying that there might be a surprise redefinition of the June 4 incident," he said, citing an eternal hope by Chinese reformers that the 1989 protests would be declared patriotic and not counter-revolutionary, a revision that people hoped would signal political reform. "Overall, the political atmosphere in China is better."

The informant snickered. "There are more prisoners of conscience. That is an objective fact."

The group grew quiet, and then Mrs. Huang adjourned the session for another month. Everyone got up and cast quick glances at Wang Bin. He remained seated, cleaning his fingernails with the edge of the Bible and shaking his head in disgust.

12

Beijing: Ascending the Mountain

People often say that Chinese look backward, dragged into the past by their thousands of years of history. But in daily life, people are impatient, arriving early at events as if to force the future to arrive sooner. Today was the thirtieth day of the third lunar month, which made tomorrow the first day of the fourth lunar month, the start of the Miaofengshan pilgrimage. But the truly pious never arrive then. They know that the best time to make the pilgrimage is tonight, the first night—the eve of the event. Today they could savor the moments until the clock struck midnight, the month turned, and the moon was at its darkest. Only then would the ceremony make the most sense: as a progress from dark to light, ending fifteen days later with a full moon and life renewed.

Jincheng had told me this from his hospital room—arrive early, he had commanded—but I made the mistake of thinking that 4:00 p.m. was early for a midnight event. It wasn't. The parking lots were already full. Cars that had come later were parked haphazardly on both sides of the road, strewn like spent rocket boosters floating in Beijing's powerful orbit. Men with security armbands ordered people to ditch their cars, but I pointed to a backseat full of supplies and said I was with the Whole Heart Philanthropic Salvation Tea Association. The words had a talismanic effect. The guards let me through, and I soared up to the accordion gate at the main entrance.

The temple complex was small, perched on a tiny plateau like an observatory up to the heavens, or down to the city below. I walked along a path that widened after one hundred yards to a small square with a large pine tree in the middle and a giant stone with the words "Origin of Fate" inscribed on it. Beyond it was the final, small rise holding the temple to Our Lady of the Azure Clouds. Off to the left was a row of one-story buildings: the home of the pilgrimage associations that would spend the entire fifteen days up here, offering tea, rice porridge, beans, and steamed buns.

In front of the first building, a group of men sat around a card table, drinking tea and making boisterous jokes. As I walked over, I was intercepted by a short, stout woman in a bright red down jacket and a helmet of permed hair.

"My name is Qi. Jincheng gave me a call. He can't make it because of his back. If you need anything, I'm to take care of you. That's the way it will be. Got it?"

I nodded meekly. I had met Qi Huimin before at the Ni household. She had been sitting in a back room with the women when I went in to see Old Mr. Ni, but she was hardly a retiring female of the inner chambers. She smoked the same Great Qianmen cigarettes as the men, and she took nonsense from no one. I quickly figured out she ran the place.

She instructed me to put my bags in the shrine. It was housed in a twenty-foot-long building, built in the traditional Chinese style of gray brick walls on the side and back and a front made of red wooden bay doors. The roof was of curved tiles that jutted out into the air. Out front was a huge oak tree, and beyond that the final rise in the mountain that led up to the goddess's shrine. To one side of the tea association's shrine, and down a small slope, were administrative offices of the complex, as well as a restaurant and toilets. On the other side, up a small rise, were more Chinese-style buildings housing half a dozen other pilgrimage associations and their shrines.

Inside the Ni family's shrine was one of the most unusual altars I had ever seen. It was a wooden table covered in yellow silk and decorated with dozens of porcelain teapots, varying in sizes and shapes, painted with Daoist and Buddhist deities and inscribed with the association's name: Whole Heart Philanthropic Salvation Tea Association. They had been custom-made in the southern city of Jingdezhen, the historic center of China's porcelain industry. They were decorative but so numerous that it was almost impossible to see the yellow silk underneath, as if to say, "Here are people so devout that they will slake the thirst of any number of pilgrims." The teapots surrounded a four-foot bronze statue that normally stood in

Jincheng's shrine atop his house. It was Guanyin, the Buddhist goddess of mercy. Even though Miaofengshan was devoted to a Daoist goddess, this was perfectly normal. They were just different paths up the same mountain. Flowerpots holding big yellow lilies, ceramic censers, and candlestick holders filled the rest of the space—a cornucopia of devotion.

Strung up behind the altar from ceiling to floor was a bolt of yellow silk. Behind it were cots where some of the group members slept at night. Affixed to its front so it hung just above the goddess were four characters, *pu du zhong sheng,* or Universal Salvation. Affixed to the silk screen behind the goddess was an enormous single character: *cha,* or tea.

Mrs. Qi turned on a small box that looked like a vintage transistor radio, except that the round station dial was replaced by an image of Guanyin illuminated with psychedelic swirling lines that blinked on and off. A small digital display showed which holy song was being performed. Mrs. Qi had dialed up "The Great Compassion Mantra," a teaching by Guanyin of about four hundred words. The first line went, "Bow to the noble Lord who looks down, the enlightened sentient being, the great being, the merciful one!" It sounded like this:

na mo a li ye wo lu jie di shuo bo la ye.

This doesn't mean anything in Chinese. It was transliterated phonetically from the Sanskrit and meant to be used as a mantra, to sing or listen to as a way to calm oneself or meditate. It would be as if Jesus's Sermon on the Mount were transliterated phonetically from ancient Greek into English and chanted in order to become compassionate, or perhaps similar to how Catholics and some Protestants sing Kyrie Eleison—Greek for "Lord, have mercy"—sometimes without knowing what it means.

In one corner of the shrine was Mrs. Qi's husband, Chang Guiqing. He had stick-thin arms and legs and a stylish slouch hat over shoulder-length hair. Next to him was a supply of tinned Yanjing beer. As always, one was open in his right hand, which he hoisted at me in greeting.

sa wo sa duo na mo wo sa duo na mo wo jia mo fa te do

The mantra ended, and Mrs. Qi turned it back on.

an xi dian du man duo la ba tuo ye suo wo ha

"This is good for your health. It also helps your family. You can repeat it over and over again."

I asked her how long she had been a believer.

"Since January 1990. I believe in Buddhism. I really believe. I believe in all this," she said, motioning to the altar and the shrine. "But I'm also superstitious!"

I stifled a laugh. She had used the taboo word *mixin*, the one that Chinese governments had used to discredit much religious belief over the past century. But she had used it unassumingly, as if it were another system of belief.

"I do all that stuff. I can read fortunes and tell people how to set up their rooms."

"Fengshui?"

"Yes! I can do all that. I pick the days when people get married and buried. I can do that, absolutely, yes. People say I'm good at superstition."

"Do you think that's superstition? Is it more superstitious than Buddhism?"

"Ahhh," she looked down the pilgrim's road, her face back to its usual scowl. "That's what they call it, superstition. I don't know what it is. It's just what we believe in."

I thought of their little courtyard, the mahjong tiles, the teapots in offering to the goddess, the thick dust, and the musty smell. Was that superstition? It was inseparable from their beliefs. It was their life.

"The key is prayer. You can't skimp on it," she said. "I'm up at 6:00 a.m. and pray. I have sutras I say. You can pray in bed or sitting in a chair. It's up to you. Everyone has their own way. Then in the evening, maybe for another couple of hours, sometimes just listening while cleaning up. That's what works."

"And your children?"

"My son didn't believe, but he's starting. He's coming up this year for the first time. He's had some problems and wants to start doing this. We'll see if he's suitable for it."

The shrine was filling up with relatives, friends, and colleagues who supported the tea shrine and donated money. Many had brought along newcomers curious about the pilgrimage. I asked one woman if she believed.

"I guess I do," she said slowly. "I don't know. I'm still working things out. I know there's something bigger than us that guides us. I heard about Miaofengshan from my husband's friends, and we thought it would be interesting to come here. I want to learn about this."

Mrs. Qi sat next to her, nodding and puffing on a Great Qian-men cigarette. It was now 10:00 p.m., and the midnight ceremony was drawing nearer. Easter and Qingming were two weeks past, so we were now on the first day of a new solar term: Grain Rain. As if on cue, a rain cloud had enveloped the mountain in a cozy mantle. The tea association's shrine was lit up by small halogen lamps mounted on the eaves of the buildings. In front of us was an open area and beyond it the road leading up to the main temple and down to the parking lot. The path was marked by more lights, but the mist turned them into blurry halos. Our world seemed to shrink to this one peak, this one evening.

Slowly, ordinary pilgrims arrived. They were not members of the associations that performed or set up shrines like the Ni family's, but in terms of numbers they were in the majority; thousands of them would arrive tonight to pay respect to the goddess. The better connected drove cars up through the main entrance, using their *guanxi* to get past the guards. Most arrived by car or bus in the village below and walked up. People piled into the temple, holding long sticks of incense. Many made their way straight up to the temple to get their prayer in before the midnight crowd and eventually found their way down to the shrines donating free food and drink, like the Ni family's. One of the family members sat next to the censer and hit the bronze bowl with the small wooden mallet. It rang out constantly, punctuating the rain and the music, tolling across the small square.

A letup in the rain allowed Mrs. Qi to make her own offering. She lit a dozen foot-long sticks of incense, pressing them tightly together so they flamed up and formed a small torch. She clasped the bundle in her two hands and planted it on her forehead, the burning ends pointing outward and flaming like a holy fire. She bowed three times. The sticks burned quickly, and glowing embers began breaking off. She paid no heed. Suddenly she twirled with surprising dexterity, stopping at each of the four cardinal directions to bow, before dunking the fiery offering in the censer. Others from the family now began to do their duty too and light incense, but none were as imposing as Mrs. Qi. Her obeisance seemed to mark the real start of the pilgrimage.

Around eleven, we were joined by Wang Defeng, the stocky manager of the temple. He had the powerful, ruddy look of a local farmer but had a detailed and sophisticated understanding of Miaofengshan's history that was the match of any scholar's. Toward the pilgrims he cultivated a fatherly attitude, often admonishing them for not cooperating better as they shared this small outcrop overlooking Beijing.

Wang had been a local Communist Party official sent to help rebuild the temple in 1986 as part of the effort to roll back some of the destruction caused in the Cultural Revolution. When pilgrimage associations heard the news, they quickly began to form again and in 1990 made the first ascent in decades. In 1993, the local government created a state-owned tourism company and listed it on the stock market. Its revenues came from gate receipts of all the temples in western Beijing, including Miaofengshan. It charged 40 yuan, or about $7, for entry.

Many of the pilgrimage associations might have rejected Miaofengshan at this point. People like Old Mr. Ni, for example, forbade worshipping at commercialized temples. But it was a tribute to Mr. Wang that he kept the pilgrimage going. He cultivated ties with all the groups—visiting Old Mr. Ni on the second day of the Lunar New Year, for example—and he understood their prickly pride. He invited them to the temple and waived the entrance fee. Counterintuitively, he also won them over by not offering them money. Pilgrimages are also called temple fairs, and over time the commercial connotation of that term has come to dominate. Some give performing groups money to appear, hoping to attract more visitors, who pay entrance fees and buy concessions. Not Mr. Wang. The performing groups did not have to pay to enter the temple grounds, but that was it. They got no money to perform and nothing to offset their transportation costs. Instead, he offered something better: the honor of participating in Beijing's most famous pilgrimage. That guaranteed that those who came were not after material gain. At the end of their journey, the associations took home a pennant, and that was all, but it became a coveted sign of being a real, respected pilgrimage association.

Now sixty-one, Mr. Wang was a year past the official retirement age but had been asked by the government to stay on; everyone thought he was indispensable.

Tonight he was again the diplomat, making the rounds to touch base and receive the associations' thanks for having organized the temple fair with such grace. He had been plied with enormous amounts of liquor by the time he showed up at the Ni family's altar. But the fair's imminent opening did not seem to make him happy. His weather-beaten face was flushed as he turned to me and talked for a few minutes.

"You guys—I don't mean you foreigners—but you academics and writers and researchers and journalists, I don't have time for you. You come here and take something that will make you famous and then you leave. But what about me? I'm sixty-one this year and came up here in 1986 to rebuild the temple. But what do I have to show for it? I'm not corrupt, so I don't have money, I don't have a car, and I don't even have an apartment. What has this brought me?"

"Everyone respects you and says it's the best temple fair in Beijing."

"It's true that when they talk about Miaofengshan, they say this," he said, sticking his thumb up in the air, "and don't say this," sticking out his little finger. "I do it for Our Lady. That's my service, to make sure she is respected properly."

"You're a Communist Party official," I said delicately.

"That's right. I am a materialist," he said. Then he tried to explain.

"My faith is here," he said, touching the center of his chest, symbolizing the Confucian ideal of the golden mean. "It's not here," he said touching his heart. He meant that his job was to make sure that the pilgrimage in honor of Our Lady of the Azure Clouds was run properly. That was his duty. And yet, of course, this form of righteousness has been a Chinese ideal since at least Confucius's time twenty-five centuries ago. The amount of effort far exceeded what any person would normally put into a job. At the very least, this was his passion, his life's calling. Others might call it faith.

"It's hard to explain all this to higher-ups," he said. "They don't get it. They ask how many are showing up, and I say, 'With folk believers, you can't be so exact.' They come or they don't come. It's not so clear why or when. Everyone wants exact numbers, but it's not like that."

Wang Defeng moved on to another pilgrimage association to complete the evening of toasts. Our small hall was getting crowded. The men looked like sports fans dressed up for a big game, each cultivating an eccentricity. Mr. Chang had his shoulder-length hair and slouch hat. At one stage, a man came in with a bagful of fedoras and handed them out. It was just an idea he had: let's wear fedoras. And so for this evening, we all did.

I wandered the grounds, stopping at one pilgrimage association that offered free *mantou*—steamed buns. A red sign announced plans for how many buns would be donated each day. Tomorrow, the first day, would be the busiest, with six thousand pounds of buns donated. The group had been founded by Beijingers more than one hundred years ago but was now being run by businesspeople from Taizhou, a coastal city south of Shanghai—about a thousand miles away from Beijing.

"We've been doing business in Beijing for a while and heard about this association," said Mr. Bai, one of the partners. "The person who had founded it had died, and it was going to close because his children weren't interested. We thought, what a pity to allow this tradition to die, so we banded together to keep it going."

As he spoke, a minivan pulled up and people began unloading huge bags of *mantou*, which were stored behind an altar similar to the Ni family's.

"In the past, pilgrims were hungry, so the associations offered food. But now everyone can eat enough," Mr. Bai said. "So we do it for health and happiness. The *mantou* are blessed by the prayer and make you blessed if you eat them."

Back in the Ni family shrine, a tall, striking man was sitting at a folding table, writing names on a five-foot-long sheet of bright red paper. He was in his early fifties, with a shaved head and long graying muttonchops that met under his chin, making him look a bit like a bald Amish man. His clothes, though, were working-class hipster: a wicker driving cap with swirly zebra stripes, jeans, and a black leather jacket. Two thick stone signet rings adorned his hands, and his right wrist was encircled with a bracelet of camphor beads.

It was Ni Jintang, the younger brother of my friend Jincheng. He looked and acted very much like his brother: strong, gruff, and prone to outrageous comments. But he was more at ease in social situations; people gravitated to him, and even before his father's incapacitation he and Mrs. Qi had been quietly assuming a bigger role in the pilgrimage association. Jincheng might have felt that as the older son he was responsible for keeping it running, but he was happiest in his private shrine on the roof of his house. Organizing the chaos of the first night of a pilgrimage was not for him; for Jintang, it was something he eagerly awaited.

He had spent most of the past hour on one of the association's most important tasks: writing the names of all the group's members, friends, donors, and pious individuals on the paper. He wielded a traditional writing brush expertly, calling out to Mrs. Qi occasionally to confirm a name. He was almost finished. He had affixed the seal of the tea association at the bottom but needed another chop—that of a steamed-bun association run by Zhang Baojing. He was an old family friend who every year donated several thousand *mantou*. Mr. Zhang did not have the money to run his own shrine like the wealthy Taizhou business owners, but Old Mr. Ni had taken him under his wing and allowed him to set up a card table outside the family shrine and hand out buns on the first day of the temple fair. The old man had also always made sure that Mr. Zhang's seal was affixed to the paper that would be burned at midnight, to make sure the goddess knew of his charity. But with an hour to go, Mr. Zhang was missing in action.

Jintang rolled up the sheet of paper and stuffed it in his pocket, muttering to himself. He headed for a small building in a back corner of the temple grounds. It was a dorm that at this hour should have been empty, but his instincts were right: Mr. Zhang was there, passed out on a cot. He was wearing a red silk padded jacket and baggy black trousers, but his outfit was slightly stained with food and drink. Jintang pushed his shoulder, and Mr. Zhang awoke, groggily rolling off the bed and onto his feet. "We need the chop, hurry up," Jintang said, pushing the red bundle of paper in front of Mr. Zhang.

Mr. Zhang sat down at a table to affix his association's seal to the holy document. But suddenly time seemed to slow down into a painful sluggishness. He moved his enormous hands clumsily, as if controlling them from a wire.

"I've got to make the envelope first," Mr. Zhang said. He had started this project hours ago and was determined to finish it. It was an envelope to hold the sacred red paper with the signatures. He clutched a paste-it stick and tried to guide it over the edge of a sheet of half-folded yellow paper. But he couldn't get his hands to follow his brain's commands. The glue zigzagged across the paper. Mr. Zhang stared at the mess he was making.

"The seal," Jintang said. "Forget the envelope. We've got envelopes. We need your association's seal."

Mr. Zhang checked his pockets. It should have been easy to find: a seal, or chop, is a piece of stone with a name carved on the bottom. He was supposed to dab it in ink and stamp the letter. He searched the same pockets over and over, always coming up empty. It was infuriating. Finally, Jintang exploded.

"What the fuck is wrong with you! Are you out of your mind? You don't have the chop? Where is the chop? We've always had your damned chop on the paper."

Mr. Zhang mumbled something about having misplaced it or that it was in a bag but he wasn't sure where.

"Find it!" Jintang roared, his eyes bulging like a door god's. "You good-for-nothing nincompoop! It's just this one task you have to do and you can't do it! That's enough. That's fine. Stop. I can't watch this.

"You people from Daxing, shit, what's wrong with you? You're good for nothing. You lost the seal. You can't find this. You misplaced that. I can't believe our families were neighbors."

He rumbled on, his anger like a straw fire that everyone knew would soon be out.

"You're going too far," Mr. Zhang said in his slur. "You, you, you." But he couldn't really get angry with Jintang and went back to folding the envelope. Jintang got up to take a walk.

Another man came in and sat down. He stared at me with mock hilarity. A foreigner. He wanted to make sure I understood what was going on tonight.

"This is culture," he said, drawing out the word. "C-u-l-t-u-r-e. This is not religion. This is not politics. Got it?"

Mr. Zhang looked up and mumbled something, then put his head down on the desk to take a nap.

"Okay," I said.

"This is culture. It's also not politics. You get this. We aren't doing politics here! I'm not Bo Xilai and you're not Wu De."

Bo Xilai was the disgraced former member of the Politburo, but who was Wu De? I asked him.

"You're a foreigner. It must mean something to you. Wu De. You must have heard of him. He's a foreigner. He's English. Dead. Wu De is dead."

Wu De. Wood. Neil Heywood, the man poisoned to death by Bo Xilai's wife, a big scandal at the time.

"I am not Bo Xilai, and you're not Wu De! Got it! Ha-ha, I'm not Bo, and you're not Wu! I won't kill you! We're friends! Friends!"

"SHUT UP!"

Jintang had returned.

"What are you doing here, babbling like an idiot? What will foreigners think of us if we act like this? Act seriously, please."

"I'm just telling him this is cul-ture, not religion."

"Get out of here. We're going to see Our Lady."

Mrs. Qi walked by ringing a little bell. It was time to leave. Jintang snatched the half-finished envelope from Mr. Zhang's clumsy hands and told him he'd finish it. "Let's go."

We walked back to the tea association altar, Mr. Zhang stumbling behind us mumbling. "I'm . . . You're too fast . . . This isn't fair . . . The envelope isn't finished . . ."

Mrs. Qi lit more incense. Jintang folded the envelope quickly and stuffed the bulky red paper inside, without Mr. Zhang's seal. It was now almost midnight, and everyone headed up the path to the peak. The temple loomed on a promontory, its red walls descending to meet us as we walked up.

A broad staircase led us up the final incline. It was jammed with people trying to get in at midnight. The temple itself wasn't big: one courtyard with buildings on its four sides. The yard was filled with people and a giant incense pot. People pushed forward to toss bundles of incense in it; unlike on a normal day, there was no way to carefully place incense sticks or kowtow on the kneeler in front. In fact, the steel container was so stuffed with incense that staff wearing masks and wielding metal rakes pulled the overflowing bundles off the top so they would fall behind it to an area on the stone floor that they had cordoned off.

It was crowded but orderly, and the Ni family's representatives made their way toward the cauldron, Mr. Zhang trailing by a few feet. Jintang quickly tossed the envelope with the names into the fire, which consumed it in a matter of seconds. He watched to make sure it was gone and the names on their way up to heaven, then he made his way back toward the entrance to survey the fiery scene.

Mr. Zhang stayed a bit longer, staring, his mouth open, almost frozen in place. The paper didn't have his chop on it; would the goddess know that he was here again and had donated a few thousand steamed buns? Then he thought, but she knows everything. But then he thought, what she cares about most is sincerity. That was the important question: Was he sincere?

It was now well after midnight, and a long night stretched ahead. Back down at our shrine, some of the Ni family's friends were sitting half-asleep on chairs, while others played cards doggedly, hoping the time would go faster until dawn. People would arrive all night, although the real crowds would pick up again around 6:00 a.m.

I looked inside and saw Mr. Chang, seemingly bound to his chair. He croaked a greeting and raised his tin of Yanjing beer.

"What are you doing up?" I asked him.

"The old man couldn't make it," Mr. Chang said, referring to Old Mr. Ni, ill in bed back in Beijing. "It's my vow. I'm keeping watch through the night."

For millennia, Chinese have revered mountains as intersections of heaven and earth. The kings of China's first recorded dynasty, the Shang, offered sacrifices to *yue*, a mountain, probably Mount Song in central China. *The Rites of the Zhou*, a classic from the third century B.C.E., lists five holy mountains that match the five cardinal directions in Chinese geomancy: Mount Tai to the east, the birthplace of the goddess worshipped on Miaofengshan; Mount Hua in the west; Mount Song in the center; Mount Heng in the south; and another Mount Heng in the north, the mountain that the Li family took as the name for their Daoist music group. Over time, these five imperial mountains were supplemented with innumerable other mountains around China. From places that themselves deserved worship, the mountains became abodes of the immortals, or the sites of Buddhist and Daoist temples. They were places of serious contemplation. As the fourth-century Daoist Ge Hong put it, "Never enter lightly into the mountains."

From the eighth or ninth century onward, pilgrimages to sacred mountains became popular among all social classes. Mountains were so linked to pilgrimages that the term for going on any pilgrimage is *chaoshan jinxiang:* "paying respects to the mountain and presenting incense." With time, the idea became overriding; holy places were called mountains regardless of their shape. One of China's most popular Buddhist pilgrimage sites, for example, is Mount Putuo near Shanghai—a rocky island barely above sea level.

Miaofengshan lies at the start of the Taihang Mountains, the rugged chain of mountains that runs down to central China. Its highest point is only 4,235 feet above sea level, and the actual height from the village at its foot is about 1,000 feet. If you park in the village below and walk up "the path of a thousand elbows," the climb is easily done in forty-five minutes. Miaofengshan's history is equally short. But since its first recorded pilgrimage in 1689, the mountain has become one of China's most famous. One reason is that its chief deity, Our Lady of the Azure Clouds, is one of the most popular goddesses in northern China. She is often simply called *Songzi Niangniang*, or the Goddess Who Gives Children, a kind of fertility goddess, but also an important part of the Daoist pantheon. In years past, Beijing had eight major temples devoted to her: the five peaks and the three mountains. The five peaks were small temples in the city's north, south, east, west, and center. The three mountains were located in Beijing's suburbs. Two, Yajishan and Tiantaishan, were favored by the imperial court. Miaofengshan was reserved for the common people.

Miaofengshan's location near Beijing also helped spread its fame, linking it to the imperial family and the city's vibrant cultural life. Stone steles record visits by pilgrimage associations in the eighteenth, nineteenth, and twentieth centuries. By the mid-nineteenth century, records show that entertainer organizations began climbing the mountain. The peak might have been 1899. A stele from that year records that the mountain was visited by 141 associations.

By the twentieth century, Miaofengshan had become something else: a site for academic pilgrimages. In the 1920s, Gu Jiegang, a young scholar of early Chinese history, and other iconoclastic intellectuals helped found folklore studies in China. Miaofengshan became a prime location for their research. For people like Gu, folk traditions like Miaofengshan's were authentic history compared with the official histories compiled by dynasties and recited by generations of Chinese schoolchildren. Folk practices were seen as "living fossils" that showed modern people how the past used to be organized— a wildly romantic view of the past, especially for a pilgrimage that was only a couple of centuries old. Gu made several trips to Miaofengshan and wrote the first of dozens of books about the mountain published through the years.

Foreigners, such as Sidney D. Gamble (of the Procter & Gamble family), visited China to carry out sociological surveys. Gamble made an astonishing fifteen-minute film from footage shot during three visits he made to Miaofengshan between 1924 and 1927. The scenes seem out of another era: one man is encased in an instrument of punishment called a *cangue*—a wooden board with holes for the hands and head—while another is walking on all fours like a horse, his back saddled. While these scenes no longer exist, the rest of Gamble's report seems very similar to today. He said that over one hundred pilgrimage associations attended, including associations providing services, such as food and drink—like the Ni family's tea association today—and other groups that performed for Our Lady: walking on stilts, martial arts, dancing lions, and others.

Then as now, the associations were self-organized and self-funded—autonomous organizations largely independent of government control, as most religious life had been through Chinese history.

In May 1938, *The New York Times* picked up on the remarkable pilgrimage, writing, "The Canterbury pilgrimage of Chaucer's tales has a Chinese counterpart in the annual pilgrimage held this month up the slopes of Miao Feng Shan, some seventeen miles north of Peiping." The new Japanese occupation of northern China did not seem to dampen the pilgrims' ardor; on the contrary, the *Times* reported that the Japanese organized militias to protect the pilgrims from bandits.

Two of Gamble's friends were L. Carrington Goodrich and his wife, Anne, both children of missionaries. Carrington went on to a distinguished career as a professor at Columbia University, while Anne became an excellent amateur anthropologist. In 1998, at the age of 103, she published an account of their visit to Miaofengshan in 1931. According to information she gathered at the time, roughly half a million pilgrims visited Miaofengshan that year. After walking up the mountain with another couple, she and her husband took a tiny guest room in the temple.

> *The temple guest rooms were small, holding not more than a camp cot. They were on a terrace at the very edge of the high cliff which presented one with a glorious view of the mountains and the plain to Peking. To wake up there before sunrise and look at the clouds snuggling between mountain peaks catching the glow of dawn and the sun turning the clouds crimson, is an experience that one never forgets.*

Best of all, Goodrich wrote, "before the year was out our friends had a baby girl and my husband and I had twins. Had we pleased the goddess?"

The Ni family's tea shrine groggily awoke at six o'clock the next morning. Mrs. Qi, Jintang, and a few others would spend the full fifteen days up here, but many others had come only for the first night and today's performances; they had tried to get some sleep in their cars or on camping chairs and were now staggering about, looking for tea and congee. Mr. Chang was still in his seat, his slouch hat low on his head, and a tin of Yanjing in his right hand. He squawked a greeting and waved the beer at me.

I waved back but sat down next door at the Deqing Fresh Flower Association. It was adjacent to the Ni family's altar, separated only by a narrow corridor just wide enough to squeeze through, and dedicated to the flower goddess, a folk deity. It was a smaller shrine, with plates holding stacks of biscuits and fruits, as well as twenty potted poinsettias, hyacinths, and tulips. Instead of a bronze statue, the altar held a small wooden tableau of dark lacquered wood. Inside was a photograph of a woman dressed in traditional costume with flowers in her hair.

Out front was the association's namesake, Chen Deqing, an eighty-six-year-old friend of the Ni family's. She sat on a folding chair, the picture of beauty in old age: a full head of thick silver hair combed back to her shoulders, a red cardigan over a smart blue blouse, and a permanent smile highlighting a full set of white teeth. This was the high point of her year, the culmination of countless hours spent organizing and saving for the pilgrimage.

"You're back," she said to me, and motioned for me to sit next to her and drink a cup of tea. In the 1980s, when she was already in her fifties, Old Mrs. Chen rode her pedal-powered trishaw all the way here from Beijing to deliver flowers to the goddess. The forty-mile ride from her home took her two days, including the last fifteen miles of steep dirt roads when she had to push the cart.

This year, she and her family had spent several thousand dollars on the flowers, the food, and the expense of spending fifteen days on the mountain. She slept on a cot behind the altar, waking at dawn and keeping watch out front. Every time a pilgrim kowtowed to the flower deity, she struck a bronze bowl with a mallet. This was her service to the community. For this period, she was like a priestess, a mediator between heaven and earth. As is usual in most Chinese religion, she had no formal credentials. Instead, she was legitimized by her commitment. This is what gave her the credibility in the worshippers' eyes to carry out this sacred function. Many simply called her a *huofo*, a living Buddha, a person whose piety and devotion were worthy of veneration.

Like many of the people who ran these benevolent associations, Mrs. Chen was a person of few words. I thought of Wang Yi and the self-reflective Christians who produced reams of articles, essays, and books explaining—almost justifying—why they were Christians. Mrs. Chen just did it: she believed in the goddess and made this offering. It reminded me of Stephen Jones, the British academic who publishes books on the folk music of northern Shanxi, including the Li family's rituals. He titled one accompanying DVD *Doing Things*—a perfect description of folk religion. Theory and history were for other people—the academics and writers who loitered and took notes. For real practitioners, actions were what mattered.

There were two kinds of pilgrimage associations: "civilian" (*wen*) and "martial" (*wu*). We were the civilians, sitting in our shrines and offering services for the entire two weeks. The martial groups got their name from the activities they practiced: staff fighting, tossing huge poles with military insignia, sword fighting, and feats of strength. Others danced or offered absurd skits—cross-dressers, mock smokers of opium, or silly monks swinging enormous prayer beads around their necks like hula hoops. No matter, they were all classified as martial groups. Each group had about thirty to forty members, including performers, musicians, and family members. Their arrival was staggered so that at least two or three came each day, with up to a dozen arriving on big days like today, the first day. They arrived early, marshaling in front of the "Origin of Fate" stone.

Old Mrs. Chen still marveled how it all came together, how everyone journeyed here because of the goddess, and how she was a part of it, the Deqing Fresh Flower Association. She looked at me and smiled again, a warmth that needed no words.

In the distance, the martial groups' music—mostly drums and cymbals crashing and banging—filled the air. We watched the first group ascend, a troupe of dancing lions. Almost all were dressed in yellow, holding pennants and flags, with their musicians bringing up the rear as they walked up the path. After performing for the goddess, they would come down to play for us. This was always accompanied by ritual greetings and a handwritten letter of thanks to the associations like the Ni family's that would stay here the entire two weeks. These visits were when Old Mrs. Chen was in her element, bowing and clasping her hands to greet the performers. All the associations knew the story of the old flower lady who used to ride her trishaw all the way from Beijing to worship the goddess. That was how religious life had been reborn in China, by these single, heroic acts.

Every pilgrimage association had similar stories of old men and women who had remembered the past and taught their children and grandchildren how to perform with swords and staffs, to dance on stilts, or to sing old songs. One troupe of women would toss six-foot wooden tridents in the air, catch them on their shoulders, and let them roll down their arms before flicking them aloft again, an amazing display of strength and grace.

Still, everyone agreed that the performances were less impressive than even twenty years ago, let alone in the scenes that Sidney Gamble had captured. Many groups lacked the repertoire. The actions weren't as daring or precise. This isn't surprising: in the modern world, few people have the time to practice staff fighting or stilt walking for hours a day. Rituals have become simplified everywhere, in almost every religion. The key was that the people came, participated, and found a deeper meaning. And as fun as it seemed, for many people it was as profound as Ge Hong's admonishment. It wasn't something they did lightly.

Toward the end of the morning, I was sitting in front of the shrine, drinking the Ni family's tea, and watching the crowds roll by. Mrs. Qi's Buddhist music wafted into the mist. It was a choir simply chanting over and over again, "Homage to the bodhisattva Guanyin," or as it sounded in the Chinese transliteration of the Sanskrit:

Nan Mo Guan Shi Yin Pu Sa

It was one of Chinese religion's most famous chants, and the syllables stretched and stretched out through the rain.

Nan Mo Guan Shi Yin Pu Sa

This was just the first day. Two more weeks remained. My mind wandered over the sacred land, back to Beijing, where Old Mr. Ni

was dying and where his older son, Jincheng, was having back surgery. He would be released tomorrow and in a week make the trip
up the mountain for Guanyin's birthday, which falls on the eighth
day of the month—a highlight in the pilgrimage. A week after that,
it would end. By then, sixty-nine "martial" pilgrimage associations
would have made the trip up, dancing, fighting, twirling, and singing
in honor of Our Lady of the Azure Clouds. The Taizhou merchants
would have doled out 40,200 steamed buns. More than 100,000 people would have visited the mountain: some as pious pilgrims, others
as tourists, most somewhere in between—lighting incense and finding their way.

Nan Mo Guan Shi Yin Pu Sa

In Shanxi, the grain rains meant the Li family's neighbors could
plant their summer crops. In Sichuan, Wang Yi was preparing to train
seminarians in the mysteries of ancient Greek. In the political world,
demons were being purged so the ritual change of power could take
place in the autumn. The clear and bright days were over, and soon
the humid summer would arrive.

Nan Mo Guan Shi Yin Pu Sa

The music went on and on, an endless loop that accompanied the
rain and the pilgrims. Toward the end of the morning, a group of
five people walked up to our shrine. I was sitting next to the censer,
a giant rusting bucket that was smoldering lightly, the incense almost
out. The visitors were in their twenties and thirties, white-collar professionals probably, and I guessed they had driven up for the day.
They stood as if sizing up the building, talking quietly among themselves for a moment until a young man caught my eye.

"What is this building for?" he asked.

"It's a shrine to Guanyin," I answered, "the Buddhist sister of Our
Lady of the Azure Clouds."

They laughed, and I asked if they weren't going to offer incense.

"We didn't bring any," said a bored-looking young woman in an
expensive outdoor jacket, dressed for a hike in the mountains.

Nan Mo Guan Shi Yin Pu Sa

Mrs. Qi stepped out from the shrine. She took a bundle of incense from the family's stack and silently handed it to the young woman. She hesitated and then took it, at the same time pulling a wallet out of her pocket.

"Charity!" Mrs. Qi said brusquely, and the woman looked surprised.

Nan Mo Guan Shi Yin Pu Sa

The young woman stood there with the incense clutched in her left hand. A young man stepped forward, flicked open a metal lighter, and set the bundle alight. The two of them walked to the giant metal pot and tossed the burning sticks in. The smoke poured out, and the couple stood there, uncertain what to do.

"Kowtow," Mrs. Qi said. "Three times. And pray."

"How?" the woman said.

"To kowtow?"

"To pray. What should I say?"

"Say something that's in your heart. Isn't that why you're here? Just say it silently."

The young woman strode up to the kneeler, but when she stood there alone, facing the goddess, her face lost its fixed expression and became softer, as if she were searching for words.

Mrs. Qi picked up the mallet. The young woman gingerly lowered herself to her knees and then prostrated herself for the first kowtow. Mrs. Qi flicked her wrist. The bronze bowl reverberated, and a clear note sounded.

PART IV

SUMMER HARVEST

The six mini-seasons that make up China's summer are about heat and passion, growth and harvest. This duality is symbolized by one of the most important of the summer solar terms, *mangzhong*, a compound word meaning harvest and planting. *Mang* means the ear, or grain-bearing tip of a plant—the period when grains like wheat, barley, and peas already have grain in the ear and must be harvested. *Zhong* means planting, because this is also when autumn crops like maize, sorghum, millet, and soybeans must be put in the ground; any later, and they won't be ripe before the autumn frosts. This time in early June is so important that until recently even city people could ask for time off work to go back to their homes in the countryside to help out.

Now the earth is seventy-five degrees on the plane around the sun, and the next solar terms mark the height of summer: *xiazhi*, or Summer Solstice in late June, when the days are the longest, and then Little Heat and Big Heat in July. By then the hottest days are already past, and even if it does seem early, the next solar term is Autumn Commences in early August.

The summer is home to two of the year's most colorful festivals. One is the lunar calendar's second festival of the dead, the Hungry Ghosts Festival, which falls on the fifteenth day of the seventh month, usually in August, when people who died unhappily have to be placated so they do not wander the world and bother the living. The other big festival is *Duanwu*, or the Dragon Boat Festival, the second festival of the living—the others are the Lunar New Year and the Mid-autumn Festival. *Duanwu* celebrates the life of the fourth-century B.C.E. poet and statesman Qu Yuan. But like most holidays in China, death is part of the story. Qu was disgusted with his government, spoke up against misrule, and eventually committed suicide; the dragon boats are often said to be searching for his corpse.

Qu Yuan also left one of the most important bodies of poetry in China, especially "On Encountering Trouble," an autobiographical poem that tells of his frustrations with politics and describes shamanistic encounters with mythic beings. In this excerpt, he invokes the lush vegetation south of the Yangtze as an allegory for his disappointment and concern for his country's future:

> I had tended many an acre of orchids,
> And planted a hundred rods of melilots;
> I had raised sweet lichens and the cart-halting flower,
> And asarum mingled with fragrant angelica,
> And hoped that when leaf and stem were in fullest bloom,
> When the time had come, I could reap a fine harvest.
> Though famine should pinch me, it is small matter:
> But I grieve that all my blossoms should waste in rankweeds.

13

Chengdu: Recitation

arly one Friday morning in July, Wang Yi was leading a prayer group of twenty men and women. We sat in a circle, in the open area in front of his office, rubber mats cushioning us from the tiled floor. Some squatted, others knelt, a few crouched on all fours. It felt like a team meeting before a football game, with the players psyching themselves up by forming a primordial circle, heads pointing toward the center. We belted out an old Presbyterian hymn, sweating out the lyrics in the muggy Chengdu smog. As usual, we sang all the verses; there were never any shortcuts in Wang Yi's church. Then we repeated the first verse, which in English reads,

> Beneath the cross of Jesus I fain would take my stand,
> The shadow of a mighty rock within a weary land;
> A home within the wilderness, a rest upon the way,
> From the burning of the noontide heat, and the burden of the day.

"This was a time before air-conditioning and before electric fans, but this was a way to keep cool!" Wang Yi joked as we wiped our brows and sat down on the mats. Then we read aloud an excerpt from Matthew, explaining how to pray:

> And when thou prayest, thou shalt not be as the hypocrites are: for they love to pray standing in the synagogues and in the corners of the streets, that they may be seen of men.

Wang Yi noted that the message was not to pray in a showy fashion. This was common in many Chinese churches, where people prayed aloud, as if they wanted their neighbors to hear their sins and hopes. Wang Yi didn't like this. To him, it wasn't proper—certainly not the way it was done in the overseas churches he took as a model.

"Small children pray aloud, but as we mature, we pray silently," he said as everyone nodded. "It's also less boastful. It's between you and God."

We sang another hymn and prayed again, and despite Matthew's admonition, everyone spoke out their prayers in turn. It was as if they needed to make their views clear—*biaotai* in Chinese, a way to show you are part of the group. Some wished that today would be successful, others that they would be diligent. All hoped that the Bible would enter their hearts. Then more public prayer, this time everyone speaking together like a swarm of bees.

"I have been unfaithful; make me more faithful."
"Open my heart."
"Make me a better person."
"Stop me from sinning."

The group was mostly men, clean-cut professionals in their forties. We focused on Wang Yi, his charisma and logical arguments holding us despite the heat and discomfort. After all, we were here because of his latest daring move: opening a seminary to train house church pastors.

It was an audacious step. China's State Administration for Religious Affairs runs not only the country's churches, temples, and mosques but also its seminaries. It determines who gets to be a priest, monk, nun, or imam. It sets the curriculum. It decides what version of a religion's history is taught, which ceremonies are acceptable, and which are "superstitious"—that vague, almost meaningless word used over the past century in China to discredit other people's beliefs. And, of course, the government also inserts political courses in the training programs so the clergy of all faiths know the latest slogans. In some ways, it was useful for religious professionals to know the party's latest policy lines, but the training often turned them into government parrots. This was especially true in churches, where sermons are so important. In government-run churches, pastors and priests studiously avoid problems in society, delivering at best bland homilies. Churches like Early Rain offered an alternative—a mighty rock offering shade from the noontide heat.

Friday's classes in the seminary were given over to biblical Greek. The students were using an up-to-date Western primer, *Basics of Biblical Greek,* translated into Chinese and published in Hong Kong. The goal was to read the Gospels in the original Greek. But the room was full of doubting Thomases. Some still hadn't really mastered the Greek alphabet, while most seemed flummoxed by the endings attached to nouns.

"We understand the idea, but we can't memorize all of this," one of the students called out to much laughter.

"You've been learning a lot of practical things, like how to form a church or a council, but this is important, too," the teacher said. "This is your chance to read the Gospels in their original language." That reminder silenced the students, and they focused on the grammar. He summarized, saying that Greek had twenty-four letters and nouns with three possible genders: male, female, or neuter. Some people began to doze.

Sitting up in the front row were Wang Yi and his wife, Jiang Rong. They sat quietly, exchanging the occasional glance, former childhood sweethearts still in love. Later that year, Wang Yi would write, "Twenty years ago, I had a dream. I hoped that in class the teacher would suddenly say, 'Wang Yi, go over and sit together with Jiang Rong.' God is so great. He has allowed my wife to become my desk mate in His own time, making the hope for my first love come true."

Love was at the center of today's class. The teacher wrote the word for unconditional love, *agapē.* The students wrote out the root "agap" and the endings. Then the teacher did the same for "word," or *logos,* as in the word of God.

The two dozen students wrote out the declensions, faces pressed close to their notebooks as they struggled with the foreign letters. About half of the students were from Chengdu, including Early Rain church members who wanted to improve their knowledge of Christianity. The rest came from other parts of China—some as far away as the east coast. Over the next year, they would attend courses that lasted four to six weeks and teach them theology, history, and organizational skills. Most were in their forties or fifties, about three-quarters men, almost all sent by their congregations. Today's class might seem impossibly difficult, but they at least wanted to be able to use the word *agapē* in a sermon, and I recognized the same sense of wonder I had when I had picked my way through my first classical Chinese poem. But to them this was much more important; it wasn't just a window to a different culture but the language used to record God's word.

During a break, I talked to a student from Fuyang, a city in a poorer part of China's otherwise affluent east coast. Forty-five years old, he had converted twenty years earlier and become active in his local church. His skin was still darkened by years in the field, even though he had moved to the town a decade ago along with many able-bodied men and women to look for work. He was dressed in a polo shirt and jeans, and everything about him was unremarkable—a man one might see hundreds of times each day in a Chinese city.

"The countryside is emptying out," he said as we sat in Early Rain's main hall of worship, a converted conference room with a big cross on the far wall. "There's just old people and kids left, so the church's work is in the city.

"But people are changing now. It used to be charismatics who ran the churches in the villages, but people are not so satisfied with that. They want more content."

That led his congregation of about sixty to sponsor his three-year study. Costs were minimal: he took an old, slow train to get here, and a local Christian family provided room and board. Tuition and books cost about $1,000 a semester, and he survived on about $100 a month in spending money, enough for buses and maybe the occasional bowl of noodles when studying late. Next month he would head back to Fuyang and spend two months there on self-study and helping in the congregation as an assistant to the pastor.

"It seems a long way off," he said with a laugh, "but in a few years I'll probably have my own congregation, and hopefully I can teach some of these ideas."

Earlier this week, the seminary had offered a class that seemed more practical: Church Planting. It was taught by two teachers from New York, who used a dozen books translated from English, including *Church Planter's Toolkit*, *Indigenous Church Planting*, *Planting Churches*

Cross-Culturally, Starting a New Church, Church Planting Landmines, Planting Missional Churches, and *Churches That Multiply.*

Church planting was one of the hottest topics among Christians in China, and one that directly affected Early Rain. The church was already overflowing, and its leaders were beginning to discuss planting a new church elsewhere in Chengdu. The technique had been tried around the world: find a part of town that needs a church, and send a core group of reliable members there to start services. People coming to the old church from that part of town would begin to go there too and possibly start bringing friends. If done properly, a new church would take root.

I wondered what the seasons are for planting a new church. How does it take root? Right now, the soil did not feel fertile. A party congress was coming up, and the government was putting its resources behind China's traditional religions, not Christianity, as well as tightening social control. But as Wang Yi had said to me at Easter, the Chinese political calendar was always full of sensitive dates and anniversaries; here at the grass roots, these events faded, and life unfolded according to more lasting rhythms.

After the Greek class ended, Wang Yi and I had a simple boxed lunch of rice with stir-fried vegetables—the same quick, $1 meal that the students were wolfing down. What we had just experienced— the prayer meeting and then learning the abstruse rules of ancient Greek—seemed so far removed from Wang Yi's previous life as a human rights lawyer. I wondered if there was a direct link. People like the filmmaker Yuan Zhiming had converted directly after the failed democracy uprising of 1989; was this his catalyst, too?

"June 4, from my perspective, destroyed the Communist Party's position in society, so I became a believer in freedom," he said. "I thought that freedom was the most important thing in society."

"So you felt that without Christianity, political reform would not occur?"

"It's not a question of achieving political aims. If you believe in a God above and in the passing of life, and if you believe in an eternal soul, then what matters here is not crucial. Of course we wish for a free, democratic system. We think it fits the Bible better, but having a democratic society isn't the key. If God wishes it, he can make his people live in a nondemocratic society. He can still love these people and care for them. What matters is the freedom in your heart."

"So it's not about politics?"

"No, it's about knowing the word of God."

It was 12:30 and time for the midday break. Wang Yi would spend the afternoon studying more ancient Greek. I went back to a little hostel where I kept a room and checked my messages. One was from an old friend of Wang Yi's, the exiled writer Liao Yiwu. He was also from Sichuan and had written about Christianity in Yunnanese hill tribes. But Liao hadn't converted and had later found his freedom by walking across the mountains to Vietnam. He now lived in Germany with his new wife and young daughter. But he was still involved in the daily battles for political freedom that concerned Ran Yunfei and other activists and that were once the center of Wang Yi's life.

Liao was reminding the world that the trial of Li Bifeng, another Sichuan writer and activist, was starting soon. In years past, Wang Yi might have championed Li Bifeng, perhaps even defending him in court. But now he was silent. In fact, he rarely met his politically active friends like Ran Yunfei, focusing instead on Early Rain.

One day during a trip to Washington, I had met another one of Wang Yi's old friends, Yu Jie. He had converted Wang Yi in 2005 and now lived in the United States. Unlike Wang Yi, Yu had not founded a congregation. Instead, he remained closely attuned to politics, authoring a biography of the jailed Nobel laureate, Liu Xiaobo, and criticizing Chinese political problems. A young, severe man, Yu spoke carefully but forthrightly.

"God has chosen Wang Yi to be a pastor, but on the other hand I regret that he's no longer that much of a public intellectual, a writer, or a legal thinker. He's written a lot less than in the past. He has a lot of concrete work in the congregation that takes his time. I hope in the future, when the congregation is more mature, that he has more assistants who can run the congregation and allow him time to think."

Perhaps one day Wang Yi would become politically active again, but I thought of it from another perspective too: As a public intellectual in a repressive state like China, what could Wang Yi really achieve through activism? House arrest and a blocked Internet connection? An appeal to free Li Bifeng that no one would see? As a pastor and seminary teacher, Wang Yi could influence hundreds of people and help plant congregations across the country. At the very least, here he was creating his own society—a tiny cosmos of order and justice in the middle of one of China's largest cities.

One of Chengdu's holiest spots is the Palace of the Bronze Ram, a well-preserved Daoist temple with a lively teahouse under a canopy of trees. I always imagined that the temple would be best appreciated there, drinking a cup of green tea and contemplating the Dao under the old oaks. Unfortunately, the experience usually ended up being something more like this: You went to the counter to buy tea. No one was there. You waited. A grumpy old lady appeared and ignored you. When you finally attracted her attention, she said she wasn't responsible for whatever it is you wanted. Finally, you located someone in charge, usually another grumpy old lady who grunted out answers. She flung the cup, saucer, and a packet of tea. You wandered the grounds for fifteen minutes, trying to find an empty chair; there were plenty, but people invariably claimed they were reserved for someone else. When you finally sat down, the man pouring the water almost never arrived. After an hour, you'd wish a Daoist Jesus would drive these money changers out of the temple.

One Saturday I stopped by to attend a course on Daoist massage, or *tuina,* offered by the temple's Laozi Zhuangzi Academy, a public education center started two years earlier. It was part of an effort by Daoist temples to appeal to the better-educated urban class, many of whom were attracted to churches like Wang Yi's. In the past, Daoist temples were secretive and rarely open to the public. And when they were, it was just to offer their halls as places to burn incense or perhaps have one's fortune told. Ceremonies, scriptures, or the ideas behind Daoism—all of this was kept a mystery. Today's event was an effort to claim ownership of traditional Chinese healing arts, some of which originated with Daoist ideas about the cosmos and the human body. In the Communist era, they had been stripped away from religion, which left many Chinese wondering what Daoism was all about—what had it contributed to Chinese culture? Offering massage classes at the temple was a chance to show that this physical practice originated in Daoism.

But the class had been canceled with no notice, and so I spent a miserable hour attempting to drink tea. Then I remembered that the temple sometimes had Saturday afternoon readings of the *Daodejing*—*The Way and Its Power*—founding text of religious Daoism. I located the room and stuck my head in. Its sole occupant was a man in his sixties walking around an immense wooden table that ran the length of the hall. It had twenty-five seats around it, and he seemed to be searching for a place to sit.

"Come in and sit down," he said to me, as if my action might help him decide. "Sit anywhere."

I chose a chair near the door. The man sat down across from me. He looked distracted, his face overwhelmed by big, 1980s-style glasses that hung precariously off the tip of his nose. He handed me a name card. His name was Huang Niu, and like everyone else in China he had a seemingly infinite array of positions, honorifics, and posts—so many, in fact, that the name card folded out twice to list all his titles and tributes. He advised governments how to obtain intangible cultural heritage. He served on a committee to promote the *Daodejing*. He chaired a commission on Daoist philosophy. He taught calligraphy. He made wooden screens. He designed inkwells. As I admired his card, he slid a copy of the *Daodejing* across the table toward me.

"I edited this," he said. "You see, it has pinyin, so you don't need to understand the characters to read it."

He was referring to the system of converting Chinese characters to letters.

"We're going to read this out loud," he said. "Join us."

"You're going to read the whole thing? Why?" I glanced at my watch. "And how long will this take?"

"It creates merit for you if you read it out loud, but even if you just want to understand it intellectually, the only way to really understand it is to read it one hundred times."

"That's good," I said uneasily. "But how long will it take?"

"It's only got five thousand characters, so you can do it pretty quickly. It takes about an hour or an hour and a half to read it through once. So if you really concentrate, you can read it one hundred times in a week. We'll start by reading it once today; that will give people an idea of how to do it. Mainly, I don't want them to rush. People are used to rushing through Buddhist texts because they're just transliterated Sanskrit and don't mean anything to most people. But you can actually understand the *Daodejing* because it's an original Chinese text.

"The next thing you have to do to understand a text is to copy it out by hand. And then last thing you do is memorize it," he said, "although by the time you've read it and copied it, you probably have almost memorized it."

I had grown up in an era when memorization was disdained. You can always consult a reference book, our teachers from elementary school onward had told us. I only realized the error of this advice later in life. Even if you have reference books at your fingertips, they are no substitute for calling up verses in your head. I envied my father, who could recall poems and verses from Shakespeare, all of which had been hardwired into his brain. My generation had memorized pop songs and lines from sitcoms. Maybe learning this text by heart wouldn't be a bad idea.

People began arriving. Two young women sat down next to Mr. Huang.

"How would you explain Daoism?" an aggressive young woman said to him in a challenging, almost flippant tone.

"Everyone talks about Christianity nowadays," he said, looking at me. "In the West, people say that God is supreme. There is one God and he rules everything. But Daoism is different. We believe in God too. But above God is *ziran*. It is much more mysterious and powerful than a mere god, no matter how powerful that god."

Ziran is a term often translated as "nature," but it means something more like the cosmos, or the natural, spontaneous flow of life. Behind Mr. Huang were twenty dark wood panels with the entire *Daodejing* carved into the wood. On either side, two pillars were decorated with couplets meant to inspire and warn us:

> *Among the disciples is a saint*
> *Without* ziran, *there is no Dao.*

He pointed to the first line and explained that the saint was Confucius. He is an important person, Mr. Huang conceded, but he
didn't get the big picture. Sure, the sage's rules and rites mattered, but
without the Dao they were empty.

By now another dozen people had floated in, and it was 2:30, time
to start our recitation. I couldn't read the characters fast enough, but
Mr. Huang's pinyin below each one made it easy to speak the words
out loud. I found even on this first pass that some phrases suddenly
became clear because I was reading it out loud. It felt like a first stab
at understanding.

An hour later we were finished. When we had read the last lines—
"The Dao nourishes by not forcing / By not dominating, the Master
leads"—we looked at each other in a daze. The world outside felt far
away, and the text felt present in our bodies.

The *Daodejing* was still ringing in my head as I headed across town to
Dacisi, the Temple of Great Charity. This was the Buddhist temple
that Ran Yunfei had written a book about, and we met there so
he could show me around. It was an unimposing, smallish temple,
mostly reconstructed after the Cultural Revolution, but it reminded
me of an important distinction that Old Mr. Ni had made at the
start of the year: sometimes the best or most historic temples weren't
real centers of religion. Miaofengshan in Beijing, for example, had
been rebuilt from scratch after the Cultural Revolution. These temples might not have the cultural treasures of a famous temple or
holy mountain, but that didn't matter. What counted was what you
invested in the practice, not the age of the statuary.

Ran's temple also reminded me of how Buddhism was much better organized than Daoism. The theories about this difference were
legion, and all of them had a kernel of truth, but the upshot was
that Buddhist temples simply had more events and activities. The
first thing I noticed in the temple was a large banner announcing
several classes on Buddhist philosophy. Meanwhile, in the main hall,
a ceremony was being held to induct fifty new lay worshippers—
volunteers and activists to distribute scriptures, staff booths, and
help visitors understand the precepts of Buddhism. The men and
women knelt, stood, and chanted according to a monk's instructions.

Next door was the office of local Buddhist charities. A professionally produced report detailed the first six years of the foundation's work. It cost just 120 yuan, or about $20, to join the foundation, which undertook all manner of work, from releasing animals into the wild (a symbolic act of renouncing violence against sentient creatures) to supporting poor schoolchildren. I couldn't help contrasting all this to the Temple of the Bronze Ram. We had recited the *Daodejing* there, but the other event had been canceled, and for the rest of the week the temple had no activities for lay believers.

Eventually, I found Ran in the teahouse. He was his usual rambunctious self, gleefully telling me about a government social media hack who had been beaten up by a female journalist in a Beijing park. I sat there enjoying his rapid-fire delivery, his mind shifting so fast it caused his body to jerk up and down as if convulsed by electricity. His head was shaved for the summer—he'd just gotten back from the barber—and I thought this was a good idea because it might allow his mind to cool off a bit.

Our conversation turned to our mutual friend Wang Yi and the path he had chosen.

"Everyone has their role in life and he's doing his part. I tell you, he'll be more influential in China as a pastor than as an intellectual. The churches are really becoming big now. They are absolutely crucial to China. They're the only really independent organizations in China. These temples are government run. I like them, don't get me wrong, but it's not the same.

"I'm reading the Bible myself. I read a chapter from a book every day. That's how to read it, right? You don't read too much of it; you read a chapter a day and savor it. I read it almost first thing. I get up and make sure nothing is urgent on my e-mail. Then I read the Bible out loud."

On Sunday, it was Wang Yi's turn to recite. He was wearing a light blue oxford shirt, short sleeved, with a striped tie. He bounced forward on the balls of his feet, grasping the pulpit like a pogo stick. He talked about today's reading, which was the story of Jesus's feeding five thousand people with just a little fish and bread—a miracle.

"China's congregations are like this today. You hear so many peo-

ple say, especially intellectuals like I used to be, 'Christianity can promote economic development. Capitalism is brought by Christianity.
It can help clothe and feed us. It can promote a more civilized form
of commerce based on trust.'

"Christianity can bring democracy and human rights. It can make
us a constitutional country based on rule of law. In other words,
Christianity can allow us to feed ourselves like the manna from
heaven or the loaves of bread. Christianity can bring a truly harmonious society.

"But the Gospels aren't about this. What is the relationship between the Gospels and capitalism? There is no relationship. What is
the relationship between God and democracy? There is no relationship. What is the relationship between Christianity and eating your
fill? There is no relationship.

"This doesn't mean we won't push freedom and democracy and
people eating their fill. But this isn't what the Bible is about."

Instead, he said it was about God revealing himself through
Jesus. It started with individuals' taking responsibility for their own
actions, he said, and it started with the Greek verb "to be." And then
he began to recite.

"*Ego eimi,*" he said in ancient Greek: "I am."

I am the bread of life.
I am the light of the world.
I am the way, the truth, and the life.
I am.

14

Practice: Learning to Walk

Beijing's north and east are its carefully groomed public face. Here, within easy range of its main airport, are its boisterous bar streets and foreigner enclaves, its university district and gentrified *hutongs*, its business district and big hotel chains. The city's south is an after-thought: the poor part of town, an army of housing towers rolling endlessly into the cornfields of Hebei, punctuated only by high-speed rail lines whisking people to China's prosperous south. But the capital's mystery and power lie hidden in its western reaches, which rise slowly toward the city's holiest grounds along the northern end of the Taihang Mountains, here simply called the Western Mountains, home to Miaofengshan and almost every famous temple from imperial times: the Temple of the Sleeping Buddha, the Temple of Great Perception, the Eight Great Sites, the Temple of the Ordination Terrace, and the Monastery of Clear Pools and Wild Mulberry.

The Communists built on this tradition. Directly west of the Forbidden City is the Zhongnanhai leadership compound, a walled complex of buildings scattered around two lakes that were once a royal park. Then come a chain of ministries and housing for the country's political elite. The most famous is the Nanshagou housing compound, its entrances manned by soldiers and its sixteen buildings nicknamed *bumen lou*, or ministry buildings, because each structure housed a different ministry or agency. Building Six: distinguished academics from the Chinese Academy of Social Sciences. Building Eight: Ministry of Electrical Machinery. Building Ten: Finance. Building Twelve: Construction Materials. Many well-connected party officials also lived here, such as Xi Jinping in the 1970s and 1980s before he set off to make a name for himself in the provinces.

This part of the city is sedate and its power expressed quietly. In the east, people flaunt their wealth in Lamborghinis and Ferraris; the west has well-ordered streets and expensive restaurants camouflaged inside dull hotels. Its wealth only pops out occasionally, such as a row of town houses along the Yongding River Canal. Awarded to senior generals and officials for their service to the state, each unit is said to be over ten thousand square feet. When officials or their families need cash, the units can be sold; the minimum selling price was $2.5 million. These stories are never publicized but are known to people who live nearby, who see the heavy dark sedans prowling the streets and notice the renovation work that signals a new occupant. It's no wonder that the Communists built the country's diplomatic districts and foreigner housing out east—keep the barbarians as far away from us as possible, please.

The party's places of power culminate in a complex of military sites—the apparatus that brought the party to power and keeps it there. Grouped tightly together is the Ministry of Defense, its sister organization the Ministry of Railways, and the Military History Museum. Down the road is the Babaoshan Revolutionary Cemetery, where the party's martyrs and loyal servants are buried.

North of the military district is the strangest celebration of China's modern religious state: the Millennium Altar. Built in 1999 by the former leader Jiang Zemin, it was meant to celebrate a new age: the Chinese century. Decorated with stone friezes of garlands and a giant hammer and sickle, it is a gargantuan sundial-like object set on a concrete bunker. It looks tawdry now, its base streaked with water and dirt and the pointer aiming at the heavens like an anti-aircraft battery. But it does emanate a talismanic power—a crude building that taps into China's wellspring of magic and spiritualism. It speaks of the era of *qigong* fever, just before the Falun Gong crackdown, when China was a little less straitlaced and dared to express some of its ancient belief in destiny and fate.

One day in July, Qin Ling summoned me and several other practitioners to the city's west for a week's worth of internal alchemy. Her home at Muxidi was just south of Nanshagou and a few blocks from the Pool of the Jade Abyss Park, a former imperial park of 326 acres, about half taken up with a deep, emerald lake—the abyss around which paths and flower gardens were built.

"Cultivation isn't just internal," she said to me over the phone. "External cultivation is important too. We'll learn how to walk."

I had thought that Daoists flew on clouds, but Qin Ling taught us that they are more like Olympic-style power walkers, with arms pumping and legs motoring almost at a jogging pace. It seemed comical, but then I realized how tough it really was. Our gait was linked to breathing. The simplest method was to inhale every six paces and exhale every six paces. Another option was to inhale every three, hold one's breath for three, exhale for three, hold the breath for three, inhale for three, and so on. Also, she instructed us to keep our heads up, chests out, and arms moving back and forth so the backs of our hands almost touched the buttocks on the back swing and then were hurled forward. "Look like a leader inspecting the troops!" Qin Ling commanded, but I couldn't help feeling I was Monty Python's Minister of Silly Walks.

The Pool of the Jade Abyss Park was the perfect place for our walks. Although it is one of Beijing's bigger green spaces, its location in the city's west keeps out most tourists, and crowds are relatively few. We were faster than anyone on the path and were constantly overtaking, a convoy of arm-swinging Daoists among the ambling masses. From a Western point of view, it seemed incongruous that Daoists would be the fastest walkers, but then again Westerners are constantly misreading Daoism, thinking it has to do with taking it easy and going with the flow. Instead, like all serious spiritual practices, it is hard work.

The day was hot and humid, the sun hidden by low clouds and a layer of smog. The heavy atmosphere covered us in silence as we focused on our rhythm, internalizing it, and calming our minds. But after we marched for an hour around the deep lake, clouds began to gather—the start of one of Beijing's summer rainstorms. Huge drops fell, splattering onto the hard, dusty soil and breaking the spell. With a yell, we broke off, running piecemeal back to Qin Ling's home a few blocks away.

For ten days this was our pattern: exercise in the park and then meditate according to the *Golden Flower*. It felt right in this combination. Because we were loosened up from our walks, the meditation wasn't so painful, and I could sit for over an hour and a half without fidgeting.

We sat on thick straw mats in the back of Qin Ling's apartment, in the usual small room. When we assembled, Qin Ling would put a small photograph of Master Wang Liping on a bookshelf, and then she would sit behind us, like a captain on a barge, keeping an eye on our external form. As always in China, form was the key. What happened inside did matter, but you couldn't do one without the other. It was the antithesis of the modern mantra that all that matters is what you feel, that outward signs—clothing or grooming—are empty superficiality. In the Chinese tradition, rituals are vessels that hold the meaning.

We started with the breathing we learned last time, breathing in and out, sitting quietly for half an hour, trying to let the reel of daily events unwind. Finally came the heart of the session, which was the focus of this week's lesson on the *Golden Flower*. First, we brought the light into our body, then circulated it through the organs to purify them. Then came a process called *anshen zuqiao*, or "calming the spirit at the ancestral portal." We put our hands in an "eight trigram" position, which means in our lap with the tip of the thumb and middle finger of the right hand touching. The thumb and middle finger of the left hand are in a similar position, but the thumb is under the middle knuckle in the palm of the right hand, and the left middle finger is on top of the right hand's middle knuckle. The idea is to keep the body's energy channels linked.

> *Lift your head.*
> *Look without looking.*
> *Look at a distant place.*
> *Look at something you really want to do, a real thing.*
> *Look at that distant place.*
> *Is it bright? Shining?*
> *Look without looking.*
> *That distant place, make it small, bright.*
> *Bring that light back to the space in between the front of*
> *   your eyes.*
> *And start* anshen zuqiao.

Focus the light.
Move it forward a bit.
Pull it back clockwise.
Focus it; make it very small, very bright.
Keep your eyebrows spread.
Look without looking.
Relax your whole body.

Inhale and bring the light down into your abdomen.
Send it down along two channels from the eyes.
From the central field (in the upper abdomen) to the dantian
Our eyes are looking inward.
It flows: eye to nose, nose to heart, heart to belly, to the lower
    field.

Inhale!
Hold the light!
Use your qi to surround it.
Hold it in the dantian.
Inhale, contract the dantian.
Exhale, expand your dantian.
Use your eyes to look at the dantian.
Everything is relaxed
Two wrists, two arms.
Look at the dantian.
Lift up your head.

I always found this part of the meditation slightly dubious. We were to focus on something we wanted and pull it into us, making it our own. Of course, it could be a good thing, but there were no instructions about this. What if it were something selfish, or evil? What if this tradition were linked to political power?

When I first went to China in 1984, one of my favorite places to visit was the White Cloud Temple, one of the oldest and quietest temples in the city. Located in the western part of the city, it was usually empty, except for the odd Daoist walking by in a blue gown and black cap over a topknot. During the first decades of Communist rule, the temple's size had shrunk considerably. Halls were torn down or expropriated for other use. The neighborhood was gutted, including an enormous temple to Zhenwu, a warrior god in the Daoist pantheon. By the early 1980s, White Cloud Temple was surrounded by Communist-era housing and a belching power plant. But it remained a noble and ancient structure, dating back nearly a thousand years.

Over the years, the temple began to recover its original size. After the debacle of the Cultural Revolution and the start of economic reforms, the Chinese government was weak and had little money. But starting in the 1990s, the state began to rebuild its power. It boosted tax revenues and began to invest in government services, improving health care, professionalizing the police force, and raising the pay of civil servants. It more effectively monitored dissent, and built itself palaces to run the land. These were not as grand as the Great Hall of the People, but in almost every town they were the best buildings: tall, mirrored structures surrounded by gardens and hidden behind high walls and accordion-style barriers. These were gated communities of power, remote places off-limits to the public. People used to explain this with an ironic statement: "The Communist Party is now rich!"

The five official religions began to benefit from this government largesse too. The White Cloud Temple reclaimed some of China's traditional medical heritage by opening a clinic in a newly refurbished wing of the temple. It built a new school to train Daoists in the ways of officialdom: how to balance a temple's books, set up a website, apply for government funding, and efficiently monitor the Daoist priests in their district. The Chinese Daoist Association, which is headquartered in White Cloud Temple, also invested in real estate, including a shopping strip across the street from its main entrance. And many Daoist practices began to benefit from the government's support of "intangible cultural heritage," such as the Li family's rural music. The government even began promoting Daoist ideas among bureaucrats.

But Daoism still retained an aura of being less controllable and more magical. Glimpses of this could be seen across the street from the White Cloud Temple in a storefront bookstore. It was just a few blocks from Qin Ling's apartment, and after we got out for the evening I used to go see if it had any material on internal alchemy. The store was unremarkable and tiny—just ten feet wide and twenty feet deep. But because it was not run by the Chinese Daoist Association, it was filled with material that official Daoism would prefer to forget. Stacked from floor to ceiling were piles of books, magazines, pirated manuals, and photocopied treatises from the *qigong* craze of the 1980s and 1990s. These included magazines, now closed down, such as *Qigong* and *China Qigong*, as well as scores of autobiographies and hagiographies of the great *qigong* masters.

The magazines were a mishmash of short scientific-sounding articles, such as "New Qigong Treatments for Malignant Tumors in the Middle Stomach Duct," as well as reports of miraculous healings that had accompanied *qigong* treatment ("Within a week of practicing, a long-standing illness that I suffered from, bleeding gums, had completely stopped"), ads for martial arts equipment, and a full-page color ad for the "Mysterious Electrical Qigong Teacher"— a contraption that emitted electrical impulses through wires that were clipped to the body.

The books included Master Wang's autobiography and practice manuals, but most told wilder tales of a great master curing a famous person or discovering such and such a method on his own in the wilderness before deciding—for the benefit of humanity—to teach it to a select few. One, by a young man named Chen Zhu, was called *Chinese Superman: Chen Zhu's World*, with a picture of Chen on the cover, wearing a Western suit, his hands apart as if grasping a beach ball. Superimposed between his hands were red, green, and blue lights in a circle. Another, darker book was called *A Qigong Practitioner Warns: Possessed by the Devil*. The second part of the title came from the Chinese expression *zouhuo rumo*, or "walking through fire and being possessed by a spirit." This referred to practicing something to an extreme and was often used to describe cults. These more skeptical books began appearing in the 1990s, as a debate was building over *qigong*, with orthodox Communists squaring off against *qigong*'s proponents.

One of *qigong*'s biggest backers was also one of China's most popular novelists in the 1980s and 1990s. Ke Yunlu grew up in Beijing and attended the prestigious 101 Middle School, where he came into contact with offspring of China's ruling elite. During the Cultural Revolution, he was one of tens of millions of young city people whom Mao sent to remote parts of the country to labor for the better part of a decade. These experiences convinced him that China's traumas could only be resolved through spiritualism.

One of Ke's best sellers was a 1989 novel called *The Great Qigong Master*, which sold 700,000 copies. It told the story of a young man who attempted to uncover the meaning of life through traditional Chinese concepts, such as *yin* and *yang*, and great books such as the *Book of Changes*. In his quest, he comes across a great *qigong* master. The two confront a stubborn bureaucrat who refuses to believe the master's miraculous powers even after seeing them with his own eyes. In his preface, Ke writes that "at present, man needs a new spirit. Our era needs to find a new meaning," and then he issued a call for a spiritual revival:

> *We will be more open, more direct, more sincere, more altruistic, more toler-*
> *ant, more artistic, more relaxed, more natural, more able to put into practice*
> *our historic cooperation and our mission in life.*
> *We will be like a golden baby.*
> *We will be like the dawn sun.*
> *We will be positive, transcendental and radiant.*
> *We will enlighten the world.*

Ke's books were products of an earlier era, when China's course was not yet set. In the 1980s, when even politics was up for grabs, public figures openly advocated democracy. That discussion ended with the 1989 student protests and massacre. But the spiritual free-for-all lasted a decade longer, with charisma and magic playing key roles until the 1999 Falun Gong crackdown. None of this was ancient history. The people running the country now came of age in that era. These were some of their most formative experiences.

Even though Ke never became an internationally famous author—none of his novels have been translated, for example—he put his finger on two key events from that era: the *qigong* religious revival and the rise of new leaders who were children of the first generation of Communist leaders. He described this new political nobility in

another best-selling novel that told the story of a young party secretary who was the son of a famous revolutionary leader. The young
man volunteered to go to a bastion of Maoism to push through
the new policy of capitalist economics. The novel was immensely
popular when it was published in 1984, and the main character, Li
Xiangnan, became a household name, especially after the book was
made into a television series.

Almost immediately, political aficionados tried to guess who the
young party secretary was based on. Rumors swirled; Ke, after all,
had grown up with the children of senior party officials and knew
them all. And several famous sons of top leaders had similar career
trajectories. Many believed that the main character was a compos-
ite based on three men. One was Weng Yongxi, a brilliant agricultural reformer who was later sidelined politically. Another was Liu
Yuan, the son of the former top Communist leader Liu Shaoqi and
a future general in China's military. The third was Xi Jinping. The
novel's prophetic title: *New Star*.

15

Ritual: New Star

The master said to the steward of the temple, "Where have you come from?"
"I've been to the provincial capital to sell the millet," answered the steward.
"Did you sell all of it?" asked the master.
"Yes, I sold all of it," replied the steward.
The master drew a line in front of him with his staff and said, "But can you sell this?" The steward gave a shout. The master hit him.
The chief cook came in. The master told him about the previous conversation. The chief cook said, "The steward didn't understand you."
"How about you?" asked the master. The chief cook bowed low. The master hit him, too.

—THE RECORD OF LINJI

The North China Plain stretches languorously toward Beijing along a dusty, dense swath of farming villages anchored by small, gemlike towns: Anyang, the birthplace of Chinese writing; Handan, a wellspring of so many myths and legends that it became the capital of Chinese idiomatic expressions; and Dezhou, the once-wealthy city where taxes used to be collected on boats traveling up the Grand Canal. In time, these small towns were eclipsed by faceless newcomers, such as the sprawling railway junction of Shijiazhuang. Some of their cultural treasures were forgotten or fell into disrepair. By the late twentieth century, they were backward provincial towns, far from the exciting economic reforms taking place on the coast.

In 1982, two men arrived in another one of these eclipsed cities to restart their lives. Their new home was Zhengding, the birthplace of one of Zen Buddhism's most important schools and home to some of China's best-preserved temples. One of the men was Shi You-ming, a famous Buddhist monk who had taken his vows at age six and been a respected religious figure by the age of thirty. But then the party persecuted him for three decades, forcing him to leave his calling and labor in the fields. Now sixty-six, Youming was taking his final posting in the ruins of one of Zhengding's legendary temples.

The other was Xi Jinping, the twenty-nine-year-old son of a top Communist Party leader. Just like the character in Ke's novel, he had volunteered to serve in a rural county to put in a mandatory stint in the provinces, hoping to burnish his résumé by showing party elders that he could work in a poor part of the country. During the Cultural Revolution, Xi had been forced to live in a poor mountain village, but all young people had similar experiences, and so it did not count as a real posting. This is why many ambitious young officials took rural positions in the 1980s, even though almost all had labored in the countryside in the Cultural Revolution.

Zhengding was an unpromising place for either man to make his mark. Located a day's drive south of Beijing in Hebei Province, it was dominated by subsistence farming. At harvest time, farmers took over two of China's major north-south roads: after collecting their wheat, corn, and sorghum, they would spread it on the roads for cars and trucks to drive over—a crude kind of threshing. Resolving this congestion was one of the local government's priorities. In official documents, Communist Party administrators summed up Zhengding in three words: "Chaotic, dirty, and backward."

These two men had experienced the Cultural Revolution in surprisingly similar ways. Youming had been expelled from his temple, made to renounce his vows, and forced to work in a factory. Xi had been sent into exile as a youth and labored on a farm. Now, they were making up for this lost time. Xi wanted to build the sort of political career his father had once enjoyed. Zhengding was an important first step up the ladder, and he needed to show success. For Youming, it was possibly more important—the culmination of his life's struggle.

Zhengding was the site of Linji Temple, the birthplace of Zen Buddhism's Linji school, which is better known abroad by its Japanese name, Rinzai. This is one of the most famous forms of Zen, with odd and enigmatic stories—*koans* in Japanese or *gongan* in Chinese—that were meant to shock the listener into enlightenment and often ended with the master trying to beat the dreamer awake. These were collected as *The Record of Linji* and learned by generations of Zen practitioners around the world. But after the chaos of the previous decades, all that remained of the temple was a solitary stone pagoda from the sixth century. Youming liked to say that "the temple is for promoting Buddhism and cultivation; it has no contact with the earthly realm." But even a teacher of koans needed a temple, and to rebuild his, Youming needed Xi's help. Xi, meanwhile, had to show tangible success in this forlorn posting. These were the initial, hesitant steps toward the Communist Party's eventual embrace of traditional religions.

Early in their history, China's Communists were not especially antagonistic toward religion. Before winning the civil war in 1949, the party had found refuge in China's northwest. Its numbers reduced by disease and attacks, the Communist Party could not afford to alienate locals, be they non-Chinese minorities like Tibetans and Hui Muslims or pious Chinese farmers. So even though formally atheistic, the party took a pragmatic approach to religion during this period, mostly leaving it alone as long as it didn't directly challenge party rule. Mao himself understood religion's power, calling divine authority one of the "four thick ropes" binding traditional society together. (The other three were political authority, lineage authority, and patriarchy.) In the 1950s, when Mao entered the final, twenty-year megalomaniacal phase of his life, he would try to sever the rope of religion, eventually presiding over the destruction of tens of thousands of places of worship and banning religious life. But in its early years, the party was much more cautious.

Xi Jinping's father exemplified the party's pragmatic faction. In the late 1940s, Xi Zhongxun had been head of political affairs for the Communist-occupied western provinces of Gansu, Ningxia, and Shaanxi—areas with significant Muslim and Tibetan populations. Known for his ability to work with religious leaders of faiths in this region, the elder Xi became an important voice in the party's religious affairs work. Later, Xi Zhongxun was purged because of his opposition to Mao and spent fifteen years on the sidelines while China went through its atheistic apogee in the Cultural Revolution.

After Mao's death in 1976, the older Xi returned to power. Beginning in 1980, according to his own account, he headed the party's religious work. Two years later, still on his watch, the Central Committee issued what to date is its most important paper on religious policy: Document 19. This eleven-thousand-word paper warned party members against taking actions to forbid religious activity or expecting it to disappear quickly. It also called for temples, mosques, and churches to be restored, religious professionals rehabilitated, and a new generation of clergy to be trained.

That same year, Xi Jinping arrived in Zhengding. His attitude toward Youming and the temples in the old city was motivated by many factors. Unlike China's prosperous coast, Zhengding was isolated, and its arid environment limited possibilities for economic development. Its cultural wealth, however, could be parlayed into tourism. Xi used his family ties to lure to Zhengding the filming of a big historical drama based on the classic novel *Dream of the Red Chamber*. Just like in other parts of the country, Xi Jinping probably saw religion as part of an economic development strategy.

I visited Zhengding several times before and after Xi took power. People I talked to uniformly said that Xi was a pragmatist who wanted to develop the town but also that he was motivated by genuine respect toward Buddhism. Xi became a regular visitor to Linji Temple, helping to smooth bureaucratic hurdles while Youming raised money, especially from Japan, for the temple's reconstruction. In 1983, Xi approved the temple's reopening to the public, even though the site was still in ruins and Youming was living in a small hut next to the pagoda.

The next year, Xi helped secure approval by China's cabinet, the State Council, for Linji Temple to be recognized as a legal place of worship and for Youming to be approved as its abbot. The young party secretary helped set up a meeting to formalize Japanese aid for the temple. Reconstruction of the main hall began, as well as dormitories for the growing number of monks who had followed Youming to Linji Temple. Xi also pushed ahead with reconstruction of eight other temples in the city. While a number of party officials elsewhere in China would later see temple reconstruction as worthwhile for gaining political promotion, Xi was one of those in the vanguard, taking risks that many of his generation avoided. It was a remarkable period of reconstruction, and reestablished Zhengding as a religious center in northern China.

Shortly after Xi arrived in Zhengding, he decreed that all officials—himself included—move to a village to see how peasants lived and worked. Xi's village was Tayuanzhuang, a collection of mud-and-brick farmhouses surrounded by cornfields. Now it is a suburb of Zhengding with new ten- to thirty-story buildings that some investors from the town have started to buy.

This high-speed urbanization wiped out the old village where Xi lived, but Tayuanzhuang is still a monument to Xi. In the summer of 2012, as Xi was readying to take power, local officials were making sure that the place where Xi served looked as impressive as possible. The town had recently built traditional arches, pavilions, and a long wall about ten feet high with huge propaganda billboards. They listed the duties and powers of officials and displayed diagrams for new parks and lakes that were planned for the region. Next to photographs of local leaders was a billboard with their predecessors, including Xi.

Linji Temple had also changed dramatically. The pagoda was now part of a much bigger complex of rebuilt halls, a library, and monks' quarters. Youming had died in 2010, and his quarters were turned into a little shrine. They were decorated with calligraphy, an altar, and display cases along the walls.

As I walked through the shrine, the current abbot walked in. His name was Shi Huichang, and he lived in a small, dark room next door. "That's actually where Youming lived," he said. "We built this [shrine] in his honor afterward."

Huichang had come to the temple in 1989, well after Xi had been transferred to a bigger post on the coast. But throughout the 1990s, he said—long before Xi's rise to the top was likely—Xi continued to visit the temple and Huichang.

"Xi did a great service for Buddhism," Huichang told me as we inspected the display cases filled with Youming's clothes, books, and photographs. "Even when he was working in the south, when he went to Beijing, he would stop by and visit. He showed respect. I'm not sure he was a believer, but he respected it. He knew more about it than most people."

We stopped and looked at a picture from 2005, when Xi was head of Zhejiang Province and about to return to Beijing to take his position as leader-in-waiting. The only temple he visited was Linji, and again Youming gave him a tour. Xi walked through the temple hand in hand with Youming, admiring the new halls and statues that surrounded the old pagoda.

Then we looked at a picture of the two from the 1980s. They were an odd couple: Xi tall for a man of his generation at five feet eleven, with the thick black swept-back hair of a Korean movie star. Next to him, Youming was a wisp in saffron robes, his head shaved, laughing like a Zen master; what could be more absurd than my present situation, he seemed to be saying, walking with a representative of the party that tried to wipe out my faith? What koan could we write of this scene? Who would beat whom?

The past fifteen years have not been kind to Ke Yunlu. After writing the two novels that captured the rise of a new class of political leaders and the country's spiritual revival, he fell victim to his success. In 1999, when he was fifty-three, Falun Gong was banned. That marked the end of the *qigong* movement and of Ke's role as a public figure. He had written four major books on *qigong*, but all were suddenly banned. *New Star* was still in print and still generated royalties, but when he returned to political themes, his luck left him. He began a series about the Cultural Revolution, writing five novels and one work of history on that era of his youth, but they were banned or the media barred from publicizing them. He became a nonperson.

But as China entered the era of Xi Jinping, I couldn't help but think of Ke. It wasn't just that he had astutely identified Xi in the early 1980s as an up-and-coming politician. That was remarkable enough. But he had also chronicled the country's spiritual revival in a way that no one had since. I knew from my own experience that many of these old styles of physical practice were making a comeback. I wondered what had become of him.

Through intermediaries, I wrote him an e-mail explaining my interest and own practice of internal alchemy. To my surprise, he wrote back a few days later. "You say you have read some of my works, so I am sure you can understand how I have been misunderstood on some topics. I once wrote 'I entrust my hope with time,' and still hold to this conviction."

I wrote back saying that time had indeed justified his views: traditions were coming back; his faith had not been misplaced. That started a yearlong correspondence between us. He declined to meet, but in our letters he was candid. One key point I wanted to clarify is what had spurred the *qigong* revival.

"I believe it was because of the craving for the liberation of the mind in the post–Cultural Revolution era," he wrote to me. Extraordinary powers, he said, became marginalized because the "dominant ideology"—his euphemism for the Communist Party's ideas and its taboos—"is not ready to tolerate and digest such an issue."

I also asked him about *New Star*. I could almost hear him sighing through the e-mails: that question again. I asked him about the theory of the main character, Li Xiangnan, being based on Xi Jinping. He answered diplomatically:

> *I would rather let readers decipher it. If you definitely want to say something, you can say that I paid attention to the kind of young politicians like Li Xiangnan's generation, and knew them well, and in fact knew them much better than many people. I hope we can stop this question at this point, and you will permit me to not say anymore.*

But I couldn't resist a follow-up question and wrote back, asking what we could learn about politicians of this generation. They had come of age in the era of *qigong* fever and tolerated it. Unflaggingly polite, Ke answered,

> As I said previously I knew people like Li Xiangnan. If they headed an administration, there would be some special characteristics, such as:
>
> 1. *They are comparatively strong. They dare to act.*
> 2. *They have a consciousness of reform. In some areas they are not sticklers for the legacy of their predecessors.*
> 3. *They have a strong consciousness of national revival.*

Zhengding was not a one-off in Xi's political biography. When he left to serve in Fujian Province on the coast, he likewise backed cultural preservation, on two occasions stopping real estate developments to protect key cultural monuments. During a 2005 visit to Zhengding and Linji Temple, Xi told national media that he had ordered a Buddhist leader from Zhejiang to visit the temple to study its reconstruction—a clear sign that his work in Zhengding was meant to be an example of how government and religion should work together. He also called on Buddhists to unite to promote China's biggest religion.

Does any of this prove Xi's own religiosity, or was he just a politician taking calculated risks? Leaders' faith is a taboo topic. As Communist Party members, they are required to be atheists. When they talk of faith, they usually mean in the Communist cause, and when they honor the dead at Qingming, they lay wreaths at the Babaoshan Revolutionary Cemetery.

And yet people want to believe that their leaders have faith, and some evidence points to their having at least strong sympathy toward religion. One of the oldest and most credible rumors was about the former leader Jiang Zemin. His wife was widely seen as a pious Buddhist, and I have seen pictures of the couple making private visits to temples. These are not propaganda pictures taken as part of an official visit—the sorts of things that all leaders do in an official capacity and that do not signify personal piety. Instead, these were personal visits, and in one Jiang had incense sticks in his hand. The photographs were amateurish—clearly taken by a believer or clergy member—and later posted on the temple's bulletin board.

Jiang also secured for his hometown of Yangzhou an enormous campus of the Foguangshan religious movement. Based in Taiwan, Foguangshan is a Buddhist missionary organization, not a charity like the Taiwanese Buddhist group Tzu Chi. As one of the few foreign religious organizations allowed into China, it could be seen as a sign of Jiang's sympathy toward the faith.

His successor, Hu Jintao, was not seen as a religious man, but his premier, Wen Jiabao, was widely considered sympathetic toward

Christianity. This is not quite as far-fetched as it seems; Western and Chinese academics who have carefully analyzed Wen's speeches found that he used the Chinese word for love, *ai*, in a Christian way—in the sense of love of one's neighbor and charity toward others. In 2009, Wen reportedly told students visiting the Zhongnanhai offices, "Everything depends on love. We hope that you children understand love, cherish love, learn and master love. You must turn love into practical action."

Likewise, Xi's rise to power in 2012 made his beliefs a topic of intense speculation among people of faith in China. Chinese who knew him well believe he looked favorably on Buddhism, just like his father. One childhood friend of his who was also later his neighbor in the 1980s spoke to a U.S. diplomat. According to a record of this transcript later released through Wikileaks, Xi's friend—referred to in the diplomatic cable as "the Professor"—said he visited Xi in Fujian, shortly after having left Zhengding. Xi, according to the Professor, "displayed a fascination with Buddhist martial arts, qigong, and other mystical powers said to aid health, as well as with Buddhist sacred sites such as Wutaishan." The Professor said he did not know if Xi was truly religious but that he "was extremely surprised by how much Xi knew about the subject and Xi's seeming belief in supernatural forces."

If Xi was favorably disposed toward Buddhism, he seems to have had more troubles with Christianity. From 2002 to 2007, he served as party leader of Zhejiang Province, where his administration received a black eye when it confronted local Christians. A congregation in the township of Xiaoshan had built a church, but the government declared it illegal and tried to demolish it in 2005. Police moved in, but members of the congregation quickly organized, and hundreds of believers flooded into the area. Although the government eventually succeeded in tearing down the church, it became one of the most embarrassing episodes in Xi's period in Zhejiang.

In the summer of Xi's ascension to power, people in Linji Temple felt that Xi was on their side. One woman I talked to said she had been there since the 1980s, when she was one of Youming's earliest lay disciples. Sitting in front of the temple's main hall, she was embroidering cloth and making sure people did not take photographs of the statues inside. I asked her if she had known Xi.

"Xi?" she said. "Of course, we all knew him. He came here often."

"And did he believe in Buddhism?" I asked her.

"Of course, how could he not?" responded the old woman. "He believed in Buddhist law."

This probably was not literally true; as a Communist Party official, and a savvy one at that, Xi would not have actively worshipped at the temple. I mentioned this to the woman.

"Well, of course he would not have lit incense," she said. "But when you look at what happened during his term, how this temple was rebuilt and how he kept coming back to see the old master, how else can I express it? Actions speak louder than words."

16

Beijing: The Flower Lady

At 5:30 on a sticky July morning, believers were already pouring into one of Beijing's smallest temples: the Temple of the Central Peak. The turmoil of the twentieth century had greatly reduced it in size; in fact it was only one courtyard. But on this day, the first day of the sixth moon, the temple was celebrating its annual fair, and so men and women had crowded into this small space to light incense and pray. The object of their devotion: Our Lady of the Azure Clouds, the Daoist deity also worshipped on Miaofengshan. She was widely known as *Songzi Niangniang,* or the Goddess Who Gives Children, and I had always assumed she was part of a fertility cult. But it seemed to me that most of the hundred or so predominantly women in the courtyard had not been of childbearing age for quite some time.

I approached the youngest woman I could see. She was in her fifties, with red-tinted hair, and held a bundle of incense over a candle, waiting patiently while it caught fire.

"These women surely aren't praying for children," I said to her.

"They're all too old!" she said.

"It's called a *Songzi Niangniang* temple."

"They're looking for peace and continuing the family. But not to give birth themselves. That's too narrow."

"So you mean for their children—that their daughters and sons can have children and the family continue?"

She thought for a moment.

"Sort of like that, but bigger. It's life from generation to generation," she ventured. "Children mean the future. They are praying for a better tomorrow."

Many religions would say eternal life has nothing to do with this world; it's something God gives you or that you earn and exists on another plane. But this realm does possess its own kind of eternity. You die but live on through your offspring or others with whom you share your experiences or teach. It is your essence being transmitted onward: mixing, swirling, forming the future. While the big world religions ask their followers to believe in an invisible and unprovable hereafter, Chinese religion offers its proof here: in the steles that commemorated departed people like Old Mr. Ni, or the ancestral tablets worshipped by the living, or the care taken to sweep tombs.

A short, gray-haired woman walked up to me, slightly stooped but vigorous and strong. She held a cane in one hand and wore what seemed to be a permanent smile.

"Do you remember me?"

I stared for a minute.

"You don't! Think. You know me!"

"Old Mrs. Chen!" I said. Of course, it was the flower lady from Miaofengshan, Chen Deqing, the woman with the shrine next to the Ni family's tea association—the woman who in the old days had carted her flowers to Our Lady on a trishaw for dozens of miles through the mountains. "What are you doing here?"

"This is my village," she said. "I'm the only one with a pilgrimage stand here. Come outside and take a look when you're free. The thirteen are here."

"The thirteen?"

"The thirteen pilgrimage associations," she said in her low, hoarse voice, laughing at me as if I'd forgotten something incredibly basic. Beijing traditionally had thirteen kinds of pilgrimage associations. Nowadays, the thirteen only appear together at two temple fairs each year: Miaofengshan and this one, the Temple of the Central Peak. But why would they come here? It was hard to find, and one of the smallest in Beijing. And yet people took days off work, rented vans, carted equipment, hired makeup artists, and performed—all at their own expense. Why?

Beijing once had eight temples devoted to Our Lady of the Azure Clouds: three in the mountains, including Miaofengshan, and five in the city. Those five were located in the city's north, south, east, west, and center. Even though Beijing is about as flat as it comes, each of these five temples was called a "peak"—a reminder of how mountains and spiritual pursuits are almost synonymous. Two of these peaks are gone. The Temple of the East Peak used to be in the Zuojiazhuang neighborhood not far from the fancy MOMA apartment complex, where foreigners and well-off professionals live. It was torn down in the 1950s when a housing complex was built. So too the Temple of the South Peak, which once lay near Dahong Gate in the city's south. Until the mid-twentieth century, its main gate still stood, with the inscription "Teach the People." But then even that fell, and today not a trace remains.

Two others are standing and in various states of use. The Temple of the West Peak in the Landianchang neighborhood had been used as a convalescent home and then as a rubber factory, but its main gate and halls survived, and now it was a fully functioning temple, with three old Daoist nuns living there—although with no pilgrimage. The Temple of the North Peak lies just south of the "Water Cube"—the aquatics center used for the 2008 Olympics. According to an article that is reposted every few months on Chinese social media, it was supposed to have been destroyed to make way for the swim center and the stadium, but as they were about to demolish it, several workers died under mysterious circumstances—the goddess if you believe the article, an accident if you do not. Regardless, the delay gave preservationists time to save the structure, even though it is mostly closed to the public.

None of these four, however, are as important as Old Mrs. Chen's Temple of the Central Peak. It is located in the former village of Xitieying, a neighborhood that felt a lot like the Ni family's Temple of the Tolling Bell—cheap tenements built on former agricultural land. In 2014, the buildings would be torn down, but the government's new focus on preserving traditional belief meant that the temple would be spared, even though dwarfed by high-rises. Of the five, it is the only one that functions fully as a pilgrimage site.

I had first visited the temple in 2011 with Bao Shixuan, one of Beijing's most knowledgeable people about the city's temples and religious life. He was a tall, rangy professor at the Beijing Institute of Ancient Architecture and has published dozens of monographs and books on the temples in Beijing's western suburbs. He was something like the historical memory for the pilgrimage associations. Whenever they had big events or ceremonies, they invited Professor Bao and gave him a place of honor at the head table. It was Professor Bao who had introduced me to the Ni family and who had shown me why this tiny little temple played such a big role in the city's religious life.

We had met near the Yongan Gate and taken a taxi south. He had kept a sharp lookout at the rows of shops along the right side of the road and suddenly told the driver to turn right, just before the high-speed rail line to Tianjin. At the end of the road was a small square with the temple and the neighborhood government offices. Inside, we met a sixty-eight-year-old village elder who said the temple had housed a company's offices until the village had been given control of the temple. He and others had renovated it and installed some smashed relics that people had hidden in the Cultural Revolution.

I asked him if this was religion.

"Religion," he said, almost visibly shrinking at the word. "No, no, it's not religion. No, not at all."

"But they burn incense and come by the thousands to prostrate themselves before Our Lady of the Azure Clouds."

"Ahh, well, that's not religion. That's belief. That's culture."

Later, Professor Bao laughed but said this was typical of the government's ambivalent approach to religion. According to the way religion is organized today, this temple should belong to the Chinese Daoist Association; after all, the main deity was Our Lady of the Azure Clouds. But religious organizations are among the weakest in China, so their property is easily taken by tourism bureaus or the local ministry of culture, both of which try to run them for profit. The Temple of the Central Peak was controlled by the local village government, while its activities were sponsored by a new government office dedicated to preserving "intangible cultural heritage," the amorphous term that covered all sorts of quasi-religious and cultural activities. Placing activities like temple fairs under the realm of culture could be seen as a setback for religion, but it was actually better than the alternative. A temple designated a "religious activity center" has to be approved and controlled by the State Administration for Religious Affairs. Calling it culture is simple.

"Everything is mixed up in China. You have a listed stock company running temples, and the government running temple fairs," Professor Bao said with a sigh. "That's China; it's chaotic."

For people like Old Mrs. Chen, none of this mattered. The key was that they were allowed to worship. Like the Ni family's tea association, her flower association was centered on her family and friends, especially her daughter, her eldest son, and a close family friend.

A few years earlier, I visited her home and learned her story. She was born in 1926 and already twenty-three when the Communists took over. "I am basically illiterate," she told me during that visit and every time I saw her. "I can't recognize one character."

She had seen her father participate in one of the traditional pilgrimage associations. But in the first decades of Communist rule, everything was banned.

"I was afraid for a while," she told me during a visit one day to her home. "You know, after liberation they didn't let us burn incense. They wanted to know what you were doing there. Are you causing trouble? Why are you doing that? I was afraid to go."

But then she retired in 1976, the year Mao died. Slowly, religious life returned and she made the pilgrimage, hoping to imitate her father's piety. For several years in the early 1990s, she rode all the way to Miaofengshan on her trishaw. Word spread. Inspired by her action, family and friends pitched in to set up the Deqing Fresh Flower Association. I asked her what she had learned from all this.

"Do good works, don't say bad things," she told me. "That's what I've learned. What more is there?"

As the fair gathered pace, Mrs. Chen took her post at her flower shrine. It was a smaller version of the altar at Miaofengshan. Instead of housing the flower goddess in a wooden structure, her family had set up a tent with an open front. She had the picture of the flower goddess and various banners and scrolls of calligraphy, as well as a few hyacinths. She sat on a folding chair to the side. A small child crawled up on the kneeler and tried to kowtow. People crowded around. Cameras whirred and clicked.

I sat down next to Mrs. Chen, and then another friend came over: Mr. Ni the Younger, or Ni Jintang, my voluble friend from Miaofengshan. A few days earlier, I had returned from a trip and learned that Old Mr. Ni had died. Jincheng told me that the funeral had lasted three days and all the main pilgrimage groups had come and performed in his honor. Now, sitting here in the summer sun, Jintang said he was still trying to come to grips with it.

"His body had been bloated from the water. We couldn't have an open casket. It was too hot, and he was disfigured from the disease. . . ."

His voice trailed off. Then he restarted.

"Last weekend I went back to Miaofengshan to look around."

"Yourself?"

"Yes, I drove up and walked around a bit. It had been thirty days since he died, and I wanted to pay respects, light some incense."

He was lost in thought. Then he pulled out a new packet of cigarettes and busied himself with removing the cellophane and silver wrapper. He said he was getting more active in the Ni family tea association now that his father was gone, and his older brother, Jincheng, was still struggling with a bad back. Plus, Jincheng's daughter was not interested in pilgrimages while his own son was. That meant it could be passed down to his son.

Today's event was too short to warrant carting the tea shrine over here and setting up all the teapots. The government only wanted it to last half a day.

But he had come to show his solidarity with Mrs. Chen and was dressed for the event: a straw fedora on his head and a silver-and-black-polka-dot suit made of satin.

"She's why we're here," Jintang said to me, pointing to Old Mrs. Chen. "She's, you know, something special."

As if on cue, thirteen men walked up to her, representative of the thirteen "martial" pilgrimage associations: martial arts troupes, stilt walkers, men who tossed around huge poles, and others who performed feats of strength with heavy stones. The men carried their ceremonial flags in one hand. They stood in front of her and then bowed, putting their right leg forward and letting their flags dip in honor.

"Respect and honor!" they called out in unison.

Mrs. Chen stood up, smiling. She clasped her hands in greeting and respect. Her smile was radiant, and her eyes danced. "Thank you, thank you," she said.

The men moved on to the temple to pay their respects to Our

Lady. Mrs. Chen sat down. A city government employee, wearing a blue T-shirt issued by the temple fair and carrying a walkie-talkie, smiled at Mrs. Chen.

"Are they, uhh, worshipping you?" the young woman asked. "They bowed to you...."

"Ahh, you don't understand," Mrs. Chen said. "It is to the goddess, not me!"

The woman looked relieved. Of course, the goddess was being worshipped, not the lady. But so much respect, who was she again? What position could an old woman possibly hold? She opened her mouth to ask more questions but was not sure how to start.

Inside the temple, the martial pilgrimage associations offered incense and then performed. Their next stop was the village square, which lay in front of a high-speed rail line. They planned to give a public performance there but first had to wait for the government's rituals to conclude. A podium had been set up with two rows of tables and chairs, enough for twenty or so officials to watch the proceedings. Speeches began, and as if on cue their god appeared: a sleek "Harmony" bullet train, decelerating as it approached Beijing. The speeches were drowned by the rush, but no one minded.

Just as the pilgrimage associations had their flags, the party had its slogans. Printed on big red banners, they festooned the square:

PROMOTE CULTURAL VALUES, DEVELOP A CULTURAL INDUSTRY, INSPIRE THE VILLAGERS' SPIRIT.

PROMOTE THE BEIJING PARTY CONGRESS'S SPIRIT, SPEED UP THE INTEGRATION OF XITIEYING WITH THE CITY.

Parsed, these two slogans meant

CREATE NEW VALUES BECAUSE NO ONE BELIEVES IN COMMUNISM, MAKE MONEY OUT OF CULTURE, MAKE THIS POOR AREA FEEL LESS HOPELESS.

DO WHATEVER THE LATEST PARTY CONGRESS INSTRUCTS, TEAR DOWN XITIEYING AND MAKE IT ANOTHER SUBURB.

An announcer read out the names of the dignitaries present: the head of the Beijing Daoist Association, a local representative of the Beijing Municipal Congress, various experts and officials, too numerous to list. Chief among them were representatives from the Intangible Cultural Heritage office. I thought back to the local official from my earlier trip here: it's not religion; it's culture. Worshipping a goddess is just culture. Repeat after me.

Then the performances could begin. The thirteen groups danced, fought, heaved, and tossed for the crowd. The sun rose. Today was the first day of the sixth lunar month. The year was coming to its midpoint, and on the fourth day of this month would be the solar term *dashu*, or Big Heat. It was also the end of the major public performances for the pilgrimage associations this year. In traditional society, people would be busy with summer chores and harvesting; that's why most fairs are in the spring and early summer, before and after the planting. Few temple fairs took place in the autumn or winter; that was the time to harvest and rest up for the New Year.

Beijing's summers were once enjoyable. In the 1980s, the summer was hot and sticky, but the city got strong, cooling breezes. People ate watermelon and drank sour plum juice to *qingre*, or expel heat. No one had air-conditioning, and it really wasn't necessary. The city was just hot for six or eight weeks, and one could get through it with a fan. In fact, in just twenty days would be *liqiu*—the official start of autumn. Although that would only be the beginning of muggy August, the calendar was telling us that the hottest days were most likely behind us and the earth was slowly but surely cooling.

All of this made more sense before people lived in megacities of twenty million and couldn't feel the earth turning, and often couldn't see the moon marking the passing of the days. On smoggy days like today, it wasn't even possible to see the sun clearly: it was a small red disk behind a white haze.

By eleven in the morning, it was almost over. The leaders though still had to give one more speech. I thought no one would pay attention. And yet all the groups turned up, waiting to obtain ceremonial banners declaring that they had been participants. The final award went to Mrs. Chen.

A recording began of an orchestra playing something like the beginning to *Chariots of Fire:* a flourish, a fanfare, and emotional music building to a climax. A professional announcer stood up and told us Mrs. Chen's story, of how she had ridden her trishaw all the way to Miaofengshan and had donated so much.

"Because Chen Deqing has a pious heart, she has left behind the beautiful name 'the Old Flower Lady,' a name that everyone knows, no matter here or on Miaofengshan."

And with that, the officials all stood up and clapped. Mrs. Chen walked up to the stage to take her award, a banner. Her daughter stood next to her. Over her shoulder, the younger woman carried a red bag with the motto of Mrs. Chen's flower association: *Bai Zhi.* On those two characters hung all the pilgrims' law and practice. It meant, simply, "Worship It."

17

Shanxi: Source of the Divine

Half a mile across the cornfields from the Li family's home in Upper Liangyuan Village is Lower Liangyuan Village. The two are about as similar as their names: one-story homes made of brick surrounded by adobe walls, gates fashioned out of old branches lashed together with baling wire, cows and horses tethered on the shady side of the street, pigs sent out to snort through the trash. Beauty is accidental but defining: sunflowers waving over mud walls, poplars rustling over green fields, dirt roads glinting like streams in the late summer moon.

The one difference is a temple. The Li family's village once had seven, but by the end of the Cultural Revolution all were gone. Miraculously, one survived across the fields in Lower Liangyuan Village, the Temple of the Source of the Divine. When it reopened in the early 1980s, it barely existed. Its main halls had been torn down. Its gold-leafed statues burned in a bonfire. Its ritual implements smashed. Its liturgies torn and scattered. One room had escaped by doubling as a grain warehouse for fifteen years. It contained a fragment of a mural from the Qing dynasty, and that was enough to secure its status as a historic building, preventing its final destruction.

The temple began to grow back its severed limbs. It now had four new halls, including statues to the temple's main deity, Dragon Hu, or *Hulong*. This was the spirit of a man surnamed Hu who had been a successful official in imperial times and since then had been honored as a protective saint. Three of his representations were garish and new—ten-foot papier-mâché statues colored with splash-bright paint. But the temple possessed one wooden statue that dated from the 1980s. It was much smaller, only about three feet high, but the work of a talented craftsman, an anonymous and unknown master who I imagined had been trained before the Communist takeover. It represented a man in swirling robes, with a furrowed, angry face, his deep crevices setting off burning eyes. All the villagers considered this the real representation of Dragon Hu, and today was his birthday, the seventh day of the seventh moon. The small statue would be carried out of the temple in a sedan chair, regaled with opera, and preside over a complex ceremony to bring his spirit down to earth, bless the village, and allow it to thrive in peace over the coming year.

But first, the petty affairs of humans had to be addressed. For years, the Li family had performed the music and rituals on Dragon Hu's birthday. Old Mr. Li could recall playing here in the 1950s and also for the thirty years after religious life revived in the late 1970s. But now the temple had a new manager, surnamed Yuan, and he had not invited the Li family. For several years now, he had asked another group, headed by a lay Daoist named Yuan Lishan (no relation to Manager Yuan). Financially, this did not mean much to the Li family. The performance fee was just 800 yuan, much less than the 2,000 they received at funerals. Still, they had always led the summer ceremony, and Old Mr. Li had been insulted that they had been disinvited. He was too proud to say anything, but Li Bin decided to use his contacts in the city to set things right. He spoke to the officials at the cultural bureau in Yanggao Town. They told Manager Yuan to invite the Li family, and so he did.

At 8:00 on this late summer morning, Li Bin, Old Mr. Li, Wu Mei, and the rest of the band were sitting in a room of the temple waiting to perform. The windows gave us a panoramic view of the main courtyard: the new halls to Dragon Hu on the left, the kitchen across the yard, and a pine tree bristling against the dark blue sky. The windows were bright and clean, but the glass was old-fashioned and warped.

Li Bin busied himself on his phone, trying to track down friends who had grown up nearby but were now living in the nearby city of Datong. These were the kinds of people he wanted to impress. He fingered his Italian belt buckle, which he would show off to them in a few hours.

"Okay, then it's a deal. You pick me up at the fair at 11:30, and we'll go to the restaurant. I'll tell you all about my trip."

His father looked at him crossly. The group had always eaten together at funerals or temple fairs. It was a way to build camaraderie inside the troupe and with the hosts. But for Li Bin, these new ties represented the future.

Manager Yuan walked into the room. He was short and bald, and today he wore the gray gown of a Buddhist monk along with Daoist-style shoes—black cloth with white trim. He had a small aggressive face like an angry rat and the deep raspy voice of a man about to lose his vocal cords.

"So you're all here?" he said, surveying the room. Old Mr. Li dragged on a cigarette, eyed him, and nodded.

"Yeah, well, it's like this. You're welcome to perform. I never had anything against that, right? Ha-ha. I had no choice. Money was tight, and we hired a local band. They're good too—you know them? Yuan Lishan's group."

"We know them," Old Mr. Li said uncharacteristically fast and hard. The two Daoist groups went back generations. The Yuans had been Daoist musicians too but had lost everything in the Cultural Revolution—all their books and all their instruments. Yuan Lishan's father had died before the end of the Maoist era and hadn't been able to teach his son much. When the chaos ended, Yuan Lishan was in his twenties and had never performed. But he was determined to restart the family tradition and so went to Old Mr. Li's father, Li Qing. The old man had taught him and through his connections managed to round up a couple of the Yuan family ritual manuals that had survived in other people's homes. And for those he couldn't find, Li Qing gave the young man copies of his own books. After a few years, in the late 1980s, Mr. Yuan left and restarted the Yuan family group with the Li family's blessing.

The two groups were drifting apart. The Yuan family was still centered on rural life, while the Li family was split, with Li Bin in Yanggao Town, and Old Mr. Li left back in the family homestead. This put the burden of keeping up informal ties on Old Mr. Li. He was bad at schmoozing: allergic to alcohol, and too tired to host the endless meals needed to win over a person like Manager Yuan.

"Well," Manager Yuan continued, "they've been performing, and now there are two groups, which is fine. We're so lucky. Thank you.

But one will have to go first, and they've been doing it regularly; they'll go first."

"We know," Old Mr. Li said, cutting him off.

"And, well, you'll all figure it out, ha-ha!" He nodded a few times and backed out of the room.

In a small room across the courtyard, a crowd had gathered around a woman in her forties, hair pulled back in a bun, face smooth and unworn by wind or sun. She wore pointy pink plastic glasses inlaid with rhinestones, a loose dress patterned with black-and-red swirls, and black tights. A big black leather purse lay beside her, its contents strewn over the *kang*.

Across from her sat a man, who was fidgeting nervously as he told his story. He was in his sixties, quiet, but erect and broad shouldered. His right hand was in a cast, supported by a crude sling made of cardboard and a ribbon that cut into his neck. A stalwart of the temple-fair organizing committee, he had fallen in the rain rushing on an errand for the temple and broken his wrist.

He asked her why. What had he done wrong? He had been trying his best to organize the fair. Had he displeased someone?

The woman listened quietly, stubbed out her cigarette, and began singing in a rough, high-pitched voice that did not seem to be her own. In fact, it wasn't. She was channeling a god:

> *You are diligent,*
> *And a good man.*
> *But your home is disorganized.*

"How so?" he asked.

She stopped channeling the spirit and began using her right index finger to count the joints of the fingers on the inside of her left hand. Starting at her wrist, she touched her thumb joint, index finger joint, its knuckle and tip, then worked down the middle finger and up the fourth finger and down the pinkie. It reminded me of the joints we had learned about during *qigong* classes: each had a name and was associated with fields of energy.

"Your gods are misplaced in your home," she said in her normal, raspy, smoker's voice. "What statues do you have on your home altar?"

"A god of wealth and Lord Guan," he replied.

They discussed the direction that the gods faced.

"They are misaligned. The energy is flowing improperly in your home," the woman said firmly. The man looked perplexed and embarrassed. He was an important member of the community, and this implied his home was not run properly.

His reaction seemed excessive until I remembered something else the man had said earlier at the start of his talk. He had mentioned his daughter. She was in her late twenties and still living at home—late in urban China but scandalous in the countryside. When the woman said his family was "disorganized," was she referring to his unmarried daughter? Preoccupied with his family's worries, was he perhaps not truly devoted to the temple's needs? At the very least, his family life did not conform to the tightly proscribed life in a village. His accident, which some people might have put down to bad luck or clumsiness, had become symptomatic of a broader moral failing—an embarrassment to a prominent member of local village life.

The man thanked her and left, discreetly putting 10 yuan, or about $1.50, on the *kang*. She ignored the money and then turned her attention to a group of women waiting to talk to her. Some of them were standing in the courtyard and had pushed open the windows, sticking their heads through to watch. The woman talked to them about childbirth, weddings, and the best day to start construction on a project. Most of this was fairly standard fortune-telling—the sort of work that Li Bin and his father did regularly. After each consultation, the visitor left 10 yuan, or sometimes half that.

After a while she took a break to stretch her legs in the courtyard. I went out with her, and we talked as we watched the Li family go into the main shrine to perform. I realized that a form of sex segregation occurred at these temple fairs. The musicians were male, and they performed in the main hall in front of the deity. Next to the musicians were the village elders, all men, who sat along the wall watching. Except for me and the troubled man, I had just been in a room full of women. That was their area. It was a side room, but arguably more powerful; the musicians were worshipping and calling on the deity to appear, but here, through this woman, a spirit had already manifested itself and even criticized a leading member of the community.

She said her family name was Zhang and she lived in the neighboring city of Datong. She was forty-five and no longer worked at a regular job; instead, she said she earned a good living organizing trips by city women to temple fairs and solving problems for people like the man. To this fair, she had brought a group of five women. They were pious and prosperous; they had cars at their disposal, and tonight they would leave and go on to another temple to the south. She would not say exactly how much she earned, but based on my experience, the exact amount was not important. It might depend on the women; if they came back satisfied, they would probably give her a few thousand yuan, a few hundred, or nothing, to be paid another time in other ways: access to a wider circle of prosperous people, help if she had her own troubles, expensive meals, or even trips abroad.

"People call me a *ding shen*," she said—a spirit medium.

"Which god are you channeling when you speak?" I asked.

"It varies," she said vaguely. Throughout the Mao era and well into the 1980s and 1990s, spirit mediums were discouraged as superstitious. Even though they have made a comeback, they remain on the fringes: appearing on their own, almost always women, often in their forties or fifties, and free from familial duties. They are not affiliated with a religious hierarchy and usually not invited by the organizing committee. They are tolerated because they represent not themselves but the voice of the divine.

Half a century ago, Yanggao County was filled with temples. With more than 250 villages, it had at least five hundred temples; the Li family's village alone had seven, and older people say that almost every village had a couple. The temples were not formally affiliated with any religious organization, and only the rarest of temples would have had full-time Daoist or Buddhist clergy. Instead, they were organized like most temples in traditional China: by local people like Mr. Yuan, the temple manager, who hire religious specialists when needed.

That was the role of the Li family. Each of the temples would have some sort of annual pilgrimage—a celebration of the residing deity, usually on its birthday. The scale and frequency of the festival would depend on many factors, such as how prosperous people were. But before the cultural destruction of the twentieth century, the Li family and other troupes spent a large percentage of their time on these activities—a contrast to today, when funerals dominate their work.

Temple ceremonies resembled a funeral. The musicians get a room in the temple, just as they are given a room in the home of a deceased person's family. They perform several times a day, with the temple altar replacing the coffin. About half the pieces are the same as at a funeral: works like "Opening the scriptures," and "Recite the scriptures," and "Obtaining the water."

But the temple fair also has specific pieces, particularly later when the god is taken out of his hall and the temple purified. That is key for believers because without the temple's being ritually prepared, the god's spirit won't manifest itself. If that doesn't happen, the event is pointless. The musicians make the event divine, which makes today more than just an especially lively market day in front of a temple, which is what it might look like to outsiders.

How to describe the music? In style, there is little difference between temple or funeral music. It is powerful but lacks the ecstasy of Qawwali music from the Indian subcontinent or the complexity of a Western choral work. The Li family were accomplished musicians who knew their trade well, but fundamentally it is meant to accompany a ceremony.

The pieces generally have a uniform structure. They start out slowly with cymbals and drums. Other instruments join in, and then the piece builds over the next minutes—some pieces as short as seven minutes and others twenty minutes long—until they crescendo in cymbals, drums, and other instruments wailing, everyone playing hard. I enjoyed it most when I let myself go and fell into something of a trance, allowing the buildup to take place. Inevitably, I would be tapping my foot and waiting for the cymbals to crash. But it wasn't something one would necessarily want to listen to for an hour or two. The forty-five-minute concerts that the musicologists had developed seemed about right.

The temple rituals themselves have their own pattern. Just as during a funeral, the initial events are low-key: The scriptures are opened. Then they are recited. The events grow in complexity: Holy water is fetched, which sends the musicians out of the temple and through the village to a well on the outskirts of town. The water is put in a ceremonial vessel and transported back to the temple, or the deceased's home, to be used later. This public act draws in people, moving the ceremony increasingly into the public realm. The culmination brings out emotions. In a funeral, it is the burning of offerings and then the burial. Here, it is the temple's purification and the god's removal from the temple to sit outside, symbolizing his presence in the community. In a funerary or a temple ceremony, the goal is the same: a controlled eruption of emotions.

In the afternoon, Ms. Zhang was back in action. But instead of advising a member of the community, she was critiquing Manager Yuan. She was in his office, sitting across from him on his *kang*. The room was crowded with women. The sole man in the room, Manager Yuan squirmed uncomfortably, looking around the room incredulously as the medium sang in her high voice:

> *You are worthless*
> *And only think of yourself*
> *You don't work too hard*
> *And don't serve the people*
> *Now you're the manager*
> *You're like a dictator!*

Ms. Zhang went on for ten minutes, wagging her finger and telling him off. I couldn't judge any of her accusations, but I knew how Manager Yuan had treated the Li family and couldn't help but notice that the event was even more chaotic than most temple fairs I had visited over the years. It had been under way for half a day, but Manager Yuan's staff was still putting up decorations, such as colorful flags and bunting. The canteen food had been atrocious as well. I wondered how he had obtained his job.

The medium stopped. Manager Yuan shifted uncomfortably. Everyone looked at him.

"Okay, I accept your criticism," he said gruffly. "I'll work harder, but it's more complicated to run this than you think."

The woman shook her head and started on again, each syllable dragged out as if she were singing an aria:

> *Exhortations*
> *Can save people from evil*
> *Beware*
> *Of hell*
> *It pulls*
> *In sinners.*

The left side of Manager Yuan's mouth twitched, and his left nostril flared into a snarl. He looked furious, and in other circumstances I wondered what he would have done. But his eyes slightly closed in fear, and he put a tight smile on his lips, backing out of the room and looking from side to side. He bobbed his head and left.

The medium looked around. Several women crowded around her, smiling and readying to tell their problems. But she shook her head tiredly and lit a cigarette. The spirit had gone, and she was just another person at the temple fair.

The next day was Dragon Hu's birthday: the seventh day of the seventh lunar month, double seven day. This day has morphed into what the marketing world calls Chinese Valentine's Day—the day when two constellations meet: a cowherd and a weaving girl, who are part of a story about unrequited love. But it is also a time when many temple fairs take place. This is the peak of summer, and this year the solar term Big Heat also started on this date. This marked the last hot weeks of summer and a time to anticipate the autumn harvests. The sun was free from clouds, and the sandy square in front of the temple was like a reflecting bowl. The streets were crammed with cars, and visitors jostled as they pushed into the yard and then the temple.

The fair had attracted visitors from far beyond the village, people like Zhang Wei, a lanky man in his forties, wearing expensive outdoor clothes and heavily tinted aviator glasses. He had brought his wife and daughter in their new Jeep Cherokee over from Yanggao Town. As we spoke, he slid a thick beaded bracelet off his wrist and began quietly counting off the small stones with his thumb and forefinger, the sign of a Buddhist believer.

"You see that?" He pointed to a flag in front of the temple that read *yu shun feng tiao*. It literally meant that the winds and the rains come at the right time of the year for agriculture, but it was also a saying from an ancient military classic about knowing the correct time to act. "That's what this is about," Mr. Zhang said, "adjusting our lives so they work."

The worshippers moved into the main hall, where the Li family were setting up. Many dropped money in the donations box, the amount recorded by a scribe. I peeked over his shoulder. Some people gave as little as 10 yuan. But most gave ten times that amount— not bad for an area that still relied on agriculture.

Many visitors wanted their fortunes told. As in most every temple in the Chinese-speaking world, worshippers first lit incense sticks outside and placed them in a giant steel censer, which today was billowing huge clouds through the courtyard. Then they entered the hall and took a long, narrow jar, usually made of bamboo. In it were about two dozen sticks about the length of chopsticks. Each had symbols denoting a chapter in a fortune-telling almanac. The worshippers kowtowed, held the jar sideways, and shook it until one of the sticks fell out. That stick's symbol was checked with a reference book, and sometimes adjusted for the person's age or the current year. Then the person got a slip of paper with a fortune. It was written in very sparse, poetic, classical language, and sometimes the meaning had to be interpreted.

Here in the Dragon Hu temple, the interpreting was done by the three old men who sat on a bench next to the wall, smoking, chatting, and hauling out the tattered, hand-copied reference book. It dated from the early nineteenth century and had survived the Cultural Revolution wrapped in an oilskin and buried in a pigpen. When they had a difficult answer that they couldn't interpret, they sent the person to an even older man who lived in the back of the temple.

"He's old," one of the old men told me. "He's seen a lot. He knows a lot."

"He's old," another one chimed in.

"Old," a third said, with a definitive nod of the head.

The Li family began playing "Offering the Incense," a long, winding piece that went on for twenty minutes. It started with Wu Mei on the *guanzi*, floating precariously over the drums, cymbals, and two *sheng*, which were playing rhythm.

People crowded in as the music picked up pace. Old Mr. Li might have been the oldest, but he was the most vigorous of the group, smashing his cymbal as if to urge on the others. Li Bin wailed on the *sheng*, his fingers flying back and forth on the holes drilled along the base of the instrument. Wu Mei thrust his *guanzi* up in the air as if blowing toward the heavens. He closed his eyes and played over the drums, the cymbals, and the *sheng*, riding over them like a jazz improviser soloing over the rhythm section. Except it wasn't a solo; it was a tightly scripted piece meant to open the heavens and let in the offerings from down below on earth: the prayers, the incense, the candles, the bunting, the people praying for their future, all of it housed in a shabby little temple that was transformed for just a few hours into an access point to heaven.

Then came the culmination of the festival. Dragon Hu was carried outside on a palanquin. Four posts had been set up in a twenty-foot-by-twenty-foot square, with a fifth in the middle—just like the five holy mountains that demarcated traditional China, or the five temples in the city of Beijing to Our Lady. Each pole had a red strip of paper pasted on it with black characters written with an old-fashioned writing brush. They proclaimed the god of each direction, while the post in the middle represented the polestar.

The two groups of musicians walked out into the square playing their instruments. They walked past one post, then another, then cut to the middle, then back to another, their colorful robes swirling, until they stopped at the first pole. Manager Yuan quickly put a small table in front of it to create an improvised altar. One of the temple elders threw himself in front of the altar, kneeling and kowtowing. He was dressed simply in blue cotton trousers and a white tunic. His feet were bare. Unlike the spirit women, he didn't speak or acknowledge anyone else, but his eyes rolled crazily in his head, and his mouth was permanently agape. The worshippers surged around the outside of the posts, like crowds at a bullfighting spectacle waiting for blood.

Manager Yuan gave the madman a bundle of yellow paper, which he lit on fire as an offering. But he didn't put it in a container of any kind; there wasn't any. Instead, he let the flames consume the paper as he held it, only dropping it at the last second to the sandy ground. The late summer breeze started to blow the paper away, but he patted it down with his hands. He touched the paper quickly and lightly, recoiling slightly from the heat, until it was ash.

Then Manager Yuan splashed holy water onto the ground. The possessed man lit a stick of incense and offered it to the pole, kow-towing over the yellow earth, the ashes swirling around him as if alive. Meanwhile, the troupes had lined up on either side of him and were accompanying his actions with a piece, "The planter with no name."

The Daoists paraded around the space again, ending up at the next pole, where they performed "Completely extinguishing sin," during which the possessed village elder again threw himself on the ground, set more yellow paper on fire, let it burn in his rough hands, patted it out, lit incense, prostrated himself, and knelt in prayer until the music ended. Then the next, until all four poles—the four directions—had been honored. Finally, they ended up at the pole in the center of the square, the polestar, the heavenly body that guides us unfailingly. Yuan Lishan pulled a cord, and a giant banner unfurled from atop the pole. Coins and candy flew out all over the square. Kids ran up to grab them to applause and whoops from the audience.

Many in the crowd were filming: the lucky ones in front holding their phones steady, those behind reaching over the top, desperate to get some sort of image. The heavy sun and persistent wind, the warm ground and barren surroundings, the broken walls and fenced-in sunflowers—all of this made it feel as if we were in another era, one that people wanted to record as some sort of vanishing folkway that they suddenly realized was their own. Here I was, at this event, yes, really, I was here, back in the second decade of the twenty-first century, back when everything was different—a past to be salvaged for the future.

After lunch we rested at Old Mr. Li's home and got back to the fair around 4:00, but it was almost over. After playing two final pieces, the musicians packed up quickly and left. This always happened at Chinese events. It was the anticipation that mattered, the run-up. The events themselves always felt perfunctory, and the endings hasty and embarrassed.

The bunting sagged. The sun was setting, and the earth was cooling. Soon the Temple of the Source of the Divine would be another small, hidden temple with no traffic jam to mark its location. The ceremony had been like a hurricane that had formed, blown through, and disappeared without a trace.

MID-AUTUMN

The First Night, or *Yuanxiao*, is the moon's grand entrance—the first full moon of the year. But the moon is celebrated most festively only now, seven months later, in the autumn, on the fifteenth day of the eighth lunar month. This is the Mid-autumn Festival—the third and final holiday for the living in the Chinese calendar.

Its stories are many, but its most famous is of a great archer who saved the earth by shooting down nine extra suns that rose in the sky one day. As a reward, he was given a potion of immortality and awarded kingship. But he proved to be a tyrant, and his wife drank the potion so he would not live forever. Incensed, he chased her, trying to shoot her with his bow, but she flew up to the moon with her pet hare. He is now himself a god called *Tuerye*, or Lord Hare, a severe, martial animal with a fierce glare, who wields pestle and mortar, mixing medicine to save humanity from plagues, his outline visible on the lunar surface.

The holiday falls just after the solar term Autumnal Equinox, when the earth is halfway, or 180 degrees, on its journey around the sun. The next solar terms, Cold Frost and Frost Descending, herald a new, harsher period.

The moon is a lonely symbol, and Chinese poets have long used it to reflect the quiet and sometimes disturbing thoughts that come to us when we are alone, in mourning, or thinking of the future. In "Anchored Overnight at Maple Bridge," the eighth-century poet Zhang Ji gives us the image of a traveler, lonely on a moored boat, autumn approaching, the moon setting, the temple bell ringing. This poem has inspired people across East Asia for over a thousand years. Even today, tourists from China, Japan, and Korea go to the Jiangnan city of Suzhou (spelled below "Suchou") to see the temple and look at the bell. This translation is by the Buddhist Bill Porter, the scholar-recluse whose book on Buddhism had so interested Ni Jincheng earlier in the year. Porter abandons punctuation to let the images flow together, like the time on earth slipping away, leaving only the bell tolling:

> Crows caw the moon sets frost fills the sky
> River maples fishing fires care-plagued sleep
> Coming from Cold Mountain Temple outside the Suchou wall
> The sound of the midnight bell reaches a traveler's boat.

18

Practice: Learning to Sit

woke at 5:00 and hiked up the hill toward the pagoda. The early morning moon was so full and so bright that it made the familiar strange. It left shadows on the asphalt, which gleamed and shimmered in the supernatural light. The road was newly hacked out of the mountain's side, and its dark red soil bled down the precipice to the village, the temple, and the dam, its water a dull, luminous blue, trying to suck away the light.

Another twenty minutes up the road was a pagoda, made of raw concrete and smelling of urine. It was another eyesore, but the location was perfect. From under its eaves the village revealed itself fully, the white buildings reflecting the moon's pale rays. Nearby was the Daoist temple to the Great Immortal Huang, where we would meet twice a day for the next ten days. The mountain rose up to the north, protecting the valley from winds and storms. Its ridges rippled like taut muscles. Caves opened into the earth's womb, forming quiet retreats for self-cultivation. Outside, the landscape was rich, soft, and forgiving. I understood why temples to Huang had been built here for seventeen hundred years.

Dawn broke. Roosters crowed. Clouds took shape and form. The sun rose over the mountain and came into line with the moon, which faded but refused to disappear. The sky turned a light yellow. A plane soared overhead, going to one of the nearby Jiangnan cities: Suzhou, Hangzhou, or Shanghai. The jet's faint rumble was drowned out moments later by the temple's 5:30 morning bell. Low and sonorous like a gong, it reverberated up through the landscape, stopping, then echoing as it reflected off the rocks, the trees, and the people. It was slow but insistent, a call for us to start our day.

In 1986, a woman living down the hill in the city of Jinhua had a vision. She knew that a great master was leaving his hermitage in a faraway mountain range. He would arrive and meditate in the mountain's caves, just as the Great Immortal Huang had done centuries earlier. He would perfect himself here and then teach ordinary people, helping to spread the ancient arts. Just as she prophesied, a thirty-seven-year-old man arrived a few weeks later and introduced himself as someone who was on the final step of a spiritual journey. His name was Wang Liping, and now, decades later, he was back in this valley to teach immortality.

After the Falun Gong crackdown of 1999, the great *qigong* masters disappeared from view. But by early in the second decade of the twenty-first century, the government's attitude toward traditional religion was shifting. From being viewed as superstition, or a cause of unrest, it was perceived as a source of morality and social cohesion. In 2008, Wang began offering public lectures at the temple to the Immortal Huang, and about two hundred people had come.

Wang was the mentor of my teacher, Qin Ling, and his picture stood on a bookcase in our meditation room. Wanting to meet the great master, I joined the retreat last year. By then, the number of participants had surged to five hundred, including many who seemed as if they belonged in Qin Ling's 1980s *qigong* home movies. There had been a man who walked around in a squat, thrusting his legs out in front of him like a Russian dancer. Another walked backward the whole time, stumbling and falling up and down the path from our hotel to the temple. A woman dragged her half-delirious mother to the session, hoping that Wang could cure her. An autistic teenager howled during meditation and was only quieted when Wang stuck acupuncture needles in his skull. And an old granny handed out shoe insoles that she had made by hand, as well as laminated pictures of Wang with an overexposed streak over his head. "It's his dragon spirit, but it's too bright for the film," she told me, pressing a copy in my hand. She was the one who had foretold of Wang's coming and was eager to tell of miracles associated with his presence. It was a rough, raw setting, like a Chinese outdoor movie lot with endless extras and little direction.

This year was more sober but in some ways more remarkable. One of Wang's close associates told us that the era of miracles was over and that this was an era of "traditional culture"—a smart idea because it meant being on the right side of government policy. Flying under the radar is never a good idea in China in the long run, especially not when the new leader has a firm hand. And now that the times were supportive of traditional culture, government officials had been invited. The Jinhua retreat rebranded itself for this new era: the people from the Ministry of Silly Walks stayed home, and the people hoping for faith healings didn't show up in public. And yet five hundred still attended. I meditated with lawyers, businesspeople, musicians, painters, and filmmakers. Like most Chinese religious life, it was run by volunteers, who took off work to make the event run smoothly. They had come not to see someone shoot energy out of his hand or levitate—although few would have objected—but to rediscover their spiritual traditions.

Our venue reflected the government's approval. The Great Immortal Huang had been a local shepherd who meditated in caves in the surrounding mountains. He was later deified and grew into one of Daoism's most popular gods, especially in overseas Chinese communities. In Hong Kong, the temple to Great Immortal Huang (Huang Daxian in Mandarin, or Wong Tai Sin in Cantonese) is so big that it lends its name to a highway overpass, a subway stop, and a neighborhood. The mother temple here in Jinhua had been destroyed during the Cultural Revolution and rebuilt in the 1990s with Hong Kong money. Like many new temples in China, it was a modern version of the past. It had all the elements of a Daoist temple: the right number of candlesticks, bowls of fruits, incense burners, statues of cranes, inlaid wood, and murals on the wall. But its proportions were gargantuan: the main hall soared 150 feet, with massive pillars and an oversized statue of Huang holding a Daoist pill of immortality. It gleamed and shone but felt like a new car that hadn't been started.

Our retreat was an experiment in using this new vehicle. Daoist ceremonies are usually like this: Priests or priestesses dressed in colorful garments sing or speak liturgy written in classical Chinese that almost no one can understand. They make highly symbolic but obscure movements in front of the altar—bowing, kneeling, kowtowing, and twirling—that are designed to purify a holy space. Then they execute a request, such as calling on a god's help or bringing peace to a community. They are beautiful but arcane rituals that many Daoists wanted to change.

And so instead of obscure pomp, we were greeted at the door by a fifty-four-year-old bespectacled musician named Guo Lin'an. He handed us sheets of music with words by a thirteenth-century poet named Bai Yuchan. He had written a poem called "Spirit of the Dao" that Guo had set to music. We settled on our thick woven straw mats in front of the statue, and Guo sat down in front of an electric organ set up next to the altar. Its presence alone shocked me; I had never seen modern instruments in the scores of temples I have visited over the years. We were to sing the poem like a revivalist church hymn, belting it out in unison to the catchy tune. The problem was, no one knew how to sing it. We mumbled a few words, and Mr. Guo broke off halfway through. He stood up.

"Come on, listen to how I sing it," and he sang the hymn in a strong voice. Then he sang the notes Western-style: do-re-mi-mi-do-rei-mi, do-do-do-rei-mi. "Like this," he urged the group. Then he played the notes on the organ and sang. People began to nod. Then we sang it together:

> White clouds, yellow crane; a Daoist's home
> One zither, one sword, one cup of tea
> His robes, colored like smoke and clouds,
> His disciples, not contaminated by the outside world.

> Ordinary people of the world laugh:
> Why does he travel around the four seas
> Suffering so long to cultivate the true Dao,
> His disciples not contaminated by the outside world?

> Common people look and laugh,
> But why are they struggling for fame and fortune?
> Better to turn back and waken to the great Dao
> In the home of the immortals, free from care.

Listening to the piece was like being in a church, which I began to think was the point. We were supposed to participate, not stand back in awe at the priest. It recalled the redemption societies of one hundred years ago or the *qigong* masters from the 1980s and 1990s. They also had tried to modernize China's old religions but had been challenged and defeated by the state, which had seen no place for them. It was a sign of the new era that we were in a government-sponsored temple about to receive the government's benediction.

The hymn over, political leaders stood up to bless our retreat. Astutely, the temple's managers had plastered the entryway to the temple with slogans proclaiming, "Warmly Welcome the Eighteenth Party Congress—Study Wellness Culture—Serve a Harmonious Society." The officials riffed on these incantations. They were the usual array of middle-aged Han Chinese men in charge of religious work, with representatives from the United Front Work Department, the local Political Consultative Conference, and the provincial academy of social sciences. Each spoke in turn, based on his bureau's standing in the government hierarchy. Almost all of the speeches were the same. One used the words "harmonious society" five times and "scientific development" two more times, all within two minutes. They were the slogans of the outgoing government, which would be replaced in a couple of weeks at the party congress. The new administration would come up with its own slogan, the "China Dream," which would be incanted at next year's retreat. The blessings over, our quest for immortality began.

Our first sitting was the usual public event in China where people are supposed to be quiet but no one is: phones went off, messages bleeped, and people fumbled around with their personal belongings. The door to the temple rarely stayed shut because there was always someone who just had to get in or out; in their minds, they were always the exceptions. With five hundred participants, it meant we were tested at every session. But that led to a valuable insight: meditation and hermits play such a prominent role in Chinese tradition because of society, not despite it. How else could you get away from this self-centered racket unless you climbed a mountain and sat in a cave? Less charitably, I thought this might be a result of the Daoist idea that each person was a microcosm of creation. If I am my own little universe, does anyone else matter?

After an hour, the room settled down. The sun was beautiful and the temple illuminated by a warm glow. I thought again of the *fengshui* that went into the temple; someone knew that the light would be moving across the sky like this and built the temple in the right direction. At its simplest, this was merely because it faced south. But it also felt as if the temple were really nestled in the arms of the dragon, shielding it but opening it to the warmth.

After an hour I began to feel hot and dizzy. I had caught a cold a day earlier, and instead of relaxing, I broke out in a sweat and thought I was going to faint. I gained control of myself, put on my glasses, picked up my shoes, and stumbled to the row of pillars to the right. One of Wang Liping's senior instructors came up and asked if I was okay. He helped me on with my shoes. I leaned against the pillar, breathing heavily. He gave me a bottle of water and quietly urged me to drink. I did and began to feel better. Now I was the self-centered universe, spinning out of control, disturbing the others.

The session was nearing its end, so I sat in the back and watched. We had been issued blue cotton jackets and trousers, and the group formed a pleasing uniformity. About a hundred students sat in a dozen rows in front of the altar, with the ten-foot statue of the Great Immortal Huang. On each side were another dozen rows of twenty people each. Like me, about half were struggling with sitting cross-legged. I thought only Westerners had such problems, but of course that's wrong. If you grow up in the city, always sit in chairs, and use Western-style toilets, you probably can't squat or sit cross-legged very well. Lifestyles had changed, and many Chinese physically could not do this.

With about ten minutes to go, Wang's assistants began circling the room, watching to make sure everyone was okay. I could see that many were in pain. It was so physically demanding; I wondered how many people truly practice this. It revealed a contradiction: internal alchemy was being sold as "wellness" (*yangsheng* in Chinese), but you actually needed to be in good health to practice, something Wang and his disciples constantly reminded us. It wasn't as soft or pleasing as Tai Chi; in fact, you rarely moved. It was an internal exercise to purify oneself. Achieving it required physical sacrifice.

But I also noticed that some people were sitting in awesome stillness. One old lady was like a rock, not moving, and breathing lightly. Qin Ling had said that form was the key because sitting straight meant your channels were open and your insides could relax. It was like the Daoist recitations of the *Daodejing* in Chengdu, a physical act that helped internalize ideas.

The first class set the tone for the rest of the retreat. We started with the Daoist hymn about the lonely priest. It was the only one Mr. Guo had; a popular Daoist hymnal had yet to be written. Then Wang or one of his teaching assistants lectured mornings and afternoons for about an hour. After each lecture, we meditated for about ninety minutes. Then we went to lunch or dinner. Evenings were given over to optional classes or our own adventures.

Wang's lectures were chaotic and almost useless. People with wildly varying levels of ability were present. It was a bit like a one-room schoolhouse with students who ranged from kindergarteners to graduate students, all being taught by an eccentric recluse. Thankfully, we had been given an 850-page book of Daoist texts and evening cram sessions with the teaching assistants to pull us through. But in a way, Wang's lecturing abilities were beside the point: he was the great master, and we were there to be in awe of him. For the true believers, his very presence added meaning.

A few times, though, Wang would snap into form, the way his students say he used to teach. One morning he explained how most Daoist cultivation techniques stemmed from Qiu Chuji, a twelfth-century Daoist who traveled to Central Asia to see Genghis Khan. The White Cloud Temple in Beijing was founded by him, as well as the most important school in Daoism, the School of Complete Perfection. Wang directed us to read the chapter on Qiu's self-cultivation method. Turning to page 149, he pointed to a diagram showing the relationship between the body and the universe.

Daoism, he said, often speaks of the world's being divided into three parts: heaven, earth, and man. This was paralleled by the body's three main cavities: the head, the lung area, and the lower abdomen. Our spirit resides in our head, our qi is pulled in through our lungs, and our essence—the life force that keeps us alive and of which we have a limited amount—is in our lower abdomen. He went on, adding ideas and concepts. Around me, scores of people were taking notes in little diaries that the organizers had handed out. Some people held up mobile phones to video his talks, while many had placed recording devices on a table near him. I was doing all of this, too, building up gigabytes of information about how to leave the material world behind.

Most days, though, were incomprehensible ramblings, and some of his older students were upset at his poor teaching and the undercurrent of financial gain. Since the Falun Gong crackdown, all classes except for the Jinhua retreat were taught privately to a handful of students in his hometown or in Europe. They were expensive; a week with him in Dalian cost $5,000. Some students said he seemed to covet material trappings: he owned a Mercedes SUV and a Leica camera that he did not know how to use, and he talked incessantly about money. These sessions in Jinhua were much cheaper: 5,000 yuan, or about $800, for ten days, including room and board. That was fairly reasonable considering that the room alone had a list price of $50 a night. The organizers certainly got it cheaper, but they also provided meals. If you figured $50 for both room and board, that meant he was only charging $30 per day for two lectures. Of course that was multiplied by five hundred, but he had costs, such as paying for his assistants' travel expenses and probably a fee to the temple. Was this low profit the reason why he didn't lecture too hard? Some of his older disciples were damning in their criticism, saying he surrounded himself with rich people, many with dubious sources of income.

I wasn't so quick to judge. He was still very charismatic, in his early sixties, trim, with a crew cut and sharp, clear eyes, a solicitous host, and at times uncannily sharp. Once while meditating in a cave, I had had to leave early. About half an hour into the meditation, I had a vision of my mother, who had died a decade earlier. Feelings of sadness welled up inside me, almost uncontrollably. I tried to focus on the breathing, but it didn't work. After ten minutes, I fumbled for my flashlight, grabbed my things, and lurched out into the sunlight.

I was sitting at the mouth of the cave, breathing heavily, when Wang came up. He greeted me, and we talked about what I had seen.

"This isn't a problem. It's good. It had to come out," he said. "You should write about it."

The next day, without mentioning me or any specifics, he said that sometimes meditation brings up painful memories but that we should try to deal with them by reflecting on them. This made me think of Jung's introductory essay to the *Golden Flower*, where he wrote that meditation offers a chance for regular, quiet reflection—a rarity today. Then Wang had said, "The earth is our mother, and when we go into the caves, we're going back to her. We go in and we'll be changed when we come out. How we are changed, it's hard to say. Use your ears to listen to the mountain move and speak. Listen to the earth. You can hear it moving. It's beautiful. Think of your own mother and father. It's okay what you find. These are things worth knowing."

A few months after the Tiananmen massacre in June 1989, something miraculous happened to Chen Kaiguo. The forty-five-year-old had been working at the State Agricultural Commission, an institute that was at the forefront of Deng Xiaoping's economic reforms. It had been the home to some of the sharpest minds of China's reform era, including Weng Yongxi, the brilliant agricultural economist who along with Xi Jinping and Liu Yuan had been the basis of Ke Yunlu's novel *New Star* about the smart young official who takes on entrenched interests in the countryside. Even though Chen had been older than most of the student protesters on Tiananmen Square, he had participated, calling for more democracy and transparency in the government. He had not been a key player, and the purges that swept through the government left him untouched. But like many officials, he had nothing to do while he waited for the commissars to root out closet democrats and bring his institute more firmly back under party control. Chen found himself talking to a young colleague, Zheng Shunchao. Zheng had just graduated from university, so there was a twenty-year age gap, but they became friends, especially when Zheng began to tell him of a remarkable man he had met: Wang Liping.

The story Zheng related went like this: When Wang was a young boy, three old Daoist priests had knocked on the family's front door, dressed as beggars. Wang's pious mother had offered them food and lodgings. They then revealed themselves and said they had been sent to teach Wang ancient Daoist arts. The parents agreed. The men rented a farmhouse on the outskirts of town, and the boy went there every day after school, submitting to a sometimes brutal training regimen. To make sure he kept the right poses, the priests tied Wang up or forced him to sit in a pit. With time, his ability to sit for hours on end improved. When the Cultural Revolution struck in 1966, the four of them took to the hills, wandering the highlands of rural China, while the political chaos consumed the cities and towns in the valleys below. By the 1980s, Wang had been publicly teaching these once-secret arts for a few years and had a huge following.

Chen had seen that political action was impossible, so this more spiritual orientation held out hope. Fascinated, he began to write down everything Zheng told him. Soon they hit upon an idea: What if they wrote Wang's story and published it? They called Wang and he approved. Then Chen contacted friends at a government publishing house, and *Opening the Dragon Gate* was published, a book that went into multiple reprints and even today is popular enough to be sold as a bound photocopy edition.

Chen and Zheng were attending the retreat and met up with us one day. The discussion soon turned to miracles. One person, an old man with silver hair and a beard, asked how we should understand the book. Even with some of the miracles removed, it was still a pretty difficult story to believe: Wang really had trained with three old Daoist masters for years next to his family home? Then, when he was a teenager, he had really traveled with them over hill and dale, eluding Red Guards and learning Daoist magic and doing good deeds?

"When I tell people I study this, well, they—they say it's not a real story, right? They say it's like a fable or something," the man with the beard said.

Chen sat at the front of the room with Zheng. Chen was now already seventy-one years old, with thinning hair, glasses, and the hesitant air of an old Communist Party official who has been through so many political campaigns that he no longer knows what he thinks or what is acceptable to say. He deferred to Zheng.

"You can't prove that Jesus was crucified, but this doesn't prevent Christians from believing," Zheng said. "I used to be interested in proving the miracles, but I realized this wasn't the point."

The room exploded in agreement.

"I can see an aura around him."

"When I practice during sleep, I have seen Wang appear. He comes into my bedroom and talks to me."

Later, I talked to Chen alone. For many years he had lost touch with the movement. Even though cleared of participating in the demonstrations, he felt that the political atmosphere was oppressive in the capital. Like many others, he had fled to the faraway economic reform zone of Shenzhen and gone into business. He retired in 2002 and only resumed contact with Wang in 2009, when the Jinhua retreats restarted. Now, he said, he was planning a new version of the book.

"What we're going to do now is emphasize traditional culture," Chen said. "The age of miracles is over."

Whenever I doubted Wang Liping—his erratic teaching and his well-paid lifestyle—I reminded myself that he inspired people. He enabled all this to happen—not just the meditation in the temple, but people like Mr. Guo, who now had a chance to modernize Daoist music. If Wang had flaws, he also created a platform for a lot of good people to explore traditional ideas in new ways. That seemed like a real accomplishment. If he was also able to make money on the side offering courses to Russian oligarchs, well, it wasn't exactly inspiring behavior but not too different from how many other religions get their money.

One of the brightest stars in Wang's orbit was Shen Zhigang, his chief teaching assistant. Shen was in his early fifties, careful and reserved when talking about himself but energetic and engaged when discussing internal alchemy. An engineering teacher in western China, he had been a student in Xi'an's Jiaotong University when he met Wang in 1986. "His aura was so bright," Shen told me one day, "that I knew this was a remarkable person. I wanted to know what he knew."

For the thirty years since then, Shen has taught Wang's Daoist school of internal cultivation, including the *Golden Flower*. Here at our retreat, he was a volunteer whose evening classes were a big draw. They lasted about two hours and were crammed with about one hundred students. Shen was popular because he could put Wang's cryptic and incomplete message into context, filling in the missing bits and speaking to us in a clear language we could understand.

But what I found most useful was his willingness to draw pointed conclusions. One evening he stated that China was the last ancient culture still alive. How many Greeks and Egyptians, he said, could read their classical texts or draw on their ancient practices?

In China, though, the language was still roughly the same. Learning classical Chinese is not easy, but it is still taught to all students in school and is much easier than, say, a Westerner learning Latin. Any Chinese person with a high school education and a bit of patience can plow through one of the classics; in fact, that's what Daoist priests like Li Bin do. Few of them even have high school diplomas, and yet they master difficult texts.

"In the West, most of this kind of knowledge was lost or suppressed," he said. "But in China, through Daoism, this prehistorical knowledge was transmitted."

Shen wasn't exactly right—some New Age ideas draw on pre-Christian beliefs—but overall it was an important point. No one reads ancient Greek texts to re-create religious life in modern-day Athens, but in China precisely this is happening. People build school curricula based on their reading of Confucius and chant the *Daodejing* for inspiration. They cite the *Book of Songs* to encourage filial piety and comb ancient literature like the *Golden Flower* for clues to meditation. Westerners often talk about how Chinese culture is lost or destroyed, but part of this is because the West puts a high value on the antiquity of structures. In Chinese culture, the written word is supreme, and it has survived.

Shen's lectures were journeys into this mystical world. He talked passionately, filling his whiteboard with swirling diagrams and bullet points that followed one after the other. He put them up so fast, drawing pictures of our organs, the stars, and circulated qi, that his assistant could hardly erase the board fast enough before he filled it again with more and more words from China's inexhaustible past.

Other volunteers contributed in more prosaic but moving ways. One day in the hotel lobby I met Zhang Xiaofei, a smart-looking young woman in her late twenties bouncing her two-year-old son on her lap. She was in charge of registration and logistics—a tough job, given the five hundred self-centered universes attending the event. I thought she might have been a local official, perhaps seconded to this job for a couple of weeks. But she told me that she normally works in a nearby town for an insurance company.

She looked the role, modestly turned out in black slacks, a purple blouse, and a black blazer. Her hair up in a ponytail, she was a no-nonsense person, with limitless patience but a tough edge that allowed her to get things done. Lightly marking her cheek was a long, faint scar, probably a childhood wound, now almost like a beauty mark.

"I've always been a believer," she said to me, putting her son down and letting him walk, fall, and crawl across the shining tiled floor. "Around here, with this history, a lot of people go to temples. When they said they needed help, I volunteered."

That was in 2009, when Wang restarted the classes. She told me that her company isn't happy about her taking the time off. The autumn is the busiest time, she said, and so they fine her 100 yuan a day—about $15. So she not only uses up her annual leave of ten days but also pays out of pocket for the privilege of volunteering. I said it was a real sacrifice.

"No," she said, as if that were a very narrow and strange way of looking at it. "It's *yuanfen*"—the Chinese word that can be translated as "fate" but also has a sense of destiny, duty, or sometimes even luck. "I do it. It's what I want to do."

I also saw how everyone—from Wang to the abbot to the hundreds of people on the retreat—treated her with respect. This was something that must give her life a deeper meaning, and I thought of my parents, who had themselves volunteered at the churches we had attended. In Tampa, my mother had been the church's junior warden, a thankless job involving every sort of logistical issue that others don't want to handle. One year the church needed a new roof, and she chased down contractors' bids for months, saving the church thousands of dollars. I don't think she ever received formal thanks, but it was a source of pride.

As Ms. Zhang and I chatted, a thin Tai Chi master walked in. Like Ms. Zhang, he was on the organizing committee. It was to meet tonight to discuss why we couldn't get into Jinhua's most famous cave, Double Dragon Cave, to meditate. Rumor had it that the government tourism authority wanted to sell tickets and would only allow us to go during normal business hours. That wouldn't work, because during the day the cave is floodlit with red, green, and blue lamps. People tramp through it. Who could meditate in such circumstances? The authority's only concession had been to offer a discount on ticket prices. The thin Tai Chi master shook his head sadly at the turn of events.

"We can only do what we can do," he said. "In this case, I think there's nothing we can do."

The Tai Chi master wore baggy black pants and a gold top decorated with the eight trigrams. The outfit was made from what looked like velour curtain material. It was a bit bizarre, but he wore it with dignity, as a badge that he was a recognized Tai Chi master and head of the local Tai Chi association. He was short and almost gaunt, but when he put on his black-and-gold uniform, he was transformed into a master of the eight trigrams, a defender of Chinese culture. If the local bandits who ran the cave wouldn't yield, he would retreat a step and counterstrike next year.

Toward the end of my stay, I decided to try my own luck at Double Dragon Cave. The year before, a group of us had snuck in through the exit and had a quiet few hours without tourists traipsing by. So one night I made my way there, only to find that the tourism trolls were a step ahead of me. They had built a giant fence around the exit with a revolving gate that was locked. They had also hired a family to patrol it. The family had a dog. It barked, snarled, and snapped. Water defeats stone, one day, but not today. I left.

Nearby was a stream with a huge concrete pavilion. One day, I told myself, this will be replaced by something wooden. One day, when everyone is richer, better educated, better traveled, and so on, it will look great. One day I will be dead.

But I caught myself. The aesthetics of concrete pagodas wasn't the point. The idea was to meditate in the moonlight next to a gurgling stream. This idea could be realized. The moon was still intensely bright. The stream gurgled. My eyes would be closed; who needed an ancient wooden pavilion? The idea was enough.

I placed my mat on the grass next to the stream and closed my eyes. I could hear the stream and feel the bright moon reflecting on the trees. To my right was a pagoda and below me the earth. The images from the past came up: the supernaturally clear road, the wave of nausea in the temple, the people debating miracles, the woman with the light scar—all of them rolling forward randomly until the reel emptied. I looked off into the blackness, beyond the rocks, far into the distance. I saw a light. It was bright. I drew it toward me and turned my eyes inward to see what was there.

After returning to Beijing a few days later, I got an e-mail from a Hong Kong friend, Ken Peng, writing to tell me that Master Nan had died. In the coming days, the Web was filled with reports of his cremation. His ashes reportedly contained colorful beads and marbles, proof that he had developed miraculous powers. The reports were not carried on major news sites, but they were sent around via social media, gaining currency and becoming true.

I called Ken to thank him and to tell him about the retreat. Earlier in his life, Ken had been vice head of the Hong Kong Qigong Association. He was familiar with Daoist-style practices. He told me why he now preferred Master Nan's Zen-style meditation.

"A problem I find with the Daoist practices is there's so much time spent directing energy and qi around your body that the mind never really calms down."

He asked if there had been people bouncing around during meditation like in the old days, or other strange behavior. I could tell he now disapproved of this. Zen was more mainstream, and people did not act quite as strange.

I said it had been under control. Nothing really out of the ordinary.

People crying? He asked. People disturbed?

Not exactly, I said, but I told him how I had broken off my meditation after being confronted with memories of my mother's death.

"Strange, right?" I said to him, guessing he would find this bad—an example of the unbridled emotions that internal alchemy could release.

"No, not at all," he said. "That's something to treasure. We don't know what we find when we look inside."

19

Beijing: The Sacred Slum

From the newly opened subway stop on Line Ten, the Temple of the Tolling Bell neighborhood looked the same as always. It was a cold October night, and people bustled about, dodging the potholes, the broken sidewalks, the grease slicks, and the fruit stands lit with extra-white lights. A faint noise drifted through the air. Drums and cymbals clashed and clanged, growing in intensity as I walked down the street. It was nighttime and too late for a celebration. Music at this time could only mean one thing: death.

It was the send-off for Yu Xiurong, Old Mr. Ni's wife, marking the end of a cycle of death for the tea association. The old man had died in June, almost twenty years after Our Lady of the Azure Clouds had given him a new lease on life. Then, two months after that, Mrs. Qi's husband—Chang Guiqing, the friendly man at the temple fair with the tin of beer always in his hand—had died. Now, another two months had passed, and Mrs. Yu had departed. She died of lung cancer, which within a month had overwhelmed her.

The departure of such an important woman called for the representatives of the thirteen pilgrimage associations to attend, and they all did. None even had to be asked, because as soon as she had died, word had gotten out, and everyone knew what was expected. When you asked people why they were there, they looked surprised. It was common sense. Old Mr. Ni had helped rebuild the thirteen associations after the Cultural Revolution. This was his wife, his partner for sixty years. How could they not attend?

"If you don't know human nature, then you can't accomplish anything in this world," Old Mr. Ni's elder son, Jincheng, said to me later in the evening. "Even the Communist Party officials came to see us. They understand how life is here."

The last one hundred yards of their alley was filled with a twenty-foot-high tent made of steel scaffolding and covered with a green canvas tarp. The tent had one antechamber, which held the coffin. Sitting around it was a troupe of ten Buddhist musicians very similar to the Li family's group in Shanxi. They had brought their own small metal statue of a Buddhist god, *Yuedu Wangling*, or Delivering the Departed Spirit. The god was there to make sure that Mrs. Yu would make it to the otherworld safely. The statue was set on a table, and the musicians sat on stools around it, hitting drums and cymbals and blowing through *sheng* pipe organs and *suona* horns.

A dozen paper wreaths surrounded the glass coffin, which had a small glass window that revealed a yellow silk shroud over Mrs. Yu's body. Stitched with Buddhist prayers in Chinese and Tibetan, the shroud lightly revealed the outline of her face. At the head of the coffin was a small altar with a black-and-white photograph of her, surrounded by fruit offerings and incense sticks. Hanging from the top of the tent were brocaded silk banners with the names of Buddhist deities, such as Guanyin and Maitreya.

I walked through an archway into the main part of the tent, a vast dining area with stools and card tables covered with plastic and set with chopsticks and paper plates. In the back, a kitchen had been set up, and half a dozen cooks in white chef hats were preparing a feast.

Jincheng called out. He was sitting with a group of friends near the archway and motioned for me to sit next to him. He was dressed smartly, but his hair was grayer than ever, and he looked drawn and exhausted. I expressed my condolences and asked him how he was doing.

"I'm tired!" Jincheng said to me. "But that's the way it is. Your mother is dead. You're tired."

Soon dinner was served, and we cracked open bottles of grain alcohol. I thought of all the times I'd rejected alcohol—tired, headache, health, and so on—but I saw that they never refused. It was part of the ceremony: you drank, or at least made the effort, especially at a time like this. Some people liked to drink, but it was also a form of respect. Plastic cups appeared, and mine was filled to the brim with the clear liquid.

Jincheng's mood swung between his normal jocularity and intense sadness. He made jokes with people at our table but refused to eat. He went on a mandatory tour of the fifteen tables filled with guests, offering each table his thanks and toasting them, but when he came back, his glass was still full. He sat down with a groan and stared blankly at the table.

His younger brother, Jintang, came over. "The Ear of the God," he whispered. Jincheng's eyes lit up. "They have arrived," he answered, and rose slowly.

Outside, a dozen men dressed solemnly in yellow silk, as if officials of the emperor, awaited. They walked out of the darkness, into the light of the alley, in four groups of two men each. Between each pair was a pole that suspended an enormous gong. Following them were several musicians. In front was another robed member wearing a neck brace. A pole came vertically out of the brace up the back of his head and then bent at a ninety-degree angle so it ran over the top of his head and stuck out in front of him like a fishing pole. Hanging from it, a foot in front of his face, was a tiny gong. He held a mallet wrapped in red silk and stared expectantly at the gong in front of his nose.

Mrs. Qi was already standing outside, her bulldog face showing the faintest smile of recognition. The Ni brothers were busy with mourning duties, so she was the standard-bearer, and she clutched the tea association's flag in her right hand. It was an honor to receive a visit from any of the great pilgrimage societies, but on this night they were special. A key part of a Chinese funeral is getting a message to the other side. If anyone could do it, it was a group of musicians with four giant gongs.

"From the ancient lineage, fourteen generations, the Ear of the God has arrived!" one of the yellow-clad men bellowed out to Mrs. Qi.

"Accepted and welcome!" she shouted back.

The troupe leader stepped toward her and bowed forward, dipping his ceremonial flag. Mrs. Qi simultaneously did the same with the tea association's colors. The percussionist from the Buddhist group crashed two big cymbals together to punctuate their bows. Then they did it again and then a third time, the cymbals marking their mutual respect.

The conductor with the contraption on his head waved his mallet with a flourish and struck the little gong, making a tiny *boinging* noise. That was the signal: the teams of men behind him swung their mighty mallets, and the old neighborhood shook from the low rumble: a bell tolling not just for Mrs. Yu but also for us. We savored the sound, which lingered until the conductor hit his tiny gong again, triggering more reverberations, and then a third time. Three peals, three kowtows, three marks of obeisance for the old woman and the pilgrimage association she represented.

Then, an apparition: Jincheng, at the entrance of the tent, ghostly, backlit by the bare bulb, supported on both elbows by younger relatives. They were mandatory, to give the impression that the chief mourner would collapse without their support, but in this case it was not a show. Jincheng's eyes were glassy, the bags under them dangerously dark and heavy, and his body sagged. He nodded with a smile to the men from the Ear of God. They stepped forward three paces, and the leader bowed down again three times toward Jincheng. Jincheng responded by dipping his mourning scepter, a stick wrapped in white paper with cloth strips attached to the top, each white slip covered in handwritten calligraphy of prayers and devotional sayings.

More troupes arrived until all thirteen of the major associations had paid their respects to the elder son of the departed. None of the others performed; this was a funeral, and martial arts or skits would have been inappropriate. All that was necessary was the mournful peal of the gong, echoing through the neighborhood.

The Temple of the Tolling Bell violated a law of physics that governed Chinese cities: space is equal to quality over time. If you go back in time, you end up in run-down spaces like this. Or if you go far enough away from Beijing, you find these kinds of neighborhoods. But these communities are not supposed to exist near the center of a big city like Beijing; instead, the area should be filled with high-rises and shopping malls. Its existence was a wrinkle in the space-time continuum of Chinese urban planning. They were called *chengzhongcun:* an urban village.

Eventually, this anomaly would be ironed flat. The tenements would be replaced by modern high-rises. The lanes turned into boulevards. The shops replaced by malls. But when that happened, something would be lost. Even though not ancient, the small buildings and alleys had been like the old city's *hutongs:* built to human scale and intimate. Here it had been possible to re-create the old city's sacred way of living. Here you could march through the alleys, and your neighbors knew you. They set out offerings. They stood in their doorways and watched. How would it be living in a housing silo, not knowing your neighbor? What communal spiritual life would survive? It would be different, more personal, more like Jincheng's private piety punctuated by occasional visits to temples like Miaofengshan. But those were just the rough contours; the future was only slowly coming into focus.

The mourners marched through the streets like a Chinese-style New Orleans funeral rag. The Ear of the God led the way, gonging to attention everyone who might be near. The men walked slowly, dignified, their call rumbling through the neighborhood.

They were followed by a group of men carrying silver-coated paper parasols and several large paper animals and other symbolic offerings. Along the way we stopped every one hundred yards or so in front of a shop or doorway. These were homes of people who wanted to pay homage to Mrs. Yu and had set up little stands with plastic cups of tea and plates of sunflower seeds and oranges for the performers. The idea was to make sure that the dead person had enough food and drink on her path through the underworld.

We passed down the narrowest of alleys, past tiny hotels catering to relatives of people at a nearby hospital, hole-in-the-wall convenience shops, and apartment blocks made of rough brick, with tenement-style staircases. It was about as gritty as it got in the capital, but for that evening the mourners turned it into its holiest ground.

Our guide was the moon, full tonight as if on cue, the hare staring down at us, pestle in hand, unable to provide the medicine that might have delivered Mrs. Yu. Last month, the eighth of the lunar year, had been the the moon festival but tonight's moon seemed brighter, perhaps because the sky was free from smog. The heavens seemed aligned to make the funeral a success, the reward of a good life devoted to faith and charity.

We ended up at a T-intersection and a small traffic jam. The road was narrow. Bikes, scooters, and cars jostled to get past. But for our group, none of this mattered. For ten minutes, they transformed this urban planning mess into a portal to the otherworld.

The Ear of the God occupied the intersection first, and the yellow-clad men shooed back a taxi that wanted to turn down our street. The driver knew what was going on. He quickly backed up, parked, turned off his engine, and waited it out patiently. Not so other drivers, who were in a hurry and thought they might just get through. The Ear of the God stopped them by standing in front of the cars, the men hitting their gongs, as if imbued with magical power: cars are now at our command, and for once we don't have to scurry out of their way. They halted all traffic and formed a square in the center of the intersection. The drivers grudgingly turned off their engines.

The other pilgrimage associations and mourners arrived. Everything that they had been carrying went into a pile in the center of the intersection. They tossed the paper horse, the silver parasols, the remaining paper money. A crowd gathered. Everyone knew what would happen next.

One of the younger men pulled out a cigarette lighter. A bonfire quickly erupted, the flames roaring across the plastic-covered paper and leaping up ten feet in the sky. A police officer sauntered past, studiously avoiding the pyre. Did they have a permit to set up a bonfire at the intersection at night? This was one mystery he would not attempt to solve.

The performers stripped out of their garments. The Ear of the God men took off their yellow silk robes and suddenly became gray, green, brown, and blue like everyone else: men in windbreakers and slacks, with wrinkled faces and rough hands, fumbling for cigarettes and talking in big voices.

Everything disappeared, even Jincheng's white mourning scepter. He tossed that into the fire too, and it was soon consumed. When the fire burned down, the ritual was over. The cars reclaimed the road and drove over the ashes.

We walked back toward the Ni family's alley, suddenly just a group of people like any other. We passed a small park. Even at 10:00 at night and the temperature around freezing, people were out doing fox-trots or swinging back and forth on simple exercise machines.

Across the way, the restaurants gave way to cellphone shops, convenience marts, and storefront restaurants with just a couple of tables. Somehow, this slum has become the family's neighborhood, even though it had no city wall, no century-old houses, no temple, no bell tolling. They had been exiled here, but they had made it their own. And now it would be torn down.

Jincheng stopped and sat down on a cement block at the side of the road. "Go on," he said exhaustedly, waving his hand. "You go your way. I'm resting here for a while." He could not lift his head. Everyone stood around, unsure what to do. After a while, two young men put their arms under his, hoisted him up, and helped him stagger back home.

Tomorrow the hearse would take the coffin to the crematorium at 5:00 in the morning, but one more ritual was required. Like many others, it had to do with food. The Buddhist musicians started up and played for ten minutes with the senior member reciting prayers. Then Jincheng summoned his energy. He knelt in front of the small altar at the head of his mother's coffin and held a large glass jar out in front of him. The relatives lined up, about twenty of them, and took turns using chopsticks to take morsels of food and place them in the jar—Mrs. Yu's final meal before her body left the earth. Jincheng had no words and no bluster. He was just exhausted.

"He's the elder son, you know, he has to do it," his older sister said to me with tears in her eyes. "That's how it is."

The music eventually stopped, and the hard-core stragglers paid their last respects to the family and then to the coffin. Jincheng came back to his seat.

"That's it," he said. "Tomorrow she's gone."

20

Ritual: The New Leader

n spring, Premier Wen had presided over Chinese politics' spring
ritual, the National People's Congress. Now it was time for the
autumn ritual, which this year was grander than most. Most years,
the party holds a secretive plenum at this time of year, but every five
years it holds a full-blown party congress. And so it was this year
in mid-November that the Great Hall of the People—that gargantuan, tragic building off Tiananmen Square—was transformed into
a temple of Communist Party power. The ceremony's name was the
Eighteenth Party Congress, and its *fashi* was Hu Jintao. His goal was
to immortalize himself and anoint a successor.

The event got under way at 9:00 in the morning with large screens
showing propaganda films touting the achievements of the outgoing government. Space exploration, responding to the 2008 Sichuan
earthquake, and strong economic growth were explained as something
that government leaders had given the people. The video flashed to the
earthquake: Hu stood next to nervous officials, all wearing hard hats,
as he squeaked out barely comprehensible clichés about how he had
come in the name of the entire Chinese people to succor the victims.
I thought of Wang Yi's congregation, whose members had actually
driven for days through the mountains to ferry supplies to the area,
or Tan Zuoren, who had discovered why so many children had died
in the disaster. That was faith and commitment; this was affectation.

A blue sign flashed on two large screens on either side of the
rostrum. Delegates were urged to take their seats. The screens
announced that 2,230 delegates had arrived. Most were sitting in the
audience. The center of attention was the stage. The back of the
stage held an elevated rostrum of six rows of forty-six seats filled

with current and retired government leaders. These roughly three hundred distinguished party veterans had no function other than to confer legitimacy. They looked down like a choir on a long desk at the front of the stage. This was the dais, empty now, but soon to be filled with Hu's closest associates and the country's most powerful officials. Almost everything was red: the poinsettias, the carpet, the seat covers, the table covers, the bunting hanging like curtains over the back wall. The only exception was a saffron wall hanging with an enormous golden hammer and sickle. It lent a golden hue, just like the yellow backdrop to the Ni family's shrine and their enormous symbol, the character for "tea."

A dozen women walked up to the rostrum, taking positions at the middle and end of each row, waiting, quiet and poised. They were officially known as "ritual girls," *liyi xiaojie* in Chinese, chosen for their looks and ability to keep a reserved but friendly distance. None smiled, focusing carefully on their tasks. They were like nuns, and in fact they signed up to live for four years in all-female dorms where modesty was so strictly enforced that they could not even wear pajamas in the hallways, let alone leave the dorms unescorted in case they met "outsiders." The women were recruited from the countryside; Beijingers were ineligible out of fear that they might be tempted to return home. Only after the congress was over could they resume contact with the outside world.

At an unseen and unheard command, they leaned over and with one hand slid the lid off the porcelain teacup that was in front of each delegate. In their other hand they wielded a stainless steel thermos and poured water into the cups. Tea leaves pre-positioned at the bottom swirled to the top. Almost exactly at the same time they replaced the lids and walked to the next seat to repeat the procedure. Everyone had to have tea, even though none would drink it; it was part of the ceremony, symbolizing that the delegates were ordinary Communist Party officials like the millions of other party members around the country, with their mugs on their desks, piling through work reports, reciting numbers and slogans, conscientiously carrying out their tasks just as the delegates were doing now. Gods and humans: in the Chinese religious world the two overlapped and imitated each other.

Finally, the leaders walked out. First came Hu, a small cautious man, his skin pasty and pallid—a man who had spent too much of his life in meetings. He was often criticized for being too passive, but his form of *wuwei* had allowed religion to thrive. Back in the south where he came from, it was possible to imagine him strolling in a park with his grandchildren, a retiree from the hydroelectric company. He walked along the front row of the rostrum, shaking hands formally. A few steps behind him was his predecessor, eighty-six-year-old Jiang Zemin, who had been rumored dead last year but was now appearing in public again and had managed to place several of his underlings in the new government's ruling bodies. The rest of the men came out several steps farther back, indicating that Hu and Jiang were in a class by themselves.

A deep-throated announcer asked for everyone to stand up and join a moment of silence for departed leaders, such as Chairman Mao, Liu Shaoqi (whom Mao had essentially murdered), Deng Xiaoping (the man Mao had feared most to be his successor but who had in fact succeeded him), Chen Yun (the economic conservative opposed to Deng's reforms), and others. These had been fierce enemies men but now were arranged in a straight line, like emperors on a timetable of history.

Hu eventually spoke. Like a Daoist priest, Hu emulated an immortal, but instead of wearing the richly embroidered robes of a god, the sixty-nine-year-old followed modern convention: dyeing his hair jet-black to make himself look ageless, and surrounding himself with propaganda banners conferring immortality (*wansui*) on the Communist Party. The chief banner, each character about two feet high, hung across the balcony of the main plenary room, reading, "Long Life to the Great, Glorious Communist Party of China." I thought of Wang Yi and his eulogy for Auntie Wei. Who gets to confer immortality?

Hu's recitation came in the form of a work report. He declaimed only a few excerpts, because at sixty-odd pages it would have taken longer to read than the *Daodejing*. The report listed Hu's accomplishments over the past five years and predicted what his successor, Xi Jinping, would do. There was little of substance in the report, but it was not meant to be substantive. It was an incantation, a list of talismanic phrases and words that showed that he was still *ling*, or efficacious. If he failed to do this, his *ling* was fading.

How to become an immortal? The key was to have one's ideas enshrined as part of China's guiding ideologies. The Communist Party was officially based on Marxist-Leninist thought, which didn't really mean anything specific; China no longer followed Marxist economic theory, and Leninism was followed only in the sense that the Communist Party was an authoritarian organization structured loosely on Lenin's ideas. But mentioning these ideas and the people behind them conferred legitimacy, like a list of ancestors known in Chinese as a *jiapu*. After Marxism and Leninism came Maoism, much of it convoluted and circular in reasoning but still some sort of coherent body of work. Then Deng Xiaoping Thought would be mentioned, which was really just a collection of ideas rather than a vision or philosophy. Next came Jiang, the first of these giants who was still alive. Perhaps because of this, his ideas did not carry his name; instead, they were called the "Three Represents," which meant that the party has to represent more classes than just workers and farmers. It was a thin idea but important because it opened the party to the businesspeople who actually had power and money in the country.

Hu had pushed two ideas: "Harmonious Society" and "Scientific Development." Scientific Development was fairly empty, meaning perhaps that one should listen to experts and not follow utopian visions, which had been Mao's way of operating. Harmonious Society was a sop to traditional ideas, such as creating cohesion by appealing to the past. The key, however, was for Hu to mention his terms as much as possible. Repetition created reality.

The players knew their parts well. Hu had no charisma or oratorical skill; it was as exciting as hearing a grocery list. But a modern speech demanded high points and applause, so to signal this, Hu occasionally raised his voice to a shout. "We will resolutely fight to achieve a moderately prosperous society!" Everyone applauded.

At times the prompts were poorly executed. Hu didn't seem always to know when to raise his voice or did so too late in the sentence, causing the delegates to applaud too quickly. Something was missing, like music or at least the drums and cymbals of the pilgrimage associations on Miaofengshan.

Hu, though, did have a pleasing voice. It was measured, and he did not stumble. Clearly he had been reading similar work reports for decades, starting at the local level and working up through the hierarchy. And compared with the political-religious cult of Mao, this was tastefully done. Hu did not bask in the adulation of hundreds of thousands of frenzied followers nor plaster his face on billboards around town. He was a low-key man—an exception in the pantheon of Communist leaders.

In any case, Hu's spells worked. A week later, with no public announcement or explanation, China's new leadership team appeared in the Great Hall. Hu and most of the leadership had vanished, replaced by the new party boss, Xi Jinping, the future premier, Li Keqiang, and five other new faces who would rule China for the next five years.

Xi made fixing China's moral malaise his top priority. Thirty years earlier he had rebuilt Zhengding's temples and allied himself with a Zen master to move a county ahead. Twenty years ago, he had watched with great interest the *qigong* movement and told an old friend about his interest in Buddhism. Now he undertook two main tasks. One was a corruption crackdown. Whatever one thinks of this—as a power play or a genuine attempt to rein in malfeasance—it was instantly popular. The other change was harder for outsiders to understand or even take seriously: a massive nationwide campaign to promote the Communist Party's embrace of traditional values. In fact, the two were related. They were his answers to the lack of minimum moral standards.

In pursuing these goals, Xi was following the script set down by his rival Bo Xilai, the former party chief of the city-state of Chongqing who had been jailed after his wife had killed a British businessman. Bo gained national attention for addressing two of China's biggest systemic problems. One was corruption, which he had tackled by arresting big-name gang leaders. The other was China's spiritual vacuum. Bo tried to turn back to the Mao era, instituting a program of "singing red songs." Companies and government organizations were ordered to stage glee-club-type meetings and competitions where old Communist songs were sung. Forward-looking Chinese were appalled at romanticizing the Maoist dictatorship, but when I went to Chongqing shortly before Bo's downfall, some people I met spoke fondly of the exercises as something done collectively; in a country with few opportunities to meet in a public sphere, be it in politics or religion, these gatherings forged a sense of community.

It was easy to see the parallels in Xi's anticorruption campaign and support of a new system of public morals. The main difference was how Xi and Bo approached the spiritual vacuum. Xi probably realized that a purely neo-Communist approach of glorifying Communism would not work for everyone. The genius of Xi's strategy was to meld Communist tradition to China's ancient heritage.

Ten days after taking office, while touring the National Museum of China, Xi invoked the phrase "China Dream" for the first time, linking it to China's national rejuvenation. Many observers immediately saw this as copying the idea of the American Dream, but most Chinese would probably have understood this as drawing on imagery in Chinese statecraft, philosophy, and literature. For thousands of years, Chinese rulers framed questions on how to rule as interpretations of dreams, while dreams have figured prominently in Daoist philosophy and famous Chinese novels. Even early twentieth-century thinkers described their utopian visions as dreams. In 1902, the great reformer Liang Qichao wrote a futuristic novel in which a descendant of Confucius delivers a lecture at the 2062 World's Fair in Shanghai on how democracy has come to China.

But how to define Xi's dream for the twenty-first century? And how to sell it to the public? After Xi's speech, propagandists and thinkers began to brainstorm the practicalities. By the New Year, they had found an answer in China's past.

21

Chengdu: The New Calvinists

The streets around Wang Yi's church were echoes of a fading past. There was Polished Splendor Temple Street, named after a Buddhist place of worship; Hall of Educating Children Street, named after a Confucian academy; and Small Lord Guan Temple Street, named after a Daoist shrine to a warrior god. All these temples had been torn down in the twentieth century, but many of their ideas remained, part of the traditional religious culture that had survived the destruction.

Overlaying this old shell was something new but invisible: a sacred landscape that the churches were fashioning. Early Rain had come of age in 2009 after the congregation had bought half the nineteenth floor of the River Trust Mansion. When police had blocked members from entering the building, they had congregated along the Jinjiang River, holding outdoor prayer vigils until they were allowed in. The canalized, polluted waterway had become their river Jordan, a sacred body of water where their congregation had been baptized into a new era. Today, a church conference room displayed a map of Chengdu, the Jinjiang snaking through the downtown and around it pins showing homes and offices where Bible study groups met every week. Not too far away were allied churches and prayer groups that met quietly: not permitted by the government, but also not forbidden. Like the pilgrimage societies in Beijing, they were hidden to outsiders but defined the lives of thousands of believers.

One November morning I wandered east from Early Rain to visit one of these sacred spots: the Spring of Life Reformed Church run by Zha Changping. A bookish professor at Sichuan University, Zha taught in the Department of Religious Studies' Christian Research

Center. His specialty was the Bible—not to train pastors like Wang Yi's seminary, but as an academic topic taught to students majoring in Western religions. Spring of Life was his personal project, and like Early Rain it was an unregistered church. Along with another pastor, Peng Qiang, they formed a triumvirate of dynamic, unregistered church leaders in Chengdu.

I had met Zha earlier in the year, and he had asked me to buy two reference books the next time I was overseas: English and German translations of the Septuagint, which is the translation into Greek of the Hebrew Bible. It was the version most familiar to early Christians, making it a key to understanding how those founding generations had read and understood the Jewish tradition from which they sprang. Zha was planning a new translation of the Bible into Chinese and wanted the volumes to check his understanding of ancient Greek. Single-handedly translating the Bible into Chinese was an enormous undertaking but typical for China's new, urban churches; this was their founding era, and almost nothing seemed beyond their ambitions.

Zha's church was located partway down Small Lord Guan Temple Street. Like Wang Yi's, it was hidden from the outside world, with no cross on the roof or plaque outside. It simply occupied the third floor of an old four-story schoolhouse. But the rooms were bright and cheerful: painted a luminous white, their windows decorated for the coming winter season with paper snowflakes, silver icicles, and cutout fir trees. It was cozy and familiar but strange: this was a humid, subtropical city, not New England or northern Europe.

I found Zha at his desk. A slim forty-six-year-old with short hair and round, wire-rim glasses, he looked studious and austere, almost monk-like in a black jacket and black scarf wrapped around his neck. But he was no dour intellectual; he loved to joke in an understated way, especially about himself and the struggles he had with his congregation. Unlike Wang Yi, he was not a onetime media star who attracted people to the church by force of personality. He had taken over an existing congregation twenty years ago and managed it like a harried schoolmaster trying to control unruly adolescents.

"I'll show you around the church," he said with a wink. "We've made some changes."

We walked straight to the back wall, and with a flourish Zha pointed to his latest achievements. At first glance, it seemed strangely dull: a newly framed list, about two feet long and one foot wide, titled "Our Identity." It started out simply enough, but suddenly got very complex:

1. *We are Christians. We repent and reform. We trust in the God of Jesus Christ as revealed in the Bible to be our personal Savior and Lord.*

2. *We are Christians. We accept the Apostles' Creed, the Nicene Creed, the Athanasian Creed, and the Chalcedonian Creed as confirmed by the Holy and Apostolic early church, as the standard expression of Christian faith.*

3. *We are Reformed-denomination Protestants. We accept the Second Helvetic Confession (1566), the Westminster Confession of Faith (1646), as the complete, balanced and authoritative expression of Christian faith.*

4. *We are an ecumenical church in China. We support the principle of separating church and state.*

5. *We are Presbyterian Protestants. We choose the selection of Presbyters as the appropriate governing model for our church.*

6. *We are members of the Spring of Life congregation. We believe that the Trinity of Father, Son, and Holy Ghost is the well-spring of renewing life.*

The beginning and the end were clear enough, but the middle section was tougher. My problems began with the second point. The Apostles' and Nicene Creeds are familiar to regular churchgoers: they lay out fundamental tenets of Protestant faith. But the Chalcedonian Creed? And the Helvetic Confession of 1566? I needed a refresher course in church history.

"What's the *Ya-ta-na* Creed?" I said.

"Ah," he said. "Of course you are familiar with the English: Athanasian Creed."

"No," I said, slightly guiltily.

"You should look that up!" Zha said. "It's part of church history."

"And your congregation," I said to Zha. "They all understand this? The, ahhhhh, *Wei-si-min-si-te* Creed?"

"Westminster Creed!" He laughed but then blew out a sigh.

"There's still a lot of opposition," Zha said. "Some members don't want this, but we're going to continue with it. They don't understand it and reject it."

"Reject what?"

"Being a Reformed church," Zha said. "We are adopting Reformed theology and want to make this as clear as possible. That's why this list."

Reformed Christianity was a Protestant denomination sometimes also known as Calvinism, Presbyterianism, or Puritanism. Over the past few years, it had taken off in China, where many believers felt it was the most authentic and original form of Protestantism. Based on the teachings of the sixteenth-century French theologian, John Calvin, Reformed Christianity is a conservative, austerely beautiful form of Protestantism that gives primacy to the word of the Bible. Worship allows only that which the scriptures explicitly endorse, and thus few overt rituals, such as bowing and crossing oneself, or ecstatic experiences like speaking in tongues. Early on, even music was banned. This was later lifted, but Reformed Christianity retains a puritanical streak, often codified in strict rules—appealing in a country where some people had rejected traditional religions and were still looking for new guidelines in life.

Wang Yi's church had wholeheartedly adopted Reformed theology. Over the summer, his congregation had read the sixteenth-century Heidelberg Catechism, a statement of the Reformed faith based on 129 questions and answers, each one backed up with extensive footnotes.

QUESTION 11: *Is not God then also merciful?*
ANSWER: *God is indeed merciful, but also just; therefore his justice requires that sin which is also committed against the most high majesty of God be also punished with extreme, that is, with everlasting punishment of body and soul.*

That sort of moral certainty appealed to many Chinese, but other parts of Reformed churches were controversial. Zha explained that Reformed theology has two key sticking points for Chinese congregations. One is the baptism of infants. This might seem a small point—what does it hurt to baptize an infant? In the view of Catholics and some Protestants, it is an insurance policy so the child will go to heaven in case of an early death. But for other Protestants—especially in China—the idea grated. Many Chinese feel more comfortable with the idea that adults should decide for themselves, perhaps because they have had enough of someone else choosing their path.

The other concept that challenged many Chinese was the idea of presbyters. These are supposed to be a handful of wise elders who run the congregation—a system that in some ways resembles traditional Chinese political thought, or even today's political system. In Wang Yi's church, the position was not elected. He and one other pastor were the presbyters, and they ran Early Rain. The church had once had a third presbyter, but he had been expelled when his wife insisted that women could be pastors, too. Wang Yi had objected and told them to leave.

"Maybe one could be more flexible," I said. "Not all churches are organized like this. Some have elections."

"No," Zha said. "We need the system of presbyters. In the past, we just had a big chaotic meeting every year, and nothing got done. We need structures, and for that we need a culture of contracts—the idea that things are done a certain way that we agree upon and that not fulfilling it has consequences. China doesn't have this. Chinese people lack this. There is no idea of a contract in the Chinese mind. That's an objective opinion."

I began to understand why Zha had rushed me back to see this framed list of beliefs. It was a public contract that everyone agreed to follow. This was another version of the new urban churches' commitment to radical openness: these were Zha's ninety-five theses nailed to the door. Either you agreed or you didn't. There was no room for ambiguity. I asked Zha why he felt that this kind of a public statement was so important.

"China needs the culture of contracts, for society and the people. People don't have this feeling. If you set an appointment for 4:30, people come at 6:00."

"Are people ready for this?"

"Last weekend we argued about the issue of infant baptism," he replied. "Finally, we just had to vote on being Reformed or not."

The result, he said, was that 66 percent of the congregation supported it. "That's two-thirds, that's enough."

We walked back to his office, and Zha handed me a book of interviews conducted by Wang Yi and the writer Yu Jie with Protestant pastors from around the Chinese-speaking world. Zha's chapter was called "Christianity in a China Transforming from a Society of Knights-Errant to a Society of Public Citizens." The title described how many people in China saw their country—as a lawless land where good deeds were done, but only as individual acts by noble people and heroes.

Zha wanted something else: a society of law upheld by active, engaged citizens. It paralleled the political reform movements of the first decade of the twenty-first century, such as the New Citizen Movement. This had been an effort to use laws to defend civil rights and culminated in Charter 08, a blueprint for political reform in China. But the Communist Party had detained or sidelined most of its supporters, especially the Nobel peace laureate Liu Xiaobo. For the party, laws were tools to rule the country, not a framework for guiding society or for conferring rights on citizens. This was one of the stumbling blocks for political reform in China: Some people were above the law. Laws and rights were not God given; they were created by the Communist Party. But here, in these Reformed churches, was an effort to create something based on higher loyalties.

The early twentieth century was a high point for missionary work in China. In 1900, a quasi-religious group called the Boxers had massacred foreigners, especially missionaries, until it was finally quelled by Western armies. But this violence only spurred more foreigners to rush in and try to save China. The number of missionaries rose from thirty-five hundred in 1905 to more than eight thousand in the 1920s, divided along denominations and ideas. For Protestants, there were Anglicans and Baptists, Methodists and Presbyterians, Lutherans and Episcopalians, not to mention the growing rift between fundamentalists and modernists. And of course there was Catholicism, with its own splits into various orders and national interests: Italians versus French, Franciscans versus Jesuits. One summer I visited Mount Jigong in central China's Henan Province. Overlooking the

North China Plain, it had been a popular summer retreat for missionaries in the early twentieth century. The mountain was dotted with three hundred villas that were once used for the missions from twenty-four countries—each denomination from each country had its own retreat. It was a babble of spiritual advice, each villa a center of a different idea for saving China.

The only people missing from this army of advisers had been Chinese. In 1907, Protestants held a big conference to mark the centenary of the arrival of the first Protestant missionary to China. Held in Shanghai, it was attended by 1,170 delegates from around the world. Only 10 were Chinese. By the 1920s, many people questioned the missions' usefulness. Bureaucratic and costly, they were dominated by expensive expatriates who raised funds by traveling back to their home country at great expense to give celebrated keynote addresses about saving the heathen Chinese. Many critics thought that the denominations were particularly destructive; what China needed was one unified church to spread the word, not the complicated divisions between Protestant groups, whose splits seemed often more about style than substance.

Many prominent Chinese Christians like Cheng Jingyi questioned the need for missionaries. At the World Missionary Conference in 1910, he electrified the audience by calling for Chinese to take over leadership roles from the missionaries. He also fervently objected to the Protestant denominations, saying China needed a unified Chinese church. Progressive foreigners like Pearl S. Buck had similar views. A child of Presbyterian missionary parents, she won the Nobel Prize in Literature in 1938 for novels such as *The Good Earth*. A few years earlier at New York's Astor Hotel, she had stunned the audience by giving an address called "Is There a Case for Foreign Missions?" Buck portrayed missionaries as arrogant and ignorant of China and only halfheartedly endorsed their continued presence in China. Seventeen years later when the Communists expelled missionaries, many Westerners did not object too strenuously. Missionaries seemed like a relic of the colonial past. The fact that Christianity grew fastest after 1949 seemed to reinforce the fact that outsiders had been superfluous.

But Christianity is a global religion, and when China opened its doors again a few decades later, contact resumed. What happened, though, wasn't a wholesale adoption of Western ideas. Instead, the Western experience of Christianity was treated as a tool kit that Chinese could choose from selectively.

Ursula Seidt grew up in prosperous postwar West Germany and in the 1980s landed a job as a public servant in West Germany's Finance Ministry. But Ursula had a nonconformist streak. She attended church regularly, and instead of worshipping at a government-supported church, she went to a "free" church that emphasized evangelism. Inspired by her faith, she took a sabbatical in 1986, traveled to Hong Kong, and became a mule.

Her cargo was Bibles, and her boss was Dennis Balcombe, a forty-three-year-old Vietnam War veteran who became a legendary figure in missionary circles for smuggling into China hundreds of pounds of Bibles at a time. But Balcombe was more than courageous. Like the sixteenth-century Jesuits, he knew that understanding language and culture was important. He had mastered Cantonese by reading the Gospel of John out loud over and over for three months, and he told Ursula that if she wanted to do more than be a mule, she had to use her head. So she studied Chinese for a few years and finally traveled to China, supported by her savings and a missionary society.

"I wasn't sure what city to visit, so I traveled through China. When I got to Chengdu, I felt it was different. We were at the main train station. You know what it's like; it's crowded, so crowded with people. Even chaotic. But I felt something in the air and thought, this city is welcoming me."

It was April 1990, not even a year after the Tiananmen uprising, and foreigners were still spooked by the massacre. As one of the few foreigners in town, she was welcomed at a local university to study Mandarin. She began to make friends, including Christians, and invited people to her apartment to bake cookies, talk about the Bible, and pray. Progress was slow, but in 1994 she met Zha, then a young theology student at Sichuan University. Eventually, Peng Qiang—the third of Chengdu's most influential pastors—joined too.

"We would hold our meetings outside in parks. It was like a close family, and we shared everything. We ate together and shared experiences together."

When I met Ursula, she had been in China for more than twenty years. She was a warm woman in her fifties, with dyed-blond hair, thick mascara, a strong southern German accent, and the comforting air of a person who regularly bakes. She had recently returned from Germany with her new husband, Manfred, a committed Christian who was eager to help Ursula in her mission work. We met at the west gate of Sichuan University and looked for a place to sit down, finally settling on a local chain of Western restaurants called Peter's. They drank plain black coffee, carefully sipping it, looking out of place among the Chinese eating carrot cake and slurping expensive lattes.

Increasingly, this was no longer a world Ursula really understood. It wasn't just the prosperity that was different. People's attitudes had also changed. Back in the 1990s, she had taught Zha, Peng Qiang, and the other young Chinese Christians something very different from Reformed theology. The Free Church movement that she represented was charismatic and had minimal hierarchies—not do as you please, but a rejection of formal structures. She used to bring a ukulele to the park and sing simple songs of praise to God. She taught what she valued as a child of the freewheeling postwar West: a suspicion of authority.

But Zha and the other new Christians wanted these very structures that her generation of Westerners had rejected. Their development over the past twenty years left her baffled. What especially annoyed her were the hymns. At Wang Yi's, Zha's, and Peng Qiang's churches, everyone sang out of Western hymnals, with songs written one or two hundred years ago. Manfred cautiously made a point.

"What they seem interested in is not tradition but traditionalism. We reject that. We see the Holy Spirit as living. We're like on a river and we started somewhere and are going somewhere, but the Holy Spirit is in our hearts; it guides us and lives in us. It doesn't live in a ritual that was adopted by someone else at some point earlier on the journey. To us, that's not the meaning of it.

"Christianity didn't start then. They say these are the time-tested or proven hymns, but this certainly isn't the case! Look at the West now—who sings these hymns? Where did all of this lead the West? To no one going to church and no one worshipping God. The spirit is too easily extinguished in these heavy structures."

Ursula said Wang Yi is justified in how he builds his church. His congregation is new and centered on him. People joining it know it is his creation. But she was more disturbed when I told her that Zha's church had voted 66 percent in favor of infant baptism. She felt that Zha was pushing the congregation in ways it might not really want to go. Two-thirds might sound good, but it isn't that much of a majority when people are being guided by their pastor.

"Many of these people have been there for twenty years, so this is completely different for them."

"And the hierarchy," Manfred said. "They want this triangular, pyramid structure just like in Chinese politics. Why?"

Ursula said this is reflected in how members of congregations are sometimes treated as subjects and pastors as rulers. When she was visiting Germany a year earlier, two members of her church decided to leave her small congregation and join Early Rain. Instead of just going themselves, they tried to take the entire congregation with them, as if it were an army that could be brought over en masse under their flag.

"I've never heard of this sort of thinking before," Ursula said, shaking her head. "It's like they're your people and you control them."

Increasingly, Ursula and Manfred felt that their time here was running out. One problem was visas. They used to be easy to obtain, especially back when China needed "foreign experts" to help it engage with the outside world. Now they were tough to obtain and required proving that one was really engaged in some sort of productive business. Perhaps this attitude filtered into the house churches as well. Outsiders were still needed and useful but only if they brought the religious equivalent of high tech: knowledge in ancient Greek, running a seminary, or church planting. By contrast, Ursula and her ukulele seemed part of an earlier, almost embarrassingly naïve time. Chinese often praise the word *guifan*—standard. A company should be *guifan*. A city should look *guifan*. A housing complex should be run in a *guifan* way. Ursula was definitely not *guifan*. Her Christianity was about finding your own way and rejecting structures—the very things her converts prized.

"I am happy with our lives," Ursula said. "I always said that missionaries' first goal should be to make themselves superfluous."

She had also told me this at the start of our talk, as a way to preface everything and to make clear that what would come next were the experiences of someone who was nearing the successful end of a quarter century of missionary work, not an embittered or nostalgic person. She had talked without regret, but with detachment, as if referring to a child who had ended up strangely different: an accountant born of hippies.

"We do feel that if it's God's will to go back, we will," Ursula said, and Manfred added, "Yes, if we go back, then that's God's will. It's fine."

The two had each other, and this made it easier to start a new life. When we left, they were walking hand in hand, a middle-aged couple taking the pedestrian bridge to the buses that depart for the remote suburbs.

A few miles south of the Jinjiang River is another invisible center of Christianity in Chengdu. Located in a new, more prosperous part of town of tree-lined roads and busy restaurants is the Trinity Bookstore and the offices of Enoch Publishing. These businesses belong to Peng Qiang, who joined Zha and Ursula's fellowship in the 1990s. Unlike Wang Yi, guarded and focused on his visions, or Zha and his intellectual ambitions, Peng was open and dynamic, and he connected easily with other people. Entrepreneurs in China have to court government officials and generally get along with other people, and Peng seemed perfect for the part: short and compact, he was also handsome, with a full shock of hair and an easygoing smile.

Back in the early 1990s, Peng was following a very different career track. He was studying at the Communist Youth League's training center in Beijing. This was a high-level academy that was headed by China's current premier, Li Keqiang; in fact, Peng's diploma is signed by Li. His major was "youth ideology education," but he gradually grew disillusioned with the party. If he continued on this path, he would work for the government in the propaganda apparatus, as he put it, "helping to brainwash students." This was just a few years after the Tiananmen massacre, and he wanted no part in continuing the party's rule. He heard about Christianity on campus and soon converted.

After graduating in 1994, he returned to Chengdu and fell in with friends who had found an unusual niche publishing books. Most publishing houses were government run, and they were allotted a certain amount of ISBN numbers each year, allowing them to publish books. But these state-run companies had little idea what would attract readers. Most lost money. Some started selling their ISBN numbers to middlemen who used them to publish popular titles on doing business, self-help, and psychology. This was Peng's role: a broker trying to figure out what excited and moved Chinese people, without running afoul of government censors.

At the time, his faith was not strong, but it grew after he met Ursula and Zha and joined their fellowship. In 1997, when he got married, he asked Ursula how to perform a Christian wedding. They rented a hotel ballroom, decorated it in white—which in traditional Chinese culture is the color of mourning; red is for festive occasions—and put a cross and flowers on the stage. Zha presided over the ceremony.

Peng began to hone his business model. Many books related to Christianity could be sold through the same method he used to sell pop-psychology books. All books still had to pass censorship, but a book on church history would be approved if given a straight historical title. But unlike most history books, these had a broad audience of Christians, making the publication profitable. So, too, books on Christian ethics or historical figures like Calvin and Luther. A book on Chinese theology would be banned, but if presented as part of Western history, ideas like Calvinism could be printed.

Peng studied Reformed theology in 2000 when he went to study at the International Theological Seminary near Los Angeles. There, he read about the former Dutch prime minister Abraham Kuyper and his 1898 book *Lectures on Calvinism*. Kuyper argued that Christianity should penetrate every part of society: politics, science, the arts, religion. This, Peng thought, was exactly what China needed— a replacement for the Communist ideology that had taken over society a few decades after the imperial system had collapsed a century ago. It was exactly the opposite of what Ursula had offered, but it made more sense to Peng.

"Chinese society has been dominated by Marxism, and Marxism is a complete system toward every aspect of society," he said. "Calvinism is the only holistic worldview in Protestantism."

Unlike Marxism or even traditional Chinese culture, Christian-ity allowed people to work together as equals. He felt that this was crucial to its success.

"Chinese society hasn't solved the relationship between the indi-vidual and society. If you say 'collective,' it becomes 'totalitarian.' If you say 'individual,' it becomes 'chaotic.' Today, only a faith com-munity has a better response. We have personal conviction but also liberty of conscience."

Reformed Christianity also fit the needs of many newly urban Chinese. The Christianity that had taken root in rural China during and after the years of Maoist persecution had appealed to another, ecstatic side of China. It often revolved around messianic preachers and millennial predictions. Centered on rural, poorer provinces like Henan, this charismatic style was fading as Chinese left villages for the city and became better educated. New, city-based churches like Early Rain were ready-made for modern urbanites, with an educated pastor, an emphasis on intellectual inquiry, a plain aesthetic, and a body of presbyters, or elders, to run church affairs. Mostly, it pro-vided firm guidance.

Many Chinese churches emulated Zha's statement of faith. The Shouwang Church in Beijing, for example, had a twenty-page manual of rules and regulations, including prohibitions on premarital sex, extramarital sex, homosexuality, narcotic drugs, and idol worship. Fredrik Fällman, a Swedish historian who has studied what he calls "New Calvinism," wrote that the list of prohibitions closely mirrors early Calvinist communities in Reformation-era England, Scotland, and New England.

These ideas are often associated in the West with Puritanism. Chinese Christians like Wang Yi, Zha, and Peng also saw the Puri-tans as influencing their thought, but more in a political than a moral way. The Puritans fled oppression in England to practice freely in the New World, and many of their ideas were adopted by the politi-cal theorists who drove the American Revolution. A key point was that rights were God given, not bestowed by a monarch or a politi-cal party. To many Chinese Christians, this intersection of faith and action is a key to saving China as a whole.

Peng told me that something else was at work too. Chengdu's

unregistered churches show how people are organizing groups outside the government sphere.

"People can't believe how corrupt society has become," Peng said. "In the past, it was just businesspeople or government officials who were corrupt. Now it's monks, priests, pastors. So what's the reaction? Found your own church, your own home Daoist temple, your own study group of the classics. Do it yourself."

This was how religious life had been organized in China for centuries, but it was also a political statement. Like governments in the imperial era, the Communist Party saw itself as the arbiter of morality and conscience, but unlike the dynasties of the past it was much more powerful, able to wield the levers of a modern bureaucratic state. And its leaders were now eager to renew their claims to guide China's spiritual life.

WINTER SOLSTICE

*D*ongzhi, or the Winter Solstice, is the year's darkest hour. It is the shortest day of the year, a time dominated by *yin*, whose main property is darkness. But Chinese prefer to look ahead. Instead of darkness, they see it as the beginning of the ascent of *yang*, or light—the ultimate expression of the Chinese saying *wu ji bi fan:* "When things reach their extreme, they must move in the opposite direction." In politics, this means that extreme openness will move toward contraction, but also the opposite—a reason for optimism during a time of oppression. We often see China in clichés—booms and busts, contractions and crackdowns—and are constantly trying to define it by today's headlines. This extreme day reminds us to take the long view.

Now, as we are 270 degrees through our journey to spring, the chilliest solar terms await: Lesser Cold and Greater Cold, which fall in January. Chinese count off these icy days with a numbers game. The final eighty-one days to spring are divided into nine periods of nine days each—the nine nines. The days start cold, then begin to warm until finally the fields can be plowed, as in this popular rhyme:

> *One, two, hands freeze outside*
> *Three, four, ice supports your weight*
> *Five, six, willows start to green*
> *Seven, rivers open*
> *Eight, geese return*
> *Nine, add another nine, and*
> *Oxen fill the fields.*

22

Practice: Following the Moon

The key to walking is breathing. Inhale for three steps. Hold for three steps. Exhale for three. Hold for three. Repeat.

Three in. Three stop. Three out. Three stop.

This helps focus the mind on the body, keeping it away from the trivia of daily life. It breaks down the barrier between the two and internalizes ideas of oneness, of relaxation, of going blank. It is the essence of physical practice: reforming one's mind by reforming one's body.

Three in. Three stop. Three out. Three stop.

My daily walks reflected this circularity. My neighborhood in Beijing had no nearby parks, so the only option was to walk around Workers' Stadium, an athletics complex that was rarely used for sports and instead housed restaurants and clubs. It was bounded on two sides by big roads, but the traffic rarely turned in to the stadium, allowing one to walk straight. Lining the road were plane trees and firs; focusing on them and the breathing made it possible to imagine that nature was nearby; the idea was what mattered.

Three in. Three stop. Three out. Three stop.

A key was to get out early. One reason people often give for practicing early is to "get into contact with the earth's qi" (*jie diqi*)—the qi that emanates from the ground. But for me it was simply easier to walk between five and six in the morning—it was quieter, with less traffic and fewer people on the pathways. In China, that makes a big difference because of the population density. Power Daoist walking down a crowded sidewalk is impossible.

But the best reason to get out early was the moon. It wasn't always there, and sometimes would slip away quickly when the dawn came, but it kept me grounded in the calendar and the passing year. I felt less alone in the big city and began to look for it. During the day, I would check its location and size on calendars and websites, but over the months I started to know its cycles.

I'd see a sliver on the wane and think, a new month is approaching. Or I'd see it wax and anticipate the full moon, which seems to grow in size in the sky during the year along with the crops, burning like the sun during the mid-autumn festival in September when the final harvest is due. In the winter, it seems cloudier, just like the year winding down.

The moon guided me back to the constellations. Even though the bright lights and pollution of Beijing blocked most of them, the moon was always there, and often the North Star too. That helped me understand why Wang Liping and other Daoists put such an emphasis on that heavenly body: the North Star was constant and easy to find. Even in a big city, with mapping apps and subway diagrams, I found comfort in looking at the sky to know where I was.

Three in. Three stop. Three out. Three stop.

I realized why the moon was a better marker of time than the sun. The sun has its rhythms too, rising earlier or later in the day, higher or lower in the sky, sometimes burning brightly and other times a pale disk. But the moon is more expressive. Its phases give more information. The sun burns and blinds; the moon is there to enjoy, to stare at and ponder. We can see a boat moored near a temple and hear the bell tolling across the water. We can see the clever wife of an evil king and the fierce Lord Hare mixing his potions to save humanity. It might be cool, but it is habitable, while the sun is fiery and uncontrollable—a steed we can barely harness. The moon has space to project our hopes and desires. Its trajectory is like the nighttime watches, reminding us when to rise, what to do, and how to live our lives.

Sometimes, my walks were more about the moon than anything else. I changed my course so I could see it through the buildings, charging toward it three in, three stop, three out, three stop, circling the stadium like the moon around the earth. From my quiet orbit, I could watch people, and wonder.

––––––––

The bars in Workers' Stadium close very late, around 5:30 or 6:00 a.m., so customers would be staggering out while I circled past. Tired but unrelenting men and put-upon women would stand around looking for cabs, while poor migrants from the provinces tried to sell them balloons—was this the final step in a one-night stand? Some people were hungry and found food at nearby stalls. Others got into arguments, still able to arouse their passions.

One morning in late November, two men yelled at each other at the stadium's north gate. They stood on the pavement, next to a balloon seller. One was a short man in tight trousers and a dress shirt, badly drunk, his eyes angry and bulging, his nose bleeding. The other in jeans and a polo shirt, hair flopping forward, laughing, a woman behind him, eyeing the scene coolly.

The short man ran back as if drunk.

"Hit me! Hit me!" he yelled.

The taller man backed up, hands in front. The woman took a step back. It was a duel that had already ended, and the short man had lost. Everyone knew it was over. Maybe the bloody nose was part of the deal. Perhaps he had been wrong and deserved it. But he had to show that he still had pride. He had lost, or paid some sort of penalty, but he was still there, still alive.

"Hit, hit, hit," he said, now tired, his arms sagging. The couple stood still. It was over. Each side turned away.

Three in, three stop, three out, three stop.

On the next corner, I saw a small pile of charred paper money. It was always there on the mornings after the thirtieth and fourteenth days of the lunar month. The holy days are the first and the fifteenth days, but in China events are anticipated earlier. Shopkeepers burned their paper the night before, just at midnight, and then a walker on the streets a few hours later would encounter the charred remains and know that the moon was either empty or full.

23

Shanxi: City People

Li Bin drove through the Garden of the Peaceful Masses and pulled up in front of an apartment building with a small fabric tent out front. The tent was decorated with bendable plastic tubes filled with blinking red and white lights. Winter was already upon us, and the wind shook the tent. Li Bin finished his cigarette and stared through the windshield. The lights reflected off his face, red and white, red and white—the same colors as the ceremonies he performed: red for happiness; white for grief.

The temple fair in the summer had been a red day, a celebration of the god's birthday, a reaffirmation of its support for the community. Today was a white day. The tent shielded a coffin that held the body of a forty-four-year-old woman who had lived in this small housing complex in the center of Yanggao Town. She had left behind two children and a husband, a math teacher in a local middle school. He had contacted Li Bin a week earlier and asked for a price. Li Bin tallied up an offer of 12,000 yuan, or a bit less than $2,000. Most of that money would be paid to others—including a dozen pallbearers, a carver for the tombstone, and a family business that prepares the sacrificial food for the altar. The schoolteacher balked. His wife's illness had set the family back nearly 70,000 yuan, he said. He looked over the list and struck the Li family music troupe.

"We'll make do with *suona* players," he said.

Li Bin blanched. These were the crudest of musicians, capable of just a few pieces that all sounded the same—a sort of whining, wailing music that drove any sober person to distraction. But Li Bin knew better than to argue with city people. This was how the world was moving, and he wanted to move with it. If they didn't want the music, he would strike 2,000 yuan for his family's music troupe and handle the rest.

"That's fine," Li Bin had said. "I'll find a *suona* group and bring them early the next morning."

Now the sun had risen, and everything had to be crammed into a day and a half. We jumped out, breathing in the acrid air of winter in northern China, and walked over to the casket. The tent was adorned with scores of paper flowers and a big white character, *dian:* "Make offerings to the dead." Below it were four characters, *chentong daonian:* "Mourning with deep grief."

To the side of the tent were three big wreaths made by Li Bin and his wife, Jing Hua. Inside the entrance, the oak coffin was illuminated by a naked bulb hanging from a wire, and below it a picture of the woman. She was wearing a red wool coat, her long hair running down her shoulders, her eyes fixed directly into the camera's lens, her face expressionless. Set in front of her were offerings of biscuits, wrapped tangerines and apples, and two candles with plastic windscreens.

Her husband ran out to meet us. He was a bookish man, slight and nervous, oblivious to everything except getting the funeral taken care of as quickly as possible. He didn't seem upset, but the appearance was misleading. Normally focused and fastidious, he couldn't concentrate on the long list of things to do and seemed befuddled most of the day. He was wearing the white clothes of mourning over thick winter garments, giving his body a formless appearance. His face, however, was thin and angular and carried a disquieted expression. The teacher had a university degree. Li Bin was clearly his social inferior. But suddenly the *yinyang* man was ordering him around on this important day.

"These have to go up," Li Bin said, handing the husband four pieces of white paper on which he'd written with a large calligraphy brush the characters *song zhong li chan:* "The rite of repentance for burying a parent." The phrase applied to the man's two children. A husband could remarry, but the children were forever motherless; their loss was central.

The husband took the sheets of paper and began pasting them over the entranceway to the tent. "Like this?" he said. One sheet was crooked. Another curled at the end.

Li Bin silently took a pot of glue and a roll of tape and walked over. He helped the husband affix them and two more strips of calligraphy that he had written the night before. He took out the formal announcement, an elaborate piece of calligraphy written with black ink on white paper. It is sometimes said that Chinese are private people, but at times I was not so sure. The paper read,

> My late mother, of the Chen family, née Wang, given name Mei, on this day, although only 44 years old, lies in this coffin. Born in the happy year of 1968, on the 7th month and 19th day. The bereaved son, shorn of his mother, cries tears of blood.

We tidied up and went inside. The family lived on the first floor, their glassed-in balcony overlooking the tent. Like so many Chinese homes, it was spartan, as if no one were really sure what to do with the space. The only signs of habitation were an overstuffed sofa and two easy chairs pointing toward the television. China Central Television's military channel was on, featuring a news show announcing the military's new emphasis on science and technology. Later someone switched it to China Central Television's news channel. Its twenty-minute loop was centered on a storm that had covered northern Europe in a shroud of snow. Throughout the day, the news never varied: the cities were blanketed in white, and people kept digging out.

The apartment began filling up with mourners, each of them wearing something white. Some just had a bolt of white cloth affixed with a safety pin to a sleeve. Others wore white hemp jackets over their winter clothes. In China's big cities, people sometimes wore black ribbons in imitation of the Western style, but here everything was white like the snow in Europe.

The dead woman's children stuck together silently, the boy fourteen and the girl twelve. They had wiped all emotion off their faces, but their eyes were half-closed in disbelief as they stared at the people violating their home. These people—some family members, others strangers from their mother's school—traipsed around their apartment, fussing endlessly, making plans as if a military maneuver were being launched. The children were ignored by everyone, standing against the kitchen wall like mannequins in an ethnographic exhibition: "A Chinese boy in mourning, early 21st-century, rural Shanxi Province. White trousers and jackets tied with a white rope belt, white cloth shoe covers, white hats in the form of a mortarboard, decorated with hemp string. The subject's clothing gives the impression of forsaking normal life to live as a hermit in order to mourn one's relative." But in this real-life tableau, the children didn't have to act; they were stunned—the only ones who seemed to grasp that their mother had been lying in a coffin outside their living room window for three weeks.

Li Bin ignored the fussing relatives and set about writing the strips of calligraphy that would be used to decorate the family's apartment. He wielded the writing brush expertly, filling strips of red and white paper with characters announcing grief and sadness, the phrases worn and tired but still true.

Then he took a small earthen tile out of his bag and placed it carefully on a coffee table. He opened a bottle of black ink and used a writing brush to write onto the tile the woman's name, when she died, where she was born, and which family she belonged to. When the coffin was in the ground, it would be placed on top before the hole was filled in. This was insurance in case one day her tombstone toppled and someone dug up the coffin. Then those people in the future would know who was inside. The notice needed heavenly protection, so Li Bin fished out a plastic bag holding a broad, flat seashell. He carefully poured red ink into the shell and used another brush to add swirling, talismanic symbols in red ink. These gave it a divine provenance that would warn any believer against disturbing the dead woman's rest.

This was a task Li Bin had performed countless times since he began working with his father as a teenager. But to the dead woman's family members this was almost magical. All had more formal education than Li Bin, but he had beautiful, strong calligraphy, and he could write the standard characters used for centuries in pre-Communist China, not the simplified peasant Chinese that the Communist Party had pushed for the past seventy years. They stared at him as if he were from another planet. He worked quickly and efficiently, sitting on the edge of the sofa, the strips of paper filling up with characters and symbols they barely understood.

The *suona* group arrived, dressed in dirty clothes and carrying battered instruments. They set up in the parking lot in front of the coffin: two speakers, an electric keyboard, and a microphone, all powered by an extension cord that snaked up the side of the family's balcony and into their living room. The musicians had brought large bricks of coal, which they tossed on the pavement and lit to warm themselves. They held out cracked hands to catch some warmth, the sooty smoke billowing around their heads.

Soon, they were blaring the only two songs they knew—a contrast to the rich repertoire that the Li family might have been performing at this moment. Of course no one had asked the neighbors about all of this, and why should they? The woman had died, and now there was a funeral. Protesting against the noise would be like complaining about the weather.

Li Bin rallied the family again.

"Come on, it's time to go out and kowtow."

"What, now?" The husband said, looking around nervously. "What about lunch?" It was going to be a big affair, with several tables at a restaurant. But the funeral had a timeline that was unalterable, even for city people. "You're going to the village this afternoon to burn the other offerings, and then tomorrow is the burial. Now is the time."

"Oh, right, right, right," the man said, and pushed his children out the door.

The three of them plus other family members knelt in two rows to the left and right of the altar, the coffin above them. The picture of the dead woman looked down at them.

"Now," Li Bin said. "Kowtow!"

They did it three times at Li Bin's command and went back inside.

"These people don't know anything!" Li Bin muttered under his breath.

"City people?" I asked.

"People in the city never know that much about these things, but he's the worst. A teacher! A bookworm. What does he know?"

———

Li Bin's son was home for the weekend but was invisible. Li Binchang was a quiet boy of eleven who spent his time on the computer, zapping monsters and sending messages to his friends. He had the fair, smooth face of his parents but seemed disconnected from their lives, just as they were from his. They worked nonstop in their downstairs store, but he had no idea how to bend bamboo or write an elegy. And they could look at his grades but could not help him with his homework. His parents knew how to deal with the world of spirits, but he was trying to succeed in the world of the living.

Sometimes, it felt as if he weren't really here, but the couple always explained their move to the city as being strictly for him. They had left the village a few years ago so he could have better schooling, and Li Bin hustled up new business to pay his monthly tuition of nearly $500, a huge sum for a *yinyang* man in a poor part of the country. The boy's picture was everywhere in their little apartment, especially two big ones taken at a professional studio on his last birthday. A round picture about two feet in diameter showed him wearing the white outfit of a tennis pro and carrying two badminton rackets over his shoulder. In another photograph, the boy wore a white tuxedo in front of a bookcase crammed with leather tomes and DVDs. He held a magazine in his right hand and looked slyly at the camera. Next to him were the words "Beautiful Story" in Chinese and "Cover Story" in English. Underneath were the lyrics to an imaginary song:

> *I must be dreaming*
> *Or am I really lying here*
> *My dreams are coming true*
> *Just one touch.*

Li Bin looked blankly at the computer screen when he entered the room, then asked his son in a sharp tone if he had completed his homework. The boy answered with a distracted nod. Li Bin grunted, then headed out to lunch. Squatting on the floor in front of a half-completed funeral wreath, Jing Hua shot him a disapproving look—a waste of money, she seemed to say, and how about helping out here? But the meal was free, and the person who had invited him would also pay him $50 to help choose a date for a store opening. So it was a business meal, and a lucrative one.

But it was true that there was something not quite right about this sort of lifestyle. At the very least, it was ruinously unhealthy. In the countryside, even a Daoist *yinyang* man like Old Mr. Li had chores to do. And in China's large cities, a consciousness of wellness was taking hold. But here in these provincial towns, people had the money to smoke, drink, and eat too much and nothing to prevent them from doing so—no hard work and no traditional strictures. Every meal was a series of bad choices accepted as part of being a good host or guest. The more the better; refusal was not an option. It was understood as tradition but felt more like a misunderstanding.

Over lunch we also discussed an idea that the two of us had been hatching. My home was in Berlin, and I thought it would be fun if his group performed in Germany. I could show him around, and they could see a new country. We called up Steve Jones, the musicologist who usually accompanies them on their trips. He agreed, and in the coming months we began organizing the paperwork.

After lunch, Li Bin and I drove to the south end of Yanggao Town to look at the future. The government was building twenty towers of twenty floors each, with each floor home to four apartments. That would be sixteen hundred apartments. If each had three people, then that would mean about another five thousand fewer farmers.

Li Bin drove slowly. He approved. This was new; this was modern. This is what he had done. There was one crucial difference: he had chosen to move to Yanggao Town, while these towers were part of an experiment in social engineering. The government was moving 250 million people into cities over a ten-year period, ending in 2022. Over the previous decades, China had urbanized fast—from 20 percent living in cities in the 1980s to nearly half by the middle of the second decade of the twenty-first century. But officials thought this was not enough; modern countries were urban, not rural. So urbanization, natural or forced, must be good. And now that the government was flush with cash, it went full tilt.

The plan worked like this: the government tore down villages and gave the farmers a free apartment in a neighboring town or city. This was possible because all land was owned by the state; farmers might feel they had "their" family land, but the Communist revolution had actually ended all private landholding. People held leases for only a set amount of time—typically twenty to thirty years for farmland and seventy for apartments. In addition to the free apartment, the government calculated how much grain they could have grown on their old plot of land and gave them the cash equivalent—the idea being that at least they could afford to buy grain if they could not find work.

In exchange, the government got the farmers' land. If it was near a town, the land rights were often sold to developers, and the proceeds used to build the new housing areas and to pay government operating budgets for a few years. If the land stayed agricultural, governments encouraged industrial farming of profitable cash crops. And in some cases it reforested the area, especially in mountain regions where overpopulation in past centuries had pushed desperate farmers to clear land for planting.

From a technocratic point of view, all of this made sense. But none of it was voluntary, and it treated farmers' most precious and emotional asset—land—as an abstraction. Some people welcomed the new policies, especially people like Li Bin, who wanted to make the move anyway. Perhaps they already had a job driving a taxi or working in a factory. For them, a free apartment in the city was a bonus. But many people actually had emotional ties to their homestead. Their lives were now confined to a thousand-square-foot apartment a hundred feet up. Many ended up on antidepressants, while social workers in these housing projects spoke of suicides. Gone were the days when they could step out of their front door onto their land and shape their future with their own hands—to *jie diqi*, to touch the earth's qi.

As we drove past tower after tower, I thought how a big country like China with such a long history should have striking regional variation. But increasingly it all looked the same: a homogeneous landscape of highways and high-rises. Trees would be planted, and public transportation made available—the government, after all, is brilliant at infrastructure—but none of it was attractive or special. The outcome wasn't surprising: the country had one landowner, the state, with one aesthetic style, utilitarian-fascist. Housing was functional, while public buildings were meant to make visitors feel small.

I asked Li Bin what city people asked for the most when they consulted him. He craned his head forward over the steering wheel to look up before answering.

"In the countryside, people have very concrete questions, like when to marry or hold a funeral," he said.

I nodded and remembered the spring when the woman asked Old Mr. Li if she should divorce her husband, or when the man asked the spirit medium why he had broken his wrist.

"But in the city the questions are much more vague," Li Bin continued. "They don't know what the future will hold, and they want someone to reassure them."

Like everything in China, the woman's burial began early. Already at 6:30 the next morning, a gang of migrant laborers had returned to dismantle the tent around the coffin. They did so in brutally efficient, almost violent fashion. They tore down the paper decorations that we had affixed yesterday. The calligraphy declaring the loss of a parent, the scores of paper chrysanthemums—all went into a bonfire in the parking lot. They worked fast and hard, wielding wire cutters to snip the cables holding the screens of flowers. The wreaths would go to the tomb, but the tent served no more purpose here. The altar offerings that had been carted here yesterday were tossed aside and the coffin laid bare.

Only a dozen relatives—half the number of the day before—were there to escort the coffin to the village. It was bitterly cold. The children put on down jackets under their white mourning clothes, preparing for the walk.

Soon everyone formed a procession. The scrappy *suona* players began their one-tune concert, the horns wailing as we walked out of the Garden of the Peaceful Masses. Teenage nieces and nephews of the deceased led the way, lighting off firecrackers to purify the area. We turned west. In front of us was Dragon Phoenix Mountain, part of the Taihang Mountains that run up to Beijing and Miaofengshan. After fifteen minutes, we stopped on the outskirts of town. The coffin was put on a flatbed truck decorated with the wreaths. The laborers jumped up on the truck to accompany the dead woman, and everyone else squeezed into cars. We drove slowly along the country road heading west out of town.

We paralleled Dragon Phoenix Mountain, which began to glow from the sun. Along its ridge were modern windmills, their blades like a bullfighter's banderilla stabbed into the back of a defeated animal. I wondered what they did for the mountain's *fengshui*.

After fifteen minutes, we turned sharply left, almost doubling back on the road. The husband's ancestral village came up quickly after a ridge, a group of forty or fifty small brick homes. Almost no one was outside, but the chimneys puffed coal smoke, giving the village a cozy look in the morning light. We drove along a rutted dirt road past banks of hard-packed loess soil. The yellow earth colored everything in the village, even the houses, making it at once warm from the color and bleak from the monotony.

"There," Li Bin said, and turned left along a narrower road, almost a path. We only stopped when we ran out of graded earth. Behind us was the flatbed truck with the coffin and a dozen workers. I wondered what their ride had been like in the cold. They jumped off, shovels and pickaxes gripped tightly in their bare hands. They began clearing earth from the edge of the grave site so they could better position the coffin. A relative from the village set off firecrackers and small rockets to scare away the ghosts.

I realized that almost none of the city relatives had come. It was just Li Bin, the workers, the husband and children, and me. The dead woman was in the ground within half an hour. The husband told the men to start putting in the earth.

"Stop!" Li Bin said. As usual, the husband had almost botched the ceremony.

Li Bin ran over to the grave and crouched next to it, so close I thought he would fall in. He pulled out a *fengshui* wheel and stared at it. He looked at the mountains and down at the woman's grave. He grunted. She was pointing in the right direction. He had had an argument with the husband a week earlier when he'd suggested one location for the grave. Li Bin had gone to visit it and noticed that it was surrounded by trees. "*Qiu*," he had said simply. It meant imprisonment and was written like this: 囚—a person, 人, inside four walls, 囗. The woman would not be free surrounded by the trees. The location had been bad.

When he told me the story, he'd shrugged his shoulders at the husband's ignorance. The man had been accompanied by his three

elder brothers. They had lived longer in the countryside before moving to the city and had immediately understood the problem. The
math teacher couldn't get it until Li Bin had written out the character
and explained that the walls were the trees. What a bookworm! Li
Bin had thought to himself.

The new plot looked fine, and Li Bin called for the tile. He handed
it to a worker who jumped down into the hole and placed it on the
coffin. Li Bin nodded his head. Now the coffin could be covered.

They labored quickly and silently, the sound of their movements
drowned out by the wind tearing across cornstalks. Impaled by their
jagged ends were small plastic strips that swung like hundreds of
small flags in a storm. These tiny shreds were all that was left from
sheets laid over the field in the spring to keep the newly planted seeds
warm. When the sprouts emerged, farmers had torn away the plastic
sheets but did not bother to dispose of them properly. Rural China
was full of this detritus, part of its transformation from the center
of Chinese civilization to its garbage dump. But today, the plastic
strips added a surreal feeling. Whipped uncontrollably, caught by the
low sun, bursting with white light, tearing at the stalks, whirring like
locusts, they heaved as if the ground itself were trembling.

A gust picked up one of Li Bin's paper wreaths and flung it cart-
wheeling across the field until a worker ran it down. We bent over
and waited for the wind to pause. Finally, the workers put up the
tombstone. Li Bin put a *ling peng*, a spirit branch, on it. It marked the
grave.

Everyone stood around dumbly until the foreman, one of Li Bin's
most trusted contractors, raised his eyebrows: *When would the children
sweep their mother's grave?* Without that final act of filial piety, the ceremony couldn't end.

Li Bin raised his eyebrows. *I'm not going to do anything more for these
people,* he answered back silently.

"Here," the foreman said, brusquely handing a broom to the girl
and a shovel to the boy. "Sweep. Clockwise. Sweep the loose earth
up onto the mound. Clean up the grounds."

The children froze, unsure what to do.

"Go!" the foreman called out sharply.

The girl took the little hand broom and began sweeping madly at
the dirt, pushing it toward the mound. The boy followed, shoveling

the earth onto the pile. A well-tended grave has a proper mound, not one flattened by the rain and the wind. It has to be regularly tended, ideally by the deceased's children. This is part of the concept of *xiao*, or filial piety. Being a good child doesn't end with a parent's death; duty continues until one's own death and is then picked up by the next generation, the living never forgetting the dead, a debt that can never be repaid: the living existing to placate the departed.

The children went around and around the grave, tossing the earth up so the mound grew. The girl lunged furiously at the loose clods, whacking them toward the pile that marked her mother's corpse, tears streaming off her face onto the dry ground.

Her brother stooped and straightened like a marionette, his face slack in disbelief. The two hadn't known what to do, but now this was all they knew. This was for their dead mother. Around and around they went, shoveling the earth, building a small pyramid.

The foreman bowed his head in embarrassment. He hadn't meant to be so cruel. He bit his lip and stepped forward, stopping them by gently putting his hands on their shoulders. He nodded his head at them: enough. They had done their duty. They were good children.

Their ritual was over for today. But each Qingming they would return to sweep the earth back onto the funeral mound, a lifelong battle against the wind. The children bowed their heads, and now even the boy started crying. Their mother was gone. A few feet away, the husband stood awkwardly. How to bury one's wife? How to comfort one's children?

The workers began burning the paper wreaths and the garbage. It all burned quickly, whipped by the wind. The paper seemed to disappear in a second, with only the sunflower stalks crackling for another few minutes. Two days earlier, Jing Hua had carefully built all of this in the family workshop, and now it vanished.

Li Bin placed the woman's picture in front of the tombstone and dug out three little holes with his right pinkie. He lit three sticks of incense and put them in. Then he walked around the grave and sprinkled the mound with the *wu gu,* the five grains: millet, barley, sesame, soybean, rice. These guaranteed prosperity or abundance in the afterlife.

The husband looked at him gratefully. It was another thing he hadn't thought of, but this strange *yinyang* man had. His wife had been given a proper send-off. Everything possible had been done to ensure a peaceful rest. The ceremony was finished.

Back home, the children symbolically washed their hands and faces of the grave's earth. Then everyone sat on the sofa in front of the television, blank now for the first time in days.

The bill came to 9,988 yuan, most of it money for subcontractors: the workers, renting the tent, the coffin, the tombstone, the musicians, and so on. The math teacher carefully went over every line of Li Bin's handwritten bill.

"You're charging 500 for the tent. It should only be 300."

"I don't set the price. That's a subcontractor's amount."

"But it was supposed to be 300."

"That's for the first ten days. You had her out there in the parking lot for nearly three weeks! Each extra day was another 20 yuan."

"Look," the math teacher said, "let's not argue about money at a time like this!"

"I agree."

"So 300 is okay? That's it then."

"I don't set the price! Call him and ask if you don't believe me."

"Oh, let's forget about it. Three hundred."

"You're acting like you're conceding, but you're not!"

"But it should be 300."

"Okay, fine: 9,788. I'll take the loss."

"Here, let's make it 9,800," the teacher said magnanimously. On this day of his wife's burial, he had just saved 188 yuan, or about $30.

Li Bin took the money and left.

"I didn't even charge him for the calligraphy paper and a lot of other things. If I'd known it would be like that, I would have itemized everything. I have to cover the 200 now."

Li Bin drove back to his store and greeted Jing Hua, who was cooking lunch in the back room. He handed her the money, and she carefully wrote it in their ledger. Within a matter of minutes, a stream of creditors came calling: the foreman collecting money for his laborers, the *suona* musicians, and the man who had rented out the tent. When he heard the story about the cheap husband, he would only accept 300 from Li Bin; after all, they were old friends. After a long argument, Li Bin insisted he take the full amount; a deal was a deal. Jing Hua looked over and nodded her approval. They were townsfolk now, but they still had their principles.

Finally, Li Bin could relax. He went upstairs to look for his son but then remembered that it was Monday already. The boy was off at school for the week, leaving nothing but photographs.

24

Beijing: The Great Hermit

Ni Jincheng lived atop the city, looking down on it as if astride Miaofengshan. His hermitage, though, was not perched on a mountain or a skyscraper but was a roughly built penthouse on the roof of a three-story brick house. From the outside, the building looked like a combination of Florentine palazzo and New York tenement block. Fortresslike, it could only be entered through a combination of locked doors and staircases. But they were only precariously bolted onto the back of the structure like a rickety fire escape. You ascended up a few stairs but were stopped by a metal door in a frame protected by bright spikes sticking out in all directions. There was no buzzer, only his sharp-eared dogs, whose barks alerted Jincheng and sent him tramping down to let me in. Then he would lead the way up. His stairway bypassed the first two floors, which were rented out. At the third-floor landing, we would wave at his wife, Chen Jinshang, and then climb the final flight to his hideaway—proof of the Chinese saying that anyone can be a hermit on a mountain but "the great hermit lives in the city."

Today was a windy November afternoon, and when we got upstairs, he closed the door behind us. The walls and door were made mainly of glass; through them, the city's poorer southern suburbs stretched out to the horizon. The only distinctive marker amid the concrete was the high-speed rail line to Tianjin, the same one that whizzed past Old Mrs. Chen's village and the Temple of the Central Peak. When we sat down on old armchairs to chat, all we could see was the bright blue sky and thin clouds that streaked across the horizon.

Jincheng was wearing a gray pinstriped Chinese-style jacket, black trousers, and a felt fedora. When he took the hat off, I saw that he had shaved his head.

"Are you taking your vows?" I joked.

"Ha! No, not me. It's just more comfortable this way."

But there was a change. Jincheng was quieter. He had also lost weight, having sworn off alcohol and heavy food. Over the next year, he would even start walking regularly, which would allow him to stop taking medicine against high blood pressure and diabetes. I began to notice this among other pilgrimage society members. The boom years had been good to everyone but had wrecked their health with too much food, too much drink, and too much tobacco. Now a rethink was taking place. The ancient Chinese belief in *yangsheng*— nurturing life—was reasserting itself.

To our left, behind a glass wall, twenty European racing pigeons cooed and strutted.

"Your air force," I said to him.

"I've got an army and navy too." He pointed to three small dogs scampering around on the floor.

"And your navy?"

He pointed to a huge blue-and-white glazed porcelain vat in the corner. I got up to look. It was a giant fishbowl that rose three feet off the ground. Inside were four fat goldfish. A tube attached to an air pump kept it aerated.

"Let me tell you why it's there," he said. "This coming year, wealth is coming from the east and the south. That's why the fish are on the east side of the balcony."

Fish, or *yu* in Chinese, is a homonym for the word "abundance." So the fish would attract the wealth. I got that. And the south? He got up and opened a glass case. In it was a *ruyi* scepter made of jade. It would also attract the good forces in life.

"This year, evil influences are coming from the western direction," he said, walking to the west side of the room and pointing to a golden gourd-shaped container. It held Buddhist scriptures. They would deflect the evil.

None of this was affected or on the advice of someone he had hired. It was actually how he lived. In the past, all of this had been part of life in the *hutongs*. It was a set of physical objects and intangible practices that were hard to separate: the city planning, the architecture, the religion, the hobbies, the relations among people. The first two did not exist anymore in a meaningful way—not just in Beijing, but across China. The rest of it—the beliefs and practices, the ideas and relations among people—was trying to find a home in these oversized cities and depopulated villages. Not everyone tried as hard as Jincheng to make it work, or knew as much, but the effort was everywhere to see: the shelves devoted to traditional teachings that could be found in almost every bookstore; the heavy bracelets that men wear to show their piety; the religious icons placed on the dashboards of taxis; the temples filled on holy days; the burned paper on the sides of roads; the growing number of lay believers; the popularity of Buddhist or Daoist websites; the smartphone apps that explain the solar terms. They were pieces from the past settling into a new pattern.

The practices often did not fit into organized religion, but then Chinese religion has always been run by ordinary people, with little input from authorities or clergy. It has always been held together by daily routines—like the unseen forces of an atom. And it is how more and more people experience spirituality around the world: as private events, sometimes unnamed but which hold great meaning.

This did not mean that Jincheng embraced the new era. He saw the old ways of organizing religious life—the traditional pilgrimage associations with their arcane rules—as the proper way to do things. They provided structure that helped guide people. Now even the pilgrimage associations were less strict than before. In the past, all were based on volunteer work; the idea of accepting money to perform at a temple would have been insulting. But now some of the groups—especially those engaged in martial arts or other colorful performances—did it for money. They were hired by stores for their grand openings or went to commercialized temple fairs for a fee. Some even performed at funerals for money. To Jincheng, this was shocking, even immoral, but I did not find it so strange. What funeral home in the West offers its services for free? Or even a church? Of course, Jincheng was not naïve. He understood the forces that pushed money to the center of many considerations.

"Say you want to participate in a friend's funeral. How do you tell your boss you're doing that? In the past, you could just say you can't work because a friend is having a funeral. People understood that.

But now you have to take vacation. And people now live far apart. It's not just down the street. You have to rent a truck or van to carry the performers or for us to transport the teapots and the altar. So people ask for money as compensation. They say it's travel and eating money; that's how they justify the money. But for some there's even a profit. Society has changed."

"Your father said that not everything new is bad."

"I know, but he was against commercialization."

"What did he think of associations that aren't properly recognized?"

The old way of doing things was clear. Groups that were not recognized by other pilgrimage associations were "black associations." Recognition came through building ties, working piously, and getting sponsors. At the appropriate time, the elders of the associations approved you. Then you held a giant feast called *hehui*, or celebrating an association. At the festivity, all the participants signed a giant piece of red cloth. When you ascended Miaofengshan for the next three years, you wore the cloth to show you were legitimate. You also began to carry a little triangular flag with the name of your association. Cloth streamers were added from that point on. They were white, and handwritten on them with a calligraphy brush were the dates of each major pilgrimage or event that you attended. They were your history, there for everyone to see.

But many groups no longer bothered with that. They simply went to Miaofengshan. They did not know how to greet each other. They did not understand which groups were once sponsored by the last dynasty and which had been formed last week. They could not even perform very well. They just came to the temples and danced a watered-down version of a routine that anyone could learn in a few days. Worst of all to purists like Jincheng, they seemed satisfied and happy.

Jincheng flipped on the television and inserted a disc. It was a ninety-minute documentary of their own *hehui* in 2003. I have been to several of these celebrations over the past decade, but this was many times bigger. The entire street downstairs had been blocked off with an eighteen-foot-high tent. The leaders of all the key associations begin arriving, pulling up like VIPs arriving at a film festival.

Old Mr. Ni and Jincheng were waiting for them, Old Mr. Ni in a flashy yellow scarf, black-and-yellow silk blouse, and silver trousers, with his head shaved, just as Jincheng's was now. Jincheng had a full head of thick black hair and a tight Chinese jacket showing off his broad shoulders. As the dignitaries got out of their cars, they produced their flags and then gave something like a curtsy—one leg forward, one back, and a slight bow. At the same time, they dipped their association's flag. Old Mr. Ni did the same thing. It was repeated three times, each one punctuated with cymbals and drums.

"He's dead," Jincheng said of the man. "Him too, and him. Dead.

"There, look at that," Jincheng said. It was a complete set of porcelain from the old imperial kilns at Jingdezhen.

"Liu Licai, Wei Shizhong, Zhang Fengliang. They all came," Jincheng said, pointing to more people on the screen. "Most of them are dead."

"Well, people do die," I ventured, and Jincheng looked at me as if I had not really gotten the point. These women and men who had rescued the pilgrimage after the Cultural Revolution, who had restored tradition after the ravages of the twentieth century, most of them were gone. Left behind were just people like him and his brother or Mrs. Qi. How could they compare?

The scene cut to a stage. An emcee strode atop.

"The king of hawkers," Jincheng said glumly. "He had a really loud voice. He's dead too."

The Hawker King wore a blue silk gown, a red silk vest, and a black skullcap. He bellowed out everyone's name in a deep, beseeching baritone.

The camera panned over Old Mrs. Chen. She was much younger then, with some black in her hair, radiant, dressed in a red silk dress. The two associations had held their ceremony at the same time.

"She's alive," I said.

Jincheng rumbled an inaudible comment.

The Hawker King read out a formal statement declaring the family's fealty to Our Lady of the Azure Clouds and then shouted out grandly that they were formally initiated. There was a loud cheer, and then the fun began. The performing associations did their martial arts, comic skits, and lion dances. Finally, a giant banquet of one hundred tables with a dozen people each. Everyone drank a special grain alcohol that Jincheng had ordered, *Zuijiuxin*, or the Heart of Inebriation.

"I wish you could have been there," he said.

"Me too," I said. "I like the name of the liquor."

"I've still got some. I'll give you a bottle."

Jincheng's wife had heard the television and walked up to join us.

"The old films!" Chen Jinshang said with a laugh. "You should have come here ten years ago when all these people were alive! Dad wanted you to write his story. We said okay, but then he departed."

"But you—you are alive."

"I'm getting old," Jincheng answered.

"You're only fifty-six. People of your generation are running China. And you saw a lot of the old ways too. You're like a bridge."

"That's true too."

"You learned from the old Daoists living next to the old family home. What did you do back then?"

"I was just a small fellow, and really mischievous. On this or that side of the temple wall, I was always getting into trouble. Our eaves touched the temple wall. Our house had a small yard, and I'd climb the wall and drop down into the temple. When everyone was lighting incense, I'd steal some of the fruit off the altar! That old Daoist, Daoist Han, I called him Grandpa or Master Grandpa. Daoist Han and our family, we were all disciples."

"What was the most important thing you learned from him?"

"Respect. I learned to respect other people."

We retired to the third floor, where Chen Jinshang began boiling noodles. We talked about Old Mrs. Chen, the flower lady. Over the summer, she had been the focus of the Temple of the Central Peak's pilgrimage. But later that summer the inevitable happened, and her neighborhood was torn down to construct high-rise apartments. The temple was spared, but the family had to move out for a few years until the new towers were complete. The family members split up, each one staying with relatives or renting. But Old Mrs. Chen was having a hard time, staying with her daughter in a sixth-floor apartment.

"They have an elevator, right?" I said.

"That's not the point," Jincheng said. "You don't understand what it's like if you're a farmer and you're used to going out the door and seeing the land. You are in touch with the qi from the land. That's called *jie diqi*. If you've never worked the land, you'll never understand."

"She's become a bit confused," Chen Jinshang said to me.

"I saw her at Miaofengshan and talked to her. She seemed fine. And at her village's temple fair, it was she who walked up to me and greeted me."

"Sure," Jincheng said. "Then she was fine. In the spring, she was fine. In the summer, she was fine. But then they tore down her home. Now she's confused."

We ate, and then it was time for me to go. I looked over at Jincheng and complimented him on his jacket. It seemed like a perfect blend of East and West: gray pinstripes but collarless and with Chinese-style knotted buttons.

"It's yours." Jincheng got up, took off the jacket, and handed it to me.

"I didn't mean it like that. I like it, but I don't want it."

Jincheng laughed; I had said I admired it, which was basically like asking for it. We spent the next five minutes arguing.

"I'll just take a picture and have it copied."

"The tailor who made these is dead."

"But another tailor can surely copy it!"

"No. They are all dead."

"That can't be true!"

"Dead."

"I don't want it."

"It's yours! Take it!"

"No, no, no!"

"You're funny! It's now yours, not mine. Take it!"

"But you can't get new ones made! The tailors are all dead!"

Jincheng stopped, took a breath, and looked me in the eye. "You don't understand. A jacket like this only has meaning if it's passed on to someone who wants it. It's yours now. I'm passing it on to you. Get it?"

25

Ritual: Eastern Lightning

One winter day while I was walking through the streets of Chengdu, a text message popped up on my phone:

The Judgment Day isn't trustworthy, cults cook up nonsense to conceal their calamitous heart; they trick people out of money, into having sex and joining religions; joining them invites disaster. Eastern Lightning is a cult, its false claims about Judgment Day disturb people's hearts. Science opens our eyes; cultish monsters become nothing. Shanghai Anti-cult Association.

Spurred by a popular Mayan prophecy that the world would end on the Winter Solstice, China was awash with doomsday predictions. Most Chinese people took these prophecies with a grain of salt, or at least a dose of entrepreneurial spirit. One Chinese businessman built an ark out of wood to carry the lucky few to safety. A Beijing office worker constructed what he said was a cataclysm-proof bunker high up on the Tibetan plateau with an $8,000 entry fee. I checked my watch. It was noon, December 21, the day the world was supposed to end. Either all of this was a hoax, or I had a maximum of twelve hours to live.

Of all the groups in China touting the world's end, only one was truly feared: Eastern Lightning, a Christian splinter sect also known as Almighty God. The group had been active in the 1990s but then fell quiet. Perhaps inspired by the Mayan forecasts or deeper premonitions, its members began meeting in large groups again around 2012, repeating the biblical doomsday prophecies that are part of its theology. This revival had spurred the Shanghai Anti-cult Association to send out its message, and the government to round up roughly one thousand believers. According to official reports, the group was behind forty riots and generally stirring up unrest.

Like Falun Gong before it, Eastern Lightning managed to anger both the government and other religious groups. For authorities, the main concern was political. The group attacked the Communist Party as the "great red dragon," and claimed that its rule was so plagued with catastrophes that biblical doomsday prophecies were coming to pass. As early as 1992, government officials had declared it "counterrevolutionary" and pledged to eradicate it, sending members to thought-reform classes. For their part, Christian groups rejected Eastern Lightning's theology as heretical and its methods as criminal. They said the group hijacked entire congregations, most famously in 2002, when it allegedly held thirty-four church members in a house until they converted. It was also accused of using femmes fatales to seduce and blackmail mainstream pastors into taking their entire congregations over to Eastern Lightning.

Almost no one felt the group was worth defending—especially after a family that is alleged to have followed Eastern Lightning bludgeoned a woman to death in a McDonald's restaurant in 2014. But even before that, it was routinely denounced as a cult by everyone from the *People's Daily* to *The Daily Beast,* with Western reporters relishing its members' odd beliefs, especially the use of "flirty fishing" methods. Angry, resentful, and secretive, Eastern Lightning seemed like the perfect cult.

Qianlong was one of China's greatest emperors, reigning from 1735 to 1796 in what he immodestly called the *shengshi,* or the Prosperous Age, an era of affluence and glory for China. Under his long rule, the Qing Empire doubled in size. He built lavish palaces, had himself portrayed in paintings as a Buddhist saint of wisdom, penned forty thousand poems, and oversaw the compilation of a thirty-six-thousand-volume encyclopedia. When the British envoy George Macartney visited in search of expanding trade, Qianlong famously rebuffed him, writing that the empire "possesses all things in prolific abundance and lacks no product within its borders."

But at the peak of this self-satisfied era, Qianlong's empire was beset by attacks from sorcerers. They plagued China's richest region, terrifying the population through an unusual practice: they clipped hair off people's heads and chanted incantations to steal their souls. Panic spread across the region. Mobs attacked people suspected of witchcraft. One man was set upon when he tousled the hair of a child on the street. Local magistrates tortured false confessions out of the accused, and the emperor sent panicky instructions to his subordinates to handle the cases with utmost severity. All of this took place in Jiangnan, the wealthy region of silk, tea, and rice around the Yangtze River—then as now the most prosperous part of China and the economic backbone of the empire. And yet it was here that people succumbed to mass hysteria. Why?

The case fascinated the historian Philip Kuhn, who wrote a book about the era called *Soulstealers*. He pointed out that this was a period of great economic change. Silver from the New World was flooding into China. Trade became the way to gain wealth and get ahead, undermining the Confucian ideals of farming, scholarship, and propriety. A huge gap between rich and poor opened. The population boomed. The ecology deteriorated. Overseeing this fragile state was a brittle political system. Dominated by ethnic Manchus like Qianlong, it lacked broad support among the Chinese majority and was hypersensitive to unrest of any sort. Although Qianlong declared his age glorious, the Qing's best years were behind it, and China was about to enter the turbulent nineteenth century: "the eve of China's tragic modern age," as Kuhn put it, when there was "a widespread perception of ambient evil, of unseen forces that threatened men's lives."

Although we shouldn't misuse the past as an allegory for today, it is hard to miss the parallels. Today's China is also undergoing rapid urbanization that has brought wealth and an improved standard of living but also destroyed traditional social relations. Its environment is severely degraded; its political leaders brook no direct criticism. Reflecting the ruling systems around them, society's heretical members are hierarchical and undemocratic, while society's reaction is harsh and brutal. Even though unlikable, these marginal groups, Kuhn argued, are keys to understanding ourselves:

Many aspects of our own contemporary culture might be called premonitory shivers: panicky renderings of unreadable messages about the kind of society we are creating. Our dominating passion, after all, is to give life meaning, even if sometimes a hideous one.

In the 1920s, with foreign missionaries on the wane, a Pentecostal revival swept through China and created new Christian groups, many of them rooted in Chinese ideas about spirituality. These new denominations—in today's parlance they might be called sects—offered spiritually hungry Chinese ecstatic practices, such as prophecy, divine healing, and speaking in tongues. Some lived communally in the countryside, with seers among them traveling to heaven and returning with visions. Others like the True Jesus Church—the one that Xu Jue encountered when she lived in Germany after her son's death—were based on visions that a Beijing cloth dealer experienced. Sternly dogmatic evangelicals like Wang Mingdao rejected Western missionaries, especially those advocating liberal ideas, in favor of literal interpretation of the Bible. Another critic of foreign influences was Ni Tuosheng, or Watchman Nee. He developed his ideas at the height of China's nationalist movement after World War I, stridently opposing foreign denominations as unscriptural. Instead, he set up what he called "Local Churches" in villages across China. Also a mystic, Watchman Nee developed elaborate millennial views of the world's end that he set out in volumes of books.

When the Communists took power in 1949, they created the Three-Self Patriotic Movement to unite the country's Protestant churches under an umbrella organization that the government could control. But this government association mainly took over the old mission churches. Some indigenous church leaders were co-opted, but most were banned. Preachers like Wang Mingdao spent decades in labor camps for refusing to join the Three-Self churches, while Watchman Nee died in prison in 1972.

Their ideas, though, did not perish. Some of their followers found safety abroad, such as Watchman Nee's church, which further developed its indigenous theology. One idea that grew was to "call out" God's spirit. This movement became widely known as the Shouters and spread through many Chinese-American communities.

Inside China, Christianity did more than survive; it flourished. This was for two key reasons. One was the unimaginable famines and political campaigns of the Mao period, which seem to have driven people to religion—especially to groups with a strong millenarian streak. In addition, the government's political campaigns crippled its own religious apparatus. The Three-Self Patriotic Movement ceased to function effectively for more than a decade. With government churches shut, Christians organized on their own.

When the Mao era ended, the underground groups were bolstered by an avalanche of books, pamphlets, tracts, audiotapes, and videos sent in by their brethren living abroad. This was the start of a new great wave of religious innovation. With the official church decimated by Mao, groups like the Shouters flourished, especially because they emphasized personal charisma and spiritual gifts over theological training and a formal clergy. Throughout the 1980s and 1990s, wave after wave of new Christian groups rose up: Established King; Lord God; Narrow Gate in the Wilderness; and Three Grades of Servants. These groups, according to the historian Daniel Bays, represented "one of the largest examples in Christian history anywhere of creative cross-cultural adaptation."

Most of the leaders of these groups were declared counterrevolutionary. After the 1999 Falun Gong uprising made the government especially sensitive to religious groups, these sects were broken up and senior leaders executed. One, however, survived. It drew its name from a prophecy of Jesus's return in the Gospel of Matthew 24:27:

For as the lightning cometh out of the east, and shineth even unto the west; so shall also the coming of the Son of man be.

Eastern Lightning was founded in 1991 by a former member of the Shouters, Zhao Weishan. While traveling in Henan, the thirty-nine-year-old Zhao met an eighteen-year-old woman named Yang Xiangbin. Zhao declared her to be the "female Christ"—the lightning in the east prophesied by Matthew. The group used the lexicon of Watchman Nee and his successors to press the idea that the end of time was imminent. Zhao and Yang reportedly fled to the United States around 2000, but the group continued to live on inside China.

Groups like Eastern Lightning are often dismissed as heretical—how can the Christ reappear in China? And of all places in Henan? And as a woman? Truly understanding the mind-set of Eastern Lightning believers would require many in-depth interviews with believers—something that has not been possible because of the group's secrecy. But reading the group's literature and thinking of recent Chinese history give clues to its popularity.

One is the group's birthplace in Henan. With 100 million people, it is China's most populous province, but it is also an area traumatized by history and poverty. Some of the Mao era's most disastrous experiments were centered here, such as the Great Leap Forward, whose famine is often reckoned to be the worst in history. Although we sometimes see events like the famine as ancient history, they were just thirty years in the past when groups like Eastern Lightning were founded. For someone like Zhao Weishan, the founder of Eastern Lightning, it would have been the defining moment in his life—as a nine-year-old watching people starve to death.

Even today, the province is one of China's least promising. Its poverty is not because it is particularly mountainous, which is often the case in China's impoverished borderlands, such as Yunnan and Guizhou Provinces. Instead, Henan is overpopulated, lacks resources, and depends on agriculture. It has little of the dynamism found in China's coastal region and instead is widely known for its crime and social unrest.

I thought of this one summer while traveling through Henan with Zhang Yinan, a local historian of Christianity and church leader. There were few reminders that this had been a cradle of Chinese civilization, home to two imperial capitals, and the birthplace of many famous historical figures. The cities were flat and faceless, the countryside a monolithic face of waving corn and wheat fields, and so many villages were devoid of even one temple. Thanks to the Communists, it was tabula rasa when the Mao era ended and religion was permitted again.

"They destroyed almost all the temples, and Confucianism was destroyed too," Zhang said to me. "It was a blessing from heaven."

These apocalypses are reflected in Eastern Lightning's theology. It holds that humans have gone through three eras of roughly two thousand years each: the Age of Law (which is also the time of the

Old Testament, or Jewish Bible, and its prophets); the Age of Grace (the past two thousand years since Jesus Christ's arrival); and now the Age of Kingdom. Just as Jesus superseded the Old Testament prophets, so too is Jesus's work now "outdated," according to the group's main work, *The Word Appears in the Flesh*. This is an era of turmoil, especially in China, which is referred to as the "great red dragon," drawing on vocabulary in the book of Revelation:

> *Because it has disintegrated within and its internal affairs have been in chaos, the great red dragon is doing the work of self-defense, preparing to flee to the "moon." But how could they escape from the hand of God? As God says, "They will have to drink the bitter cup they themselves create." When the internal disorder takes place, it will be the time when God leaves the earth. God will not "stay" in the country of the great red dragon any longer.*

Besides its portrayal of a China in disarray, Eastern Lightning's vocabulary, its images, and its femininity probably also helped to win followers. In describing God, the group did not use the standard Protestant term *shangdi*, instead preferring *shen*, which is primarily used in folk religion. Another familiar touch were the parallels to the Mao cult in the Cultural Revolution. Having a savior come from the east would be familiar to many worshippers, who grew up in the Mao era singing, "The East is Red, China has brought forth a Mao Zedong!" The new Christ being a female must have been another attraction. The majority of worshippers of China's unregistered churches are women, but the pastors are almost always men— think of Wang Yi's church and his expulsion of a church elder who advocated female pastors. Putting a woman at the center of worship would be a welcome change and hark back to popular Chinese deities, such as Our Lady of the Azure Clouds and the Buddhist goddess of mercy, Guanyin.

As for the paranoia and violence, it is hard not to see the parallels to China's recent violent past. The church's defense is that it did not order or inspire anyone to murder, calling the murderers "psychopaths," but the circumstances are unclear, making it hard to draw conclusions. At the very least, it is clear that the group uses confrontation and deception to win over adherents.

One widespread charge was that the group kidnapped other

Christians. These allegations are usually vague, and the charge of using sexual favors to lure pastors seems dubious, and probably reflects an effort to discredit the central role played by a woman. But the charges of bullying and of trying to hijack congregations are so common that they must at least reflect a fear among China's unregistered churches—a primordial unease, a feeling that believers' faith in the established churches is so shallow that their souls could be stolen.

26

Chengdu: Searching for Jesus

As Christmas arrived, it seemed that Wang Yi's church might not be able to hold a service. This was usually the high point of the year and a key chance to recruit followers; many Chinese are curious about the Western holiday but don't really understand it—who is the fat guy in the red suit, and what does it have to do with Jesus? The Christmas service was an opportunity for the congregation to invite friends to a fun evening, and maybe win over a few people. Usually these services were so popular that Early Rain rented out a ballroom. But this year, every time they booked a hotel's ballroom, they got a call an hour later from the manager apologetically backing out— clearly the result of government pressure. I began to wonder if it had all been too much: the seminary, the expansion plans, and linking up with other Reformed churches.

I visited Peng Qiang to ask him what he thought. He had his own church and had known Wang Yi for years. What did he think of these tensions between churches and the government? Was this a serious conflict? We sat in his chilly offices, like most buildings in southern China unheated in the winter. The damp Chengdu winter penetrated every room, every layer of clothing, but Peng was buoyant and laughed good-naturedly at my question.

"Let me answer your question by telling you about a dream I have. I have always wanted to make a movie about Christianity in China for my friends back in Los Angeles. People there just hear about the crackdowns and arrests, and they get worried for me. Some guy gets arrested a thousand miles from here and they call me up: Are you okay?

"I remember back when we were celebrating out by the river—

you remember, back in 2005 when Early Rain was locked out. Do you know what it was like? Was it suffering? Yes, it was suffering. We didn't know what would happen. But mostly, it was fun! People were happy and enthusiastic. I always say that Christians and revolutionaries have one point really in common: when you go to face a problem, you have *joy, you have hope*," he said, emphasizing the last few words by speaking them in English. "A revolutionary is like that, right?! I'm locked up and I'm facing death alone, but I'm happy about it!

"So if I were writing a screenplay about these events, it would be like this.

"They'd see the police blocking their door, saying, 'Sorry, you can't go inside.' Some brothers and sisters, their hearts are angry, but others say, 'Forget it, let's go down to the Jinjiang River.' And they'd find a place in the park by the river. The sun is coming out. It is beautiful. And then they'd start to sing. And these mamas from the church, they'd see the people in the park in the morning and say, 'Hey, young people, you should believe in Jesus too because then you'll understand why you're living.'

"Chengdu is full of teahouses, and they'd split up and go to drink tea. Everyone's really happy. And the plain-clothes police are following them. But it doesn't matter. People are talking, sharing, and praying. They're excited; they're happy.

"Then they go and eat hot pot, and the plain-clothes police are still going with them. They don't know why, but they do. And they're the sad ones. They're just following. Their lives, these police, their lives are *ridiculous*. Because every profession, it has something in it that allows *dignity* to emerge. If you're a police officer, your dignity is you're arresting bad people. Your bravery comes out. But here, what are you doing?

"So this script, it's different from what you read. It is suffering, or at least it's inconvenient, but overall there is God's grace. If God doesn't exist, then it's meaningless. But if God exists, then it makes sense."

Peng had others reasons to be optimistic. Yes, he agreed that Xi Jinping's administration was making a concerted effort to strengthen state control over society by arresting dissidents and lawyers. It was also promoting Chinese traditional values and religions at the expense of Christianity. But Peng stayed positive, not out of naïveté, but because he saw the longer-term problems in the government's hard-line approach. One is the cost of its "stability-maintenance" program, often known by its Chinese acronym, *weiwen* (pronounced "way-when"). According to government figures, authorities spend more money on *weiwen* than on national defense.

"*Weiwen* is very expensive. If someone in a housing complex hears singing from an apartment, he might call the police, but who pays for it? Police have a lot of real problems, like crime and terrorism. The police have to call up all these departments: the religious affairs office, the local constabulary, the national security, the Ministry of Civil Affairs. All these departments have to pay gas for their cars, overtime, meals. The first thing they'll all say is, 'Who's paying?' So now unless the central government issues an order to close down something, the local government is not that willing."

Talking to Peng reminded me why it was important to get out of the capital. There, the government's power seemed limitless; here it was tamed by distance. It would be naïve to downplay the hard political power of an authoritarian leader like Xi but equally glib to ignore long-term trends beyond the government's control.

Shortly before I left, Peng told me a story that summed up how life often played out in places like Chengdu. His daughter was six and a half years old and had started public school earlier that autumn. Neither Peng nor his wife wanted her to wear the red scarf of the Young Pioneers, the Communist youth group that almost all students join.

"We didn't expect it to come up so quickly, but after just three weeks she came home and said her teacher said they had to wear the scarf. We were upset."

Peng talked to her and tried to reason with her, saying she didn't have to, in fact that she shouldn't because it represented the Communist Party.

"I was too logical and she cried. She said every child will wear one. It's very colorful. It looks nice.

"But my wife is a counselor, and she used the right side of her brain to talk to her. She explained that you can be a good student without the red scarf. You are a child of God, and you don't want to wear something that isn't God's.

"So she said, 'Yes, I'm a child of God, and I don't want to wear the red scarf.' Then we prayed together."

Peng's wife went to school and thanked the teacher for being so good to the children but asked if the scarf was voluntary. The teacher said it was, so his wife told the teacher, "'We're a Christian family and it's not in accordance with our faith. But our child respects her teacher and will work hard and be a good pupil.' The teacher was fine and said, 'No problem.'"

The couple then wrote a polite letter to the teacher so she would have a written explanation in case the principal asked why one child wasn't wearing the red scarf. The daughter carried the letter to school. That afternoon, Peng and his wife met their daughter at the school gate.

"She was so happy, and I asked her why. She told us that that morning when the Young Pioneers were lining up, everyone lined up except her. But she didn't feel bad, because the teacher's assistant yelled out to the class, 'She doesn't have to participate. She's got faith!'"

At noon on Christmas Eve, I was sure the service would be canceled. With just a few hours to go, no hotel had agreed to hold them. But then I got a call from my friend Zhang Guoqing, the church's point man on social issues. They had succeeded. The service would be held at the Greenland Business Hotel, a third-rate hotel in one of the side streets near the church. I thanked him, but after hanging up, I wondered how many people would show up on such short notice.

I arrived at a quarter to seven, forty-five minutes before the service was supposed to start, but Early Rain members were already streaming through the lobby and up the stairs to the hotel's second-floor ballroom. The entrance to the room was filled with poster boards prepared for the event. They were three feet wide by six feet high and explained tonight's theme: "Searching for Jesus in Chengdu."

The posters were a bold experiment in retelling the city's history. They explained not only that Chengdu had a Christian history— that itself was something one couldn't read in any guidebook to Chengdu, in any textbook, or on any official website in China—but also that Christianity had played a huge role in the city's modernization from the mid-nineteenth to the mid-twentieth century.

One banner featured biographical sketches of the missionaries who reached Chengdu in the nineteenth century. Another, called "Precious Blood; We Cannot Forget," showed how these men and women had created from scratch all the modern medical infrastructure in the city: hospitals, clinics for pregnant women, and even an ambulance service. It stressed that anyone was served regardless of religious belief and that those working there did so out of belief, not for money. Another board showed how some of the city's most prestigious middle and high schools had been founded by missionaries. Maybe the most powerful poster showed a foundling hospital set up by missionaries and below it a picture of garbage bins in a neighboring province. There, in 2012, five babies had been dumped by a local orphanage. The contrast wasn't explained, but the message was obvious: Christianity saves lives; the state disregards them. At the bottom, in bold red letters, was a verse from the Gospel of John: "I will not leave you as orphans; I will come to you."

Reading the boards carefully, it was clear that the message wasn't that Western missionaries were good. It was that all missionaries were good—a direct challenge to the orthodox Communist version of history. It had always claimed that missionaries were bad—part of an imperialistic project to undermine China. But by the 1940s, the boards showed, many key missionaries were Chinese. A Bible study group in a university was led by a Chinese pastor. Chinese doctors took over the hospitals. The point was that Christianity was doing this; the fact that Westerners happened to have brought it to China was a historical accident.

After looking at the billboards, I walked into the ballroom. People were handing out brochures. One had a picture of the former Soviet leader Nikita Khrushchev with a quotation, "God knows I'm an atheist!" The pamphlet discussed the existence of God, noting that great scientists, such as Darwin and Einstein, had believed in God.

Another brochure attacked heresies. Eastern Lightning wasn't mentioned by name, but the flyer seemed like a clever move to show that Early Rain wasn't completely out of step with government policies. But as I flipped through the pamphlet, I realized that this wasn't the point. The back page of the brochure listed people in history who had overcome heresies. The last person on the list was Wang

Mingdao, the Christian leader who had defied Communist rule and spent twenty years in a labor camp. Implicitly, it was the government that was the heresy for having jailed Wang.

I gulped and pocketed the pamphlet. Guoqing came over, looking very nervous.

"Sit up front," he urged me. I asked if I might not be a bit more inconspicuous if I sat in the back, but he said no; he wanted me up front. "The *guobao* [state security] is here. I'm trying to manage it. It might be better if you're up front in a prominent position."

I didn't want to be part of their conflict with the state security, but I reasoned that if the government had wanted to close this down, it would have already. Barring some antigovernment propaganda during the service, it was going forward. So I sat in the front row. Before I settled into my seat, I looked behind me and counted twenty-five rows of twenty-five seats each. Almost all the seats were filled. This was easily double a normal service. Somehow, they had all come on such short notice and were gazing at the stage to see how the evening would unfold.

Wang Yi opened the service with a prayer that explained the topic of searching for Jesus in Chengdu.

"As Christians, as a congregation, as Chengduers, we don't have grounds not to know our history, to turn a deaf ear or a blind eye to the fact that missionaries helped build congregations here, as well as most of the schools, hospitals, and charitable organizations."

Another gauntlet thrown down to the state, I thought, although of course this wouldn't interest the agents at the back of the room. They were looking for something explicit that they could understand—an excuse to stop the meeting. And of course Wang Yi was too smart. He was aiming at the party's source of legitimacy—its monopoly over knowledge, especially its control of history—but this was too subtle for the agents.

"Saying this is just history is to defame the past. So we ask you, God, to let Chengdu become a city grateful to you and not let Chengdu people again be devoid of gratitude and reject the glad tidings."

Then came a one-act play called *Chengdu: This Evening We Won't Leave You Alone,* an allusion to the 2009 novel *Chengdu: This Evening Leave Me Alone* by a friend of Wang Yi's, the writer Murong Xuecan. The novel had been extremely popular a few years ago, recounting the stories of aimless, rootless friends who drink, gamble, and sleep their way through the city, with Murong describing the city like this:

> *Chengdu at night always looked gentle and soft. The colorful lanterns gave it a warm glow, and from all around came sounds of laughter and song. But I knew that for all its luster the city was slowly rotting. A tide of lust and greed surged from every corner, bubbling away, giving off a hot odor, like a stream of piss corroding every tile and every soul.*

The play was Wang Yi's answer. It involved a young couple meeting outside Sichuan University, which was founded by missionaries as West China Union University. In the opening sequence, the couple were reading newspapers and commenting on all the problems in society: unsafe food, dangerous roads, unscrupulous doctors. Then they mentioned that they had been together for a decade but were on the verge of divorce. He calls her a nitpicker. She thinks he is an arrogant poseur. Their love seems gone.

At this point, a psychiatrist came onstage, a humorous woman in her late thirties who froze the characters and pointed out what made them tick. The man's love was analyzed as lust born of chemical reactions. The woman's worries were angst resulting from insecurity. All these problems and issues could be solved with the right drugs, she said. The young people regained consciousness, and the young woman asked the psychiatrist, "So I'm just a collection of chemical particles moving, multiplying, on northern latitude 30.67, eastern longitude 104.06 degrees?"

"Correct," said the psychiatrist.

"So what sort of meaning do people's lives have?"

"Excuse me," the psychiatrist said, "but 'meaning' is not a rigorous expression."

Then the couple's old university teacher entered and asked them if they were still Christians; they were, sort of, they said, but not really practicing. When the teacher mentioned the school's Christian past, the play jumped back one hundred years to the May Fourth Movement of 1919, which called for more democracy and science in society. Radicals came on stage and bemoaned their soon-to-fail revolution, with China still not democratizing. A young man shouted, "Oppose corruption!" and was arrested by the police—the Nationalist Party's police, of course, but the parallel to today was obvious. The radicals and the couple suddenly realized that without a spiritual revolution all these efforts at political change or improving their personal relations were pointless.

The play ended with the cast members recounting their real stories. The psychiatrist had been on medication before finding God. The teacher is a leader in the church. The couple really were close to divorce before rediscovering Jesus and going to Early Rain. They now had a child. His name was Shuya, a short form for Yeshuya, or Joshua. That was the real name of Wang Yi's son and the name that Wang Yi had adopted as a pen name for several years in an effort to bypass the censors' ban on his publishing. The boy had one line to speak in the play, the last six words of which are a citation of Psalm 33:

> My name is Shuya, which is taken from "Joshua" in the Bible, because our family has been "chosen by Jehovah for his inheritance."

Wang Yi began his sermon by talking about what it had been like growing up as a little boy in the Sichuan countryside. Like most of the people in the audience—even many of the young ones just out of college, with white-collar jobs and the latest mobile phones—his family had been so poor that he had had no toys to play with. Instead, he played with ants, spending hours watching them crawl around, building their kingdoms and empires. One day, a storm cut off a group of ants from their home.

"It was like the Red Sea obstructing their way. They didn't know what to do. They had no way back. I took pity on them and wanted to help them because I could help them. I picked up every ant, there must have been one hundred of them, and put them in a bowl. Then I took it to the other side of the water, and I released them. Do you know what I felt like? I felt I was their savior," he said, and the audience laughed.

"I was only seven years old but felt I had done something really meaningful. I had delivered them. I had spent about an hour helping them, but to them it might have been five thousand years," and again the audience laughed at his reference to the five thousand years of Chinese culture—a point of pride among Chinese around the world that he was skewering as insignificant.

"Maybe one of them was really smart and later wrote a book. Maybe in it he wrote, 'The Dao that can be seen is not the true Dao / 'The name that can be named is not the true name.'"

These were the opening lines of Laozi's *Daodejing*, the Daoist classic—in Wang Yi's world, the work of ants who didn't understand the world around them.

"Thirty years later I began to read the Bible seriously. I came into contact with Christians. And I realized I hadn't been the ants' savior. If I had really loved those ants, and if I really had had the power, I wouldn't have been just a superhero. If I were God, I would have been like God's son, Jesus, who when humans had lost their way, when they were on their way to devastation, I would have given up my human form and gone to them in their midst as an ant. And not to become a king of the ants, or a flying or superstrong ant, but to become one of their most common members, one of the weak, someone vulnerable, and to give my best advice on how to cross the great sea, how to find the road home. And when it was accomplished, I might be killed by some of them."

He moved on to the passage from the Bible that they had read earlier that evening. It had been the story of the three kings' visiting Jesus after his birth. It was a fitting reading for Christmas, but also a clever choice for Wang Yi's purposes because it was one of the best-known stories from the Bible and the wise men came from the East, making them seem less foreign to his Chinese audience. That story of their quest allowed Wang Yi to segue to the theme of searching for Jesus. The kings had been searching for Jesus, and the Western missionaries, too, had been searching.

"The first Protestant missionary came to China about two hundred years ago, and he was named Robert Morrison, and he came to this country, looking in the Great Qing Empire to see if there were ordinary people who belonged to God, if there were people who knew that Jesus died on the cross for their salvation.

"About the year 1868, the first Protestant missionary entered Sichuan. He was from the London Missionary Society and was named Griffith John. He came to Sichuan. He came to this city. He came searching for sheep in the flock belonging to Jesus Christ.

"Around the year 1881, the first to rent a home in Chengdu and begin spreading the word of the Gospel, this blue-eyed, blond-haired man, he came from the China Inland Mission and his name was Samuel R. Clarke, and he came here seeking people who were seeking.

"This evening, we are also seeking. Here in this city Jesus Christ is seeking me, he's seeking you, he has been seeking people for two thousand years, for two hundred years, for one hundred years.

"In this city, there are so many traces of this. The great missionary schools are now our most famous high schools. The Huaxi Hospital is now our best hospital. West China Union University is now Sichuan University. So many street names, like Foundling Hospital Road, or Peace Bridge, they come from this history. There are so many traces of what the missionaries did here, right in our midst.

"I want you to know that Christians are in Chengdu. They are your colleagues, your classmates, your friends. They are the people next to you. And if you're willing today to accept Jesus, or even just come back to this church, if you're willing, if someone gives you a Bible, if you're willing, then please open it and read, read the word of God."

He then asked the Christians in the audience to stand up. Wang Yi spread out his arms and said, "Jesus is in our midst because Christians are in our midst."

And then he asked those standing if they would turn to those still seated. "Ask them, say, 'May I pray for you? Are you willing that I pray for you?'"

Wang Yi bit his lip and looked out. Had he connected? I followed his gaze back behind me to the five hundred people sitting in the ballroom. About half were standing and half were seated. And those standing were holding the hands of those seated, their heads bowed together. Slowly, a murmur of prayers filled the ballroom, drowning out Zhang Guoqing as he successfully convinced the secret police that they shouldn't intervene, drowning out the city outside—a cacophony of hopes and desires that could have come from any continent, any age.

"Please let me open the Bible and understand what is inside."

"Lord, I am a sinner and need your help."

"Lord, help me find peace."

"Save me."

LEAP YEAR

The miracle of the traditional Chinese calendar is that it works. It loses ten days each year but eventually corrects itself with a dramatic change: by adding a month every three years. This leap month, known in Chinese as *runyue*, pushes the calendar back into sync.

In folk customs, the extra month was a sign of longevity. Children gave parents auspicious gifts, hoping the additional month would mean a longer life. And yet the extra month could also be disturbing. It was a reminder that the traditional calendar might work but it was also flawed; a well-designed machine would not need such dramatic adjustments.

The ninth-century poet Li He captured this sense of distress toward the end of his life. In his youth, Li had hoped to pass the imperial examinations and make a career as an official. He was even distantly related to the royal family and was talented; today he is reckoned to be one of the most gifted poets of China's greatest age of poetry, the Tang dynasty. As part of his civil service examination, he wrote a cycle of poems, one for each month: wistful, evocative, and densely packed with allusions to Chinese history and myth.

Li, however, failed the examinations. The exact circumstances are not clear, but perhaps he was too free-spirited for the tightly controlled life of an official. The failure seemed to shock him into political awareness, and his poems became sharper. During these last few years before he died at age twenty-six, he added a thirteenth poem to his odes to the twelve months—a poem about life during the leap month. It is darker, referring to the rush of time and how the calendar is in disorder—a grave accusation against the government.

He even attacked the emperor directly, accusing him of wasting his time pursuing elixirs of immortality from Daoist deities instead of running the country. In this new, chaotic world, the two charioteers of the sun are not able to control their steed. The country is at risk. Order must be restored, but how?

> *Why must this year be so long,*
> *The coming year so late?*
> *The Western Mother plucks her peaches,*
> *To give to the Emperor.*
> *Xi and He let their bridled dragons*
> *Go far astray.*

27

Ritual: The Fragrant Dream

One of China's most popular folk arts are Clayman Zhang figurines: small, stout, chubby, often of children, made of red clay, and painted in garishly bright colors. They are instantly recognizable, a cross between Hummel sculptures and Norman Rockwell paintings—not high art, but nostalgia of a simpler, cleaner time: belly-laughing hawkers, willow-waisted beauties, and halberd-wielding warriors.

In late 2012, Wang Wenbin suddenly remembered Clayman Zhang statues. Wang was the head of CNTV—China Network Television, the online branch of China Central Television—and part of a brain trust of cultural officials charged with coming up with ways to promote Xi Jinping's China Dream and his call for a national renewal based on traditional values. Attending a retreat in the Beijing resort town of Huairou, Wang suddenly thought of Clayman Zhang figurines. What was cuter, more traditional—but also more harmless—than Clayman Zhang? An aficionado of traditional culture, Wang knew the studio's director. He made an appointment to visit and drove over to the studio's headquarters in the nearby port city of Tianjin.

The studios were a throwback to the Mao era of complete state control over cultural life. Nationalized in the 1950s, they were housed in a small four-story concrete building, with dim lights, linoleum floors, and whitewashed walls. The studio's artists were all government employees and worked leisurely at their own pace, often spending the entire morning drinking tea and reading newspapers. Field trips to gather inspiration were so infrequent that some had pictures tacked to their walls of outings they had made decades ago. Most figurines were subcontracted out to factories elsewhere that churned out the trademark chubby kids to be sold at souvenir kiosks around the country. That left the studio's artisans almost endless amounts of time to kill.

Wang met one of the studio's artists, Lin Gang, who showed him some of his recent projects. Most were fairly routine: a diorama of a barbershop from the 1920s, and a woman reading a book. But in a glass cabinet next to his desk, Lin pulled out an older piece that immediately caught Wang's eye. It was of a plump little girl, sitting on her haunches, her hands clasping one knee, her eyes cast upward in a wistful pose. It had been a difficult statue to make, Lin recalled later, taking nearly two months of work. Lin called it *Longing* and later told me how he had conceived of it.

"Children are very energetic and active. But they can only be quiet while resting. They are still thinking while resting. This piece of work is to show the posture of a child thinking while resting, a longing for the future."

Wang was smitten. He took it straight back to his hotel room at his retreat in the Beijing suburb and renamed it *Chinese Dream, My Dream.*

He then called up an old friend, Xie Liuqing, and asked him to come over to add some text. Xie was something new in China: a self-employed propagandist. After working for several government publications, he went freelance in 2005 to write screenplays in honor of Mao and popular histories that spun government programs in a good light. For many years, Xie wrote nationalistic, anti-Western tracts and was part of a blog called *Famous Salon* that featured famous writers who seemed to despise the West. With time, though, Xie began to realize that a more subtle message was needed. People were willing to believe a lot of bad things about the West, but at the end of the day most influential Chinese had either bought property in Western countries or sent their children there to study. A purely negative message aimed at these countries was not going to work.

In 2011, Xie had signed on to the government effort to create a new campaign that melded Communism and tradition. That year, he traveled down to a remote southern province to advise local officials on how to promote common values. His advice was to center the campaign on a local man who was inspired by Buddhism to do good. The meeting, videotaped and posted online, was somewhat surreal. Xie and several others from the *Famous Salon* blog quizzed the man about his Buddhist beliefs and asking him just how filial piety worked. "I don't want to do anything that will insult my parents," he said. Xie and the others, their eyes covered by baseball caps (which nationalists for some reason prefer), seem bewildered. Oh, this motivates people?

So two years later, when Wang called him and told him about the statue and the campaign, Xie immediately drove out to Wang's hotel. He, too, was captivated by the statue of the chubby kid.

"She could be coming from the deepest part of our culture, the ancient myths and our abundant folktales," Xie later wrote of the girl. "It is impossible for us not to be amazed by this piece of work . . . because the work itself is a legend."

Xie thought back to the myths of the Chinese past—to Nüwa and her home in the Taihang Mountains, or the giant Kua Fu, who chased the sun. Her crimson clothes reminded Xie of the Daoist peaches of immortality, and her gaze made him think of a new China, optimistic and forward looking. In a few minutes, he dashed off a poem to describe the girl and Xi's China Dream:

> You are beauty reincarnated in a sprite
> You are the dream of Kua Fu chasing the sun
> Let me softly walk in front of you
> Let me immerse myself in your childish gaze
> Let me walk together with you
> You bound-foot girl now able to run in the open fields
> Ah, China
> My dream
> A dream so fragrant.

Even before the Communists took power in 1949, they identified folk culture as ripe for exploitation. Living in the caves of northwestern China during World War II, they were directly confronted with the thick, stubborn traditions of rural China. Communism wanted to transform this, and over the coming decades the party would attack many traditions. But officials also tried to co-opt some along the

2 LE

way. The goal was not to promote traditional art as an expression of rural people's lives but to shape it into a tool to advance the party's own agenda.

Their strategy was to control how traditional cultural was taught and transmitted to the next generation. In the cultural field, artisans' skills were usually passed from father to eldest son, lineages that could stretch over many centuries. This was independent of government control, allowing a cacophony of styles and traditions in music, wood-block printing, paper making, herbal medicine, acupuncture, and dozens of other fields. The party was mistrustful of such diversity. Just as the government had created *qigong* by plucking it from its family lineages and shearing away its spiritual context, it would also try to turn other forms of traditional culture into products it could exploit.

As some of the most famous folk artists in China, the Clayman Zhang family came in for special attention when the Communists took over. Their roots go back to 1843, when a seventeen-year-old son of a small trader moved to Tianjin from southern China. He began fashioning clay figurines for friends and neighbors. His name was Zhang Mingshan, and he became the equivalent of a three-dimensional portrait photographer, making accurate likenesses of bankers, officials, and actors. Soon, he was so famous that people began calling him Clayman Zhang.

His fame spread to neighboring Beijing, where he expanded his repertoire to include figures from famous novels, gods, heroes, and the great mandarins who ran the Qing Empire. The dowager empress, Cixi, was smitten and ordered his statues in 1895 and 1905 for her sixtieth and seventieth birthdays. Even after the Qing collapsed, the works kept growing in popularity. When Zhang Mingshan died, his eldest son carried it on and also was known as Clayman Zhang, and so too his eldest son. The Nationalist Party leader Chiang Kai-shek owned pieces, as did Chairman Mao, who kept a Clayman Zhang figurine of a classical beauty in his study.

In 1950, the Chinese premier, Zhou Enlai, asked the Zhang family to send one son to Beijing to teach its craft to art students. The family sent a young man, who was showered with honorific titles, even getting to meet Mao. Eventually, that branch of the family drifted away from the profession, but back in Tianjin the tradition flourished. There, local officials followed the central government's lead, and in 1959 they established Clayman Zhang classes and a studio. By then, Clayman Zhang was the founder's great-grandson. He was made a teacher at the school and became a government employee. Fifty-five years later, it was this studio that Wang and Xie commissioned to make the China Dream campaign.

After Xie wrote his initial poem, Wang contacted the studio and commissioned it to produce others related to the China Dream. Within two months, Wang and Xie took possession of twenty figurines: heroic firefighters, soldiers rescuing people from earthquakes, young boys playing chess, or old people spending time with each other. Xie sat before each one and in a matter of minutes dashed off a poem, signing it with his pen name, Yi Qing.

By April, the government had designed and printed the posters. Most showed the statues on a white background with Xie's poem. Some advocated traditional values like filial piety ("honesty and consideration, handed down through the generations"), others outright admiration for the Communist Party ("feet shackled, hands cuffed / sturdy grass withstands strong winds / the Communist Party members on the road / the mountains can shake; their will is unshakable / hot blood and spring flowers will write today's history"), and sometimes just patriotism or nationalism ("Our country is beautiful" and "It's springtime for our fatherland's future").

This China Dream campaign was a striking contrast to the Communist Party's earlier efforts to instill moral values. In the past, posters and banners had mostly been red with white-lettered words exhorting people to follow a Communist hero or uphold this or that new policy. They blended into the background and were easily ignored. These new images were cute, beautiful, and not explicitly political. Instead, Chinese were called upon to remember their past and the old ideals of the political-religious order that had underpinned imperial China for two millennia. As Xi Jinping later put it in a famous slogan that itself became part of the campaign, "If the people have faith, the nation has hope, and the country has strength."

From 2012 to 2015, Xie and Wang's creations were ubiquitous, at one point adorning the main squares of every big city, as well as

overpasses and highway billboards, and even printed on wooden barriers around construction sites and printed on synthetic tarps used
as wind shields next to agricultural fields.

By 2016, the chubby clay girl had morphed into an animated
figure who appeared on airplane entertainment screens before and
after flights, touting the China Dream and its mixture of traditional
and Communist values. Later that year, propagandists had found a
real human who looked like the statue. She was from Mao's home
county, and they dressed her up like the girl in the statue and then
had her portrait commissioned. At a ceremony to mark this event,
they celebrated the portrait, the woman, and the statue—a bizzare
case of life imitating art as mediated by propaganda.

The Clayman Zhang China Dream campaign was such a success that Xie won a national award for an effective "public service
announcement"—the euphemistic term used for this sort of propaganda. The day after the award ceremony, I visited Xie at his office
in the Ordos hotel. It was just a small hotel room with a double bed
and a laptop on the desk. He was joined by an editor at Red Flag
Publishing House, a Communist Party company that had just published a collection of the posters and also of Xie's poetry. Xie turned
on the computer and showed me the award ceremony on CNTV. We
watched it halfway through, and he laughed.

"They said, 'Hey, we need more poems,' so I just dashed them off
quickly and now they're up," he said to me as we watched the seg-
ment end. "It's supposed to be a sixty-thousand-kilometer campaign.
That's how many kilometers of highways there are in China—we
joke that every meter of every road will be covered with it."

The campaign of the clay figurines ran deeper than just propaganda;
instead, it marked the start of a policy shift in favor of traditional
religions. In 2013, Xi visited Confucius's birthplace of Qufu, in
Shandong Province, and picked up a biography of Confucius and a
copy of *The Analects*, declaring, "I am going to carefully read these two
volumes." Then he paraphrased the sage by saying, "A state without
virtue cannot flourish; a person without virtue cannot succeed."

The state's interest is simple: Confucianism offers an instant, made-in-China value system with a long track record of holding the country together. This isn't the Confucianism found in the private sessions with Master Nan—he was too critical of Chinese society—but a stripped-down, simplified version that emphasized hierarchy and obligation to those above.

The next year, 2014, Xi spoke favorably about Buddhism while visiting Paris. Speaking at the United Nations Educational, Scientific, and Cultural Organization, Xi said,

> *Buddhism originated in ancient India. After it was introduced into China, the religion went through an extended period of integrated development with the indigenous Confucianism and Taoism and finally became the Buddhism with Chinese characteristics, thus making a deep impact on the religious belief, philosophy, literature, art, etiquette and customs of the Chinese people.*

Whatever Xi's true feelings toward religion, there is no doubt that followers of traditional religions felt he was their champion. Scholars who attended a 2014 conference about Confucius where Xi spoke told foreign colleagues that they were thrilled as much by his appearance as by the speech he gave there, because he seemed to be authorizing them to make the sage a central part of his reforms. While visiting a Daoist temple in eastern China once, I saw that nuns had put up a poster of a song written by Xi. Called "Surprising Words from Chairman Xi," it urged people to do good and be content with their lot in life:

> *If you have power and privilege, try to accomplish good things;*
> *If you don't have power and privilege, try to do at least good*
>   *deeds.*

This wasn't a government document posted in a place of worship to curry favor with the government but a genuine reflection that they agree with the sentiments. "These are good words," one of the nuns told me. "They could be written by a Daoist."

Across the country, officials started to study traditional culture. In the city of Zhanshu, tax officials read the Daoist classic the *Daodejing* in hopes of eliminating corruption. And the Chinese Academy of Governance—an elite school in Beijing that trains many civil servants—prepared textbooks that used traditional culture as a way to instill morality.

What fared less well were belief systems deemed to be foreign. Broadly, this can be seen as any sort of universal idea, such as human rights or feminism, that the Communist Party felt wasn't under its control. More specifically in the spiritual realm, it became an antagonism toward Christianity. Back when Xi worked as party boss of Zhejiang, he had been frustrated by local Christians, who initially thwarted his police from tearing down a local church that authorities said had been built without government permission.

In 2013, shortly after Xi reached the summit of Chinese politics, he was succeeded in Zhejiang by his police chief from that time, Xia Baolong. Starting the next year, Xia launched a campaign to remove the crosses from atop church steeples in Zhejiang. More than fifteen hundred churches were decapitated as part of an effort to reduce Christianity's public face in the province's cities and countryside. This was meant in a literal sense because these churches were big, Western-style structures that often dominated cityscapes, but also metaphorically because of their more socially active role and Western contacts. Based on what we know of China's leadership structure, such a controversial and long-lasting campaign could only have been carried out with Xi's endorsement.

This does not prove that Xi was hostile to Christianity, but it is noticeable that he has singled out Buddhism and other traditional systems of belief as laudable for having been "sinicized." Indeed, in 2016, he presided over a conference that required religions to localize—a clear departure from his predecessors' attempts to find common ground with China's main religions. Xi's support for mainstream religion seems limited to those with clear connections to re-creating Chinese traditional values.

The Clayman Zhang figurines seemed to tell a simple story, but they actually reflected a more ambiguous reality: one of division and violence, and of stealing culture for political purposes—in other words, the story of China's spiritual crisis.

The story began in the 1950s. Until then, the Zhang family

had run the studio, passing it down from father to eldest son. The founder's great-grandson was named Zhang Ming. He founded the government studio in the 1950s—but only because private enterprises like his family's studio were banned for being capitalist. When the Cultural Revolution began in 1966, he was forced out because of his family's links to China's past and traditions. The studio was closed. Like many teachers across China, Zhang Ming was attacked by his students. He was forced to drink buckets of soya sauce and vinegar and subjected to mock trials for carrying on the family tradition. Other family members were attacked as well. One committed suicide by throwing himself into a river.

In 1974, the Cultural Revolution was winding down. The Tianjin government reestablished the studio, naming it the Tianjin Painted Figurines Studio—carefully excising the controversial name Clayman Zhang. Zhang Ming was given an honorary title but was physically broken and stayed at home, barely able to climb the stairs without help. His son was transferred to work in a museum, and the family's link to the studio ended.

By the early 1980s, however, market-oriented reforms had taken hold, and the government studio wanted to sell the iconic figurines for a profit. It modified its name to add the more marketable "Clayman Zhang" moniker, becoming the Tianjin Clayman Zhang Painted Figurines Studio. It also secured the trademark to sell under the Clayman Zhang name. Throughout the 1980s and 1990s, Zhang Ming and his family members tried selling the figurines too but say they were stopped by the police; only the government studio was allowed to use the name Clayman Zhang. At first persecuted for being Clayman Zhang, the family was now barred from using the name. It belonged to the government.

The family sued the government studio in 1994. A Tianjin court ruled in 1996 that the family was entitled to sell clay figurines under the name Clayman Zhang. It also allowed the government studio to continue using the Clayman Zhang name but forbade it to engage in commercial activities. Instead, it was supposed to restrict itself to historical research and education. But the ruling has not been enforced—a not-uncommon turn of events when government interests clash with the law. The government studio still has stores throughout Tianjin selling under the Clayman Zhang brand. Most are not made in Tianjin, however; instead, they are made in factories elsewhere, which churn out thousands of crude clay figurines each year. The studio affixes the Clayman Zhang label and sells them for about $20 to $30 each.

From the family's point of view, the government basically stole its name and its trademark. The sixth-generation descendant of Zhang Mingshan is Zhang Yu. Born in 1978, he learned clay making from his grandfather Zhang Ming when the old man was crippled and housebound. Zhang Yu also saw his father arrested for trying to sell the figurines in the 1980s and 1990s. And now he sees the government studio sell cheap versions of the statues.

"First we were beaten for being Clayman Zhang, and then we weren't allowed to use the name," Zhang Yu told me. "How do you think we felt?"

We were sitting in Zhang Yu's studio, a semidetached house he rents in a neighborhood near the downtown. On a few desks in what would be the living room, Zhang Yu has statues in various stages of completion. Some are old warhorse favorites, such as Laozi or an image of the Buddha—popular statues he will be able to sell for high prices, often about $8,000 each.

But he wants his art to be something more than nostalgia and has been traveling the world to see how other cultures deal with their traditions. In Japan, he met "national treasures"—people recognized by the government for their skill in a special area, such as performing Japan's famous tea ceremonies, making traditional paper, or ceramics. One became a friend. A twenty-third-generation pottery maker sent his son to France to learn ceramics there, hoping to bring something different into the Japanese tradition. Zhang Yu had two sons, and it made him think about what sort of education they will receive.

"I want them to be happy and free without pressure," he told me. "After school, I let them play. I even do their homework for them so they can play."

The government campaign, he said, is a misuse of culture. If China's past and its beliefs are presented as static, they are more easily controlled. He is revolted by the idea of using Clayman Zhang to promote a government that persecuted his family.

"People sometimes call up and say, 'Hey, were you involved in *that?'*" Mr. Zhang said. "Our family wants to have nothing to do with politics."

But a bigger problem is what is promoted as traditional beliefs. Faith only means something, he said, if it is alive and changing.

"People . . . the government . . . they keep saying this can't become lost, but it's a ridiculous matter. This is a conflict I have with society. They say this must be passed down, but creativity is an individual affair. It doesn't have to do with future generations. If it's passed down, it doesn't necessarily mean it is a good or bad thing. It's not like an old piece of furniture you give to your children. Your heritage, your culture, your beliefs, they all only make sense if they are alive."

He pulled a cloth off a new work of a boy holding a string. Behind him is an elephant. The title is *I Lost My Elephant.*

"This is the real Clayman Zhang tradition. It's reflecting the reality of each generation. It's not something to make us feel good."

What does it mean? I asked him. Is he the boy?

"It reflects a feeling I have. What did I lose? What is the elephant? A sense of security, something that you want to recover but maybe can't. It's my family's past, our history, our dreams."

28

Chengdu: Entering the City

I t was January, and Chinese New Year was approaching once again. Soon, the church's annual meeting would take place, when Wang Yi would announce bold new plans for Early Rain. But first, members of the church looked back to take stock of the past year's work. Over the past year, the congregation had supported the families of political prisoners and Chengdu's homeless while trying to balance the needs of its own poor members. It had founded a seminary that was helping its own members deepen their understanding of Christianity and also training dozens of pastors from across China. It had held an inspiring Christmas service despite government harassment. And the church had formed an alliance with two other Reformed churches in Chengdu. Quietly, Wang Yi had traveled farther afield, too, making preliminary contacts across China in hopes of forming a loose coalition of like-minded, urban-based churches. Foreign contacts had also increased, online but also in person through visits by foreign missionaries.

Sometimes, these foreign contacts stimulated awkward debates. One was on abortion. In China, family-planning policies had resulted in tens of millions of women undergoing forced abortions. Sometimes—especially in the early years of family planning in the 1980s—officials marched women into abortion clinics to terminate pregnancies. More often the pressure was more subtle: have an abortion or lose one's job, or pay a steep fine, or accept that the child will never be insured or receive an education. In 2015, the policy was relaxed, but family planning still limits the size of families and heavily punishes women who exceed their birth quota (usually two per womb for ethnic Chinese living in cities, with one more allowed for rural Chinese and minorities). And the issue is still so sensitive that the government censors books and articles that discuss abortion's health risks or potential moral considerations. Early Rain wanted to challenge this.

It started its campaign a year earlier, when Wang Yi issued a call against abortion. On June 1, which is International Children's Day, he and a dozen other members of the church went to nearby hospitals and handed out brochures explaining how abortion wasn't necessary and amounted to murder. Then the efforts had died down; no one had been too sure how to proceed. They could demonstrate but to what end? How could they influence people's attitudes?

So on this Sunday before the church's annual meeting, activists in the church met in a small office next to the church crèche. Outside, the buildings of the city blurred into the smog, but inside the debate was sharp and pointed.

"According to government statistics, China has had 320 million abortions since the policy began in the 1980s," said a young man in his twenties. "We need to do something about this. We can't just sit around and talk all the time!"

Everyone around the table nodded vigorously. The group was made up of four men and four women. Later, a fifth man came in and joined the group. Five to four. But what was even more apparent was their age: except for the chairwoman, everyone was very young, and none were in relationships. For them, this was a moral outrage but an abstract one—something akin to a human rights violation in another country.

The young man handed out a flyer. It was called "The True Face of Abortion" and was authored by two Americans. It argued that modern science proved that life began at conception and that a fetus's fate wasn't the mother's alone. The paper cited *Roe v. Wade*, the 1973 U.S. Supreme Court decision that regulated when abortions could be performed in the United States. The flyer argued that the Court's ruling—that the state could only step in and terminate a pregnancy in the third trimester—was mistaken. Finally, someone spoke.

"I don't understand this; it's completely different here in China," a young woman said. "It's the right not to have an abortion!"

Two other young women began giggling nervously. They said they didn't have experience with sex.

One of the men started to discuss the mechanics of how abortions are performed. The three young women made faces. "It's like a horror movie," one said.

Finally, the chairwoman spoke up. She was in her forties and married, a lawyer who served on the church's legal affairs committee. She said she had visited abortion clinics in China and had some experience with the situation.

"The first thing is where did you get this material?" she said. "You downloaded stuff from the Internet? It's all American material translated into Chinese! It says that unwanted children can be easily adopted, but here in China it's not true."

"But I heard you could adopt!" a young woman said.

"It's possible, but it's not easy. If you're a pregnant woman, where will you give birth if you're illegal? Who's going to care for you? And then you have to abandon the baby outside an orphanage? It happens but it's rare. I'm against abortions, but if you hand out this, you're not handing out anything useful at all."

"I know," the well-dressed young man said. "But we've been meeting for months and want something to happen. We thought this material was good."

"All we do is talk," one of the young women said. "We need some action."

"Well, why don't you write your own brochures and hand them out?" the older woman said.

The group agreed. It was January. They would have the brochures done by February, then make the big push around Children's Day. On social media, church members began sending out pictures of themselves in front of clinics, sometimes holding up small pieces of paper with handwritten messages, such as "Admit it, a fetus is a life."

There was a lot to question about the church's efforts. Besides being framed in American terms, the debate was devoid of interfaith dialogue. By far, most Chinese are Buddhist, and many Buddhists oppose abortion. This is why Buddhists in some countries have temples to fetuses that die; they are considered sentient beings who deserve our prayers. But no one at the meeting had thought about this. For them, the campaign's efficacy was secondary; what mattered more was joining an international dialogue on a difficult moral issue.

In 1907, a French Catholic priest named Léon Joly published a history of Christian missions in Asia that asked a question that had troubled many of his contemporaries: After hundreds of years of contact with Christianity, why had so few Chinese converted? For much of the nineteenth century, missionaries had enjoyed unprecedented access to China. They built schools and hospitals. They traveled to the remotest parts of the empire and erected churches. And yet China had only about 1 million Christians in a population of 400 million. Joly ascribed the low numbers to Christianity's image as a foreign religion. China was too different to accept Christianity without modifications, and he proposed bringing it more into alignment with Chinese culture. Although he left the details vague, Joly provoked a lively debate in the West and set the tone for how generations of Western observers saw Christianity in China: as a failure. Missionaries had only been allowed in after China was defeated in the Opium Wars. The religion was too closely tied to imperialism. And people argued that it was too different, too foreign.

From today's perspective, Joly's most striking assumption is that Christianity had failed. Part of the reason for this is that Joly was looking at Christianity before its astounding growth in the twentieth century. But Joly might even have been disappointed today. Like many Christian thinkers of his era, he defined success based on Christianity's experiences in ancient Rome. There, Christianity had achieved quick results, converting the Roman emperor Constantine and then winning converts throughout the empire in a relatively short period of time. By contrast, even today Christians make up less than 10 percent of China's population. Compared with the grand hopes that missionaries had, it remains a small religion.

And yet, this would miss the bigger picture. Even one hundred years ago, Christianity had achieved something remarkable. Although small compared with the overall population, it was the first foreign religion to find a home in China since Islam had arrived over a thousand years earlier. And while Islam even today predominates among non-Chinese ethnic groups on the country's margins, Christianity was already part of the mainstream of China's spiritual landscape.

Scores of congregations like Early Rain are dotted across China's biggest cities, attracting educated young adherents who are influential members of mainstream society. China may not be a Christian nation, but Christians easily make up the third-biggest group of believers after followers of Buddhism and folk practices.

Another of Joly's questionable assumptions is his assertion that Christianity would have to indigenize to take root. In the first decades after he wrote his essay, his argument seemed plausible. Catholicism had problems surviving the wars and Communist persecution because it had relied so heavily on foreign missionaries; their exodus in the 1950s had dealt the faith a serious blow. Protestantism had more local leaders, and so when the Communists expelled foreign missionaries in the early 1950s, Protestantism fared better, and now the number of Protestants is many times higher than the number of Catholics. So in one sense, Joly was right: a more localized clergy would have helped Christianity grow faster in the nineteenth and early twentieth centuries.

But in terms of ideas, Joly was wrong. Christianity went through a phase of indigenization, but over the past decades local forms have weakened. In the past, Christianity had two main centers in China: the city of Wenzhou and the rural province of Henan. They were uniquely Chinese forms of Christianity: Wenzhou was home to family-run businesses whose employees often belonged to a church sponsored by the company boss, while in Henan charismatic leaders ran rural churches that often opposed the government and sometimes violently clashed with it.

By the second decade of the twenty-first century, however, these models were losing influence. Both still have many Christians, but they are not prototypes for the new, dynamic churches in China's big cities. The Wenzhou model has been weakened by the decline of an old economic model: family-style companies where a boss controls his workers the way an old patriarch runs his clan. Meanwhile, the rural churches in Henan have been reduced due to urbanization. The unique Christianity in these regions has also faded in importance because of a realization they are not standard internationally. They are outliers—outgrowths of a period when China was cut off from the world. Now that links to the outside world have been restored, people seek global norms, not local forms of their faith.

In her book *The Missionary's Curse*, the British scholar Henrietta Harrison traces the history of Cave Gully, a village in northern China that converted to Catholicism in the late seventeenth century, when local businesspeople heard of the faith in Beijing and brought it back home. They acquired prayer books and some fragmentary knowledge but no systematic understanding of the faith. The result was something highly indigenized. God was seen as another version of the Chinese concept of heaven, or *tian*. Worship of Mary was conflated with worship of popular female deities in northern China, such as Our Lady of the Azure Clouds and the Buddhist goddess of mercy, Guanyin. The Ten Commandments were a kind of moral formula, familiar to local people through Confucian texts. Western missionaries who tried to correct these practices were rebuffed.

But by the nineteenth century, China was opening up. Rail, telegraph, steamships, and other technological innovations created the first era of globalization. Catholics in Cave Gully realized that they were part of something bigger—a global Catholic Church with rules and standard theological interpretations. Soon, people looked to Rome for benchmarks of how to be a good Catholic. In other words, the opposite of indigenization took place. The religion started with the familiar—respect for a supreme deity, a popular female goddess, moral rules—but eventually moved beyond these easily digested universal manifestations of religion to uniquely Catholic ideas, such as the supremacy of the pope.

This history is reflected in Wang Yi and the congregation of Early Rain. They also longed to be part of a global movement—something orthodox, standard, and authentic, and not "indigenous." Perhaps this lesson applies not only to Christians but to China as a whole: as contact increases, international norms and standards seep into the country. Just as people want to be "real" Christians and participate in global discussions about moral issues, they also yearn for a country that really is committed to rule of law and human rights. But as Joly's frustration shows us, we should probably temper our expectations and take a long view. Like Wang Yi's congregation, we should take what has been accomplished—incomplete and inadequate as it is—as a miracle.

Early Rain's annual meeting was held on a Saturday, on the last full moon before the Spring Festival. Of course, the church does not follow the Chinese moon calendar, but it makes use of it. For many congregations, the roughly one-month period from Christmas to the Lunar New Year is a long holiday season, a period of recovering from the excitement of Christmas and preparing for the Lunar New Year. Wang Yi had told me that the Lunar New Year was another chance to proselytize, to mention to colleagues or friends the Good News and bring them into the church. So it wanted to have its annual meeting early, before the holiday started, to set plans before everyone got busy.

The meeting was efficient and informative, with half a dozen people giving presentations on different aspects of the church. We heard from a former urban planner who heads the "duty committee," a group of five people who oversee almost every activity in the church. Others represented subcommittes that handled youth work, education, legal affairs, and finances. All of them had PowerPoint presentations and spoke quickly, confidently, and firmly—not unlike the lists, plans, and goals presented by the government during its springtime meetings of parliament. But what they also wanted was passion, and this could only be offered by Wang Yi. They had heard the nuts and bolts, but they needed a vision.

Wang Yi's speech ended the meeting. The key for the coming year, he said, was growth. This would only be possible by splitting the church and moving some of the congregation away from the current home in the River Trust Mansion. Right now, Early Rain had roughly 380 worshippers each Sunday and had to turn away about 70 for lack of space. Those people would found a new church in the city's center, near Sichuan University.

This was a classic church-planting technique that was outlined in books that the seminary had studied last summer. The books had been published in the United States and translated into Chinese and were now being used as a template. Wang Yi and his deputies had discussed this for many months and decided it was a way also to protect Early Rain. If the mother church were to be closed, then the southern branch could keep going.

The church, Wang Yi said, had to grow because Chengdu was

growing too. Rural China was emptying out. So growth had to take place here, in big cities that were becoming regional and even international hubs.

As always, his lecture had a pedagogical flare: he loved to explain, and the audience loved to learn. Wang Yi described how cities have always played a big role in Christian history—the city on the hill referred to by Jesus and founders of new Christian communities through the ages. When John Calvin was laying the foundations for Presbyterianism in the sixteenth century, Geneva had just a few tens of thousands of residents. And back then, only 3 percent of the world's population lived in cities versus 60 percent now. And yet even then, cities were central.

"Ever since I was little, I thought that the city was my dream. But why do we want to live in cities?"

In the Bible, Wang Yi continued, cities are sometimes shown to be bad; Babylon, for example, was the epitome of worldly sin. But cities are also places for people to better themselves and develop their potential.

"I'll use one word: 'opportunities.' What sorts of opportunities? Hope is one. When I was growing up, we used to say, 'Hong Kong, Hong Kong, why are you so fragrant?'

"It represented capitalism, reform, and opening. It was the goal of every Chinese city to be like Hong Kong. Especially people like me who are from small towns and come to a big city, they want to stay. They hope to stay in the city. They also come for culture, for justice, and for generosity. People don't go to a village to get an education. They go to the city—to the schools or the bookstores. Petitioners don't go to a village to appeal for help; they go to the city. Beggars come to the city. They don't go to the countryside.

"Entering the city is what Jesus did in Jerusalem. Entering the city is entering a place of justice, of generosity, and of spreading the Gospel. It's a place of hope. And it's why we're in the city here, and growing here.

"In the Acts of the Apostles, when Paul was in Lystra spreading the Gospel, what happened? Some people wanted to worship him, thinking he was Zeus. But some stoned him almost to death, and when they thought he wasn't breathing, they threw him out of the city. But he got up and went back into the city. This line really shocked me. It's from chapter 14, verse 20: 'He got up and went back into the city.' He was thrown out of the city, but he reentered it.

"So if we're thrown out of Chengdu, we're going to get back on the bus and reenter the city. And the goal isn't because of opportunities, or culture, but it's because it is the city that has the chance for peace, for generosity, and for the Gospel. God wants us to be in this city."

I looked around the room. About half the congregation had closed their eyes but had light smiles on their faces, listening to a vision. It was a prophecy of struggle—of perhaps being closed by the government, but also of determination, hope, and victory. Wang Yi stood before them, looking out on his congregation, confident and firm. Then he made his pitch, his claim for them to think of their hometown as more than just another city, but that it and their lives were the center of a great movement.

"Earlier today, some disciples asked me what was the main theme of today? I said it's 'Entering the city.' And they said, 'Well, aren't we already in Chengdu? Why do we need to enter the city?' The answer is we need to keep entering the city. The city is the history of humanity's hope for the future. There's the city of God and the city of man. In the past it was Babylon, or New York, or Hong Kong, or Chengdu.

"When we talk to brothers and sisters, we should ask them, why are you in Chengdu? What sorts of dreams have brought you here? And what are our dreams? We are creating a Jerusalem. This is the city on the hill. For us, Chengdu is this city."

Shanxi: Ghost Burial

The widow sat in a little room adjacent to the coffin. She was too old to participate in the ceremonies and simply waited, watching the casket—her own personal wake. She was eighty-two years old, dressed in a purple silk padded jacket, her white hair pulled back in a bun, her face soft and creased, her eyes glassy and still. The deceased had been her second husband. Her first had starved to death in the Great Leap Forward, along with their four children. She had married into this family fifty years ago, and now she presided over it. While we talked with the help of a grandson who could speak Mandarin, the Li family's musicians assembled outside the farmhouse in front of the temporary altar. The children lined up and made the ritual offerings of money, grain, meat, alcohol, and tea. We heard this through the window while watching her husband's coffin through the doorway.

One day she would be there too, and the process would repeat itself. The tombs, though, would they survive the coming upheavals? The graves of her first husband and children had been unmarked, their corpses hastily buried in the sandy soil, where with luck only the dogs had eaten them. What would happen to this generation's dead? Would all of this be plowed over and become a subdivision or a shopping mall, a holiday resort or a dude ranch?

A little girl ran into the room and yelled a greeting at her great-granny. Her mother, dressed in mourning, followed her in and picked her up, sending her back outside.

Li Bin appeared in the doorway, and the young woman called him in. Could he tell fortunes? He smiled and laughed. "Of course," he said, and asked for her hand.

"Is it good? Will I have a long life?"

"This is your life line. It stops here," he said, pointing to it as it ran from below her little finger to her index finger—in other words, not all the way across her hand.

"Well, that's not short, right?"

"This line is long."

"What is it?"

"Your family life. You have a good family life."

"Yes, you're right," she said with a smile.

Li Bin made a crack about her family life, intimating she was close to her husband—very close. The granny cackled a laugh, and the woman shrieked, yanking her hand back. Then she turned away from Li Bin to another woman who had walked in.

"This is my life line," she said, pointing to her palm, and they started to compare their fates.

Another year had passed, and for the Li family the pattern seemed unaltered: funerals, punctuated by the odd concert in a nearby city to appease the government, fortunes told, rituals carried out. It was like the last days of yet another era, the ones that pile atop each other in China in unending succession. In thinking and writing about these traditions and beliefs, I often use the phrase "traditional China" to refer to the past. But it is only common sense to realize that there was never a golden age of unchanging tradition, when everything was right and stable—a time in the past when Li Bin's ancestors could play all the music in all the ritual manuals that now lay mostly unused in his father's house. If that period ever existed, when would it have ended? We know that the assault on Chinese religion started before the Communist takeover in 1949, so would the "traditional" period have been sometime in the mid-nineteenth century—perhaps before the Christian-inspired Taiping civil war had raged across China, killing tens of millions and laying waste to thousands of temples? Or might we conveniently mark it as 1898, when the Guangxu emperor ill-fatedly tried to convert temples to public schools?

But it might be more useful to skip forward one hundred years to 1999, the year coincidentally when Li Bin's grandfather Li Qing died. Before then, religion had been suppressed by China's elites for more than a century in an effort to forge a modern state, but overall it is fair to say that most people had still wanted it and that religious specialists like the Li family's sons had been capable of providing it; both sides were hindered mainly by government policy. When the Cultural Revolution ended, knowledgeable practitioners like Li Qing were still around, and villagers wanted what they had to offer, so the old traditions returned in force. And people like Li Qing were still young enough to train a new generation of practitioners like his grandson Li Bin. Rituals were already more simplified than in the early twentieth century; even twenty-five years ago, most of the ritual manuals that the Li family had were unused. But overall the story was recovery of past practices.

Our new era is different. On the one hand, business is booming for Li Bin and his father, but at times it feels like a straw fire. It is partly fed by all the old people left in the villages who are dying off. Their children still pay for the funerals but are not interested in the full, three-day standard ceremony. Even if they return from China's cities to retire and die in Yanggao, it is hard to imagine that their children will give them a three-day funeral. And yet there is a need for spiritual life; the question is what will coalesce out of the wreckage of the past to satisfy the future.

In this context, government programs to promote traditional culture are of doubtful value. I have watched the Li family perform in Yanggao Town and in the nearby big city of Datong on several occasions, but few people stopped to watch. Part of this was organization: because the concerts are mainly carried out to satisfy a bureaucratic project, they were arranged perfunctorily, with no publicity, no explanation, and not even seating or refreshments available. Even when it was a bit better organized, these Daoist rituals did not seem to transfer to the concert hall. In 2013, they performed at an auditorium in Zhongshan Park in Beijing, but the hall was half-empty, filled only with friends and musicologists. The program, as well-meaning as many of its founders intended it, felt like the worst sort of subsidized cultural program, aimed mainly at political ends (to prove that traditional culture was alive and well) rather than satisfying the needs of an interested audience. The best one can say about the government's support is it lends prestige and protects the practitioners from future attacks of being engaged in "superstition."

The trips abroad are even more removed from China's present. They provide an educational experience to Western audiences and give the Li family members a chance to get out and see the world. All of this is laudable but will not determine the survival of these rural rituals. Instead, the Li family's ceremonies will last if they provide something of value to local people—people like the cheapskate math teacher who had nickeled-and-dimed Li Bin a few months earlier.

The people clearest about these challenges are the members of the Li family themselves. The day after the widow's wake, I had lunch with Old Mr. Li's brother, Li Yunshan. Eighteen years younger than Old Mr. Li, he was born in 1969 and had been just seven when Mao died—a blessing and a curse for the family's tradition. He had missed most of the Mao era's ban on traditions, so unlike his older brother he had learned to play an instrument from their father, Li Qing. But he had also missed that era's closing of the schools and lack of social mobility; a good thing to have missed, but it meant he got a high school diploma and tested into a community college and then the civil service. He had a good job, but no time to play in the troupe.

His government job gave him insight into broader trends that made him wonder about the future of his family's survival in rural China. The new housing complexes I had seen in the winter, he explained, were just the first step in a new Yanggao Town that would double the city's population, adding another 150,000 people. That was almost all the remaining people in the county, I said, and he nodded; in the future, only large-scale agriculture would survive, and for that you do not need many farmers.

The implication for the old rural rituals was dire. In the 1980s, he estimated that two hundred Daoists performed ceremonies in Yanggao County. Today, he said, at most just sixty did so. And like Li Bin, few want their children to pursue such a thankless profession. As for his own family's traditions, he did not know if they would survive or how, although he said Li Bin's move to the town made sense. People want culture and traditions, he said, and the government now wants to make sure they get them.

"I remember when Li Bin was growing up," he said. "He was always so naughty, but he loved to play the *sheng* and learned from his grandfather all the time. He'd play and play and play. He was one of the best."

"But," I said to him, "you ended up as a civil servant, and you have the secure job."

"I know," he said. "But he's the one doing something different, and I'm just another official." He paused for a moment and then began to laugh. "And you know, one other thing: he actually makes more money than I do! He's like a successful businessman. Whoever would have thought that?"

I had come back to Shanxi this last time to pick up the Li family for their trip to Germany. We had organized a two-week tour, and now it was suddenly upon us. The trip would end up being enjoyable but almost an annoyance to the family members—like a big business trip that you're happy to go on but that upsets your busy daily life. Li Bin and his father rushed around for days beforehand, handling funerals like the widow's and arranging for other Daoist groups to take over for them in their absence. As usual when they traveled abroad, no one they contacted seemed overly impressed: Oh, you're going to be away for two weeks. Well, call us when you're back.

The day before their departure, Li Bin rushed out to a village home to decorate a coffin. He was now driving a new Nissan and had a Bluetooth earpiece connected to his mobile phone so he could drive and answer the endless calls that came in.

It was 8:00 in the morning when we arrived, and Shi Shengbao was waiting for us. He was a senior figure in the region who handled all matters of importance. He lived in a nearby village and was like an unelected mayor; if you had any sort of problem, from a funeral to a wedding, from a fire to a feud, you could call Mr. Shi, and he would try to handle it. That might mean contacting the local Communist Party secretary or arranging a dinner to iron out a problem. He was a broker of local affairs, a seventy-two-year-old whose prestige came from years of working honestly in the community.

Mr. Shi had been involved because the deceased was just fifty-four and his family was in difficulty. The man had died of stomach cancer, and the family was set back tens of thousands of yuan—thousands of dollars, which in this part of the country could be crippling. The dead man had three children, the youngest studying aeronautics in Nanjing and the other two working in Datong. Mr. Shi was an astute crisis manager. He called a local party secretary, who he said had owed him a favor, and they agreed to use money from a local "stability maintenance fund" to cover some of the hospital bills. Mr. Shi also contacted the son and paid his ticket back from Nanjing while negotiating with family and friends to make sure the boy would not have to cut off his studies. And he called the Li family to handle the funeral. When he heard they were leaving for Germany and did not have time, he persuaded Li Bin and his father to find some time to at least decorate the coffin properly. The deceased was a respected man in the community, and the funeral had to be done right.

Mr. Shi ushered us into the kitchen and sat on a little stool expectantly. Li Bin put a stainless steel bowl on the *kang* and pulled a jar of hardened-gelatin glue out of his bag. He used the penknife on his key chain to cut a piece of the glue out of the jar and flicked it into the bowl. Then he added hot water from a thermos and stirred it with a spoon.

From two rooms over I heard the sound of a woman's crying. A family member walked in and discreetly closed the kitchen door. The crying was more muffled now but still audible. Li Bin kept mixing: he carved out a bit more glue from the jar and then added a bit more water, stirring methodically, focused intently on the mixture. Suddenly I heard the sound of heavy knocking and then a woman's scream. I jerked my head up. Mr. Shi sat quietly, looking down at the concrete floor, while Li Bin kept stirring, staring intently at the bowl and the thickening mixture. This was an end-of-the-world wail, when you scream so much that you lose the ability to breathe. It came in waves with the cries rising and falling for a full ten minutes. It was unbearable. When the woman lost her breath, she would just sob, but so loudly we could hear it through the two walls. Mr. Shi sat uncomfortably, a hand clasping each knee, while Li Bin mixed the glue with the intensity of a heart surgeon.

After a while, the screaming stopped, and all we could hear was sobbing. Li Bin quietly blew air out through his lips as if to punctuate the moment and then stopped mixing. He opened the door to the middle room. His timing was perfect: at exactly that moment, the crying stopped. He walked through the room to the door leading to the next room and opened it. A young woman was standing next to the coffin, but through another door to the courtyard I could see others walking away. She stood staring at the coffin, her face red and puffy and streaked with tears. She was dressed in plain street clothes, not the white robes of mourning. That was for public consumption. This was where the real grief had taken place, in this quiet eruption in the privacy of her home. She stared at the coffin for another minute and then backed out.

Li Bin did not say anything or meet her eyes. He let her leave as if he were invisible and silently placed the bowl of glue on a table. Then he began cutting foot-long strips of golden-leafed paper. He pasted it on plain white paper to give it strength and then glued the strips onto the coffin. Dressed in his Italian loafers, jeans, black-checked shirt, and blazer, he looked the role of a professional and acted it too. He worked fast and silently, which was best because occasionally one of the three children would come in to stare incredulously at the coffin.

I had introduced myself to the family earlier in the day to make sure my presence would not be an intrusion. They had approved, but I tried to make myself small, sitting in a corner behind the door, my notebook in my pocket. Unlike many of the other funerals, this one felt much more private. This family straddled farm and town. Their base was still here, but the children had been launched into the orbit of city life. The funeral was traditional, but it was more personal, not the communal events I had seen so many times in the past. Even tomorrow there would be no drunken sons and riotous dinners. It was something different—more restrained and intimate.

The youngest son walked in, fighting back tears. He gasped through open lips, which he pressed hard against his teeth to control his face muscles. He lit a cigarette and set it on the wooden sawhorse holding the coffin. His father had liked smoking, and these would be his last cigarettes. Slowly the young man relaxed his face muscles and began to cry, the tears running silently down his face while he watched the coffin's transformation.

Li Bin used a brush to work the air bubbles out from under the golden paper. The room was quiet except for the sobs and the whisking. Slowly the coffin turned gold. Every so often he had to paste the paper over a dowel, and then I understood the hammering and why the wailing had begun right after. The dowels were numbered, each one a bit different because the coffin was not symmetrical. It was shaped like a small boat with a high prow, able to ride over the rough waves of the afterlife.

Two hours later we broke for lunch, but there was no siesta on this busy last day. Li Bin went right back to work, now pasting blue paper on the front of the coffin. It had a printed design on it, a fantastical swirl of red and purple. Then he mixed some ink in a bowl and pulled out his writing brush. Now I could see that the golden paper would be just a backdrop for his calligraphy. He divided each side of the coffin into rectangular sections, filling each with abstract designs or traditional symbols: a zither, bamboo, chrysanthemums, and bats.

"Do they look like bats?" Li Bin said, breaking the long silence. "I'm not really very good at this. My father is. He's more meticulous, but I'm faster. Some people take a day and a half to do a coffin. I do it in one day."

An older man walked up to me and pointed at the coffin.

"Fifty-four. He worked all his life in the fields. Two sons went to university." He spoke in bullet points to make sure I got it, that I understood what sort of person had just died. I nodded.

It was now 3:00 p.m., and Li Bin began the other side of the coffin. A few men came in to keep him company. They talked about Xi Jinping's trip to Russia as Li Bin painted bats and geometric figures on the golden paper.

Mr. Shi watched Li Bin work. He said Li Qing had been the best, but Li Bin wasn't bad—a high compliment in a country where the past is always better than the present, let alone the future. "He's a good one, but his grandfather was the best. Everyone knows that."

I sat on a stool to watch him and fell asleep, slumped against the wall. Two hours later Li Bin finished. He went over the final arrangements with Mr. Shi, again apologizing that they could not make it. Mr. Shi was satisfied. The coffin was important, and he had wanted it done by the Li family.

On our way back into town, Li Bin kept fielding calls. Someone needed a fortune told, but Li Bin persuaded him to wait two weeks until he was back from Germany. Then he made one last call. It was to a doctor in town who had called on him a few days earlier with an unusual request. He had wanted his parents dug up and reburied. Li Bin wanted to know if he still wanted that? The doctor said yes, and so Li Bin hurried home, packed his suitcase for his trip abroad, and then took a nap, setting his alarm for midnight and the tolling of the night's first bell.

The doctor's parents had died four years earlier, but they had not been buried properly. The two had died within weeks of each other and been interred in a plot in the family village, but no *yinyang* man had determined the grave or the date of burial. It had all been done haphazardly without a proper ceremony. Since then, the doctor had been uneasy. Something about the funeral had not seemed right. He was now nearly fifty and had seen the funerals of a couple of his friends' parents. One in another county had hired a *yinyang* man like Li Bin to do the ceremony. When the doctor paid his respects at the funeral, he had watched the event unfold. The meaning was not clear to him, but he felt a dignity in the music and the rituals and a sense that his friend had done the right thing for the people who had given him the gift of life. The doctor opened his heart to his friend, who advised that he should have his parents reburied. His friend pointed out something else that he said might be bothering the doctor: his parents were in separate graves. They had been a couple in life; shouldn't they be buried together? They were ghosts now, their spirits on the other side. But the resting place was still important. It would give them peace. The doctor had listened carefully and thought to himself that this is what his parents needed: they needed to be at peace.

And so a few weeks earlier he had stopped by Li Bin's shop and asked him if he did *hezang*, a double burial, which some people more colloquially call a *guizang*, a ghost burial. Li Bin went over the circumstances with him and explained carefully what this would entail. The coffins would have to be dug up. They might have rotted, and the bodies might be visible. It could be disturbing. The doctor had thought of this and said it would be fine; this was too important to his parents' well-being to let his squeamishness get in the way. Li Bin visited the site and calculated the best day and hour. It was to be the night of his departure.

Like his father, Li Bin knew the county intimately and had no trouble finding the family plot in the dark. The doctor was already there with his sister, an accountant at a coal company in the nearby city of Datong. The two were middle-aged and earnest: children of China's economic reforms who had grown up in an era when the county was already stripped of its temples and communal religious life. But this was still something that they felt they had to do, and their eyes lit up appreciatively when Li Bin arrived. The doctor had a drawn face and a worried expression, but he smiled a greeting, and his sister gave a solemn nod.

Li Bin nodded to them but made straight for the four workers who had been digging up the graves and preparing the new one.

"You found the coffins?"

"Intact."

Li Bin nodded. That was good. He had participated in messy reburials where everything had rotted. The men had already put ropes under the coffins and now hoisted them up. The pine held. The field was outside the village, lit only by the stars. Today was just the fourth day of the lunar month, and the moon was already gone, but everything was visible in the clear night sky: the low outline of the farmhouses, the trees lining the horizon, and the newly planted fields.

A short distance away was the grave that the workers had dug in the ground according to Li Bin's instructions. Li Bin walked over and checked the plot's location with a compass. The workers lifted up the coffins and carried them over, placing them side by side.

The doctor and his sister followed and stood at a distance. Then the sister stepped forward, a no-nonsense woman of forty-five and mother of a daughter in technical school. Her pale face was framed by a black wool cap and the collar of her red down jacket. She was carrying a bolt of red cloth in her hands. She stared at the coffins, pressing her lips together in sadness, and drew herself up to look at Li Bin.

"I would like to drape this over the coffins," she said.

Li Bin looked at her in surprise but instantly understood. White was the color of death; red used for a wedding. This was something he had never seen before, but it touched him and his eyes reddened.

"Good, yes, of course. What a good idea."

The doctor helped his sister place the cloth around the coffins, binding the two boxes. Five minutes later, the caskets were back in the earth. Li Bin squatted down next to the grave and carefully placed a tile on top explaining who was inside. Then he sprinkled the five grains to ensure prosperity and took a final look.

No sooner had he stood up than the first spade of earth hit the wood. There was no music, no chanting, and not even the moon, but it made Li Bin think back to his home, to his wife, Jing Hua, who worked hard every day keeping the books and making the wreaths, to his son, Binchang, who was always away at boarding school, and to their future together in the city. He thought to himself as he stood there that his job might be tough and sometimes strange, but it was also beautiful, and he wondered, will anyone do this for me one day?

Beijing: The Wondrous Peak

This year I wanted the anticipation to last longer, so I arrived earlier. But in China, you can never be first, and so my triumph at arriving at Miaofengshan at noon on the thirtieth day of the third lunar month was diminished. Jintang, Mrs. Qi, and a couple of other members of the pilgrimage association were already there and had set up the shrine. I looked inside. It was the same as last year: the teapots, the bronze Guanyin, and the flowers surrounded by hangings of brilliant gold silk. Out front, the incense already burning. The bronze bowl. The mallet. Soon, the pilgrims would come, and the bell would toll across the little square.

This was a leap year, with an extra fourth month added, so the fair was celebrated later than usual. It was already well into May, and no mists or rain blanketed our mountain. The big pine tree out front swayed in the breeze, and in the distance the mountain was a study in green. The old pine trees were dark, steadfast through the year, while the younger pines were lighter, as if still finding their way. The deciduous trees, many of them willows, were fainter still, and finally the bushes were just sprouting, smudges of khaki against brown branches.

A couple of pilgrims walked by. The man was around fifty, with a weather-beaten face surrounding deep-set, searching eyes. The woman was younger, in her late thirties, chubby and laughing, but also earnest. She had spent a month preparing for this trip, stringing together dozens of prayer beads made of about fifty small stones and meant to be wound around the wrist. She planned to hand them out to people they encountered, and she immediately gave me one. They lived in Shandong, a province southeast of Beijing, and were on their way to the holy Buddhist mountain of Mount Wutai farther west. First, though, they had decided to visit the Mountain of the Wondrous Peak to see the temple fair.

"How do you afford so much time off work?" I asked them.

"We work for money, and then we quit to travel," the wife said. "We don't take alms or donations. We just work, and then when we have enough, we try to get out for a few months."

"We've been all around China like this," her husband said. "Mount Wudang to see the Taoists, Mount Tai to see the Lord of the East Peak, Mount Song to see the Shaolin monks. If we'd met a few months ago, I could have introduced you to a living Buddha. He lived in Hebei Province."

"He knew everything," his wife said. "He could see the future and the past."

"Really incredible," the man said.

"Why spend so much time seeking these things?" I asked. "Why not live just a quiet life at home?"

"We're in a dangerous era," the man said. "Do you know Mount Putuo? It's on an island in Zhejiang, south of Shanghai. The Buddha there has a hand outstretched with a palm like this," he said, holding his left arm out with his hand raised upward at the wrist, like a traffic cop signaling to stop. "It's to protect the island from flooding. But now, for the first time, the temple has flooded. The environment isn't in balance. The Buddha can't protect them. We're in a new era of uncontrollable desire and greed."

"What do you want to find?"

"The ancients found answers in these mountains. Maybe there is something for us to learn too."

Friends of the Ni family's pilgrimage association began rolling up in SUVs. There was the stocky guy in the Land Rover who always came for the first night and an assortment of construction industry managers in Jeeps and late-model Volkswagen sedans. Family members came too: Jintang's and Mrs. Qi's sons arrived, bringing younger friends. I knew them all from years past, but now they were staying longer and bringing more friends.

It was now dangerously late to be thinking of dinner; in China, dinner is often at 5:30, but we had chatted so much that it was almost 5:00 and the table wasn't even set! The folding tables were opened, and Mrs. Qi stacked them with food and drink. Sausages were cut up and placed on paper plates along with cold noodles, buns, and platters of peanuts, salted beans, and other drinking snacks. We opened a special liquor that Jintang had bought from a distillery in Cangzhou, a small city in Hebei.

Small trucks drove past, one after another, unloading hundreds and hundreds of steamed buns, or *mantou*, for the steamed bun pilgrimage association. Its boss, a stout businessman from the south with a brush cut and aviator glasses, drove up in a Mercedes SUV. A Chinese flag was planted on the roof. On the back was a sign with the words "Mantou Sacred Association." He yelled greetings at the Nis as he gunned it up the small slope to his shrine.

Jintang talked intensely to one of the flower lady's sons. Old Mrs. Chen herself was resting, no longer as strong as she was last year. Just as Jincheng had told me a few months earlier, she seemed a bit mixed-up after being forced from her old home. Last summer at her temple fair, she had greeted me; this time around, she said, "You again!" and welcomed me warmly but could not place me. The unspoken concern was that Old Mr. Ni's passing and, one day, Old Mrs. Chen's death might lead to the breakup of these shrines—that the countless teapots and vases and statues that Old Mr. Ni and Old Mrs. Chen bought might be sold or donated to a museum. That had already happened to one tea association, whose porcelain wares were now in a temple storeroom. Old Mr. Ni had wanted his association to last for a thousand autumns and they were determined to try.

"Our associations will always be together!" Jintang said to Old Mrs. Chen's son, raising a glass. "No matter what happens, we're united!"

The son shouted his assent, and they drank.

It felt familiar and pleasant, and I thought, this is the best part—the buildup, the anticipation, the first night.

After a while, I noticed that a few people in our little group were giving me odd looks. Finally, a family member asked me where I got my jacket. I was wearing the gray pinstriped Chinese-style blazer that Jincheng had given me last winter.

"It looks like one of our family's jackets," she said.

"I got it from Jincheng," I said, nodding in agreement.

"Jincheng?" She cocked an eyebrow. "Who had it made?"

Suddenly it hit me. It had belonged to the old man. I gasped in embarrassment. Jintang saw my expression and shook his head.

"No, wear it. It's appropriate. He wanted you to write a book with him about the pilgrimage societies."

"But I didn't."

Jintang looked at me and laughed.

Sitting around, watching the incense burn. It puffs out of the cauldron like the smoke from the men's cigarettes. It billows and blankets us. It permeates our clothes like the mist, but months later is still there.

In the shrine, a seat has been left empty: the chair where Mrs. Qi's husband used to sit, immovable, keeping watch, a tin of Yanjing beer fixed in his hand. He had died of cancer less than two months after Old Mr. Ni's passing last summer. Everyone knew it had not been a coincidence. Sixty days after a person's death, the *xuanmen*, the dark gate, the gate of death, closes. Mr. Chang had died fifty-eight days after Old Mr. Ni. He had not let the gate close before joining his friend; they had passed through together.

"We shouldn't sit there," Jintang said quietly.

"We'll leave it free this year," Mrs. Qi said.

Thinking back on all these people, over all these years, Jintang began philosophizing.

"I was tight with her husband. People only get on friendly terms with each other slowly, through fate and feeling. Everyone has their temperament. You only get to understand it slowly. You only adapt to it slowly. Only if you have learned how to adapt to the other side can you be comfortable.

"Some people's temper is like this, others like that. You can't just let other people get used to you. If everyone is getting used to you, then you've got a problem. China's got this Xi Jinping. Everyone has to get used to him, but he has to get used to hundreds of millions of people's views.

"Humans are like that. Laozi, Confucius, Daoists, Buddhists, all were like that: exhort people to do good. What more is there?"

Mrs. Qi nodded toward Jintang: "This is a person you can talk to."

That evening we had dinner in the temple restaurant. The decor was simple: big round plywood tables and folding chairs. But the view was stupendous. Below us the mountains unfolded, bending their way to the city below.

"In honor of Old Chang," Jintang said of Mrs. Qi's husband, "we're starting out with Yanjing beer."

"Here's to the people who aren't with us this year."

"Don't talk about it."

We drank.

"There's someone else."

"Little Li."

"I miss him so much," Mrs. Qi said. "He was a living Buddha." Tears began to well in her eyes.

Little Li had lived in Jiangou Village at the base of the mountain and had been forty-two when he died. He had several birth defects, including a bad heart, and was mentally disabled. But during the pilgrimage, he kept watch over the temple and always lent a hand. He had lived with one of the temple managers, a hard-edged man who was a stickler for order and rules, the sort of person you would never think of as taking in a Little Li. But he had, and Little Li had lived in a room off to the side, doing chores and odd jobs and waiting for the temple fair. Then, a few months ago, he got sick. The manager and his old mother had tried to care for him, thinking it was just a spell that would pass.

The manager now spoke, still wearing his regulation blue overalls, his jaw set, focusing hard through the window on the heaving mountains, speaking in his clipped and clear voice.

"In the morning, I wanted him to drink his milk, but he wouldn't. I had to work late. I went out. I had two shifts. I couldn't come back. But when I got back, he had gone."

"Gone."

People cleared their throats. We held up our glasses.

"A good person."

Murmurs of agreement, then a pause while the group regained its composure.

"My mother cried," the manager said. "She's ninety-four."

"Ninety-four."

"A venerable age."

"To your old mother."

"The old lady."
"Long life."

Beijing was whited out from smog on the day before Sakyamuni's birthday. It was the seventh day of the fourth lunar month, and I was heading back to Miaofengshan after two days in the city to run errands. As I drove west, the mountains were hardly visible, even after reaching the Fifth Ring Road, about twelve miles from the downtown. Another six miles, at the Sixth Ring Road, and it was hardly better: the mountains were just a mile away but were still faint outlines. It began improving after I turned off the highway and passed under a huge ceremonial archway announcing "Golden Peak Miaofengshan." The road hugged the valley for four miles and then began to ascend steeply into the Mongolian foothills. The landscape was rocky, and the boulders took on a pinkish hue in the mid-afternoon light. Suddenly the particles in the air receded enough for the shapes to regain their three dimensions. The boulders popped out—*bing*. The air began to cool. It felt as if going back in time to an earlier season.

After so many curves, suddenly Jiangou Village. Then a barrier and a 5-yuan toll. The men waved me through before I even uttered my mantra: Whole Heart Philanthropic Salvation Tea Association. The final three miles were another series of switchbacks and then the end of the road: the temple.

The next day was Sakyamuni's birthday. Although a Buddhist holiday, it is a focal point of the pilgrimage to Miaofengshan. One of the main events is distributing *yuandou*, or karmic beans. This stems from a practice by Buddhist monks in Beijing who invoke the Buddha's name in prayer. To keep track, they move a yellow bean from one bowl to another each time they uttered the holy word. Thus blessed, the beans would be cooked and offered to pilgrims on the birthday of Sakyamuni. It reminded me of the practice in my hometown, Montreal, where Catholic pilgrims used to rub stiff joints with the oil from the lamp used by a local saint to read the scriptures. The church there had a display case with thousands of crutches left after the miraculous healings.

Each year at Miaofengshan, a pilgrimage association took charge and handed out bowls of tasty yellow beans, steamed and then stir-fried with onions and garlic. Unlike the Ni family or the businessmen who offered steamed buns, this group had no shrine. They simply set up a stand on the eighth day of the fourth lunar month and ladled out one thousand pounds of the beans into plastic bowls all morning long. Then they would pray and go home. If you did not understand it, the event would seem trivial, but for the dozen volunteers it was the high point of their year. And for the tens of thousands of pilgrims who came on that day, it was a key ritual.

Back at the tea shrine, Jincheng had arrived. Even a hermit has to venture out once in a while and act sociable, and Jincheng had chosen Sakyamuni's birthday to make his appearance. He had brought along some colleagues from the Ministry of Construction. One of them walked in, holding a bowl of karmic beans.

"Okay, so how do I do it?" the man said to Jincheng. The man was forty and balding and new to the pilgrimage. But he was doing his best to fit in: over his Western-style white dress shirt he wore a rich dark-blue silk jacket with a crimson lining. He had folded up the sleeves at the end so the red formed a smart border.

"What do I say?" he asked, turning to Jincheng, as he held the bowl of beans in front of him. Jincheng told him to divide the beans into two bowls, and the man did so.

"Repeat after me," Jincheng said, reciting a five-line prayer.

The man repeated it after every line.

"That's it," Jincheng said in his usual gruff manner. "No need to make a big fuss. Put the bowls on the altar, bow, and you're done. You've shown your respect."

The man carefully placed the bowls on the altar, bowed, and smiled at Jincheng in thanks. Properly, Jincheng didn't look at him; meeting his eyes and accepting his thanks would imply that he was doing him a favor. He was not. This was his duty, his honor. His glory.

It was 8:00 in the morning, and the first performing pilgrimage association came by: a group of dancing tigers. They were on their way up to the temple. After performing for the goddess, they would dance in front of their stele, the stone slab inscribed with the names of the people, now mostly dead, who had revived the traditions after the Cultural Revolution.

We watched from folding chairs near the censer. The smoke blew. The heavy metal bowl tolled. Manning it was a family friend, Wang Tiebiao. He was silent most of the time, watching carefully, and then at the right moment, when the people prostrated themselves, *bong, bong, bong.*

People stopped by for tea. They lit incense and kowtowed before Guanyin. *Bong. Bong. Bong.*

Near the Origin of Fate stone, Wang Defeng's management team had set up a table that was draped with copies of little red velour flags that each of the performing pilgrimage associations received as a reward for coming. It seemed unremarkable but was so coveted that people said it had corrupted pilgrims, making them form associations and ascend the mountain just so they could get the flag.

I examined one closely, reading it line by line top to bottom, right to left:

> *Donated by the Golden Peak Miaofengshan Administrative Office*
> *Grasping Sincere Intentions*
> *Paying Respects to the Mountain and Presenting Incense*
> *Folk Culture Temple Fair*

The two middle lines were in bold and larger font; they were the main message, a traditional phrase commemorating a pilgrimage to a holy site. It didn't seem like much of an incentive, except as a sign of pride and accomplishment. Manager Wang did not offer money to the groups. They came because the mountain had called them.

One of the pilgrimage groups making the ascent on Sakyamuni's birthday was called the Great Peace Association and was run by a twenty-six-year-old office worker in Beijing's public transport system, Lei Peng. This group entertained Our Lady with one of the oddest and most interesting performances I had seen. It was a call-and-response dance routine, where Lei Peng stumped around the center of the square, a microphone in hand, chanting lines from a song. Around him were twenty people dressed in costumes making them look like emperors and generals, concubines and nuns, together calling out responses and choruses. Ten musicians accompanied them on drums and cymbals, like the rhythm section of a jazz band.

After hearing the group perform last year, I had paid a visit to Lei Peng's home in a housing project in one of Beijing's northern suburbs. Lei Peng was a tall, heavyset young man with narrow rectangular glasses and a passion for Beijing's traditions. Just twenty-six years old, he had been raised mostly by his grandfather; the two lived together until the old man had died in 2010. Lei Peng nailed a picture of his grandfather over the door so he would see it every day, especially when he went out to work. The photograph showed the old man dressed in a blue tunic and made up in rouge and mascara. It was not a typical commemorative picture of a deceased relative, but this is how Lei Peng thought of him: as a pilgrim.

The Lei family's old home had been a courtyard house in a village named after them, the Lei Family Bridge Village. It lay on the key pilgrimage routes that ran north out of Beijing to Mount Yaji, the site of another shrine to Our Lady of the Azure Clouds. His family used to run a tea shrine for pilgrims, much like the Ni family's. By the time Lei Peng was growing up in the 1990s, the shrine had been torn down, but his grandfather had revived the Great Peace Association, and dozens of villagers met regularly to practice. The high point of their year was coming here to perform during the pilgrimage.

"In the past, everyone met at the temple, and we practiced there," Lei Peng said. "It was a nice place. We were all together."

Even after Beijing expanded and the agricultural land was converted to other use, the Lei Family Bridge Village stood apart. It was what was known as a *chengzhongcun*, or village in a city. Surrounded by high-rises, it still had its old street pattern and several old buildings, including the temple. In many cities around the world, these sorts of former villages sometimes become popular tourist destinations— think of Montmartre in Paris. In China, though, these small communities have been systematically demolished by city planners; nothing can trump an ambitious technocrat in a wealthy, authoritarian state.

In 2009, the Lei Family Bridge Village made way for a golf course. The villagers were scattered around northern Beijing many miles apart, making it hard to get together to practice. In an effort to find new ways to pass on the tradition, Lei Peng began teaching at a local school for migrant children. They learned the dances and the songs—a bit of fun in their lives and a chance for Lei Peng to win new recruits. Today, on Sakyamuni's birthday, the old members had agreed to stay home and give the children a chance to perform for Our Lady.

Lei Peng had made one small mistake: he had rented a bus that was too big for the curves on the last leg of the mountain road. So he and his troupe of two dozen schoolchildren had all gotten off in Jiangou Village and hiked up the old pilgrimage route: the path of a thousand elbows. At ten in the morning, they finally arrived, led by a fiercely proud young girl carrying the troupe's colors, a ten-foot pole with the yellow-and-red silk banner declaring, "Lei Family Bridge Village South Teahouse." She was twelve and her name was Li Lan. Her parents had come from a village in Shanxi to work in the capital. Local schools would not accept migrant children, and she was thrilled with her school and the chance to climb the mountain. She wore a turquoise silk tunic; her face was covered in a white base makeup with colorful dots and swirls radiating out like the rays of the sun. "I like the clothes best," she said, "and the flag." She clutched it tightly and planted it on the rocks next to the temple walls.

Soon, a perspiring Lei Peng arrived, along with the rest of the children. Lei Peng hurried to assemble them. Several children carried drums and cymbals, while one veteran from the old village helped keep time on a small waist-mounted drum. With a roll of the drums and a clash of the cymbals, the children formed a line and marched up the final steps to Our Lady.

"Look at them," Lei Peng said proudly as the children excitedly made their way up, none of them complaining. "I didn't know such children still existed."

The group assembled in front of the censer at the main hall. Today was a big day, and it was jammed with incense—a smoking, crackling cauldron of flames. Lei Peng pulled a piece of red paper out of his blazer pocket and read the letter to Our Lady of the Azure Clouds asking for her blessing. He had written out the children's names at the bottom. He then folded the letter and put it in a big yellow envelope that one of the children was holding. Together, they tossed it into the furnace.

On cue, the children turned right, clasped their hands over their heads, and bowed in respect. They did the same to the left and finally straight ahead, facing the goddess. Then came their performance. Lei Peng led them in the call-and-response routines, known in Chinese as *lianhualao*, or Falling Lotus Flowers. He stomped around in front of the censer, wielding a battery-powered handheld bullhorn, calling out one line while the children danced around him and called out the answers. One song told the story of a family of famous generals who lived about a thousand years ago and tried to prevent Genghis Khan's Mongols from conquering China. He would call out a name, and they would yell out that person's identity. All the while the drums and cymbals kept a complex beat.

> *Pan Renmei:*
> *The Eight Sage Kings!*
> *Yang Wuliang:*
> *The Yang Family Generals!*

Crowds watched them, some captivated by the children, others more critical. Compared with the adults who had performed last year, the children were inexperienced. They remembered their lines, but it felt forced; this was not their village tradition but just something they had learned in school, not at their grandfather's knee or at the local temple. The performance lacked the mystical, primordial feeling of last year's.

"They're just playing," a man said to me. "They don't know the meaning of what they're saying."

But this was an experiment, and several people from other pilgrimage associations nodded appreciatively at the children's effort. Teaching children these traditions in a school, maybe this was worth trying, and in fact it would become increasingly common as the government sought to aid the revival of traditional faith and belief. By 2016, schools across Beijing would be teaching these traditions. In the schools, the performances were presented purely as culture—not religion—but the children still made the pilgrimages, and their parents often came along too, some entering a temple for the first time.

After ten minutes, the children took a break, and Lei Peng decided to show the goddess and the audience what seasoned pros could do. The older man who had been guiding the younger musicians stepped forward. He had a small drum around his neck. Lei Peng pushed a kettledrum toward the censer and hung a smaller drum around his neck.

The two began a polyrhythmic beat, starting slowly and building up, trading riffs, and ramping up the intensity, Lei Peng feverishly working both drums while the older man kept the base rhythm. For ten minutes they played, their eyes closed, sweat pouring down their faces for the children, for the crowd, and for Our Lady.

By the fourteenth day, Jintang's hair was growing out—a gray-and-black stubble—while his muttonchops had become luxuriantly long. In a few days, he would trim his whiskers while letting his hair stay long. Real life was impending. Mrs. Qi walked up to me.

"She's waiting for you," she reminded me, motioning toward the mountain and the temple. I had been up to the peak many times to watch the associations perform but had not spent any time up there alone with Our Lady.

It was a Thursday afternoon, and the temple was quiet. In the center of the main courtyard, the big steel censer was slightly smoking. On either side were shrines to other deities, and in the middle was the Hall of Benevolent Salvation, the home to Our Lady of the Azure Clouds. She was made of bronze and cloaked in a cape of embroidered silk—the painstaking work of local women volunteers. On each side of her were two brightly colored statues. They were helpers, each a manifestation of the goddess's powers: Vision (symbolized by an outstretched hand with an eye in the palm); Descendants (a goddess surrounded by children); Curing Childhood Diseases (her hand forming a symbol of curing); Child Rearing (again, more children). On some reductionist level this could be explained as a fertility cult, but I thought of the woman at the Temple of the Central Peak last summer who had set me straight: This was about the future. These were universal aspirations for family, for safety, for community, for good health.

One of the old temple employees offered me a chair. I sat and watched the goddesses. Our Lady had seen the Ni family expelled from the old city, had helped cure Old Mr. Ni, and had inspired the tea association. In the end, she could not change fate, but she had been there for the family. In a 1934 novel called *Hundred Altars*, the author Juliet Bredon depicts life in a village north of Beijing in the last years of the Qing dynasty. Bredon had been born and raised in China—her uncle had been Robert Hart, the prominent adviser to the Qing dynasty—and her empathy for local people comes through in the novel intensely. A central event is a pilgrimage to Miaofengshan. One of the main characters is a woman who prays to Our Lady for a child. As the woman worships, Bredon switches perspectives, putting herself in the goddess's position, looking down on the woman. Our Lady wonders if she should help or not and asks the Goddess for Curing Childhood Diseases for advice. Being childless—what would become of the poor woman? Who would light incense at her grave on Qingming? The question, they decided, was sincerity. Was the woman sincere?

It was hard to imagine today's statues talking. The four that flanked the bronze statue were slightly cartoonish, made of wood and papier-mâché painted in bright colors—nothing a conquering soldier would want to steal and put in a museum. But the statues were just representations, not the reality. If they spoke, it was because of belief that people held in their hearts, not their beauty or antiquity. The key was that something was here now: a bridge to the future. After everything China had been through over the past century, the fact that temples were still standing was the miracle. I always tried to remember that whenever I saw a garish temple. Instead of appraising the statues, I looked at the people, to see what was in their eyes.

Down a flight of stairs from the temple was a small square. It had a commanding view of the mountains to the southeast and the valleys winding back down to Beijing. In one corner were steles—the stone markers that told the story of each pilgrimage association. I found the Whole Heart Philanthropic Salvation Tea Association's stone. Its name in Chinese—*Quanxin Xiangshan Jieyuan Chahui*—was chiseled into the stone on the front. The back contained the names of the founders: Old Mr. Ni; his sons, Jincheng and Jintang; Mrs. Qi; Jincheng's wife, Chen Jinshang; and two dozen others. This, the old man had told his daughter-in-law over a year ago, was a kind of immortality. It wasn't a statue in a downtown square or a place in a history book, but it was real—not just the stone but the lived lives: the smoke, the yells, the heated arguments, the outrageous jokes, the respect, the love.

Birds chirped and chased each other through the stone markers. Yellow-and-red flags snapped in the breeze. The fruit trees bloomed pink and white, and honeybees circled, sometimes pushed by the breeze up the steps of the temple toward Our Lady. The fair was all but over, and the temple would be quiet for another fifty weeks. Today's performers were gone, and none would come tomorrow; after all, who performed on the last day? The first day, the first night: that was what counted—anticipating the future, not holding on to something already gone.

I woke up and sat in the Li family farmhouse, the guesthouse in Jian-gou Village where I usually stayed. Last night, the temple manager Wang Defeng had summoned us for the *xiehui*—the thank-you din-ner for the pilgrimage associations that had stayed on the mountain the full two weeks. We had filled two tables in the restaurant, and Mr. Wang had given a short speech, announcing that this year had been a big success: Eighty-one associations visited, up from sixty-nine last year. He said 500,000 people had visited—another modern-day record.

My landlady, Mrs. Li, lit a dozen sticks of incense and held them at face level. Looking toward the mountain, she bowed three times. Then she stuck the incense in the vegetable garden and put a piece of cardboard on the ground in front of her. She knelt on it and clasped her hands, kowtowing three times to Our Lady.

I roused myself, said good-bye, and climbed the path of a thou-sand elbows. A few hundred yards up, I was overtaken by a group of four young people who were employed as ticket takers and security guards. A young woman in the group explained that she normally works at the Beijing International Convention Center but had been hired by Miaofengshan to work the temple fair. This was their last day, and so they were carrying their two weeks' worth of gear up the hill. Typically for Chinese travelers it was light: just a small duffel bag each.

When I got to the top, it was seven o'clock, and the pilgrimage association members were already finishing their congee and buns and getting ready to move.

Old Mrs. Chen's daughter and son started first. The son climbed up on the altar and unpinned the huge golden silk sheet that had formed the backdrop to their shrine and the tea association's Guanyin. Then he unhooked another silk sheet from the wall, and then you could see the room as it was: a concrete shell with a wooden Chinese roof. The flowers came off the altar. Old Mrs. Chen's family packed their vases and banners and sheets in big boxes. Old Mrs. Chen was tired, and so when her family finished, they set off first, packing their cars full and driving away slowly, arms out the windows, yells of good-bye. In a few days would be a pilgrimage to the Temple of the Medicine God in western Beijing, and six weeks later it would be their village's turn, just like every year. The rest of the time, they would see each other at family occasions or at ceremonies when a new pilgrimage association was formed; one was joining the ranks every few months. And of course everyone would keep in touch by social media, sending each other recorded sutras, pictures, homilies, and advice.

The tea association's shrine was bigger and required more time to pack. Tiebiao and Jintang pulled out most of the furniture from the walls and swept away the dirt, dust, and trash that had been blown under the beds and chairs over the past two weeks.

Manager Wang's cleanup crew came by to help. They filled several boxes with rubbish that had accumulated: cigarette cartons, brittle plastic used to wrap incense, food packaging, empty plastic bottles, and endless cigarette butts. After they left, we shoved two big wooden crates into the back corner, as far from the windows as possible. They were about four feet high and two feet by two feet square, painted red and emblazoned with the Chinese character for tea.

Tiebiao opened one and climbed in. Jintang jumped onto the altar and handed me teapots, which I carried over to Tiebiao, who carefully placed them in the bottom. When he was nearly surrounded by porcelain, he climbed out and placed a few blankets over the top of the first layer of teapots and then started a new layer, and then again until the box was full. We closed and locked it and then filled the other crate.

Jintang wrapped the statue of Guanyin in red cloth. He carried her off the altar and placed her into the back of his white Toyota SUV. In a few hours, she would be back at his brother's shrine, in his hermitage overlooking the city. We took down the banners and the silk curtains, putting them in other boxes. The yellow silk on the main altar table was wrinkled into a miniature landscape of mountains and valleys filled with sand blown in by the Mongolian winds. Mrs. Qi carefully gathered it into a bunch and shook it outside. The grand altar was now reduced to a plywood sheet on folding construction benches.

Everyone followed Mrs. Qi out and disassembled the tea association's honor flags that were attached to big tin drums. They doubled as storage containers and in the old days would have been carried on the end of poles. We opened the drums, packed them full, and brought them into the shrine. Then came the tea canisters and finally the card tables. It was now 8:30 a.m. Just ninety minutes had passed, but enough to turn the magical stage into a pile of boxes, and the glowing yellow walls into gray concrete.

We had worked quickly, efficiently, and silently. No one was sad; two weeks up here had been satisfying, but enough. Everyone was eager to get home and have a shower. Jintang surveyed the scene.

"Seeing the transformation is interesting, right?" he said. "It's the process that has meaning."

The tourists were out in strength today, a warm Friday in early May. It was the fifteenth day of the fourth lunar month, theoretically still the last day of the fair, but it was already over. Lingering over a dying day is not the Chinese way; better to end it quickly and move on. Jintang locked the doors to the shrine. With shouts of good-bye, we got in our cars and drove back to our new lives in the city below.

Afterword: The Search for Heaven

Old Mr. Ni made a point of telling me that the great pilgrimage associations are independent of the government. This is true, as are the spiritual lives of most of the people we followed over the past year. And yet the state played an overwhelming role in their lives, seeking to contain and co-opt them.

For some years, a strong Chinese state seemed unlikely. When Mao died and moderates took over in the late 1970s, they tried to rebuild credibility among the population by loosening control. Their goal was to push economic development and let people do as they pleased as long as they did not challenge party rule.

This period—the reform era—ran in fits and starts until sometime around 2010. During that time observers believed, or at least hoped, that this relaxation would continue indefinitely, leading to the creation of a freer society. This was an optimistic period around the world, mostly after the Cold War, when it seemed that societies were moving inexorably toward freedom and democracy. Even though China had a setback with the 1989 massacre, economic reforms and technology were supposed to result in an opening of society. And indeed during much of this period, society was increasingly free. Part of this was led by the government; in the wake of the collapse of the Soviet Union, it concluded that reforms and openness could actually strengthen control by creating more prosperity and thus dampening opposition.

But then the government has changed course. Perhaps because leaders felt that further liberalizations would challenge their rule, policy changed. Moderate critics have been locked up, the Internet brought to heel, and social movements told to obey the government or face suppression. A period of stasis has taken hold.

In the field of religion and faith, however, the government has tried harder to co-opt groups than to crush them. It has also cleverly tapped into the phrases and some of the ideas of the traditional political-religious state that ran China for more than two millennia. These trends are likely to continue, and the state—like Chinese governments of centuries past—will try to guide or control the country's moral life.

The winners will likely be China's "traditional" religions: Daoism, Buddhism, and folk religion. Seeing them as easier to manage, the state will give them more space, even while making sure they follow government policies. Here, the Miaofengshan pilgrims and the Shanxi Daoists are instructive; they face challenges, but by and large the government supports their work.

This does not mean that China will become like Russia, with a nationalistic state church and leaders who regularly worship, or that the Communist Party will morph into a Chinese version of the Indian People's Party, or BJP, advocating a nationalist-religious agenda. The Communist Party wants to hold on to power, but its grip is not yet so weak that it must resort to such a blatant instrumentalization of religion. Yet like the dynasties of the past, it will continue to push acceptable forms of faith as a way to strengthen its position as the arbiter of the nation's moral and spiritual values.

This growing state support clashes with two trends we noted in this book. One is increasing foreign ties. To some degree, the government welcomes religion's overseas contacts as a way to push soft power. Thanks to the country's resurgent Buddhist faith, for example, China has become one of the world's largest Buddhist nations and has given a permanent home in the city of Wuxi to the World Buddhist Forum. It also sponsors international Daoist conferences and meetings. But overall, the party is wary of foreign ties. This is true for the Catholic Church and its links to the Vatican, Tibetan Buddhism and its exiled leadership under the Dalai Lama, Islam with its global *ummah*, and Protestantism's international activism. As these groups expand, we can expect to see more tensions between believers and rulers. Xi's predecessors conducted religious policy with what seems now to be a remarkably light touch. The government's challenge now will be to keep a similar balance of managing religion without alienating its followers.

The strains are especially pronounced in churches like Wang Yi's. Alone among China's major religions, Protestant Christianity is growing quickly among the Chinese majority, and also has extensive foreign ties. This has led the government to try sporadic efforts at control. A key question is whether the government will allow it to continue to grow or if—in its hubris and newfound wealth—it will look to achieve complete control.

I suspect it will not. We see the temptation—for example, the campaign from 2014 to 2016 to remove crosses from the tops of unregistered churches in Zhejiang Province. But when the government held a major conference in 2016 to regulate religious life—the most important conference on religious policy in fifteen years—it did not spread the campaign. It instructed religions to "sinicize"—to become more Chinese—but in a very vague and indecisive way. We can expect more feints and thrusts from the government and growing debate among officials about how to handle religion in the new era. But in the long run, I doubt the government will try to achieve total control, in part because recent history—the Cultural Revolution, for example—shows officials how oppression can actually encourage real faith.

These foreign links are obvious problems for the government, but religion's real challenge to state power comes from something subtler that it is helping to create: a reawakened national conscience. If I could summarize the aspirations of the people in this book in one word, it would be "heaven." The concept of heaven—*tian*—is central to how Chinese from Confucius to the Ni family have thought of a well-ordered society. It carries with it a sense of justice and respect and is something higher than any one government. Christians like to say that only their religion carries with it the idea of God-given rights. This is wrong. All faiths have ideals that trump temporal powers. For Confucians, they were the teachings of the sage; for Buddhists, the ideals found in the sutras; for Daoists, the ideas of *ziran,* or the Dao; and for ordinary people, a sense of righteousness—a belief in heavenly rights and justice.

This is different from what we saw in previous decades. Throughout the years of Communist rule, the country has had dissidents, including inspiring figures such as the Nobel Peace Prize laureate Liu Xiaobo. But by and large these activists and their pursuit of universal rights left ordinary people cold. Many saw them as well-meaning but unpragmatic. When most people pursued political change, it was mainly for narrower goals: farmers protesting unfair taxation or city residents opposing the destruction of their homes. Their motivations were personal and rarely part of an overarching ideology or yearning to change the system.

The new desire for spiritual transformation is deeper and more profound. Religious and spiritual movements have selfish goals too, but they also offer systemic critiques of the status quo. It is true that faith can be an escape from politics, a pietistic flight from a chaotic society: most people aren't trustworthy, but at least my church, my temple, or my pilgrimage society is filled with good people.

And yet this inward focus is only part of the story. Faith can also spur social action. It is no coincidence that the great *weiquan* movement of human rights lawyers featured a disproportionate number of Christians or that other activists have found inspiration in Buddhism and Daoism. Even Confucianism, often portrayed as a pillar of the establishment, is part of this. In the Confucian classics, the sage advises that change begins with ordering one's own heart. But as Master Nan taught, this is only a beginning. Change flows outward to one's family, community, and nation.

In the 1980s and 1990s, faith-based Buddhist and Daoist charities in Taiwan helped turn that island into a democracy, as the scholar Richard Madsen has documented in his book *Democracy's Dharma.* On the mainland, this is unlikely to happen in the near term. The government has made clear that it will not permit nongovernmental organizations—inspired by faith or not—to set up and organize. This is why the *weiquan* movement has been all but destroyed and other religions have been limited to providing services—disaster relief, for example—but hindered from pursuing broader goals, such as trying to reform society.

But seen from a wider historical perspective, these movements are helping lay the groundwork for a broader transformation. Religion provides a morality and frames of reference for universal aspirations—like justice, fairness, and decency—that are higher than any government's agenda.

Out of this is coming a China that is more than the hypermercantilist, fragile superpower that we know. It is a country engaging in a global conversation that affects all of us: how to restore solidarity and values to societies that have made economics the basis of most decisions. Perhaps because Chinese traditions were so savagely attacked over the past decades, and then replaced with such a naked form of capitalism, China might actually be at the forefront of this worldwide search for values.

These are universal aspirations, and like people elsewhere in the world Chinese people feel that these hopes are supported by something more than a particular government or law. They are supported by heaven. As the twenty-five-hundred-year-old classic the *Book of Documents* puts it,

> *Heaven sees as my people see.*
> *Heaven hears as my people hear.*

Acknowledgments

This book was made possible thanks to two generous grants. The Open Society Fellowship made an initial award that allowed me to take the leap and leave daily journalism in 2010. I also benefited from the intellectual stimulation of the Open Society's fellows and staff, especially Tom Kellogg, Lenny Bernardo, and Steve Hubbell. Later, the Alicia Patterson Foundation provided a grant during the writing phase. Thanks especially to Peggy Engel for her support during this period.

I would not have been able to write this book if I had not been able to return to China, which seemed unlikely in 2007 when the Ministry of Foreign Affairs initially rejected my visa application. It took two years of confidence building to change the ministry's mind. I want to thank the ministry and other relevant departments for their flexibility and generosity. Thanks also to the editors at *The Wall Street Journal* for supporting my application, especially China bureau chiefs Rebecca Blumenstein and Andrew Browne, deputy bureau chief Jason Dean, former foreign editor John Bussey, News Corp.'s former government relations liaison Mei Yan, and Rupert Murdoch—all of whom took time out from their busy schedules to lobby on my behalf.

Thanks also to the editors at *The New York Times*, who accredited me after I left the *Journal*, especially managing editor Joseph Kahn, Asia editor Philip Pan, and China bureau chiefs Michael Wines and Edward Wong for their ideas, advice, and collegiality. I remain indebted to the *Times* for its enduring commitment to quality journalism.

A huge debt of gratitude is due Robert Silvers and Hugh Eakin at *The New York Review of Books*. Since 2009, writing for the *Review* has been one of my greatest pleasures. Without Bob and Hugh's support, I doubt I could have written this book. I also learned much from publishing several longer features in *The New Yorker*, where Leo Carey, Dorothy Wickenden, and David Remnick were patient editors, and *National Geographic*, where Oliver Payne was a supportive friend.

I also want to thank two institutions for helping open the doors to academia. One is *The Journal of Asian Studies*, and its editor, Jeffrey Wasserstrom of the University of California, Irvine. Jeff made me one of the *Journal*'s advising editors, allowing me to see firsthand the level of detail and commitment that first-class academic work requires. Jeff has been a constant source of support over the years and helped critique many ideas in this book.

Thanks also to The Beijing Center for Chinese Studies, an academic exchange center run by the Society of Jesus. In 2010, its former dean of academic affairs, Russell Moses, offered me a job teaching a course on contemporary Chinese religious practice. Explaining this topic to undergraduates helped hone my thinking, while also helping me to become familiar with the flourishing field of Chinese religious studies. Equally important were my regular lunches with Russ, where we watched the Chinese political calendar move and hashed out its meaning. I also greatly appreciate the close reading he gave the book. Many thanks also to Beijing Center directors Ronald Anton, Roberto Ribeiro, Thierry Meynard, and Jim Caime—true heirs to Matteo Ricci. And special thanks to my dozens of students over the years, whose questions, curiosity, and enthusiasm allowed me to see China through their fresh eyes.

Also in the academic field, I would like to thank: Philip Clart at Leipzig University for his enduring support for my yet-unrealized plan to write a history of Maoshan's reconstruction; Vincent Goossaert and David Palmer for their inspiring work on the religious question of China, and especially David's reading of chapter 2 and the "Practice" chapters; Yang Fenggang and Jonathan Pettit at Purdue University's Center for the Study of Chinese Religions for sharing ideas and thoughts over the years; Stephen Jones for his pioneering work on folk Daoism in Shanxi; Bao Shixuan of the Beijing Folk Artists Association for showing me the real Miaofengshan; Patrice Fava for all things Daoist, especially his long-term commitment to filming Miaofengshan; Kristin Shi-Kupfer of the Merics think tank in Berlin, as well as her husband, the writer and filmmaker Shi Ming, for discussions on Christianity and China's spiritual vacuum; Sebastian Heilmann of Merics for hosting several talks on religion in China and for allowing me to serve as one of the think tank's advisers; and finally to Klaus Mühlhahn of the Freie Universität Berlin for discussing several ideas around this book.

I also had enormous help from my agent Chris Calhoun, who helped carve a sprawling series of ideas into a viable book project, and my editor at Pantheon, Dan Frank, for his patience and wisdom. Thanks also to Angela Hessler for the book's beautiful maps, which adopt images from *The Classic of Mountains and Seas* to fill out the nether regions beyond China Proper.

Thanks also to the photographer Sim Chi Yin for accompanying me on several field trips and for her deep empathy for China; Ed Gargan for our two-man book club that kept me grounded in reading fiction, as well as his early reading of the manuscript; Cao Haili for introducing me to the circle around Nan Huai-chin; Zhang Yongjing, Zhao Xue, Sheng Liqun, Li Pei, and Amy Qin for research help; Xu Hong for his intellectual engagement with Christianity and for reading the Early Rain chapters; Liao Yiwu for introducing me to Chengdu from Berlin; Leslie Chang and Peter Hessler for invaluable critiques and close readings of early drafts; and my father, Denis, who remains my most fastidious editor. Finally, thanks to Elke for her patience and generosity of spirit.

I am most indebted to the people who are the subject of this book. Over many years, they let me into their homes to celebrate their marriages and births, to grieve with them for their deaths and losses: in short, to share the experiences that give our lives meaning. It is hard to convey how much they wanted me—and through me, you, the outside world—to understand the universality of our yearnings. I am not sure I succeeded, but it is not for their lack of trying.

Beijing,
December 2016

Notes

This is a work of nonfiction. Events described and facts cited in this book can be broken down into two main categories: those I witnessed directly, and those I cite from other sources. When describing how people felt or thought, I rely on subsequent interviews with them in which they described their thoughts to me.

In the notes below, I give sources—either the date of a specific interview or a standard academic citation from a previously published work. The full bibliographic information for each published work is found in the bibliography.

PART 1 THE MOON YEAR

1 Beijing: The Tolling Bell

5 **In the southeast corner of Beijing:** Material for this chapter was drawn primarily from interviews conducted on Jan. 29, 2012, and a follow-up interview with Ni Jincheng on Jan. 31. The interview in 2011 referred to in the chapter was conducted on July 17, 2011.

5 **According to local legend:** The story of the Temple of the Tolling Bell is widely told by locals, but I have not been able to find it documented in written form.

6 **Lost was a way of life:** The destruction of old Beijing has been recounted in numerous books and articles, including the second section of my book *Wild Grass*, but the most complete English-language treatment is Wang Jun's *Beijing Record*.

2 Ritual: The Lost Middle

16 **"We thought we were unhappy":** Catherine Lu Yong (a pastor of

an unregistered church in Pixian, Chengdu), interview with author, Dec. 25, 2012.

19 **religion was "diffused" in Chinese society:** see C. K. Yang, *Religion in Chinese Society*.

19 **Almost every profession venerated a god:** see Burgess, *Guilds of Peking*, 176.

20 **the city had roughly one thousand temples:** Naquin, *Peking*, 23.

20 **Primarily, they provided services:** see Goossaert, "The Social Organization of Religious Communities in the Twentieth Century."

21 **"Chinese culture was a performance culture":** David G. Johnson, *Spectacle and Sacrifice*, 10.

22 **Chinese temples were society's "nexus of power":** Duara, *Culture, Power, and the State.*

22 **Officials duplicated many of these rites:** see Goossaert, "Shifting Balance of Power in the City God Temples."

23 **China had an estimated one million temples:** Goossaert, "1898."

23 **Islam entered China:** the best overview of Muslims in China is Gladney, *Muslim Chinese*, 81–87.

23 **Islam counts at most twenty-three million believers:** China has 23 million members of ten ethnic groups that the government defines as believing in Islam. This means official statistics count every single member of these groups as Muslim—as if Islam were an ethnicity rather than a religion. In fact, many do not practice, so it is hard to know how many feel they are Muslims. On the other side of the argument, other ethnic groups, including Chinese, can convert to Islam, which could add to the total. In practice, converts are very rare, thus 23 million must be seen as a generous estimate.

24 **The impact of Christianity was radically different:** see Goossaert and Palmer, *Religious Question*, 50–62, especially for Christianity's normative effect and the creation of the categories of "religion" and "superstition."

24 **Of the two, Buddhism fared better:** see Pittman, *Towards a Modern Chinese Buddhism.*

25 **A telling example involves Sun Yat-sen:** Poon, "Religion, Modernity, and Urban Space."

25 **When Sun's Nationalist Party took power:** The definitive account of Chinese government religious policy in the Republican era is Nedostup, *Superstitious Regimes.*

27 **"forbade normal religious activities":** All citations from Document 19 quoted from MacInnis, *Religion in China Today.*

28 **One government survey in 2012:** Wenzel-Teuber, "2014 Statistical Update on Religions and Churches."

28 **In 2014, for example, the Pew Research Center:** Pew Research Center, "Worldwide Many See Belief in God as Essential to Morality."

28 **This led some Western commentators:** Keck, "Atheists of Beijing."

28 **In 2015, a WIN/Gallup International poll went further:** WIN/Gallup International, "Losing our Religion?"

29 **These studies are absurdly flawed:** Ian Johnson, "Problem of 'Religion'—and Polling in China."

29 **In a 2007 study of over three thousand people:** Yao and Badham, *Religious Experience in Contemporary China.*

29 **A 2005 survey by East China Normal University:** Wu, "Religious Believers Thrice the Estimate."

29 **Another study, the China Spiritual Life Study:** Wenzel-Teuber. "2014 Statistical Update on Religions and Churches."

29 **A government survey from 2014:** Ibid.

30 **As for Christianity, the picture is bifurcated:** For an overview of Christianity, see Bays, *New History of Christianity in China.* For an account of rural Catholicism, see Harrison, *Missionary's Curse.* For statistics on Catholics, see Wenzel-Teuber, "2012 Statistical Update on Religions and Churches."

30 **In 2008, the Beijing sociologist Yu Jianrong:** Yu, "Wei Jidujiao jiating jiaohui de tuomin."

30 **In 2011, the Pew Forum on Religion & Public Life:** Pew Research Center, *Global Christianity.*

30–31 **round-number estimates of 100 million:** See for example the Beijing sociologist Li Fan who uses 100 million, but simply saying it falls somewhere between 60 million and even higher-end figures of 130 million. Li, "Jidujiao de fazhan he jiating jiaohui."

31 **the number of Protestants could top 100 million:** Fenggang Yang, "Exceptionalism or Chimerica."

31 **Human rights groups estimate:** On the Falun Gong crackdown, see Tong, *Revenge of the Forbidden City,* for an account of government suppression, and Palmer, *Qigong Fever,* for an authoritative description of its rise in the 1990s. For a firsthand account of the movement's growth and suppression, see my book *Wild Grass,* chapter 3.

32 **Government favor is especially pronounced toward:** On loosening the ties on established religions, this is my impression based on the immense temple-building program of the past fifteen years. See for example the case of Maoshan in my article "Two Sides of a Mountain."

32 **"Middle Kingdom that has lost its Middle":** Goossaert and Palmer, *Religious Question,* 3.

3 Shanxi: First Night

33 **The Taihang Mountains:** Information for this chapter was drawn primarily from interviews conducted on Feb. 3, 4, 5, and 6, 2012.

35 **It was the dead of winter:** Temperatures in Fahrenheit.

38 **That is when a Chinese scholar named Chen Kexiu:** see Wu Fan, *Yinyang Gujiang.*

4 Chengdu: Long Live Auntie Wei

52 **When Wang Yi addressed:** Information for this chapter was primarily drawn from the funeral for Wei Suying on Feb. 24, 2012, an interview with Wang Yi earlier that same day, and an interview with Ran Yunfei on Feb. 25, 2012.

62 **"Ran isn't exactly a Christian":** Ran eventually converted and was baptized on June 19, 2016.

67 **My wife said, "I thought that you would be arrested":** Wang, Yi, "Wang Yi's Diary."

PART II AWAKENING OF THE INSECTS

71 **Each year has twenty-four—six for each season:** The twenty-four solar terms are:

Season	Longitude	Date	Name	Translation
Spring	315	Feb. 4–18	*lichun*	Spring Commences
Spring	330	Feb. 19–Mar. 4	*yushui*	Spring Showers
Spring	345	Mar. 6–20	*jingzhe*	Awakening of the Insects
Spring	0	Mar. 21–Apr. 4	*chunfen*	Vernal Equinox
Spring	15	Apr. 5–19	*qingming*	Clear and Bright
Spring	30	Apr. 20–May 4	*gushui*	Grain Rains
Summer	45	May 5–20	*lixia*	Summer Commences
Summer	60	May 21–Jun. 5	*xiaoman*	Grain Forms
Summer	75	Jun. 6–20	*mangzhong*	Summer Harvest
Summer	90	Jun. 21–Jul. 6	*xiazhi*	Summer Solstice
Summer	105	Jul. 7–22	*xiaoshu*	Lesser Heat
Summer	120	Jul. 23–Aug. 6	*dashu*	Greater Heat

Season	Longitude	Date	Name	Translation
Autumn	135	Aug. 7–22	*liqiu*	Autumn Commences
Autumn	150	Aug. 23–Sep. 7	*chushu*	Limit of Heat
Autumn	165	Sep. 8–22	*bailu*	White Dew
Autumn	180	Sep. 23–Oct. 7	*qiufen*	Autumnal Equinox
Autumn	195	Oct. 8–22	*hanlu*	Cold Dew
Autumn	210	Oct. 23–Nov. 6	*shuangjiang*	Frost Descends
Winter	225	Nov. 7–21	*lidong*	Winter Commences
Winter	240	Nov. 22–Dec. 6	*xiaoxue*	Lesser Snows
Winter	255	Dec. 7–21	*daxue*	Greater Snows
Winter	270	Dec. 22–Jan. 5	*dongzhi*	Winter Solstice
Winter	285	Jan. 6–19	*xiaohan*	Lesser Cold
Winter	300	Jan. 20–Feb. 3	*dahan*	Greater Cold

72 *"Spring approaches, bringing timely rains"*: This and all texts or poems translated by the author unless otherwise noted.

5 Ritual: Awakening the Past

73 **The golden age of China's past was the Zhou dynasty:** The parallels to the Zhou dynasty, the Zhou king's hymn, the direct quotations from the chief architect, the significance of the interior rooms, and the statement by the architectural team are drawn from Hung Wu, *Remaking Beijing*, 114–27.

74 **But the details are traditional:** On the significance of the petals, the columns, and other information about the Ten Great Projects, see Hung, *Mao's New World*. I am also indebted to Professor Hung for many very insightful conversations and exchanges over the years.

77 **Ye was a complex figure:** In 2015, a senior researcher from the Chinese Academy of Social Sciences accused Ye and another official in the religious affairs administration of taking money to designate living Buddhas. However, to date Ye has not been arrested or investigated, and in 2016 he made a public speech at Renmin University lauding Xi Jinping's program of "core socialist values."

77 **He had grown up in one of China's poorest provinces:** For Ye Xiaowen's biography, see http://www.chinavitae.com/biography/Ye_Xiaowen/full. Ye was made head of the Religious Affairs Bureau

in 1995, which was renamed the State Administration for Religious Affairs in 1998.

78 **"fielded questions like a used-car salesman"**: Aikman, *Jesus in Beijing*, 176.

78 **"If I believed in a religion"**: Interview on "Closer to China with R. L. Kuhn" on CCTV News, May 4, 2015, accessed June 21, 2016, https://www.youtube.com/watch?v=cIdG4lZ_65M.

78 **Soon, scholars critical of Confucianism**: Fenggang Yang, "Cultural Dynamics in China." According to Yang, the officials moved out included Li Shen, a student of the founder of religious studies in China, Ren Jiyu. The director of the new center on Confucianism is Chen Ming, a vocal advocate of cultural conservatism and Confucianism.

78 **Ye argued that religion**: see Laliberté, "Religion and Development in China."

78 **"Religious force is one"**: "Buddhism Contributes to 'Harmonious Society,'" *People's Daily*, April 11, 2006, accessed June 20, 2016, http://en.people.cn/200604/11/eng20060411_257467.html.

79 **The communiqué issued by that meeting**: Central Committee of the Chinese Communist Party Decision Concerning Deepening Cultural Structural Reform, accessed March 20, 2016, https://chinacopyright andmedia.wordpress.com/2011/10/18/central-committee-of-the -chinese-communist-party-decision-concerning-deepening-cultural -structural-reform/.

80 **Like every other annual session of parliament**: Personal observation in the Great Hall of the People on March 5 and 14, 2012.

81 **Wen was a thin, almost ascetic man**: Personal observation at Wen Jiabao closing press conference, March 14, 2012.

81 **As foreign journalists later proved**: David Barboza, "Billion in Hidden Riches for Family of Chinese Leader."

6 Beijing: You Can't Explain It

83 **Ni Jincheng was in purgatory**: This chapter is based on an interview with Ni Jincheng at the Titan Orthopedic Hospital on April 15, 2012.

87 **Even though this was after the Communist takeover**: Numerous books on these rules have been published in China. Especially popular among people in the pilgrimage associations was Liu, *Beijing Laoguiju*.

87 **"Who are our enemies?"**: Mao Zedong, "Analysis of the Classes in Chinese Society."

88 **When the army was sent in to Beijing**: Walder, *China Under Mao*.

88 **"We can feel the overlay of savagery"**: He, *Social Ethics*, 125.

89 **One 2014 study cited "loss of trust"**: Ibid., xxi. See also the work

of Richard Madsen, as described in Ian Johnson, "China's Way to Happiness."

90 **In place of principles, China has "hidden rules"**: He, *Social Ethics*, xxii.

91 **He became a star**: For more on Bill Porter's role in China, see Ian Johnson, "Finding Zen and Book Contracts in China."

92 **Others signed up for Tibetan Buddhism**: Johnson, "Q. and A.: John Osburg."

7 Ritual: The Caged Master

94 **Chinese culture originated**: Nan Huai-chin, interviews with author, Nov. 16, 17, and 18, 2010, and March 7, 2011. The scene and descriptions are from the March 2011 visit, with background drawn from the earlier interviews. This is the only chapter in the book that does not take place during the book's primary chronological sequence from New Year's 2012 to the spring of 2013. This is why I visit Nan on the start of the Awakening of the Insects solar term and also, in chapter 5, witness the opening of the 2012 National People's Congress on the start of the same solar term.

97 **They had discarded their traditions**: This idea is handled very well by Schell and Delury, *Wealth and Power*.

98 **Two years later, in 2001**: The story of Master Nan's property purchase was related to me by Sami Kuo, the manager of the Hall of Great Learning. The Hall of Great Learning is now easily accessible from Shanghai in under two hours by highway but at the time was fairly remote. Interview, March 4, 2011.

100 **One skeptic is Zhu Weizheng**: Interview with author, March 5, 2011.

8 Practice: Learning to Breathe

108 **I had met Qin Ling a year earlier**: The man's name is omitted and his family's details are left vague to protect his and his family's identity.

109 **"Internal alchemy?"**: This is the standard translation for the Chinese term *neidan*. For a useful short history, see Robinet, "Original Contributions of *Neidan* to Taoism and Chinese Thought."

112 **"Whoever has done mostly good has spirit-energy"**: Wilhelm, *Taiyi Jinhua Zongzhi* (The Secret of the Golden Flower), 29.

113 **The *Golden Flower*'s fame in the West**: It is also capably translated by Thomas Cleary. In addition, a website has been devoted to the text, http://thesecretofthegoldenflower.com/. Accessed Sept. 15, 2016.

113 **This was also a time when lay religious**: For an outstanding discussion of the Daoist movement in Republican-era China, see Xun Liu's *Daoist Modern*.

114 **a more neutral term is "redemptive societies":** The term was coined by Duara in *Sovereignty and Authenticity.*

114 **One survey in 1950:** Goossaert and Palmer, *Religious Question,* 107.

116 **"*Qigong* has left religion and folklore":** Palmer, *Qigong Fever,* 59.

116 **As the anthropologist Nancy Chen:** Chen, *Breathing Spaces,* 3.

118 **He was a committed Daoist:** This is a good chance to discuss the spelling of "Dao" and "Tao" and their related words "Daoist/Daoism" and "Taoist/Taoism." These are identical in Chinese. They stem from the same character, 道, which is pronounced "dow" (and yes, someone wrote a book about the Dao of the Dow). For a long time, "Tao" was standard in English and other Western languages. This reflects earlier forms of rendering the Chinese character into Roman letters, primarily the Wade-Giles system. Increasingly, however, this character is written as "Dao." This is based on the pinyin system that is standard internationally for Romanizing Chinese characters. Some people say this is irrelevant because "Tao," "Taoist," and "Taoism" became English words long before the switch to pinyin, and thus needn't change just because the government in Beijing uses a different writing system. This is an understandable position, and I sympathize with it—in the same way I would not advocate changing the Italian city of Milan to Milano or the German city of Munich to München. However, the trend seems unmistakable that "Dao," "Daoist," and "Daoism" are becoming dominant. Certainly in academic writing, no one uses "Tao"; it is seen as archaic. I do not want to be accused of following academic or political fads, but I think that this trend will continue, and so I elected to go with the flow, follow the course of least resistance, and adopt the "Dao."

PART III CLEAR AND BRIGHT

9 Ritual: Martyrs

125 **Xu Jue had the flowers:** Xu Jue, interview by the author, May 7, 2012, Beijing.

129 **In 1944, a peasant soldier named Zhang Side:** This account of Zhang Side and the term "cult of the red martyr" are drawn from Hung, *Mao's New World,* 214–32.

130 **The enormous event takes place:** "Chinese Commemorate Common Ancestors at Qingming Festival," Xinhua News Agency, April 7, 2003.

10 Shanxi: The Buried Books

134 **Early April in northern China:** Interviews on April 3–4, 2010.

138 **"The heavenly army is coming soon":** Zhou, *Great Famine in China*, 106.

139 **When people were beaten:** For a discussion of this more broadly, see He, *Social Ethics*, esp. the introduction.

11 Chengdu: Good Friday

152 **A couple of days:** Interviews on April 8–9, 2010.

160 **Compared with places like East Germany:** The 3 percent amount is based on a 1990 population of 16 million and an estimated 500,000 informers (*inoffizielle Mitarbeiter*).

163 **This might seem far-fetched:** Tsai, *Accountability Without Democracy*.

164 **About a quarter were Christians:** Estimate by one of the movement's most prominent lawyers, the non-Christian Teng Biao. See Ian Johnson, "China's Unstoppable Lawyers."

12 Beijing: Ascending the Mountain

170 **People often say that:** This chapter is drawn from interviews on April 20, 2012.

182 **"Never enter lightly into the mountains":** Schipper, *Taoist Body*, 171.

183 **Miaofengshan's location near Beijing:** For a history of the Miaofengshan pilgrimage, see Naquin, "Peking Pilgrimage to Miao-feng Shan."

184 **In May 1938, *The New York Times*:** Gardiner, "Pilgrimage of Chinese."

184 **Best of all, Goodrich wrote:** Goodrich, "Miao Feng Shan."

PART IV SUMMER HARVEST

194 *I had tended many an acre*: Qu Yuan, "Li sao," in Hawkes, *Songs of the South*, 69.

13 Chengdu: Recitation

195 **Early one Friday morning:** Seminary interviews on July 6, Daoist and Buddhist temples on July 7, church service on July 8, 2012.

200 **He was also from Sichuan and had written:** Liao, *God Is Red*.

204 **"The Dao nourishes by not forcing":** Mitchell translation.

14 Practice: Learning to Walk

207 **Beijing's north and east:** Interviews and observations from July 18–24, 2012.

207 **The most famous is the Nanshagou:** The ministries associated with Nanshagou's individual buildings were related to me by Qin Ling and

her husband, Xiao Weijian, but they cautioned that the division of ministries was not exact.

207 **Many well-connected party officials:** "Portrait of Vice President Xi Jinping."

208 **Its wealth only pops out occasionally:** Anecdote as related by senior editor at a Communist Party newspaper who lives near the villas.

212 **The government even began promoting Daoist ideas:** See the example of Zhanshu in Jiangxi Province, "Yi Daode wei Guifan Yi Lianjie wei Hexin." Thanks to Russell Leigh Moses for alerting me to this article.

213 **"New Qigong Treatments for Malignant Tumors":** "Xin Qigong Liaofa."

213 **"Within a week of practicing":** "Liangong Tihui Liangce."

213 **One, by a young man named Chen Zhu:** Chen Zhu, *Zhongguo Chaoren.*

213 **Ke Yunlu grew up in Beijing:** Ke's biographical details and comments are drawn from a series of interviews I conducted with him by e-mail between March 31 and May 5, 2015.

214 **One of Ke's best sellers:** Sales figures for *The Great Qigong Master* are from Palmer, *Qigong Fever,* 153.

214 **"We will be more open":** cited in Palmer, *Qigong Fever,* 153–54.

15 Ritual: New Star

216 *The master said to the steward of the temple: Record of Linji,* 36–37.

217 **"Chaotic, dirty, and backward":** Cited by Su, "Xi Jinping zai Zhengding."

218 **Youming liked to say:** Exhibition display on Youming's life in Linji Temple, July 12, 2012, visit.

218 **Mao himself understood religion's power:** Goossaert and Palmer, *Religious Question,* 142.

219 **Beginning in 1980, according to his own account:** Although he held no formal position as head of religious affairs, in the 1989 obituary of the Panchen Lama, Xi Zhongxun wrote, "At the end of 1980, when I returned from Guangdong to the Central Government to take charge of ethnic, religious, and United Front work, we had more opportunities to contact each other." Xi Zhongxun, "Shenqiu Huainian Zhongguo Gongchandang."

219 **That same year, Xi Jinping arrived in Zhengding:** For Xi's decision to move to Zhengding, the state of the roads, and the zealousness with which he carried out central directives, see my article "Elite and Deft, Xi Aimed High Early in China."

219 **In 1983, Xi approved the temple's reopening:** see Zhengding xian zhi [Zhengding County Gazetteer], 48.

219 **Reconstruction of the main hall began:** Interviews with author, July 12, 2012, and March 30, 2015.

220 **His name was Shi Huichang:** Interview with author, July 12, 2012, Linji Temple, Zhengding.

221 **The past fifteen years have not been kind:** Ke Yunlu, e-mail exchange with author, April 27, 2015.

223 **When he left to serve in Fujian Province:** "Xi Jinping: Xiangai Xizijide Shengming Yiyang Baohu Wenhua Yichan."

223 **He also called on Buddhists:** "Zhejiangsheng Weishuji Xi Jinping xie Furen Peng Liyuan Yixingdao Woxian Jinxing Canguan Kaocha."

224 **"Everything depends on love":** Wielander, *Christian Values in Communist China,* 56.

224 **Chinese who knew him well believe:** "Portrait of Vice President Xi Jinping," Wikileaks.

224 **Although the government eventually succeeded:** Lian Xi, *Redeemed by Fire,* esp. his notes on p. 250.

16 Beijing: The Flower Lady

226 **At 5:30 on a sticky July morning:** Interviews conducted on July 19, 2012. The earlier trip with Professor Bao was July 16, 2011. Old Mrs. Chen and her family related details of her history to me on Oct. 8, 2012, and Feb. 28, 2015.

17 Shanxi: Source of the Divine

235 **Half a mile across the cornfields:** Interviews for this chapter were conducted on Aug. 17, 18, and 19, 2012.

235 **This was the spirit of a man surnamed Hu:** The name Dragon Hu, or *Hulong,* and his identity as a successful official were told to me by locals when I visited in July 2012, but Jones in *Daoist Priests of the Li Family* identifies the god more probably as an ancient general, with the proper name Elder Hu, God Hu, or Hutu, possibly of Mongolian origin.

PART V MID-AUTUMN

18 Practice: Learning to Sit

253 **I woke at 5:00 and hiked:** This chapter is based on a ten-day retreat to Jinhua, Oct. 19 to 28, 2012.

19 Beijing: The Sacred Slum

269 **It was the send-off for Yu Xiurong:** This chapter is based on the funeral of Yu Xiurong, Oct. 20, 2012.

20 Ritual: The New Leader

276 **Now it was time for the autumn ritual:** The opening of the Eighteenth Party Congress as I observed it on Nov. 8, 2012.

277 **They were officially known as "ritual girls":** See the *Beijing News* video report, "Renmin Dahuitang Fuwuyuan Wang Qianqian 11 Nianhou Zouhong Jie Dangnian Xianbo Biaozhun." The video was originally cited in Meng, "Finding the Women at China's Big Meetings."

280 **Thirty years earlier he had rebuilt Zhengding's temples:** On Xi's time in Zhengding and his interest in *qigong*, see chapters 14 and 15.

281 **Many observers immediately saw this as copying:** On Xi's dream echoing earlier images of dreams from Chinese statecraft, literature, and philosophy, see Perry, "Populist Dream of Chinese Democracy."

21 Chengdu: The New Calvinists

282 **One November morning I wandered east:** Visit to Zha's church, Nov. 29, 2012.

287 **Zha's chapter was called "Christianity in a China":** "Jidujiao zai Zhongguo cong Jianghu Shehui zhuanxingwei Gongmin Shehui zhong de Jiaose."

287 **The number of missionaries rose:** Bays, *New History of Christianity in China,* as well as Lian Xi, *Redeemed by Fire.*

288 **In 1907, Protestants held a big conference:** Yao, "At the Turn of the Century."

288 **Many prominent Chinese Christians:** Bays, *New History of Christianity in China,* 99–112.

289 **Ursula Seidt grew up:** Ursula and Manfred Seidt, interviews with author, Dec. 23, 2012, Chengdu.

292 **Back in the early 1990s, Peng was following:** Peng Qiang interview with the author, Dec. 21, 2012.

294 **Fredrik Fällman, a Swedish historian:** Fällman, "Calvin, Culture, and Christ?"

294 **The Puritans fled oppression in England:** For a view of how Calvinists see the impact of Puritanism on the American Revolution, see Til, *Liberty of Conscience.*

PART VI WINTER SOLSTICE

23 Shanxi: City People

304 **Li Bin drove through:** This chapter is based on interviews conducted in Yanggao County, Nov. 24 and 25, 2012.

306 **"My late mother, of the Chen family"**: The names of the family and woman were changed at the husband's request.

24 Beijing: The Great Hermit

318 **Ni Jincheng lived atop the city**: Ni Jincheng, interview with author, Nov. 30, 2012.

25 Ritual: Eastern Lightning

325 **One Chinese businessman built an ark**: Jacobs, "Chatter of Dooms-day Makes Beijing Nervous."

326 **According to official reports, the group was behind forty riots**: "Inside China's 'Eastern Lightning' Cult."

326 **As early as 1992**: The group's history is from Dunn, *Lightning from the East*.

326 **Almost no one felt the group was worth defending**: An exception was an anonymous piece on the China Change website: "Eastern Lightning May Be a Cult, but They Still Have Rights."

326 **Western reporters relishing its members' odd beliefs**: On Western media coverage of the group, see Hong, "Prepare the Kool-Aid," and Shea, "Cult Who Kidnaps Christians and Is at War with the Chinese Government."

328 **"Many aspects of our own contemporary culture"**: Kuhn, *Soul-stealers*, 1.

329 **These groups, according to the historian Daniel Bays**: Bays, *New History of Christianity in China*, and Lian Xi, *Redeemed by Fire*.

329 **Eastern Lightning was founded in 1991**: There are conflicting accounts of the woman's name. Initially, and according to Bays, for example, she was identified simply by the surname Zhao. Subsequent Chinese media reports have given her the name Yang Xiangbin and provided enough biographical material to be credible. See, for example, "Inside China's 'Eastern Lightning' Cult."

330 **"They destroyed almost all the temples"**: Zhang Yinan, interview with author, July 1, 2011, Xinyang, China.

331 **"Because it has disintegrated within"**: "Why Does God Do a New Work in Each Age? And for What Is a New Age Brought About?" Excerpted from *The Word Appears in the Flesh*, accessed April 20, 2016. https://www.findshepherd.com/new-work-in-each-age.html.

331 **In describing God, the group did not use**: On the use of *shen* and parallels to the Mao cult, see Dunn, *Lightning from the East*, esp. chapter 3.

331 **The church's defense is**: On the church's denying involvement in the McDonald's murders, see https://easternlightning.wordpress.com/

category/the-truth-about-zhaoyuan-murder-case/, accessed April 19, 2016.

26 Chengdu: Searching for Jesus

333 **I visited Peng Qiang:** Interview with author, Dec. 21, 2012.

336 **At noon on Christmas Eve:** Early Rain Christmas service, Dec. 24, 2012.

339 **an allusion to the 2009 novel** *Chengdu: This Evening Leave Me Alone*: Translated as *Leave Me Alone: A Novel of Chengdu*. I used a more literal translation to make clear the parallel to the church play.

339 **"Chengdu at night always looked gentle and soft":** *Leave Me Alone*, 130.

PART VII LEAP YEAR

348 *Why must this year:* Li He, "The Intercalary Month," in *Goddesses, Ghosts, and Demons*, 38.

27 Ritual: The Fragrant Dream

349 **In late 2012, Wang Wenbin suddenly remembered:** Xie's recollection of how he came to see the figurine, as well as Wang Wenbin's role, is recounted on an online video, "Gongyi Shipin Caifang."

350 **That year, he traveled down:** see a video of Xie's meeting from Dec. 20, 2011, Xie, "Yi Qing Deng Lianxian Yan Changfeng."

351 **Xie thought back to the myths:** Xie's recollections, and the sequence of events, come from Xie and Wang, interview with author, Oct. 26, 2013.

353 **"If the people have faith":** Xi, "Renmin you xinyang, minzu you xiwang, guojia you liliang."

354 **"They said, 'Hey, we need more poems'":** Xie, interview with author, Oct. 26, 2013.

354 **In 2013, Xi visited Confucius's birthplace:** "Xi Jinping zai Qufu Zuotanhuishang."

355 **The next year, 2014, Xi spoke favorably:** Xi, "Speech by H.E. Xi Jinping President of the People's Republic of China at UNESCO Headquarters."

355 **Scholars who attended an annual conference:** Zhang, "China commemorates Confucius with high-profile ceremony."

355 **Called "Surprising Words From Chairman Xi":** Viewed at the Temple of Heavenly Creation in Jintan, Jiangsu Province. I visited the temple, saw the poster, and interviewed the nuns on March 27, 2015.

356 **More than fifteen hundred churches were decapitated:** Estimate based on official statements and interviews in Zhejiang in 2014 and

2016. See also my article "Church-State Clash in China Coalesces Around a Toppled Spire."

356 **The story began in the 1950s:** The family history is based on interviews with Zhang Yu on Oct. 19, 2015, and Zhang Fanyun on Oct. 26, 2015, when I also visited the studio and talked to Lin Gang. Some of the details were published in my article "Artistic Legacy in the Grip of China's Leaders."

28 Chengdu: Entering the City

360 **It was January, and Chinese New Year:** This chapter is based on interviews and speeches on Jan. 26, 2013.

363 **In 1907, a French Catholic priest named Léon Joly:** On Joly's argument and the idea that Christianity did not fail, I am indebted to Harrison's *Missionary's Curse*.

363 **set the tone for how generations of Western observers:** For examples of the pessimistic view of Christianity, see Gernet's *China and the Christian Impact* or Cohen's *China and Christianity*.

29 Shanxi: Ghost Burial

369 **The widow sat in a little room:** This chapter is based on interviews on April 4 and 5, 2013.

30 Beijing: The Wondrous Peak

380 **This year I wanted the anticipation:** This chapter is drawn from interviews on May 9, 10, 16, 23, and 24, 2013.

391 **In a 1934 novel called *Hundred Altars*:** Bredon, *Hundred Altars*. See especially chapter 4, "Shui Ching in Search of a Son."

Bibliography

Aikman, David. *Jesus in Beijing: How Christianity Is Transforming China and Changing the Global Balance of Power*. Washington, D.C.: Regnery, 2003.

Barboza, David. "Billion in Hidden Riches for Family of Chinese Leader." *New York Times*, Oct. 25, 2012, A1.

Bays, Daniel H. *A New History of Christianity in China*. Chichester, U.K.: Wiley-Blackwell, 2012.

Beijing News. Video report, *"Renmin Dahuitang fuwuyuan Wang Qianqian 11 nianhou zouhong jie dangnian xianbo biaozhun"* [Great Hall of the People's service person Wang Qianqian eleven years later reveals selection standards]. March 11, 2015. Accessed May 3, 2016. http://www.bjnews.com.cn/video/2015/03/11/356016.html.

Bredon, Juliet. *Hundred Altars*. New York: Dodd, Mead, 1934.

Bredon, Juliet, and Igor Mitrophanow. *The Moon Year: A Record of Chinese Customs and Festivals*. Shanghai: Kelly and Walsh, 1927.

Buck, Pearl S. "Is There a Case for Foreign Missions?" *Harper's*, Jan. 1933. Accessed July 10, 2016. http://harpers.org/archive/1933/01/is-there-a-case-for-foreign-missions/.

Burgess, John S. *The Guilds of Peking*. New York: Columbia University Press, 1928.

Central Committee of the Chinese Communist Party Decision Concerning Deepening Cultural Structural Reform, Oct. 18, 2011. Accessed March 20, 2016. https://chinacopyrightandmedia.wordpress.com/2011/10/18/central-committee-of-the-chinese-communist-party-decision-concerning-deepening-cultural-structural-reform/.

Chao, Adam Yuet. *Miraculous Response: Doing Popular Religion in Contemporary China*. Stanford, Calif.: Stanford University Press, 2006.

Chen Kaiguo, and Zheng Shunchao. *Dadao xing: Fanggu dujushi Wang Liping xiansheng* [Walking the great Dao: A visit with the reclusive layman Mr. Wang Liping]. Beijing: Huaxia, 1991.

—————. *Opening the Dragon Gate: The Making of a Modern Taoist Wizard.* Translated by Thomas Cleary. North Clarendon, Vt.: Tuttle, 1998.

Chen, Nancy. *Breathing Spaces: Qigong, Psychiatry, and Healing in China.* New York: Columbia University Press, 2003.

Chen Zhu. *Zhongguo Chaoren: Chen Zhu de Shijie* [Chinese superman: Chen Zhu's world]. Beijing: China International Broadcasting, 1993.

Cohen, Paul. *China and Christianity: The Missionary Movement and the Growth of Chinese Antiforeignism, 1860–1870.* Cambridge, Mass.: Harvard University Press, 1963.

Duara, Prasenjit. *Culture, Power, and the State: Rural North China, 1900–1942.* Stanford, Calif.: Stanford University Press, 1988.

—————. *Sovereignty and Authenticity: Manchukuo and the East Asian Modern.* Lanham, Md.: Rowman and Littlefield, 2003.

Dunn, Emily. *Lightning from the East: Heterodoxy and Christianity in Contemporary China.* Leiden: Brill, 2015.

"Eastern Lightning May Be a Cult, but They Still Have Rights." *China Change,* Dec. 21, 2012. Accessed April 18, 2016. https://chinachange .org/2012/12/21/eastern-lightning-may-be-a-cult-but-they-still-have -rights/.

Fällman, Fredrik. "Calvin, Culture, and Christ? Developments of Faith Among Chinese Intellectuals." In *Christianity in Contemporary China: Socio-cultural Perspectives,* edited by Francis Khek Gee Lim, 153–68. London: Routledge, 2012.

Gardiner, Bertha A. "Pilgrimage of Chinese: Every May Thousands Climb Slopes of Miao Feng Shan to Shrine at Top." *New York Times,* May 15, 1938.

Gernet, Jacques. *China and the Christian Impact.* Cambridge, U.K.: Cambridge University Press, 1985.

Gladney, Dru. *Muslim Chinese: Ethnic Nationalism in the People's Republic.* Cambridge, Mass.: Harvard University Asia Center, 1996.

"Gongyi shipin caifang: Zhongguo minbo shalong zhuxi Yi Qing he Tian-jin Nirenzhang yiren Lin Gang" [Public service video interview: China Famous Blog Salon chairman Yi Qing and Tianjin Clayman Zhang artist Lin Gang], Oct. 25, 2013. Accessed July 12, 2016. http://igongyi.cntv .cn/2013/10/25/VIDE1382703843638416.shtml.

Goodrich, Anne S. "Miao Feng Shan." *Asian Folklore Studies* 57 (1998): 87–97.

Goossaert, Vincent. "1898: The Beginning of the End for Chinese Religion?" *Journal of Asian Studies* 65, no. 2 (2006): 307–36.

—————. "The Shifting Balance of Power in the City God Temples, Late Qing to 1937." *Journal of Chinese Religions* 43, no. 1 (May 2015): 5–33.

———. "The Social Organization of Religious Communities in the Twentieth Century." In *Chinese Religious Life,* edited by David A. Palmer, Glenn Shive, and Philip L. Wickeri. Oxford: Oxford University Press, 2011.

———. *The Taoists of Peking, 1800–1949: A Social History of Urban Clerics.* Cambridge, Mass.: Harvard University Asia Center, 2007.

Goossaert, Vincent, and David Palmer. *The Religious Question in Modern China.* Chicago: University of Chicago Press, 2011.

Harrison, Henrietta. *The Missionary's Curse and Other Tales from a Chinese Catholic Village.* Berkeley: University of California Press, 2013.

He Huaihong. *Social Ethics in a Changing China: Moral Decay or Ethical Awakening?* Washington, D.C.: Brookings Institution Press, 2015.

Hengshan Daoyue: *Jinbei Gucui* [Hengshan Daoist music: Drumming and blowing in north Shanxi]. Materials collected for the Yanggao County Intangible Cultural Heritage Office. Internal publication, 2009.

Hong, Brendon. "Prepare the Kool-Aid: Is This the Scariest Doomsday Sect in China?" *Daily Beast,* June 20, 2014. Accessed April 18, 2016. http://www.thedailybeast.com/articles/2014/06/20/is-eastern-lightning-the-scariest-doomsday-sect-in-china.html.

Hung Chang-Tai. *Mao's New World: Political Culture in the Early People's Republic.* Ithaca, N.Y.: Cornell University Press, 2011.

"Inside China's 'Eastern Lightning' Cult." *Global Times,* English ed., June 3, 2014. Accessed April 18, 2016. http://en.people.cn/n/2014/0603/c90882-8735801.html.

Jacobs, Andrew. "Chatter of Doomsday Makes Beijing Nervous." *New York Times,* Dec. 20, 2012, A8.

Jing Jun. *The Temple of Memories: History, Power, and Morality in a Chinese Village.* Stanford, Calif.: Stanford University Press, 1996.

Johnson, David. *Spectacle and Sacrifice: The Ritual Foundations of Village Life in North China.* Cambridge, Mass.: Harvard University Press, 2009.

Johnson, Ian. "An Artistic Legacy in the Grip of China's Leaders." *New York Times,* Dec. 6, 2015, A6.

———"Chasing the Yellow Demon: Intangible Cultural Heritage in a North China Village." *The Journal of Asian Studies* 76, no. 1 (Feb. 2017).

———. "China's Unstoppable Lawyers: An Interview with Teng Biao." *NYR Daily,* Oct. 20, 2014. Accessed May 20, 2016. http://www.nybooks.com/daily/2014/10/19/china-rights-lawyers-teng-biao/.

———. "China's Way to Happiness." *NYR Daily,* Feb. 5, 2014. Accessed June 15, 2016. http://www.nybooks.com/blogs/nyrblog/2014/feb/04/chinas-way-happiness/.

————. "Church-State Clash in China Coalesces Around a Toppled Spire." *New York Times*, May 29, 2014, A4.

————. "Elite and Deft, Xi Aimed High Early in China." *New York Times*, Sept. 29, 2012, A1.

————. "Finding Zen and Book Contracts in China." *NYR Daily*, May 30, 2012. Accessed June 14, 2016. http://www.nybooks.com/blogs/nyrblog /2012/may/29/zen-book-contracts-bill-porter-beijing/.

————. "A Problem of 'Religion'—and Polling in China." *New York Times*, July 1, 2015. Accessed June 19, 2016. http://sinosphere.blogs.nytimes .com/2015/07/01/a-problem-of-religion-and-polling-in-china/.

————. "Q. and A.: John Osburg on China's Wealthy Turning to Spirituality." *New York Times*, Dec. 18, 2014. Accessed June 15, 2016. http:// sinosphere.blogs.nytimes.com/2014/12/18/q-and-a-john-osburg-on -chinas-wealthy-turning-to-spiritualism/.

————. "Two Sides of a Mountain: The Modern Transformation of Maoshan." *Journal of Daoist Studies* 5 (2012): 89–116.

————. *Wild Grass: Three Stories of Change in Modern China.* New York: Pantheon, 2004.

Jones, Stephen. *Daoist Priests of the Li Family: Ritual Life in Village China.* St. Petersburg, Fla.: Three Pines Press. 2016.

————. *In Search of the Folk Daoists of North China.* Farnham: Ashgate, 2010.

————. *Li Manshan: Portrait of a Folk Daoist.* 2015. Vimeo. https:// vimeo.com/155660741.

————. *Ritual and Music of North China: Shawm Bands in Shanxi.* Farnham: Ashgate, 2007.

Keck, Zachary. "The Atheists of Beijing." *Diplomat*, March 14, 2014. Accessed June 19, 2016. http://thediplomat.com/2014/03/the-atheists -of-beijing/.

Kuhn, Philip A. *Soulstealers: The Chinese Sorcery Scare of 1768.* Cambridge, Mass.: Harvard University Press, 1990.

Laliberté, André. "Religion and Development in China." In *The Routledge Handbook of Religions and Global Development,* edited by Emma Tomalin, 233–49. London: Routledge, 2015.

Li Fan. "Jidujiao de fazhan he jiating jiaohui [The development of Protestantism and house churches]." The World and China Institute. Accessed Sept. 16, 2016. http://www.world-china.org/bookdownload2/%E5 %9F%BA%E7%9D%A3%E6%95%99%E7%9A%84%E5%8F%91% E5%B1%95%E5%92%8C%E5%AE%B6%E5%BA%AD%E6%95%9 9%E4%BC%9A%E7%9A%84%E5%AE%97%E6%95%99%E8%87 %AA%E7%94%B1%E8%BF%90%E5%8A%A8.pdf.

Li He. *Goddesses, Ghosts, and Demons: The Collected Poems of Li He (790–816)*. Translated by J. D. Frodsham. San Francisco: North Point Press, 1983.

"*Liangong tihui liangce*" [Two criteria for learning from practice]. *Qigong*, no. 6 (1989): 278.

Liao Yiwu. *God Is Red: The Secret Story of How Christianity Survived and Flourished in Communist China*. New York: HarperOne, 2011.

Liu Xun. *Daoist Modern: Innovation, Lay Practice, and the Community of Inner Alchemy in Republican China*. Cambridge, Mass: Harvard University Press, 2009.

Liu Yida. *Beijing Laoguiju* [Beijing's old rules]. Beijing: Zhonghua Shuju, 2015.

MacInnis, Donald E., ed. *Religion in China Today: Policy & Practice*. Maryknoll, N.Y.: Orbis Books, 1989.

Madsen, Richard. *Democracy's Dharma: Religious Renaissance and Political Development in Taiwan*. Berkeley: University of California Press, 2007.

Mao Zedong. "Analysis of the Classes in Chinese Society," March 1926. In *The Collected Works of Mao Zedong*. Beijing: Foreign Languages Press, 1967.

Meng Han. "Finding the Women at China's Big Meetings." *ChinaFile*, March 8, 2016. Accessed May 3, 2016. https://www.chinafile.com/multimedia/photo-gallery/finding-women-chinas-big-meetings.

Murong Xuecan. *Leave Me Alone: A Novel of Chengdu*. Translated by Harvey Thomlinson. Crows Nest, Australia: Allen & Unwinn, 2009.

Naquin, Susan. "The Peking Pilgrimage to Miao-feng Shan: Religious Organizations and Sacred Sites." In *Pilgrims and Sacred Sites in China*, edited by Susan Naquin and Chün-Fang Yü, 333–77. Berkeley: University of California Press, 1992.

———. *Peking: Temples and City Life, 1400–1900*. Berkeley: University of California Press, 2000.

Nedostup, Rebecca Allyn. *Superstitious Regimes: Religion and the Politics of Chinese Modernity*. Cambridge, Mass.: Harvard University Press, 2009.

Palmer, David A. *Qigong Fever: Body, Science, and Utopia in China*. New York: Columbia University Press, 2007.

Perry, Elizabeth J. "The Populist Dream of Chinese Democracy." *Journal of Asian Studies* 74, no. 4 (Nov. 2015): 903–15.

The Pew Forum on Religion & Public Life. *Global Christianity: A Report on the Size and Distribution of the World's Christian Population*. 2011. Accessed July 10, 2016. http://www.pewforum.org/files/2011/12/Christianity-fullreport-web.pdf.

Pew Research Center. *Worldwide, Many See Belief in God as Essential to Morality*. March 13, 2014.

Pittman, D. A. *Towards a Modern Chinese Buddhism: Taixu's Reforms*. Honolulu: University of Hawai'i Press, 2001.

Poon, Shuk-wah. "Religion, Modernity, and Urban Space: The City God Temple in Republican Guangzhou." *Modern China* 34, no. 2 (April 2008): 247–75.

"Portrait of Vice President Xi Jinping: Ambitious Survivor of the Cultural Revolution." Confidential cable, Nov. 16, 2009. Wikileaks. Accessed July 12, 2016. https://wikileaks.org/plusd/cables/09BEIJING3128_a .html.

Ran, Yunfei. *Gushu zhi Fei: Dacisi zhuan* [The lungs of old Sichuan: The story of the Temple of Great Charity]. Chengdu: Sichuan Wenyi Chubanshe, 2011.

The Record of Linji. Edited by Thomas Yuho Kirchner. Translated by Ruth Fuller Sasaki. Honolulu: University of Hawai'i Press, 2009.

Red Pine (Bill Porter). *Poems of the Masters: China's Classic Anthology of T'ang and Sung Dynasty Verse.* Port Townsend, Wash.: Copper Canyon Press, 2003.

Robinet, Isabel. "Original Contributions of *Neidan* to Taoism and Chinese Thought." In *Taoist Meditation and Longevity Techniques,* edited by Livia Kohn. Ann Arbor: Center for Chinese Studies, University of Michigan, 1989.

Schell, Orville, and John Delury. *Wealth and Power: China's Long March to the Twenty-First Century.* New York: Random House, 2013.

Schipper, Kristofer. *The Taoist Body.* Translated by Karen C. Duval. Berkeley: University of California Press, 1993.

The Secret of the Golden Flower. Translated by Thomas Cleary. New York: HarperCollins, 1991.

Shea, Matt. "The Cult Who Kidnaps Christians and Is at War with the Chinese Government." *Vice,* July 31, 2013. Accessed July 12, 2016. http: //www.vice.com/read/the-chinese-cult-who-kidnap-christians-and -paint-snakes.

The Songs of the South: An Ancient Chinese Anthology of Poems by Qu Yuan and Other Poets. Translated by David Hawkes. Harmondsworth, U.K.: Penguin, 1985.

Su Xiaoning. *Xi Jinping zai Zhengding gongzuoshi liuying* [Some impressions of Xi Jinping's time in Zhengding]. Accessed July 11, 2016. The original article appears to have been censored from the Web, but a copy can be found here: http://www.360doc.com/content/12/1117/12/1934120 _248371581.shtml.

Tao Te Ching: A New English Version. Translated by Stephen Mitchell. New York: HarperCollins, 1988.

Tong, James W. *Revenge of the Forbidden City: The Suppression of the Falungong in China, 1998–2002.* Oxford: Oxford University Press, 2009.

Tsai, Lily L. *Accountability Without Democracy: Solidarity Groups and Public Goods Provision in Rural China.* Cambridge, U.K.: Cambridge University Press, 2007.

Tun Li-ch'en. *Yen-ching Sui-shih-chi.* Translated by Derk Bodde as *Annual Customs and Festivals in Peking.* Peiping: Henri Vetch, 1936.

Van Til, L. John. *Liberty of Conscience: The History of a Puritan Idea.* Phillipsburg, N.J.: P&R, 1971.

Walder, Andrew. *China Under Mao: A Revolution Derailed.* Cambridge, Mass.: Harvard University Press, 2015.

Wang Jun. *Beijing Record: A Physical and Political History of Planning Modern Beijing.* Singapore: World Scientific, 2011.

Wang Yi. "Wang Yi's Diary: Now I Must See My Friend Ran Yunfei Become a Prisoner," Feb. 26, 2011. Translation by David Cowhig. https://gaodawei.wordpress.com/2011/04/05.

Wang Shuya [Wang Yi]. *Tiantang chenmole banxiaoshi: Yingshizhong de xinyang yu rensheng* [Heaven went silent for half an hour: Faith and human life in movies and television]. Nanchang: Jiangxi Chuban Jituan, 2007.

————. *Wode ping'an ru jianghe: Yingshizhong de jiushu yu panwang* [My peace is like the river: Redemption and hope in movies and television]. Nanchang: Jiangxi Chuban Jituan, 2009.

Wenzel-Teuber, Katharina. "2014 Statistical Update on Religions and Churches in the People's Republic of China." *Religion and Christianity in Today's China* 6, no. 2 (2016): 20–47. Accessed May 9, 2016. http://p30969 .typo3server.info/fileadmin/redaktion/RCTC_2015-2.20_Wenzel -Teuber_2014_Statistical_Update_on_Religions_and_Churches_in _China.pdf.

————. "2012 Statistical Update on Religions and Churches in the People's Republic of China." *Religion and Christianity in Today's China* 5, no. 2 (2015): 20–41. Accessed June 19, 2016. http://www.china-zentrum .de/fileadmin/redaktion/RCTC_2013-3.18-43_Wenzel-Teuber_2012 _Statistical_Update_on_Religions_and_Churches_in_China .pdf.

Wielander, Gerda. *Christian Values in Communist China.* Oxford: Routledge, 2014.

Wilhelm, Richard. *Taiyi Jinhua Zongzhi* (The Secret of the Golden Flower). Translated by Cary F. Baynes. First published 1931. New York: Mariner Books, 1970.

WIN/Gallup International. "Losing our religion? Two-thirds of people still claim to be religious." April 13, 2015.

Wu Fan. *Yinyang gujiang zai zhixu de kongjianzhong* [The *yinyang* drum artisans as ordered in space]. Beijing: Central Conservatory of Music, 2011.

Wu Hung. *Remaking Beijing: Tiananmen Square and the Creation of a Political Space*. Chicago: University of Chicago Press, 2005.

Wu Jiao. "Religious Believers Thrice the Estimate." *China Daily*, Feb. 7, 2007. Accessed June 20, 2016. http://www.chinadaily.com.cn/china/2007 -02/07/content_802994.htm.

Wu Xiaoying. *Miaofengshan: Beijing minjian shehui de lishi yanbian* [Miaofeng-shan: The historical evolution of Beijing civil society]. Beijing: Renmin Chubanshe, 2007.

Xi Lian. *Redeemed by Fire: The Rise of Popular Christianity in Modern China*. New Haven, Conn.: Yale University Press, 2010.

Xi Jinping. *"Renmin you xinyang, minzu you xiwang, guojia you liliang"* [If the people have faith, the nation has hope, and the country has strength]. Xinhuanet. Feb. 28, 2015. Accessed Sept. 15, 2016. http://news.xinhuanet .com/politics/2015-02/28/c_1114474084.htm.

Xi Zhongxun. *Shenqiu huainian Zhongguo Gongchandangde zhongcheng pengyou Panchen Dashi* [Deeply cherish the memory of a heartfelt friend of the Chinese Communist Party, the Panchen Grand Master]. Originally published Feb. 20, 1989. Reprinted in *China Communist Party New Web*. Accessed July 11, 2016. http://dangshi.people.com.cn/GB/232052/233 953/233956/16176187.html.

Xie Luoqing [Yi Qing]. "Yi Qing deng lianxian Yan Changfeng" [Yi Qing and others online with Yan Changfeng]. *Mingbo lianxian daode mofan*, Dec. 20, 2011. http://www.gzjcdj.gov.cn/special/SpecialNews.jsp?spnewsid=19133.

Xi Jinping. "Speech by H.E. Xi Jinping President of the People's Repub-lic of China at UNESCO Headquarters," March 28, 2014. Accessed May 15, 2016. http://www.fmprc.gov.cn/mfa_eng/wjdt_665385/zyjh _665391/t1142560.shtml.

"Xi Jinping: Xiangai xizijide shengming yiyang baohu wenhua yichan" [Xi Jinping: Preserve cultural relics like our own lives]. *Fujian Daily*, Jan. 6, 2015. Accessed April 5, 2015. http://politics.people.com.cn/n/2015 /0106/c1024-26336469.html.

"Xi Jinping zai Qufu zuotanhuishang tanji Wenge dui chuantong wenhua shouhai" [Xi Jinping at a discussion meeting talks about the damage to traditional culture in the Cultural Revolution]. *Sina News*, Dec. 5, 2013. Accessed Dec. 10, 2014. http://news.sina.com.cn/c/2013-12-05 /014228887986.shtml.

Xinhua News Agency. "Chinese Commemorate Common Ancestors at Qingming Festival," April 7, 2003. Accessed July 10, 2016. http://en.people.cn/200304/06/eng20030406_114645.shtml.

"Xin Qigong liaofa zhongwanqi exing zhongliu" [New *qigong* treatments for malignant tumors in the middle stomach duct]. *Qigong*, no. 6 (1989): 256–57.

Yang, C. K. *Religion in Chinese Society*. Berkeley: University of California Press, 1967.

Yang Fenggang. "Cultural Dynamics in China: Today and in 2020." *Asia Policy*, no. 4 (July 2007): 41–52.

———. "Exceptionalism or Chimerica: Measuring Religious Change in the Globalizing World." *Journal for the Scientific Study of Religion* 55, no. 1 (2016): 7–22.

———. "The Red, Black, and Gray Markets of Religion in China." *Sociological Quarterly* 47, no. 1 (2006): 93–122.

———. "Religion in China Under Communism: A Shortage Economy Explanation." *Journal of Church and State* 52, no. 1 (Nov. 2009): 3–33.

Yao, Kevin Xiyi. "At the Turn of the Century: A Study of the China Centenary Missionary Conference of 1907." *International Bulletin of Missionary Research* 32, no. 2 (April 2008): 65–69.

Yao Xinzhong and Paul Badham. *Religious Experience in Contemporary China*. Cardiff: University of Wales Press, 2007.

"Yi daode wei guifan yi lianjie wei hexin. Zhanshu zengqiang lian zhengzhi zhidu yeshuli" [Use virtue as the rule and purity as the core: Zhanshu increases its unifying force to clean up its political system]. *People's Daily*, Nov. 16, 2015, 9.

Yu Jianrong. "Wei Jidujiao jiating jiaohui tuomin" [Desensitizing Protestant house churches]. Sociology and Anthropology China Web. Accessed Sept. 16, 2016. http://www.sachina.edu.cn/Htmldata/article/2008/12/1696.html.

Zha Changping. "Jidujiao zai Zhongguo cong jianghu shehui zhuanxingwei gongmin shehui zhong de jiaose" [Christianity in a China transforming from a society of knights-errant to a society of public citizens]. In *Wo you Xiangban Ru Hezi* [I Had Wings Like a Dove]. Edited by Yu Jie and Wang Yi. Taipei: Jiwenshi, 2010.

Zhang Pengfei. "China Commemorates Confucius with high-profile ceremony." Xinhuanet. Sept. 25, 2014. http://news.xinhuanet.com/english/china/2014-09/25/c_127030072.htm Accessed Sept. 15, 2016.

Zhang Yinan. *Zhongguo jiating jiaohui liushinian* [Sixty years of China's house churches]. Hong Kong: Fuxing Huaren Guoji Shigong, 2010.

"Zhejiangsheng weishuji Xi Jinping xie furen Peng Liyuan yixingdao woxian jinxing canguan kaocha" [Zhejiang provincial party secretary Xi Jinping and wife Peng Liyuan visit our county on a study tour]. Baidu Tieba. April 4, 2005. Accessed April 4, 2015. http://tieba.baidu .com/p/2311897694?see_lz=1.

Zhou Xun. *The Great Famine in China, 1958–1962: A Documentary History.* New Haven, Conn.: Yale University Press, 2012.

Index

Numbers in italics refer to figures.

454 INDEX
Xu Jue 徐珏: yinyang men 陰陽先生: skills of, 41
Christian beliefs, and the True Jesus funeral preparations, 373, 374–379
Church, 128, 328 see also Li Bin; Li Manshan (Old
death of her son Wu Xiangdong in Mr. Li); Li Qing
the 1989 Tiananmen massacre, Yoga:
125–127 physical practice as an aspect of
home in the western suburbs of belief system of, 118
Beijing, 125 as a spiritual practice in China, 31
involvement with Tiananmen yogi Tirumalai Krishnam's
Mothers, 128 codification and partial
tomb sweeping for her husband secularization of, 113
and son at Qingming, 125, Yu Jianrong 于建嵘, 30
130–133 Yu Jie 余杰:
Christmas visit with Wang Yi,
Yang, C. K., 19 164–165
Yang, Fenggang: interviews conducted with
China Spiritual Life Study led Protestant pastors, 287
by, 29 life in the United States, 200
on the removal of scholars critical Su Dongpo identified as his favorite
of Confucianism from key poet, 165
research institutes, 410n78 Yu Xiurong 于秀榮 (Mrs. Yu,
Yanggao County 陽高縣: Old Mr. Ni's wife), death of,
and the Li family: 269–272
Li Bin's relocation to, 36–37, Yuan Lishan and the Yuan family of
48–49, 137, 142, 237, 309 Daoist musicians, 236–237, 246
performances by the music troupe Yuanxiao 元宵 (First Night), 4
in, 236–237, 371 Yuedu Wangling 閱讀亡靈 (Delivering
location of, 33–34 the Departed Spirit), 270
temples in, 240
yangsheng 養生 (nurturing life, Zha Changping 查常平:
"wellness"), 258, 319 and Peng Qiang, 292–293
see also physical practices and Spring of Life Reformed
Yangtze River: Church, 282–287, 289–290,
and the economic and cultural 291
region of Jiangnan, 94, 327 see also Early Rain Reformed
lush vegetation south of, evoked in Church
a verse by Qu Yuan, 194 Zhang Baojing:
Yao Xiulian (Mrs. Yao, Old Mr. Li's burnt offering made by, 178–181
wife), 136, 146–147 friendship with Old Mr. Ni, 178
Ye Xiaowen 葉小文: steamed-bun association run by,
biographical information, 77–78, 178
409–410n77 Zhang Bin 張斌, shelter for the
as head of the State Administration homeless managed by, 153–156
for Religious Affairs, 77–78

Permissions Acknowledgments

Printed in the United States
by Baker & Taylor Publisher Services